PEN

THE

Andrew Wheatcroft was educated at St John's School, Leatherhead, Christ's College, Cambridge, and the University of Madrid. He is the author of many books on nineteenth- and twentieth-century history, most recently *The Road to War* (with Richard Overy). Research for both *The Ottomans* (Penguin, 1995) and *The Habsburgs* has taken him to Turkey, North Africa, Spain, Italy, Hungary, the Czech Republic, Austria, Germany, France and the United States.

Andrew Wheatcroft is based in Dumfriesshire, Scotland, and teaches in the Department of English at the University of Stirling.

D0190039

ANDREW WHEATCROFT

The Habsburgs

EMBODYING EMPIRE

PENGUIN BOOKS

PENGUIN BOOKS

Published by the Penguin Group
Penguin Books Ltd, 80 Strand, London WC2R 0RL, England
Penguin Putnam Inc., 375 Hudson Street, New York, New York 10014, USA
Penguin Books Australia Ltd, 250 Camberwell Road, Camberwell, Victoria 3124, Australia
Penguin Books Canada Ltd, 10 Alcorn Avenue, Toronto, Ontario, Canada M4V 3B2
Penguin Books India (P) Ltd, 11 Community Centre, Panchsheel Park, New Delhi – 110 017, India
Penguin Books (NZ) Ltd, Cnr Rosedale and Airborne Roads, Albany, Auckland, New Zealand
Penguin Books (South Africa) (Pty) Ltd, 24 Sturdee Avenue, Rosebank 2196, South Africa

Penguin Books Ltd, Registered Offices: 80 Strand, London WC2R 0RL, England

www.penguin.com

First published by Viking 1995
Published in Penguin Books, 1996

25

ISBN-13: 978-0-140-23634-7

www.greenpenguin.co.uk

Penguin Books is committed to a sustainable future
for our business, our readers and our planet.
The book in your hands is made from paper
certified by the Forest Stewardship Council.

For my grandmother
Bertha Regina Ware,
who gave me a sense of my past,
and who lives in my memory

and for her brothers
Otto Veit
Paul Veit
Robert Veit
Hugo Veit
Ernst Veit
the last of their line

Do you wish to understand the history of a blade of grass? First and foremost, try to make yourself into a blade of grass, and if you do not succeed, content yourself with analysing the parts and even disposing them in a kind of imaginative history.

Benedetto Croce, History Theory and Practice

Contents

List of Illustrations

by Franz Xavier Winterhalter (1806–73) (*Kunsthistorisches Museum, Vienna*) (see p. 277)
14. Katharina Schratt, the intimate friend of Emperor Franz Joseph I. Anon. (*Hermesvilla, Vienna*) (see p. 277)
15. Maria Luisa de Bourbon, the wife of Emperor Leopold II
16. Emperor Francis I at his desk, 1806
17. The traditional exequies for Archduchess Sophie, mother of Emperor Franz Josef I, in 1872, in the Hofburg Chapel, Vienna
18. Crown Prince Rudolf with his wife and daughter, 1888
19. Archduke Franz Ferdinand, heir presumptive to the throne of Austria, and his wife, the Duchess of Hohenberg, in 1914
20. Emperor Franz Joseph I in his hunting clothes, 1908
21. Karl I of Austria, his wife Zita and their children, in exile at the Château de Herrnstein in Switzerland
22. Otto von Habsburg with his family in 1966, on the balcony of their house at Pöcking

The author and publishers are grateful to the following for permission to reproduce illustrations: AGK, London: 4, 8; The Bridgeman Art Library: 1–3, 5–7, 9–14; Collection Viollet, Paris: 15–22.

MAPS

Habsburg Spain under
Philip II (1556–98)

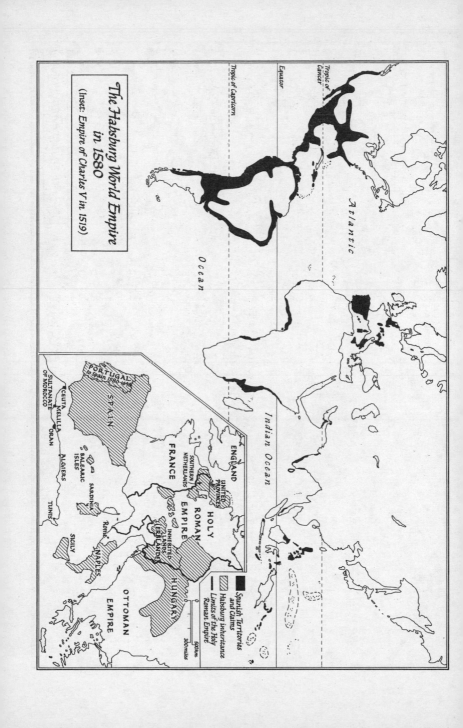

The Habsburg World Empire
in 1580
(Inset: Empire of Charles V in 1519)

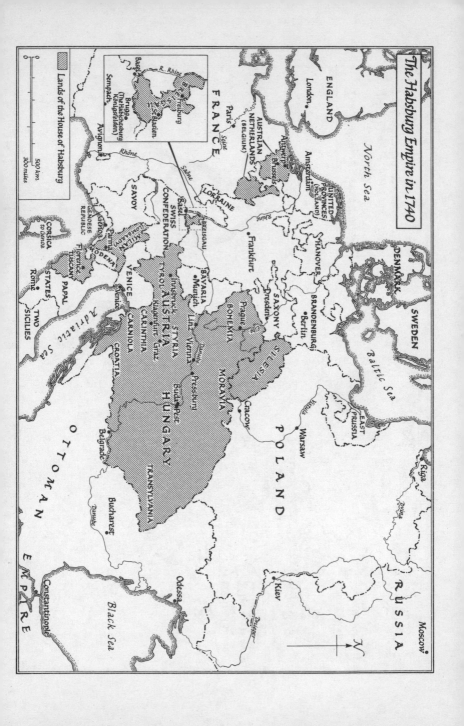

The Habsburg Empire in 1740

Lands of the House of Habsburg

0   500 km.
0   300 miles

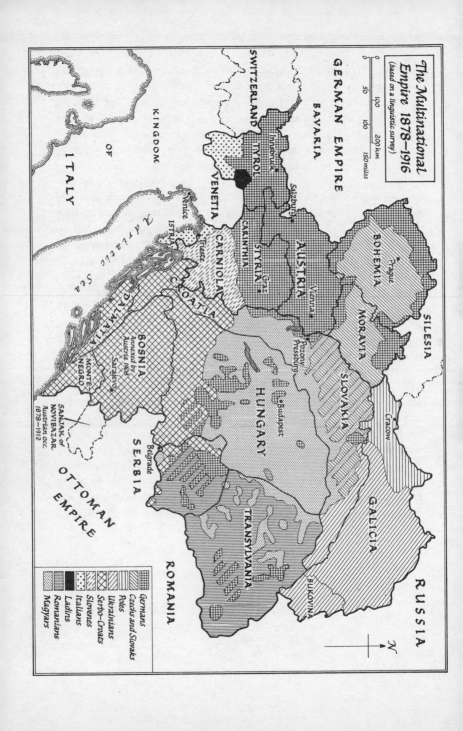

The Multinational
Empire 1878–1916
(based on a linguistic survey)

0   50   100   200 km.
0   50   100   150 miles

GERMAN EMPIRE

BAVARIA

SWITZERLAND

TYROL
Innsbruck

Salzburg

VENETIA

CARINTHIA

AUSTRIA
Vienna

STYRIA
Graz

CARNIOLA

ISTRIA
Trieste

Venice

KINGDOM

OF

ITALY

Adriatic Sea

CROATIA

DALMATIA

MONTE-
NEGRO

SANJAK of
NOVIBAZAR.
Austrian occ.
1878–1912

BOSNIA
Annexed by
Austria 1908
Sarajevo

SERBIA
Belgrade

OTTOMAN

EMPIRE

BOHEMIA
Prague

MORAVIA

SILESIA

Cracow

SLOVAKIA

Pozony
Pressburg

Budapest

HUNGARY

GALICIA

BUKOVINA

TRANSYLVANIA

RUSSIA

ROMANIA

N

Germans
Czechs and Slovaks
Poles
Ukrainians
Serbo-Croats
Slovenes
Italians
Latins
Romanians
Magyars

The Habsburgs have not, over the centuries, had a good press. At one extremity the family has been demonized: as one writer asserted in the 1930s, the Habsburgs were responsible for a 'long history of atrocities'. At the other they were long regarded rather like the dodo, as a curious living fossil, but no longer adapted to the conditions of the modern world. In fact, they have seemed out of tune with the times since the seventeenth century, if not earlier. The Habsburgs themselves contributed to this misapprehension. Not for them the fiery energy of a new monarchy. They wished, with very few exceptions, to be seen as the recrudescence of ancient power. Still negative, but sitting between the two extremes of demon and dodo, lies the mass of modern historiography. This concludes that the Habsburgs in power behaved, thought and functioned much (or entirely) like other monarchs. The great weight (in the most literal sense) of historical writing advances this central proposition. The point about weight is not flippant. The Habsburgs seem to have provoked a succession of vast books, from Lichnowsky in the nineteenth century to the thousand plus pages of Hugo Hantsch, or the nine hundred of C. A. Macartney which covered a much shorter period. Neither, of course, had to confront the issue of the *Casa de Austria*, the Habsburgs in Spain, which has generated its own vast literature.

As a result, we now know a great deal about the lands ruled over by the Habsburgs, and of some individual Habsburgs as rulers, patrons of the arts, soldiers and the like. But, by contrast, little serious study has been given to the Habsburgs as an entity, considering 'the dynasty' in much the same shorthand way that we do 'the Church'. The parallel may not be exact but it is nonetheless useful. Both were unique institutions, although they shared many of

the characteristics of other systems of power and government. Each
seemed greater than the sum of its parts, and while both presented
themselves as changeless and immutable, yet they were in a constant
state of adaptation and flux. This book is centred around this
rather metaphysical notion of the Habsburgs: its concern is more
the abstract idea of 'the dynasty' than any individual monarch or
event.

The means that the Habsburgs had available to promote this
idea of the dynasty were not especially novel. But the uses they
made of art, printed materials, architecture and public display were
unusual if not unique. There are many examples of the promotion
and propagandizing of an individual, from Louis XIV through
Napoleon, to the twentieth-century examples, notably Hitler and
Stalin. Just how the Habsburg practice differed from, say, the French
becomes clearer by comparing exact contemporaries, like Louis XIV
with Leopold I, or Napoleon Bonaparte with Francis I. In the case of
Louis the centre of attention was upon the monarch alone; with
Leopold, the individual shared the limelight with the long procession
of his ancestors gathered around him, in either visible or symbolic
form. Where Napoleon offered solitary *grandeur*, Francis proffered
Gemütlichkeit, the simple and homely ruler surrounded by his ador-
ing people. The totems and symbols of the dynasty were changed
and reconfigured to meet the needs of the moment, but the essence
remained unaltered and unalloyed.

This concern for an appropriate image may be found throughout
Habsburg history, but it surfaced most powerfully at moments
where the dynasty was under challenge or in a process of transition,
like a snake shedding its skin. Even in such non-traditional times as
the reign of Joseph II, the preoccupation with the public image of
the dynasty remained paramount. The 'revolutionary emperor' did
not deny the past of his family so much as seek to sweep away its
encrustations, and refashion it for a new era. The simple image of
the Emperor guiding the plough was as loaded with symbolic force
as the more conventional portrayals of his predecessors and successors, surrounded by their crowns.

To see the Habsburgs collectively, as a clan, with its own
mythology and covert ideology, is a perspective more familiar to cultural anthropologists than to many historians. I have benefited both

from the detailed studies of Clifford Geertz, Pierre Bourdieu and Maurice Bloch, and also from the new range of insights that emerges from reading their work. Much the same can be said of the tradition in the history of art developed by Erwin Panofsky and his successors. Richard S. Wortman's remarkable study, *Scenarios of Power: Myth and Ceremony in Russian Monarchy*, appeared just as the first edition of this book was being passed for the press. That many of his conclusions seem so similar to my own reinforces my belief that this approach has a general validity. Like Wortman confronting the Romanovs, my central assumption is quite simple: the Habsburgs' preoccupation with their own identity and mythology was intelligible. Their ceremonies were not empty of meaning, their 'cultural politics' were considered and deliberate, even if they seemed as bizarre to contemporaries as they now seem odd to us. And from all these we can glean a better sense of how the Habsburgs saw themselves and their role in the world.

Acknowledgements

Acknowledgements are invariably the part of a book that gets left until the end. In the case of this book, on which I have been working for so long, they become even more problematical than normal. My first notes are dated 1967, after which there is a sprinkling of materials in the 1970s, and then a steadily growing pile up to the present. In most cases each new stratum brings with it a new set of obligations, and the list of individuals who should feature here gets longer and longer. Adding to that the depressing fact that more and more of those to whom I feel a sense of gratitude have now died brings back to me just how long I have taken to perform a relatively simple task.

Two of those who are now part of history themselves, I think of constantly with gratitude. Professor Walter Ullmann was perhaps always a part of history; I think the Investiture Contest was more real to him than the era of the motor car. But he made history live for others, myself included. And he showed that an idea can be more powerful than any material force. With Gerhard Benecke, who by rights should still be alive and flourishing, it was the gift of friendship and a sharing of knowledge and ideas. When I reread his study of 'Max', I hear his *oral footnotes* adding and amplifying what remains a pioneering piece of work. I do not think that either John Brewer or Simon Schama is quite aware of what their friendship has meant to me, watching them as they hacked new paths through the scholarly jungle, along which I then feel able to walk with ease. Historians' revaluation of the material object, of the consumers of those objects as opposed to their producers, especially in the visual arts, has largely been *down to them* over the last two decades. From Peter Burke and Geoffrey Parker, likewise, amity and constant fresh insights.

Then there is a longer list, of those whom I have badgered for information or who otherwise unwisely offered to help me to find it. Dame Frances Yates, Dr A. J. P. Taylor, Dr Jonathan Steinberg, Professor Bohdan Chudoba, Professor J. H. Plumb (to whom my debt is large), Professor Philip Grierson, Dr Erich Gabriel, Dr Richard Luckett, David Collins, Dr José Molina, Dr Ian McGowan, Dr Neil Keeble, Hans Coudenhove, Ottó Károlyi (who has been good enough to look at the bulk of the book), Dr Judy Delin, Gordon Brook-Shepherd, Dr Glennis Stephenson, Jasper Ridley, Professor Ekkhard Helmuth, Mrs Jackie Tasioulas, Gordon Byron, Professor J. Entrembasaguas, Dr I. A. A. Thompson, Richard Stoneman, Professor Rosemarie Morgan, Professor H. H. Fernholz, Dr J. Breitenbach, Professor Carol Stapp, Professor John Bowles, Dr Vaughan Hart, John Keegan, Dr Gary Schwartz, Professor Roy Bridge, Dr Christopher Duffy, P. Luis Guillén, Professor Norman Stone, Anneyce Wheatcroft, Dr Alan Sked, P. Darío Cabanelas Rodríguez. Some have suffered more than others. Professor Anthony Goodman has read the medieval chapters, and I am extremely grateful for his careful reading and illuminating advice. He has saved me from a number of egregious errors; those that remain are my responsibility alone. Dr Celina Fox has fielded my ideas on the interpretation of pictures with great patience and tolerance. I am especially grateful to Dr Susanne Peters, formerly of Graz, who has found a great range of materials for me and smoothed my path into many institutions in Austria which would otherwise have been much more difficult. In that respect I would like to say how much I have appreciated the assistance of Hr Dr Friedrich Waidacher, former Director of the Joanneum, Graz, Hr Dr Robert Wais-senberger, formerly Director of the Historisches Museum der Stadt Wien, and the current Director, Hr Dr Günther Düriegl, the former Director of the Heeresgeschichtliches Museum, Hr Dr Johann Allmayer-Beck, and the present Director, Hr Dr Manfried Rauchsteiner, Hr Dr Wilfried Seipel of the Kunsthistorisches Museum, Hr Dr Edith Wohlgemuth and the staff of the Kriegsarchiv, the archivists and staff at the Abbey of Sankt Paul im Laventthal, and equally, at the Kaiservilla, Bad Ischl, Dr Alfred Auer and his staff at Schloss Ambras, and the administrator, Ing. Paul Kotratschek, at Schloss Laxenburg.

Then there are some whose names I have forgotten or never knew. The mayor and the people of Murtas looked after a lone visitor in the Alpujarras; I had the sense that the last one had been Gerald Brenan in the 1920s. Or the wife and family of Pepe Heredia, a good friend indeed, and Don Joaquín Hidalgo Díaz in Sanlúcar de Barrameda. This is also the case with the many anonymous librarians who have fetched and carried, or found ancient sources from inadequate references. Without Bruce Royan and his staff of Stirling University Library, Ian McGowan and those at the National Library of Scotland, Dr Paul Hess at the Zentralbibliotek, Luzern, Don Jesús Bermúdez Pareja and Sra Angel Moreno at the Archivo del Alhambra, and the Librarian and especially the Photographic staff at Cambridge University Library, the Special Collections staff at UCLA Library, Los Angeles, I could not have completed this book. Equally, since so much of the final stages has been carried out at the Library of Congress and the Folger Library in Washington, and at the library of Texas Tech University, in Lubbock, Texas, I would like to thank all of them for their quiet efficiency.

My colleagues in the Department of English Studies and in the Centre for Publishing Studies at the University of Stirling have sometimes asked each other, 'Does Andrew Wheatcroft still work in this department?' and I have tried to assure them that I do. I hope they will accept this book as a *close reading* of the cultural production (visual and textual) of the Habsburgs, which might connect to some extent with the overall goals of our collective enterprise. What I have gained from them is a sense of companionship and also access to a unique range of expertise in language, linguistics, literature and literary theory which they have patiently explained to this historian-cuckoo in their midst.

Hippolyt and Brigitte Meles in Basel, Gary and Miriam Edson in Lubbock, and David Damant, of Cambridge, London and Amsterdam, have done much more than just offer me hospitality: they have found me material, and sent me off along new lines of investigation that I would never have come to by myself.

Eleo Gordon is an editor *sans pareil*, and without her hastening me to the final goal, this book would never have been completed. I do not have the words to express my gratitude fully to her.

Nor do I to Janet Wheatcroft. Over the last twenty-five years she has, I know, given up hope of ever being rid of this incubus. We have done so much on this together – like seeing the marmoreal carnality of Maria Theresa's tomb in the Kaisergruft or looking at the postcard screens in the Kaiservilla at Bad Ischl, or watching the local peasants bemused at El Escorial on their free day ... and exchanged significant glances. Over all these years the best ideas in this book, as in all other aspects of my life, have come from her.

The dedication to this book expresses the longest and the deepest debt of all, which I can now never repay.

Preface

In a famous passage in his *Autobiography*, Edward Gibbon pin-points the moment at which the germ of *The Decline and Fall of the Roman Empire* came into his mind. Like so much of Gibbon this was a well-worked version of the truth, but the notion that there is a conceptual moment for a book is not a false one. Or not at least in my case. This book began in a small narrow room in the Palace of Charles V in Granada, that massive and alien intrusion into the lightness and openness of the Alhambra, the Moorish palace of the Nasrid kings. Piled on an array of rickety, ancient tables were the records and catalogue books of the Archive of the Alhambra. Documents are conventionally described as 'musty', but whoever first used the word can never have sat day after day amid the richly organic odours of old parchment, magnified by the heat of the Granadine summer.

Each day I walked with increasing reluctance up the long hill, the Cuesta de Chapiz, to the Gate of Pardon (with the Hand of Fátima above the portal). On the way up there were stone benches, and behind them ran a shallow rill with a constant flow of water. The sound and the scent of the water was an antidote both to the climb and to the tedium ahead. On some mornings, I would postpone my encounter with the pungent texts by lingering over a *granizado de limón* in the plaza at the foot of the slope. But latterly I had taken to stopping just before the top, to read or to write letters. In a bookshop where you could buy (and sell) cheap paperbacks I had found the only book that looked remotely interesting, a battered English translation of a book by an Austrian, Adam Wandruszka. It was called *The House of Habsburg*. Since I was, as it were, daily entombed in the house of Habsburg, I chanced the 100 pesetas for it. On the cool stone bench I raced through the first pages, and arrived very late in my monastic cell where I read the rest (it is not a long book) at a sitting. In the afternoon the manuscripts seemed to have more interest and more point to them, and as I began to fill in my file cards, the question filled my mind: *why were the Habsburgs like that?* Why had they built the cathedral in the city below, destroying the ancient mosque (perhaps the reason for that was obvious)? Why had they placed the great chancellery building on the other corner of Plaza Nueva where I bought my *granizado*, and where an archivist told me (probably entirely untruthfully) that it was a race to see if they could organize and catalogue the texts before the rats ate them?

Thus, this book began in Spain, and I am still using the file cards and the notes that I made during those months. Over the years more and more has appeared on the Spanish Habsburgs and, equally, on their Austrian cousins. At that point there was very little written in English of value on either branch. The Austrian Habsburgs existed almost mythically for me, as shadowy stories told to me by my grandmother of her Austro-Hungarian girlhood; I did not realize until many years later why she became so uncharacteristically angry when I once said that she was a German and not an Austrian. In the long years since then I have worked in both Austria and in Spain, and many other countries, besides collecting material and seeking a solution to my initial question. This book is my partial answer. It is partial because a lifetime is not sufficient to compile a complete one, and also, simply, because of personal limitations. I do not speak all the languages that would be necessary: the great Austrian savant A. F. Pribram told the young English scholar C. A. Macartney early in the 1920s that he would need to read fourteen languages to be able to do the job effectively (and I expect that this tally excluded Ottoman Turkish and the Iberian tongues).

Over time my focus and interests have, not unnaturally, changed. As I immersed myself, I began to look at matters much more from a Habsburg point of view, seeing that what once seemed (from an external perspective) to be banal or nonsensical, made a lot of sense from the inside. I came to realize that if I could trace my ancestors back for eight hundred years and could feel a sense of kinship with all those lost generations, I too would probably have a different slant on the past. But I did not want to fall into the trap of monarchist sycophancy, which was the tone of much of the work to which I was exposed. As will become clear in these pages, this is far from my viewpoint. In Austrian terms, I would be a natural 'Red' rather than a 'Black'. But this does not stop me admiring the skill and expertise with which the Habsburgs, over so many centuries, have navigated in very tricky waters.

This book began on the outside, at the Granadine extremity, and has worked its way very slowly towards the centre, Vienna. It has moved in another way as well. More and more I found that the Habsburgs expressed their sense of mission and their objectives obliquely, through a kind of code. It was a code exchanged between those who readily understood its meaning. Take, for example, the belief that the Habsburgs had been touched (literally) by the hand of God. Not one of them over all those centuries said precisely that. They talked in terms of Mission, Obedience to the Divine Will and the like. But in images I found this evasion cut away. Artists depicted the members of the dynasty touching the hand of the Almighty, or being bathed in the Divine Light. Moreover, those images persisted and reappeared over many epochs. I bought post-cards in Vienna, which showed the Emperor Franz Joseph floating above his armies like a heavenly cloud, just as his ancestor Leopold II had been portrayed two centuries before. At first this seemed to be coincidence, but I then came to understand that it was no accident. By patronage and even censorship, the Habsburgs ensured that the 'correct' image of themselves was purveyed. Following the threads back, it became clear that they disappeared into the distant medieval past, beyond Maximilian (my initial starting-point) and starting from the little castle on the hill outside Brugg in Switzerland. That experience has determined the shape and scope of this book.

Years ago, in Cambridge, a fit-looking elderly man in clumsy brown boots was pointed out to me as he strode confidently along the street. 'That', I was told, 'is Dr John Saltmarsh, the last of the Tramping Historians.' Dr Saltmarsh's pupils were expected to walk over the land, to understand the true contours of the past which they would later learn about in the dark recesses of the documents.

I never saw him again, but the image has remained, and the essential validity of his approach. I have tried to visit as many of the sites of Habsburg interest as I could, an approach which has paid off more than I could have imagined at the outset. Often there are local traditions and enthusiastic local researchers open to those who come to enquire. Frequently I found that the received version, culled by the scholars in their libraries, was simply impossible when you looked at the situation on the ground. If not precisely the Holy Grail, it certainly became A Quest.

Wrestling with this vast and amorphous dynasty, I have come to realize that the normal tools of the historian are inadequate. So I have tried to acquire an archaeologist's way of thinking, some of the insights of social and cultural anthropology, and the seeing eye of an art historian, realizing all the time that this was a slightly fraudulent accumulation of expertise: more *fancy dancing* than Deep Knowledge. Even though I grasped these techniques imperfectly, they have provided a new angle on the huge mass of material I was seeking to comprehend, and if only a tourist in these disciplines, I am certainly a respectful and appreciative one.

So much for the preliminary skirmishes. I think I have read or, at the least, glanced at most of the books written in four or five languages on or connected with the Habsburgs since about 1850, and a more selective reading before that date. The number on the list now extends into four figures. Why add another one? Simply, because none has fully answered my question. My own personal favourites, Adam Wandruszka (since that first day in Granada) and R. J. W. Evans, could not write enough to satisfy me, and what I have tried to do is simply to plod along behind them, filling in the sky and the details, so to speak, to their accomplishments. But there is one area where I think that I am mining a rich vein, and which is the justification for this book. No one has looked properly at the Habsburgs' use of image and text.

This also poses a problem. Much of my argument is visual or about the interpretation of images, and I refer to many more images in the text than are actually illustrated. I had to choose between only talking about those few pictures that the economics of publication permitted to be printed, or to demonstrate the interpretative technique on those few and to say 'trust me' when I try the same approach on those images which are not shown. To those images to which I refer but do not show, I have tried to give full references so that any enthusiasts could discover these pictures for themselves. But, as a point of principle, I have not talked about any image that I have not looked at with a great deal of concentrated attention.

One final word, about the structure of this book. It is both text and subtext. In the former I have concentrated on a narrative, trying to look both forward and backward, seeking to perceive and then present a sense of *pattern*. But the notes are not mere academic notation. They range discursively, pursue hares, tree racoons. For me, they embody a greater sense of pleasure than the surface of the text. Like the library behind locked doors in Umberto Eco's *Name of the Rose*, the seat of action lies there.

A Note on Names

There is never any ideal answer to the treatment of names in a history like this, covering so long a period. I have tried to adhere to the following principles. For *Holy Roman Emperors*, I have normally used the English version of their Latin name. So Frederick and not Friedrich, Charles and not Karl. But, inconsistently, Rudolf, not Rudolph. For *Austrian emperors* after Francis I, the most *usual* form of their names. So Franz Joseph and not Francis Joseph, or Franz Josef, Karl and not Charles. For other personal names, I have tried to distinguish, say, the fifty-seven varieties of *Maria, Theresa, Luisa, Annunziata*, etc., in the house of Habsburg, and the equivalently problematical male names.

For place names, I have tried to be consistent, but realize that, say, *Buda*, should properly be *Ofen* at a certain point in the story.

In essence, I have selected what seems to me would make sense to the reader, in the knowledge that anyone expert enough to pick up an imprecision knows enough not to be confused by my usage.

I

The Castle of the Hawk

1020–1300

On a day of stifling heat late in June 1386 the little town of Brugg was thronged to capacity with armed men. It was a natural gathering place. The contingents of knights and mercenaries from the Rhineland had crossed the great river at Basel and followed the rough road south-east until they came to the faster-moving Aare, leading south into the valley of the Aargau, and the Swiss highlands beyond. They had ridden in little groups, led by the men on horseback with a tail of more lightly armed retainers, often coming upon other bands bound on the same mission. The riders were called *gleves* – lances – and it showed the power ascribed to the man on horseback that no proper enumeration was kept of the followers and foot-soldiers. The best tally suggests that more than 3,000 lances were on the move. Gradually these groups coalesced, until there was a long, winding train of men and horses heading towards the river and south, to Brugg. On the opposite bank they could see others summoned in the same cause, riding from Austria in the East. The knights, apart from the incidentals of banners, surcoats and crests, looked much the same but their followers manifested the gulf that separated east from west. On the eastern bank, among the followers were men on little ponies, bedecked with horsetails and feathers, in rough leathers and animal skins.[1]

Many of the followers were in the campaign for plunder alone, and bound by no oath of loyalty. So too were many of the knights, although they dressed up their commitment to the cause of Leopold of Habsburg, Duke of Austria, in terms of 'honour'. The true professionals, in military terms, were the crossbowmen. Once, their weapon had been banned by the Pope for use against Christians; now it was regarded as the key to success in war, a weapon of precision. In any battle with armoured knights, or in siege craft, the crossbow was indispensable. But this enemy seemed barely to demand such elaborate preparations, nor an army on so great a scale. The duke's objective was to rout a mob of peasants, mostly foresters and mountain men, who had taken some towns belonging to the House of Habsburg, and thereby spread a contagion of disloyalty and sedition throughout the highlands. They were to be punished, perhaps annihilated, adapting Voltaire's famous phrase, 'to discourage the others'. All the same, it seemed a mighty army for so limited an objective.

Leopold III, Duke of Austria, was a figure who seemed to embody the 'beau ideal' of chivalry. Tall and handsome by the standards of the days, the chroniclers favourable to the Habsburgs described him as 'five and thirty years old . . . manly, chivalrous, dauntless . . . high minded, full of martial ardour, elate with former victories, revengeful and eager for combat . . . his indomitable spirit and personal daring knew no bounds'.[2] He was reputed to have forded the river Rhine in full armour at the flood to evade capture by his enemies.[3] His relentless ambition was also legendary, and he was determined to recover the family possessions and position that had been either lost or alienated over the decades. Earlier Habsburgs had sent their vassals to fight their wars for them, or paid others to act on their behalf. Now the duke had come himself. Accordingly, he had summoned the array to meet him at the town of Brugg, built by his ancestors hard on the banks of the river Aare, and made prosperous by its control over the single ancient bridge over the river.[4] In fact the town, where all these streams of armed men were converging, was a crossing point where three waters met. The Aare and the Reuss were, when in spate with the melting snows from the Swiss mountains, substantial rivers; the Limmat was little more than a brook. Nearly a thousand years before, the Romans had recognized the strategic importance of the place, for they had built their main legionary encampment close by, at Vindonissa. From there they could march east or west, or into the heart of Switzerland and over the Alpine passes into Italy. There had not been so many armed men in Brugg since the Roman legions had left almost ten centuries before.

Leopold's summons had attracted more than the high-born. For days, unbidden, a throng of common soldiers and camp followers had hastened to the rallying-point, within sight of the duke's castle, the place from which his family took their name, and which stood, visible for miles around, on the ridge of the Wülpisberg behind the town. It was a landmark that they could see long before the little town came into view. The castle – little more than a tower with a range of outbuildings and a ring of walls – was built of the local white limestone that shone with a dazzling brilliance in the sunshine; but neither the duke nor any member of his family lived there any longer. Even so they regarded it with affection as the *Stammhaus*, their point of origin, and others looked on it with some awe as the birthplace of a family that had imbued itself with unique rights and privileges, claiming a status greater than all the princes of the Holy Roman Empire. The Habsburgs numbered (so they said) Julius Caesar and the Emperor Nero among their distant ancestors. The castellan and his garrison were among those milling in the streets of the town below. He, too, obeyed the call to join his lord below the 'Castle of the Hawk', the Habichtsburg. For the first time in two generations, the Habsburgs were marching south in person to enforce their claims by armed force. Leopold had called his liegemen and vassals from all parts of his domain, to mount a punitive campaign against the Swiss peasants and townsmen who had expropriated his towns and abbeys and taunted his emissaries with memories of earlier defeats at their hands.

There had been little rain in the spring and the rivers were unnaturally low; the little town was quite unable to feed, water or supply the thousands who had gathered. Chaos reigned in the roiling mass of armed men that thronged the town and the fields beyond; yet to the experienced eye, there was an underlying sense of order. Leopold had planned his advance with care and skill. The heart of his battle line were the *gleves* – armoured horsemen – some in the new plate armour, the majority in the old chain-mail coats, who formed small groups, linked by region or by kinship. They were the key to the battle line, and the flamboyance of their appearance was deceiving. Almost all save the most impoverished had brought with them a string of retainers, some on horse, some on foot. All the nobles who had rallied to Leopold's call were skilled in the arts of war. They had learned to fight on foot or on horseback; most were expert with a variety of weapons, and inured to the rigours of many hours in the saddle. The Austrian knights from the east predominated, for some of Leopold's other domains in the west had found excuses for not contributing their full contingent. But many parts of the Holy Roman Empire were represented; even Italian cities like Milan, far away to the south, had sent a company of crossbowmen. In the milling and excited crowd, an observer could have picked out distinct knots of individuals. Banners, pennants and elaborate canvas surcoats, all bearing the same emblem, marked off one group from another. A few carried (or even wore) their heavy battle helmets, surmounted by a wooden crest,[5] although the wiser, already suffering from the heat, sought to lighten their burden. In battle those crests would form a rainbow menagerie, of eagles, boars, lions, bulls, bears, hawks and falcons, eagles, and other more fanciful beasts, like griffins, unicorns and basilisks. All would come jerkily to life, like some gigantic puppet-play, standing out above the pall of dust kicked up by the hoofs of the rider's horses. But in the mass of men, for all the superficial diversity of crest and emblem, it was clear that the knights were armed and equipped in very similar fashion, with (by a rough rule of thumb) the richest wearing the newest and most resplendent armour.

Among the foot-soldiers, as had been clear on the road to Brugg, diversity reigned: Flemish crossbowmen, only lightly armoured and with their precious weapons wrapped in oiled leather; swordsmen, flailmen, and wild irregulars armed with spears and axes from the Slav lands; the frontiersmen from the borders with the Ottoman Turks on stocky little ponies, and, in their thousands, spearmen. They were more lightly armed than the knights, but still weighed down with a heavy metal bassinet on their heads, a massive mail collar protecting their neck and shoulders and a short-coat of mail or of stiff leather studded with iron discs and bars. Their spears, with a solid shaft up to twelve feet in length, were topped with a stout broad-bladed point that continued with a long tang that protected the wood beneath. They also carried a short heavy sword, and some a dagger reputedly designed by an earlier Habsburg duke,[6] designed to slash the unprotected belly of a knight's horse, or to pass under the armour of a man at arms. The name of this weapon, ballock-knife, precisely described its purpose.

The gaily coloured tents that, according to the whimsical illustrations of the chroniclers, bedecked a medieval war camp were largely absent. Soldiers and knights slept on the ground, their weapons stacked close to them and sentries posted. The duke and his senior commanders kept apart. They had tents, but not the gaudy pavilions depicted in manuscript illuminations. Dyed dark browns and reds predominated rather than bright colours. It was the emblems and crests, embroidered on cloth, painted or carved in wood and vividly coloured, that both provided a bright splash of golds, silvers and crimsons, and also presented the subtle gradations of aristocratic society. The heraldic images all told a story, of family connections and loyalties, of political claims and traditional enmities. To emblazon the arms of a territory or of another family was to proclaim those connections to the world. The battle flags of later generations, flourished to enable the ignorant soldiers to know which side they fought for, grew out of this medieval practice. But in this process of development over the centuries the emblems lost most of their original meaning. Or more precisely, they gained new ones. The badge, the emblem stood for the whole nature and quality of the family that it signified. To choose a badge was no light matter for it declared a family's self-image to the world. While rules governed the complex practices of heraldry, the choice of the crest, either an animal or some other symbol, was an individual choice. Nor was it a matter lightly undertaken. As the historian Keith Thomas has observed,[7] 'In heraldry, pageantry, artistic symbolism, the creatures continued to provide a vocabulary and a set of categories to which human qualities could be described and classified.'

At one level what was happening at Brugg, on this the most extraordinary day in the history of the town, was straightforward enough: an army was gathering and preparing to march. In that sense it was a pattern repeated in countless other places over the whole of history. But this gathering and its aftermath were encrusted with a whole set of meanings that are not immediately obvious. What, then, was taking place at Brugg, and what would happen as the army headed south, along the lush farmlands of the Aargau, with the rolling hills beyond, towards its encounter with destiny outside another little country town, on the shores of lake Sempach? On the surface Leopold and his commanders were preparing for a war of punishment. There is no record that they talked of the purpose or the motive for their action, and it would have been surprising had they done so. Such matters needed no discussion. In the context of the times, the world could be divided between those who could bear arms and those who could not. The bearing of arms meant much more than the simple act of carrying a sword, a spear or a crossbow. Skill with some or all of these was a *sine qua non*, a given, among the little group that met in the duke's tent to plan the campaign that would be fought over the remaining days of June and on into July.

But 'bearing arms' carried a much more complex set of meanings. On one side it meant the physical act that legitimated the social status of a warrior, as a man of honour. War of itself was a neutral act: there was no 'honour' in killing or punishing peasants. But to kill them out of duty and loyalty ennobled the act, and made it honourable. That intricate sense of honour was made visible in the heraldic arms, the shields, crests and banners. Corporately, collectively, the sense of honour was enfolded within its emblems. In later generations soldiers would die to save the colours, the banner of their regiment or company; gunners were honour bound not to surrender their weapons. The sword, the helmet crest, became the embodiment of honour: in a few days' time, Leopold would die snatching up a banner (so the later legend went) emblazoned with the Lion of Habsburg. A vast gulf separated these men in the duke's tent – and all those who, like them, could point to their ancestry proclaimed on their shields and surcoats – from those myriad others in the town who were simply the wielders of weapons. Still more were they set apart from their enemy, who had briefly left the plough to take up the pike, sword or halberd. In a sense, the war was to be fought between those who 'bore arms' and those who merely used them.

The march into the Aargau formed part of a larger pattern. A social order already under siege was waging yet another campaign in a war to the death, to preserve rank and subordination against the threat from below. The aim of Leopold was not merely to take back the territories which had been purloined from him, but to humble those who had stepped beyond their place in the social order. He saw the people of the Swiss mountains and forests as contumacious, wilfully disobedient and defiant, and their attitudes had infested the more pliant inhabitants of the towns, like Luzern and Bern, that continued to provide taxes and revenues for the Habsburgs. They had long sustained their disobedience by force of arms. Two generations before, in 1315, the Swiss had devastated a large force of Austrian knights by lake Morgarten. On a cold November day, as the column of riders, all in full armour, traversed a narrow path beside the lake, the Swiss had rolled down huge rocks and tree trunks from the high ground above the defile, which crashed into the horsemen below. The confusion was indescribable as stallions that had not been knocked to the ground, melled and buffeted each other, terror-stricken at this surprise assault.

Many knights were pushed off the path into the icy water of the lake, to be dragged beneath the surface as their heavy armour filled with water. Most drowned, while on the path the battered bodies of horses and men impeded the retreat of the survivors. Against this remnant seeking to re-establish some sense of order, the Swiss loosed a hail of arrows, and then, dropping their bows, charged down from the heights of Buchwäldi brandishing their halberds, possibly the most deadly pole arm ever devised. (Some would contend that the Swiss pike, developed a century later, should take pride of place.) In the hands of a brawny Schwyzer, the halberd inspired terror. Swung in an arc, a blow from the massive axe blade, almost three feet long, could lift a knight from the saddle. Once the victim was on the ground, smashing jabs from the spear point, a short chopping cut from the axe blade, or thrusts from the long spike that adorned the other side of the weapon, used to burrow through the chinks in the armour, ended many a noble career.[8] The Austrians eventually carried away their dead from Morgarten, but they learned very little from that encounter. They concluded, wrongly, that these men were just mountain bandits, skilled in ambush and treachery but no match for seasoned soldiers in open combat. Not so. Gradually, the military skill of these farmers and foresters was seen to be more than beginner's luck. The Swiss repeatedly showed their skill on the battlefield as well. On a June day in 1339, 1,000 men from the Swiss forests, in the pay of the city of Bern, inflicted a shattering defeat on the knights and men-at-arms in the service of the rival city of Freiburg. The slaughter was considerable, and the nobles and rulers began to realize the deadly threat posed by the Swiss.[9]

Leopold had two other instances of how the low-born waged war. Unfortunately, the conclusions they produced were contradictory. The first concerned the Swiss. A decade before the army was summoned to Brugg, a large band of mercenaries (known as Güglers, from the pointed woollen cowls that they wore over their armour, in an effort to keep out the searing cold) invaded the Aargau.[10] They arrived early in December 1375, and ravaged the towns and villages along the valleys of the Reuss and Aare. But as they moved deeper into the heart of Switzerland, they found the people of the forests and mountain less easy to terrorize. Suddenly, they were resisted on every side. Near lake Sempach, at the tower of Buttisholz, they were surprised at night by a band of Swiss. Three hundred of the mercenaries were killed, and many more, who had taken refuge in a church, were burned alive by the enraged people of the district. In a skirmish at the village of Jens close to Bern, another 300 knights were killed, while a few days later the Swiss attacked their main encampment at the abbey of Fraubrunnen, and after savage fighting drove the mercenaries away, who left 800 dead. Battered on every side, the Güglers withdrew, and Habsburgs, among many others, began to digest the causes and consequences of their defeat. A consensus soon began to emerge. The Swiss were strong and savage, foolhardy, bold, and gifted with implacable courage. Yet they were not capable of coherent planning or military thinking. All their victories were seen as the consequence of their animal ferocity. They were both sub- and superhuman, an 'alien other', outside the bounds of European culture.

The other, indeed, the defining event which served to confirm this view, was the destruction at Roosebeke of the Flemish burgher army by the French king barely four years before Leopold's expedition into the Aargau. In the depths of winter, with a light snow on the ground and a bitter wind, the army of the Flemish cities was none the less confident of victory. It too had a heritage of success, a famous victory which had been told and retold over the years. Eighty years before, at the battle of Courtrai, armed with spears and the *goedendag*, rather like the Swiss halberd, its warriors had devastated the ranks of chivalry, after an impetuous, mad rush. Courtrai and Morgarten were the first shocking victories of the wielders of arms against the men of honour. In 1382 their chosen battlefield was about ten miles north-west of Ypres. The armies of France and the Flemish cities camped close to each other: each could see the camp fires of the other and could hear the clamour of their preparations. Some said that the noise was 'the devils of hell running and dancing about the place where the battle was to be because of the great prey expected there'. All knew that this would be a battle of great moment. If the French won, it would reinforce the traditional society of 'honour'; if the Flemings succeeded, then the supremacy of the man on horseback would be ended.

Early on the following morning, the two armies prepared to engage. The French, under the command of the constable of France and in the presence of the young French king, Charles VI, had adopted a set of tactics designed precisely to counter the habits of the Flemish way of war. The constable turned a large number of his armoured and mounted knights into foot-soldiers. Armed with spears, they stood shoulder to shoulder with the spearmen, in a solid mass, well able to resist the advance of the Flemish phalanx. The armoured knights gave the line strength and rigidity and, the constable believed, made it less likely to crumble under the weight of the Flemish assault. But the battle, he foresaw, would be won not in the centre, but on the flanks: there, mounted knights, half hidden and in reserve, would charge on his command into the unprotected burgher ranks and throw them into disruption. Thus, squeezing them harder and harder from left and right, and with an inexorable pressure in the centre, he would crack their army like a walnut, at its weakest point.

Enguerrand de Coucy, the Count of Soissons, who had led the Güglers in 1375–6, was among those who devised the plan and who was in the forefront of the battle. Artevalde had instructed his men to keep close together, 'that none might break you', and even told them to link arms or otherwise bind themselves together. In the morning, before they advanced, the Flemings bombarded the French line with arrows and crossbow bolts, but the knights' armour proved largely impervious. Then they rolled forward *en masse* on to the French spears, as the chronicler Froissart put it, like 'enraged boars'. At first they were successful, smashing into the French ranks, but without breaking them. Like so many schemes carefully conceived in advance, the chance of battle now seemed likely to destroy the French plan because the Flemish flank was no longer visible, for it had driven like a wedge into the heart of the French army. The mounted horsemen under the Duke of Bourbon and the Count of Soissons, who were to have swept in from each side, stood helpless. Then at Soissons's suggestion, they disengaged their men, and rode out to left and right; some thought that they were in flight. But then they swung around and smashed into the Flemish ranks from the rear, riding down the burgher reserves. The impact was devastating, and most of those in the rear ranks of the Flemings had no armour. The piles of bodies rose under the hoofs of the warhorses and, seeing what was happening and with a great shout, the dismounted knights began to push forward. Together, they crushed the Flemings, not like a walnut, but like a plum. Many of the burghers were crushed to death, among them their commander Philip van Artevalde. The ground was flooded with Flemish blood, and to show their contempt for their base-born enemy, the French commanders instructed that the corpses were to be left to rot, or to be eaten by wild beasts, 'the prey of dogs and crows', in Froissart's grim but exact phrase.

This was the fate that Leopold planned for the Swiss and his battle plan bore a remarkable similarity to that adopted at Roosebeke. First of all he did not intend to waste his time in besieging the Swiss cities, but hoped to draw them out into open battle. He also knew that the halberd was a deadly weapon at close quarters, one impossible for a man on horseback to counteract. A sword was simply outreached by the long haft of the halberd. The Swiss could strike blow after blow with impunity, knowing that the rider could never get close enough to slash at his tormentors. On foot, however, and using the long spears carried by the men-at-arms, the advantage shifted. Before the Swiss could use their weapons, they would need to penetrate a forest of spear points. And, while his knights on foot gripped the Swiss in a deadly embrace, as at Roosebeke, his men on horseback would dash in from the flanks and cut the Swiss to pieces. Thus he would turn their ferocity, their wild charge, against them and would clasp them close to the armoured breastplates of his knights. Once their strength was sapped, his eastern savages – Cumans, Vlachs and the like – would hunt down their shattered remnant as they streamed back into the forest. And, to show that there was no dishonour in fighting on foot, the duke himself would take his place besides his banner, spear in hand, with his knights and men-at-arms.

At a single blow, therefore, it would be possible to overthrow two generations of Swiss truculence. Once the men from the mountains had been so roundly defeated in open combat, the cities would fall back into line, dutifully acknowledging their Habsburg overlord. The force that set out from Brugg, moving west and then south through the Aargau towards Sempach and the rebel towns of central Switzerland, was confident of success The land it passed through on the way south was a hostile countryside, nominally under the rule of the Habsburgs but sullen and resentful of this new army living off the land. The expedition was intended as a punishment, to show the price to be paid by those who broke their allegiance to the Habsburgs, or had brazenly seized their possessions, as the Swiss from the Forest Cantons had done. The first to suffer for their temerity in rejecting the Habsburgs were the people of Willisau, where Leopold's army arrived at the end of June. Summoned to yield, they refused. Within a matter of a few hours, the walls were breached, all within slaughtered, and the town set alight. It was said that the acrid smoke from the burning flesh carried as far as Sempach, some thirty miles to the east, whose people had already received news of their fate. Willisau and Sempach had long been Habsburg towns, and both, under enticement, had unwisely thrown off their lord's control.

But Leopold's strategy was not just to punish little towns that had defied him. He had not mortgaged his estates and borrowed heavily to raise an army for the satisfaction of seeing Willisau destroyed. He wanted to draw out the Swiss into open confrontation on a battlefield beyond Sempach, to end their resistance for ever and to avenge the slights that his family had suffered at their hands for more than sixty years. So he marched on, skirting the side of Sempachersee, and tempting the Swiss to attack him. First he gathered his troops at Sempach on the evening of 8 July, encircling the little town and early the next day his men taunted those behind the walls. One of his knights waved a noose at them and promised that he would use it on their leaders. Another mockingly pointed to the soldiers setting fire to the ripe fields of grain, and asked them to send a breakfast to the reapers. From behind the walls, there was a shouted retort: 'Luzern and the allies will bring them breakfast.' This was what the Duke was hoping for, and soon Leopold got news that indeed the Swiss were approaching from the east. Leaving a token force at the little town, he hastened to meet them. His scouts brought news that the Swiss were camped at the forest edge a few miles from Sempach, but in no great numbers. Eager for combat, the Habsburg army straggled up the long hill from Sempach, with the commanders and the duke in the vanguard. As they crested a rise, across a small plateau, they could see the Swiss on the high ground above what seemed a heaven-sent battleground and Leopold quickly put his plan into operation. His men dismounted and took spears, forming up in a tight knot at the edge of the little plateau. They, like him, were anxious to join battle with the Swiss ahead of them. It was the ninth of July, a little after noon, at the hottest part of the day.

When they rode up the hill, Leopold and his knights were part of history; when they came down again, as bloody corpses, they were embodied in myth. The outcome, disaster for the Habsburg army, was undeniable; but precisely what happened, and why, is not clear. The tale, as carried over to later generations was so rich with detail and in incident that it cannot be wholly false. As the Habsburg army advanced,

the horses [were] fatigued by the march, and the woods [where the Swiss were gathered] were impracticable for horses, so the knights dismounted. At this moment, the Swiss according to their custom, threw themselves upon their knees and with uplifted hands, implored the assistance of the Most High. Some of the Austrians observing this action exclaimed 'They are supplicating for pardon!', but they were soon undeceived, for the confederate troops instantly quitted the woodland and poured down into the plain. A few only were in armour, some brandished the halberds which their forefathers had wielded at Morgarten; others bore two-handed swords, and battle-axes ... the Austrian host, on the contrary, were covered from head to foot in blazing armour, presented a solid range of shields, and a horrent front of projecting spears.

On the little plateau at the top of the hill, the Swiss 'confederates', brawny highlanders from the heart of Switzerland, faced an enemy who was not behaving as they had expected. Instead of a battle line of mounted knights, they were confronted by an impenetrable hedge of spear points. Nor were their halberds long enough, as Leopold had surmised, to hack their way past them and in among the Habsburg knights.

'The Swiss drew up in the form of a wedge, and rushed with their usual impetuosity to the attack, but made no impression on this formidable phalanx; the banner of Lucerne was exposed to imminent danger, and the landsmann, with sixty of his most adventurous warriors, fell before a single enemy received a wound.' It was as might be expected, with the solid ranks of the armoured warriors pressing steadily forward against the more lightly armed Swiss, crushing them on to the points of their heavy spears. The Swiss reeled back,

hesitated for a moment, regarding their enemies with a mixture of indignation and despair; while the ranks of the phalanx, advancing in a crescent, endeavoured to close in on their rear. At this awful crisis, Arnold de Winkelried, a knight of Unterwalden, bursting from the ranks, exclaimed: 'I will open a passage into the line; protect, dear countrymen and confederates, my wife and children.' Then throwing himself on the enemy, he seized as many of the pikes as he could grasp, and burying them in his breast, bore them by his weight to the ground. His companions rushed over his expiring body and forced themselves into the heart of the line; others, with equal intrepidity, penetrated into the intervals occasioned by the shock and the whole unwieldy mass was thrown into confusion and dismay.

The traditional story continued to the point of Habsburg nemesis:

The knights, oppressed with their ponderous armour and encumbered with their long spears, were unable to withstand the impetuous assault of the Swiss, or to recover from their disorder; and their servants, perceiving the general consternation, mounted the horses of their masters and left them no hope of safety by flight. The fight was for a while sustained by the efforts of personal valour and the undaunted spirit of chivalry: but the havoc soon became general as numbers fell by the sword of the enemy; many perished by the pressure of their companions and the intense heat and not less than 2,000, of whom almost a third were counts, barons and knights, were numbered among the slain.

What actually happened on that hard-fought piece of ground remains a mystery. We know that the Habsburg battle plan with the enfolding cavalry arms collapsed before it could be put into effect. We know that the Swiss suddenly broke up the Habsburg advance, threw them into disarray, and slaughtered them in their hundreds. But how? The Swiss fought in the only way that they knew.

The sun stood high; the day was sultry . . . The Swiss after their devotion ran full speed and with full clamour across the plain, seeking an opening where they might break the line; but they were opposed . . . by the numberless points of spears as by a thick fence of iron thorns. The men of Luzern . . . made many fierce attempts to break into the line, but all of them ineffectual. The knights moving with hideous rattle attempted to bend their line into a crescent, meaning to outflank and surround their assailants. Antony du Port, a Milanese who had settled in the valley of Uri, cried out 'Strike the poles of the spears, they are hollow': this was effected, but the broken spears were immediately replaced by fresh ones and du Port himself perished in the conflict. The knights, partly owing to their unskilfulness and more so to the unwieldiness of their armour, found it impracticable to form the intended crescent; but they stood firm and unshaken.

Until this point the advantage lay with the 'firm and unshaken' line of knights. The Swiss sensed that their tactic was failing. They could see movement in the Habsburg forces further down the hill and 'they became apprehensive of a movement of the [Austrian] vanguard from the rear, and nor did they think themselves altogether secure against a surprise from [the Count of] Bonstetten' (commanding the Habsburg mounted forces). What was needed was a miracle, and it duly occurred. The story of Winkelried is a pure myth: the real life Arnold von Winkelried was a sixteenth-century Swiss soldier, who was brought into the tale only in the 1530s. But the substance, if not its heroic overtones, rings true to the light of experience. Once a gap opened in the spear wall for whatever reason – some suggested that the Swiss crossbowmen, shooting into the Austrian mass, created the opening – the solidity of the front rank was broken. And Leopold, fighting close to the front rank, was instantly recognizable. In some accounts he is wearing golden armour. But in all the depictions of the battle he is distinguished by his towering crest of peacock feathers. The chroniclers made his decision to fight in the ranks of his knights into an act of heroism.

When the duke was admonished that in all engagements unforeseen accidents do happen; that the province of a chief is to conduct the army, and of the army to defend its chief; and that the loss of a commander is often more ruinous than that of half his force, he at first answered with a smile of indifference; but being urged with greater solicitude he replied with warmth. 'Shall Leopold look on from afar and see how his brave knights combat and die for him. Here, in my country, and with my people, I will either conquer or perish.'

As the Swiss broke into the Habsburg mass,

the banner of Austria sank to the ground ... Ulric of Arburg raised it anew and endeavoured to restore the fight, but he also was soon oppressed and fell exclaiming, 'Help Austria help.' Duke Leopold ran to him, received the banner now steeped in gore from his dying hand and once more waved it on high. The conflict at this moment became fierce and obstinate. Numbers of combatants pressed round the duke; many of his illustrious companions fell near him; at length all hope being at an end, he exclaimed, 'I too will fall with honour.'[11]

Once the Swiss had broken into the line, and could reach their enemy with their terrible halberds, the balance of advantage shifted. As Sir Charles Oman observed:

Swung by the strong arms of an Alpine herdsman, it would cleave helmet, shield or coat of mail like pasteboard. The sight of the ghastly wounds which it inflicted might well appal the stoutest foes; he who once felt its edge needed no second stroke. It was the halberd which laid Leopold of Habsburg dead across his fallen banner at Sempach . . . and struck down Charles of Burgundy – all his face one gash from temple to teeth – in the frozen ditch at Nancy (1477).[12]

Once the banner had fallen, the headlong retreat of the rest of the Habsburg forces was inevitable, for the battle was clearly lost. Those writing in the immediate aftermath of the battle recorded most of its key elements.[13] All the chronicles stress the heat of the day; we know that it had been a hot and dry summer, and even the dust becomes a recurring motif. As the mass of men stumbled back and forth across the little plateau, hacking at each other, the dust kicked up by their feet must have made it impossible to see what was going on from the Habsburg lines below (or indeed the main body of the Swiss above). At first the crested helmets would have been clearly visible and then only the flags waving above the battle. But when the banner of Habsburg fell, rose again from the swirl of dust, fell, reappeared, and fell to rise no more, only one conclusion was possible. The battle was lost.

The immediate aftermath was that both sides were exhausted, and it was two days before they returned to carry away their dead. More than six hundred counts, lords and knights perished under the Habsburg banner. Some sixty of the most eminent were carried north with remnants of the army, together with the battered body of Leopold; others were claimed for burial by their families. But the vast majority were buried in a huge common grave on the site of battle, where a small chapel was raised in memory of all who had died. Sempach, according to the Swiss, was a day on which God 'sat in judgement on the wanton arrogance of the nobles'.

Many medieval battles are enveloped in myth and literary fantasy. Did Roland blow his horn for relief at Roncesvalles (778)?[14] At the battle of Tours, 'The men of the north stood as motionless as a wall; they were like a belt of ice frozen together, and not to be dissolved, as they slew the Arabs with the sword. The Austrasians, vast of limb, and iron of hand, hewed on bravely in the thick of the fight; it was they who found and cut down the Saracen king.'[15] Or did they? The blind King John of Bohemia had assuredly been killed at Crécy, perhaps pointed by his knights and squires towards an enemy he could not see; but had the English king truly plucked the three ostrich feathers from the dead king's helmet crest and given them to his son the Black Prince (who thereafter bore them as his coat of arms, together with the motto, *Ich dien* – I serve)? In the world governed by honour, an act or an event was mutable; defeat could be transformed into victory, fact into legend or into myth. Sempach was unusual in that, first, the actual conduct of the battle was so shrouded in mystery – all myth and so little fact – and that, second, it was so potent a source of legend for both sides. Winkelried, as constructed, embodied the concern for family and selfless patriotism of the Swiss. 'I will open a passage into the line; protect, dear countrymen and confederates, my wife and children, honour my race' he is supposed to have cried as he buried the Austrian spear points in his body. In many of the illustrations, from the late eighteenth century onwards, Winkelried, who was early described as being of 'tall, corpulent stature, who bore the spears to the ground with his own ponderous mass', was transmuted into an epicene blond youth of surpassing beauty. In these images the fatal spear was often wielded by Leopold himself.

Leopold, tyrant to the Swiss, even the direct instrument of the fictional Winkelried's imaginary martyrdom, became in the hands of his own family a martyr himself. His name became one of the most popular among successive generations of his family, over the space of seven succeeding centuries; this was partly because an earlier ruler of Austria, a margrave of the Babenberg dynasty from 1095 to 1086, was canonized as St Leopold, and became one of the patron saints of Austria. The Babenberg St Leopold was simply colonized by the Habsburgs and made one of their own. The characters of the two Leopolds were merged, the sanctity of the former uniting with the martyr's crown of the latter. The utterances with which he was credited at Sempach – 'shall Leopold look on from afar and see how his brave knights combat and die for him. Here, in my country, and with my people, I will either conquer or perish' – which may contain some element of truth, and his dying words – 'I too will fall with honour' – which were certainly imaginary, were those appropriate for one who put honour before survival. He was made into the Dead King to fill a cenotaph, an empty shrine, already constructed. As the catafalque bearing the bodies of Leopold and his knights rolled north towards Brugg, their destination was already certain. On the other bank of the river whence they had set out was an abbey church, called Königsfelden – the king's field. It lacked only its king, and now Leopold was to fill the crypt ready and waiting for three-quarters of a century.

The martyred Leopold was the tenth generation of his family; nevertheless the Habsburgs' pedigree was not a particularly illustrious one. They had entered written history about the year 1020 when the Bishop of Strasbourg, Werner, and his brother Radbot built the white tower called the Habichtsburg above the river Reuss. Later apologists tried to prove that they were building on what had been, since time immemorial, the hereditary lands of 'that admirable family'. In fact, it was much more likely that this was an act of opportunism, an ambitious noble securing lands that were not fully under the control of any other lord. Only a few years before, the Hungarian horde had surged out of the east, looting and burning; even the walls of Basel did not prove strong enough to hold them although the cathedral (built like a fortress) survived. The Aargau remained a no man's land,[16] and it was easy to build a holding comprising a few villages and a couple of castles. From the top of the white tower it is still possible to see the entirety of the first Habsburg domain, a few thousand acres bounded by the hills to the south and the north.

By the end of the eleventh century, their possession was recognized by the Emperor, and the descendants of Werner and Radbot began to use the name of their *Stammhaus*, calling themselves 'of the *Habichtsburg*', 'of *Habsberc*', and finally, *Habsburg*. But among the magnates, they registered at the very bottom of the scale; however, the speed of their subsequent rise was remarkable. By the mid twelfth century, their domains extended both north, to the Rhine and beyond into the Black Forest, and south into Switzerland. They occupied the land by building on it not castles so much as towns and especially ecclesiastical foundations. The first of these – the abbey of Muri in 1027, became the model. First the abbey was built at the expense of the family and the community was known to be under their protection. Then in turn, the abbey acquired land and wealth, secure in the support of its patron. A century later, the Habsburgs became the protector of the abbey of Murbach, whose possessions extended from Basel down as far as Luzern. This creeping accretion of power and wealth was enhanced by judicious marriages and family alliances, and by gaining judicial rights in areas that they did not control outright.

Thus Habsburgs, as representatives of the emperor, became the legal authority – *Vogt* – over great areas south of the Rhine. In 1173, they inherited rights over Sempach and Willisau, as well as the title and rights of the Count of the Zürichgau, which gave the Habsburgs authority in the distant valleys of Schweyz and Nidwalden. Prosperous cities like Zürich and Luzern fell within the Habsburg circle, not controlled by military power but by looser ties of what were, initially, bonds of common interest. The Habsburgs provided security and the cities needed peace so that their trade and commerce could grow. The opening of the mountain passes to Italy – an extraordinary bridge spanned the heights of the St Gotthard – gave the little Habsburg towns like Brugg, Bremgarten, Maienberg, even Säckingen on the Rhine, a direct and profitable linkage to the markets of the south. Thereafter the Habsburgs grew rich from their percentage on the trade and the tolls paid as the goods passed through their towns and cities. By 1212, the Count of Habsburg was able to raise more money in support of the Emperor than the rich Bishoprics of Mainz and Worms plus four of the most powerful secular lords of the Empire. Such a positive and practical expression of devoted support was not forgotten.

This, then, was a family less of warriors than courtiers. Few of the early Habsburgs were renowned for their military prowess, but they were all noted for their loyalty and devotion to the Hohenstaufen emperors. Rudolf II, Count of Habsburg, was one of the first to proclaim his support for the young Emperor Frederick II, the future 'Stupor Mundi' – the Wonder of the World – in 1198. And he raised the 1,000 marks required by Frederick in 1212, referred to above. The compliment was repaid six years later when the Emperor stood as godfather to the count's grandson, another Rudolf, who was to become the first Habsburg emperor.[17] Other families were more flamboyant, more evidently illustrious. The Habsburgs, by contrast, seemed content to seek only riches and territorial aggrandizement; lust for glory and power seemed, to their contemporaries, largely absent.

How much did these rich but lacklustre counts conceal a vaunting, almost delirious spirit of ambition? Adam Wandruszka may well be right when he suggests that in the little family chapel of Othmerstein, built in the very first days of the Habsburgs' rise and closely modelled on Charlemagne's great chapel at Aachen, we see that from the outset there was 'a visible expression to the claim to sovereignty, [which] illustrates the family's importance and self-confidence even at the beginning of the eleventh century'.[18] Certainly, almost two centuries later, the abbey church at Königsfelden was unquestionably a shrine to the spirit of their dynasty. No Habsburg, not even the greatest like Charles V, on whose empire 'the sun never set', could happily have carried the sobriquet, Stupor Mundi. The Habsburgs even in these early days did not set out to astound the world; they sought the hidden powers that controlled it.

The first member of this large and fertile family to be more than a loyal and dutiful courtier was the child whom the Emperor Frederick had accepted as his godson in 1218. Even as a young man Rudolf of Habsburg was renowned for an 'enterprising spirit', and the list of his exploits fills the family chronicles. Tall and lanky, with thinning hair, a small head on broad shoulders, with a large and patrician nose, he stood out, literally and figuratively, from the press of lesser men. The family historians were at pains to stress his military prowess and by the time that he inherited his estates at the age of twenty-two, he was already a skilful and resourceful soldier, 'Trained to wrestling and running, [he] was skilled in horsemanship, excelled in throwing the javelin, and being endowed with great strength and vigour, gave eminent proofs of superiority over his companions.' But whatever the panegyrists might claim, the night raids, the daring seizures of towns and castles, did not justify the praise which later Habsburgs lavished on the 'Great Founder of the House of Austria'.[19] But he undoubtedly made his own fortune. His share of the patrimony from his father Albert, who died while on crusade in 1240, amounted to little more than some lands in upper Alsace, and the territory around Brugg, Muri, and the Castle of the Hawk. Within a few years he had enlarged his domain, largely at the expense of his own family, for the Habsburg inheritance was traditionally divided. Boldly, he also demanded lands from his uncle, the Count of Kyburg, one of the most powerful magnates in the region, who had the resources to crush this upstart out of hand. But in some fashion Rudolf, perhaps by his sheer energy and determination, seemed to paralyse the will of others, and the Kyburgs allowed him to have his way. Sometimes he went too far – as when he attacked the city of Basel at night and burned a nunnery, for which the Pope excommunicated him. But within a few years he was released from the papal ban, and even made his peace with his uncle.

All the records stress that Rudolf was warm in manner, open, affable. His engaging friendliness and genuine humility should not be doubted, yet there was also steel in his manner, that could terrify anyone who stood against him. To the Bishop of Strasbourg, who held the lands that had once belonged to his mother, he offered friendship and assistance, but requested the return of those territories which, after all, were only a very small part of the bishop's vast estates. The bishop peremptorily rejected his request and Rudolf quietly replied with words that strike a chill note down the passage of the centuries:

'Since you pay no regard to the greatest services and seem inclined rather to offend than conciliate your friends, Rudolf of Habsburg, instead of your ally, is become your most inveterate enemy.' Laying his hand on his sword, he added, 'While I am master of this weapon, neither you nor any other person shall wrest from me those dominions I inherit by right of my mother; and since in contradiction to every principle of justice, you grasp at the possessions of others, know that you shall shortly lose your own.'

He fulfilled his threat to the letter. In 1259, he took possession of the city of Strasbourg, and waged a relentless campaign against the dispossessed bishop, capturing all his remaining lands and pursuing him relentlessly. Soon he was dead, some said struck down by Rudolf's own hand, although there was no proof of it. The new bishop shrewdly agreed to Rudolf's earlier demands without demur and offered to ransom the towns that the Count of Habsburg had captured for a large sum. Rudolf accepted the territories that were his by right but refused the offer of money. He restored the towns and estates of Colmar, Mülhausen and lower Alsace to the bishop, winning an ally where before he had faced an enemy.

Much of this chivalric *gentillesse* is in an established literary tradition. These were the virtuous deeds expected of Great Men; but there is also much in the records that is plainly factual, and specific to Rudolf. If the heroism can be in part discarded, and perhaps the open-handed generosity, the sense of shrewd calculation, of the terror that he inspired by a quietly spoken word, must pertain to Rudolf himself. It is difficult to draw the boundary between the two. Some of the qualities attached to him – simplicity and affability, for example – were those specially remarked upon in the accounts of the first Emperor, Charlemagne.[20] This identity between Charlemagne and Rudolf was a connection which later Habsburg historians were keen to stress. But the coldness and calculation that seemed to underlie all Rudolf's actions were not the traditional attributes of a monarch. On more than one occasion he is recorded as 'having turned an enemy into a friend'; the sense, however, was that it was a friendship founded in fear. The Bishop of Basel's response on hearing that Rudolf had been elected to the vacant German throne – 'Sit fast, Lord God, or Rudolf will occupy thy throne' – is often taken as a wry tribute; but underneath lay a prickling of apprehension.

The Electors, meeting in the imperial city of Frankfurt, had finally decided on the first day of October 1273, after much wrangling, to offer the throne to the Count of Habsburg. It had been a delicate and finely judged decision. They had been anxious not to create a master, a new Frederick II. But nor had they wanted a monarch so weak as to tempt intervention from powerful outside rulers, like the King of France. They came to see that Rudolf of Habsburg met all their requirements. At fifty-five years old, he

seemed unlikely to rule for more than a few years. Nor was he at
feud with any of the Electors, indeed the chancellor of the Empire,
the Archbishop of Mainz, had benefited from his protection and
hospitality on a journey to Rome. And all were mindful that he had
dealt honourably with the Bishop of Strasbourg in the matter of the
towns captured while securing his mother's inheritance. He was
equally innocuous to the secular princes, for he posed no obvious
threat to any of them. Only the King of Bohemia, Ottokar Przemysl,
by descent a Hohenstaufen, and one of the most powerful rulers of
Europe, campaigned forcefully against Rudolf's selection. But Ottokar had been excluded from the electoral college, and his voice
carried no decisive weight. Rather, it damaged his own candidacy,
because none of the German princes wanted so domineering an
Emperor. No one could have predicted that Rudolf would rule the
Empire, with increasing authority, for more than seventeen years.

When the news of his elevation arrived, Rudolf was besieging the
city of Basel, in a long-running dispute with the bishops over land
and precedence. The chronicles suggest that Rudolf expressed amazement at his good fortune and then behaved with the utmost
modesty and circumspection. There is some reason to think that his
surprise was for public consumption, for he was aware that the
Count Palatine had been actively advocating his candidacy. But
feigned or not, his second response was a master-stroke. The
candidate 'King of the Romans' immediately sent a humble petition
to the Pope, Gregory X, who was presiding at a General Council of
the Church in session at Lyons. Rudolf as a dutiful son of the
Church sought papal approval for his appointment, and made a
promise that he would lead Europe on a crusade. The Pope's fiat
came by return, and the new king could claim that he had the
support both of the German people and of God's vicar on Earth.
Two years later there was a much-heralded meeting between the
Pope and the new Emperor[21] at Lausanne. The bitter conflict
between Pope and Emperor that had dominated more than two
centuries of European history seemed to have ended with the
absolute triumph of the papacy. The new Emperor appeared uncon-
cerned with the burning questions of sovereignty and authority that
his predecessors had fought so hard to sustain. Of the other
candidates only Ottokar of Bohemia had remained determined to

upset Rudolf's elevation, refusing to accept the election and challenging the new Emperor to contest his absorption of the duchy of Austria. This, the Empire's farthest outpost in the east, was adjacent to his kingdom of Bohemia and had been 'vacant' since the death of the last duke of the House of Babenberg in 1246.[22] The King of Bohemia had married the widow of the last duke and taken the duchy as his marriage portion. However, when he later divorced the former duchess, he retained title to the duchy, and its revenues. Whatever the rights of the issue, Ottokar was a renowned warrior, with the largest army in eastern Europe; his court at Prague was evidence of his great wealth. Rudolf's first task would be to reassert the rights of the Empire over its eastern extremity; if he failed against Ottokar, his reign would be of short duration.

It is clear that Ottokar regarded Rudolf as a mere puppet-Emperor selected by the Electors solely to frustrate his own legitimate ambitions. Rudolf made no overtly hostile moves, despite the King of Bohemia's undisguised contempt for the 'pauper count'. He remembered Rudolf as the penniless young man who had fought for him in one of his wars against the Baltic tribes. The Emperor took the advice of the lawyers of the Empire, and issued a request that the King of Bohemia attend the Imperial Diet to do homage for the eastern lands which he had acquired. This was the customary procedure, and had Ottokar answered the summons, it would have been difficult for Rudolf to refuse to grant him the fiefs to the eastern lands. Indeed, there is no suggestion that he would have withheld the duchy, since Ottokar's claims were superior to any other claimant's. There is certainly no evidence that he was determined on war with the King of Bohemia so as to provide a patrimony for his own family; if anything the reverse was true, since it seemed likely that he would fail utterly in battle against the combined forces of eastern Europe and so renowned a soldier.

Ottokar failed to answer the first summons to swear allegiance for his imperial territories at Würzburg; when called again to appear before the Diet of the Empire at Augsburg, he again failed to appear but on this occasion sent an emissary to present the case on his behalf. As the King of Bohemia's spokesman, the Bishop of Seccau, delivered his long and complex Latin address, Rudolf interrupted him. 'Bishop, if you were to harangue an ecclesiastical consistory, you might use the Latin tongue; but when discoursing upon my rights and the rights of the princes of the Empire, why do you employ a language which the greater part of those who are present do not understand.' His 'dignified rebuke' achieved the result he desired, for it 'roused the indignation of the assembly: the princes and particularly the elector Palatine, started from their seats, and were scarcely prevented from employing violence'.[23] The bishop, seeing the growing mood of anger, made his excuses and left hurriedly, returning to his master in Prague.

Rudolf is always described as good-hearted, slow to anger, modest and pious. But what the written accounts reveal, perhaps against the intention of their writers, is a man of devious political skills, even cunning. At Augsburg, he chose his moment to play the 'German card', knowing that part of the reason for his election had been a desire within the Empire for a truly German ruler, after a succession of foreigners (like Richard of Cornwall). Although he personally had made peace with the papacy, anti-papal sentiment remained strong within the Empire, and the manner in which he contrasted Latin – the language fit for a consistory – with the robust German of his fellow princes instantly secured the result he desired, and a rebuff to Ottokar. Almost to a man they rallied to him, and he was able to lead a force of 3,000 *gleves* east into the disputed lands of Austria. He marched along the southern bank of the Danube, arriving before Vienna which he immediately besieged. Ottokar, now declared an outlaw, hastened south to relieve his garrison. As he received news of the size and strength of the imperial army, and realized Rudolf's determination to enforce the decree against him, his peril became clear. So Ottokar sued for peace. Emissaries were sent to Rudolf, and a bargain quickly struck.

On 25 November, the day appointed for doing homage, [he] crossed the Danube with a large escort of Bohemian nobles to the camp of Rudolf, and was received by the king of the Romans in the presence of several princes of the Empire. With a depressed countenance and broken spirit, which he was unable to conceal from the bystanders, he made a formal resignation of his pretensions to Austria, Styria, Carinthia and Carniola and, kneeling down, did homage to his rival and obtained the investiture of Bohemia and Moravia with the accustomed ceremonies.

It was in every sense a reasonable and honourable settlement. The King of Bohemia swore homage for his lands and was confirmed in them. The bargain was to be secured in the most effective way, by marriage between the Habsburgs and the line of Ottokar.

In fact the King of Bohemia had no intention of holding to the agreement, and his only aim had been to lift the ban of the Empire pronounced against him. Once free of this anathema, he prepared for war against his Habsburg enemy. Once more secure in Prague, he abandoned the marriage plans, and issued a stream of letters disavowing the agreement, sealed only (he claimed) under duress. He called upon all his allies and vassals to join him in a final confrontation on the battlefield with the upstart Count of Habsburg. Ottokar's alliances and possessions extended from the edge of the Baltic to the shores of the Adriatic, and over the early summer of 1278, the whole of eastern Europe seemed to be on the move. Ottokar assembled not so much an army as a horde, much more colourful and 'barbarous' than the German knights mustered by Rudolf. Bands of yellow-coated Szeklers, with their long hair trailing down their backs, Tartars, and Romanians with their wide-brimmed lynx-fur hats, most armed with the short bows, sabres and lances of the east, rode towards Prague. The growing army was reinforced by knights from Lithuania carrying the long lance, the *spisa*, which they would hurl with devastating accuracy as they charged at an enemy. And the Poles wore curious conical helmets and carried heavy, studded wooden shields. Some records say there were more than 30,000 of these wild men who answered Ottokar's summons. At the end of June he began the march south towards the Danube and Vienna.

In August 955, one of Rudolf's most notable predecessors, Otto the Great, had confronted the advancing forces of the east on the Lechfeld close to Augsburg. On 26 August 1278, three centuries on, Rudolf took his battle into the enemy terrain. At dawn, the army of the German nation stood a little beyond the river March, on the flat and boggy ground known as the Marchfeld. Beside the black-eagle banner of the Empire and Rudolf's own red-lion standard,[24] a robed crucifer held the emblem of Christ aloft. Both sides, of course, were Christian, but as Otto battling with the pagan Hungarians on the Lechfeld had claimed divine protection, so too Rudolf made this confrontation into an issue of faith. Before battle was joined, the two solid masses of mailed men taunted each other across the narrow grassy strip that separated the two hosts. To the Czech battle-cry of the Bohemian army, 'Praga, Praga', the imperial army responded resoundingly with 'Rom, Rom' and 'Christus, Christus'. Some knights rattled their swords against their shields, adding to the cacophony. But above the din, the voices of the Bishop of Basel, his priests and acolytes intoning the anthem in German, 'Holy Mary, Mother and Maid, may all our grief on thee be laid', could just be heard. Then, as the imperial knights joined in the great unison, swelling the sound into a chant of triumph, the two sides spurred their horses forward into a cacophonous clash of arms.

Behind the vast rolling mêlée, the common soldiers on both sides looked on, taking virtually no part in the battle. In the first stages, Rudolf's Flemish slingers had hurled their stones at the opposing lines, and Ottokar's Cumans and Sarmatians had replied in kind with a barrage of arrows. But once the main battle was joined these many thousands of men stood like a crowd of spectators, although behind the Bohemian ranks the horde of horses and ponies responded nervously to the din and the smell of blood and sweat. What followed through the morning and early afternoon was a savage, hacking battle between the evenly matched armoured knights on both sides. Rudolf, fighting in the front ranks, was easily identifiable by his crowned helmet and the red lion of Habsburg.

Several knights of superior strength and courage, animated by the rewards and promises of Ottocar, had confederated either to kill or take the king of the Romans. They rushed forward to the place where Rudolf, riding among the foremost ranks, was leading his troops ... But Rudolf, accustomed to this species of combat ... piercing his opponent under the beaver [helmet], threw him dead to the ground.

Then a Thuringian knight of 'gigantic stature and strength' battered his way forward until he was side by side with Rudolf and speared the Emperor's horse in the shoulder. As his horse fell, Rudolf was thrown on to the ground, while the enemy rained blows down upon him. Only a timely rescue by an Austrian knight who had

seen Rudolf go down, and charged to his aid, saved the Emperor
from death. Another horse was found and Rudolf remounted,
rallied his troops, who shouted their acclaim, and pushed on
towards the Bohemian war-banners. For a moment, the battle
seemed to stand still, and then suddenly the energy and the power
to resist seemed to drain from the Bohemians and their allies. Like
a tide turning, they began to ebb away from the battlefield and this
movement quickly became a rout, as the knights in hasty retreat
collided with their own light horsemen and foot-soldiers in the
rear.

Ottokar, who had 'fought with no less intrepidity' than Rudolf,
was cut down by an Austrian nobleman with whom he was at feud
and stripped naked. The 'discomfited remains of his army, pursued
by the victors, were either taken prisoner, cut to pieces, or drowned
in their attempts to pass the March'. It was an epic battle, whose
Shakespearian dimensions appealed to the Austrian dramatist and
poet, Franz Grillparzer. His play dealing with the career and
demise of King Ottokar was written in the aftermath of Napoleon,
and deftly used the motif as Rudolf to comment on the later
greatness of the Habsburgs.[25] At the very end of the final act, the
triumphant Emperor orders that the King of Bohemia's naked body
should 'like an Emperor be interred' and that he

> Who died a lone and wretched beggar's death
> . . . have him lie in state
> Until they bear him where his fathers rest

Then, in a final scene, he has both his sons kneel before him, and
speaks to the elder of the two:

> Be great and strong; increase your race and line,
> Make it extend to regions near and far,
> With Habsburg's name emblazoned like a star!
> Stand by your brother, lend him your support.
> Should you by arrogance be led astray,
> With pride in governing raise up your head
> Think of this overweening man here dead,
> Whose misdeeds God will punish, one and all
> Of Ottokar, his rise and of his fall

> ... I hail you, sovereign now of this your land
> That, thunder like it echoes through the sky:
> Hail Austria's first Habsburg; Habsburg, hail
>
> Hail ! Hail
> Austria, hail
> Habsburg for ever

All the descriptions of Rudolf that have come down to us, like his speech at the Diet of Augsburg, or his resolute courage at the Marchfeld and its aftermath, are a mosaic, compounded in part of the real man and in part of an idealized image.[26] Where does the historical Rudolf end and the symbolic Rudolf begin? Almost from the beginning, within a few decades of his death, he had been transmuted into an emblem. 'The smiling rays of Habsburg's radiant sun[27]/That once more makes our trampled meadows green' was how Grillparzer later expressed it.[28] Nowhere is this alchemical process more clearly evident than in the legend of Rudolf and the priest. In this story the Emperor was out hunting when he came upon a village priest bearing the Host to a dying man. He stopped and climbed from his horse, and insisted that the priest should take his place on its back to cross the boiling, dirt-brown waters of a mountain stream in spate. Rudolf is reported to have said, 'It is not fitting that I should ride while the servant of my Lord and Saviour goes on foot.' Then, after they had crossed, he gave the horse to the village priest because he would not (he declared) again use for the mundane pursuits of war or hunting a beast that had once carried the Lord.[29] The first version of this tale appeared within fifty years of Rudolf's death, at a point when the fortunes of the Habsburgs were at a low ebb. This story, told and retold, and constantly depicted in images,[30] was a potent statement of the Habsburgs' claim to divine favour. They had lost the Empire and were under attack from every side. What this story presents is a lineage, in the person of their founder and great hero, that puts the service of God before its own ends; and the unspoken assumption was that in time the Lord would favour his own. *Semper patientia.*

But the story had a still deeper resonance. In 1264 Pope Urban IV established the feast of Corpus Christi as one of the main festivals of the Church, celebrating the mystical process by which the body of Christ 'became' the bread of the Holy Sacrament. Through the story of Rudolf and the priest, the Habsburgs established a connection between the body of Christ and their own destiny. Future generations of Habsburgs made it their particular feast. From Rudolf onwards, the Habsburgs claimed a special veneration for the sacrament, and until the very end of the Habsburg rule, six centuries later, the annual festivities of Corpus Christi were dutifully celebrated by most emperors.[31] The adjutant of the Emperor Franz Joseph, Baron von Margutti, described how the feast of Corpus Christi was marked in the twentieth century:

First thing in the morning the Emperor proceeded from the Hofburg . . . in a state coach drawn by six horses . . . the archdukes each in a coach drawn by four horses, preceded him . . . the coaches – a blaze of glass and gold – the magnificent harness and trappings of the horses – magnificent creams of Spanish breed – the coachmen, outriders and grooms in their black, gold-laced rococo coats, white stockings, buckle shoes and wigs under their huge three-cornered hats . . . adorned with gold braid and ostrich feathers.

After the high mass in the cathedral of St Stephen, the Emperor walked through the streets of the city as a sign of humility:

The procession was headed by the Knights of all the Austrian and Hungarian orders, in order of rank and length of membership. Next came the ecclesiastics, with the Cardinal Bishop *who carried the Host* [my emphasis] under a canopy, immediately behind was the Emperor, bare-headed and carrying a lighted candle. He was followed by the Archdukes, the higher dignitaries, the Burgomaster and the town council of Vienna, and several corporations and brotherhoods. The procession wound its way through the Kärntnerstrasse, Augustinerstrasse, the Neuer Markt, Lobkowitzplatz, Michaelerplatz and the Graben.

That is, through the whole heart of the old city, presenting the Emperor as the first servant of the sacrament to his people. 'Open-air altars had been erected in the Neuer Markt, Lobkowitzplatz, Michaelerplatz and the Graben . . . At these, gospels were read. After the return to St Stephen's, the benediction was said, and the Emperor . . . returned to the Hofburg.' Margutti described it as 'a ceremony with the traditions of centuries behind it and one of the most impressive sights in the world'.[32]

Rudolf, in the eyes of his successors, was the first model of Habsburg piety. At his coronation, the new King of the Romans had no sceptre, the symbol of temporal power, so he took a crucifix from the High Altar and declared: 'Here is the sign that has redeemed us and the whole world; let this be our sceptre.'[33] With this gesture he presented the reunited force of Church and State. In the hands of Habsburg family historians, every element in his life and legend was deployed to support this central theme. Like Charlemagne, the first Emperor of the German nation, he led armies and won great victories, bringing peace and security out of disorder. In the words of a contemporary chronicler,

His very name spread fear and terror among the licentious barons and joy among the people; as the light springs from the darkness, so arose peace and tranquillity from war and desolation. The peasant resumed the plough, which he had long neglected; the merchant whom the fear of plunder had confined to his dwelling, now traversed the country with confidence and security; and robbers and banditti, who had hitherto roved unashamed in the face of the day, now hid their crimes in coverts and wastes.[34]

In 1291, in his seventy-third year, a great age for the epoch, Rudolf felt that death was near. He had failed in this final objective, which was to pre-elect his surviving son Albert as the King of the Romans. The electoral princes had prevaricated, no more wanting a new and powerful dynasty on the imperial throne in 1291 than they had when they elected the impoverished Count of Habsburg in 1273. There could not, they loyally declared, be *two* kings on the throne at the same time. The truth was that they feared Albert more than Rudolf, for Albert had all his father's energy and political sagacity, but none of Rudolf's mildness of manner. In Austria, which the Emperor had granted to his sons after the victory over Ottokar, Duke Albert had ruled with a tight and suffocating grip on nobles and peasants alike. Appearances were telling. Rudolf had towered over his subjects, a handsome man, radiating a physical charm. Albert, dark and stocky, was disfigured by a cavernous empty eye socket, the consequence of a battle injury, and with his face distorted into a permanent snarl. He was universally known as Albert the One-Eyed.[35]

There is a huge compendium of benign tales about Rudolf, of how he would go among his people, telling tales of that 'rogue Rudolf'. Or how he would meet and remember common soldiers who had fought with him decades before. Of Albert, there was nothing so benign. He was by repute a loyal and devoted husband, but otherwise cold and controlled in his passions. All the records remark on his firmness, energy and vigour. But some also note that 'as a sovereign he was arrogant and despotic, restless and rapacious of disposition' who 'pursued his schemes for the advancement of his family with an inflexible pertinacity and with little regard either to the feelings of pity or the sentiments of justice'. In fine, Albert was judged 'Uncouth and vulgar in appearance, ferocious and unseemly in aspect, gloomy and reserved by habit and constitution, even his good qualities were obscured, and his failings exaggerated by his personal defects, and to adopt the strong language of the Swiss historians, "Virtue in him bore the semblance of selfishness."' It was Albert's 'tyranny' that the Swiss were resisting in the legend of William Tell: the hat which the tyrant Gessler set up on a pole for the Swiss to bow before represented Albert.

When Rudolf died at Germesheim on 15 July 1291, on his way to the city of Speyer, whose cathedral contained the bodies and monuments of earlier emperors (Rudolf, typically, had joked that he intended to go 'and see the kings his predecessors'), the Empire was left without a head. Even so, Albert seemed his inevitable successor, by virtue of his 'splendid talents' and also because of the 'powerful connections and affinity' that he could call upon. But when the Diet met near Frankfurt, in the following year, their fear of Albert predominated and they selected a cousin of one of the Electors as the new Emperor. Albert had learned patience and cunning from his father, so instead of resisting the princes' choice as Ottokar had done, he acknowledged Adolf of Nassau with a good grace, while secretly plotting against him. His patience was justified, for within five years, the Electors had fallen out with their creature, and declared him deposed; Albert had anticipated their judgement by killing Adolf with his own hands on the battlefield at Göllheim. When the battle was joined, Adolf spurred his horse through the throng of fighting men until he was within a sword's length of the Duke of Austria, and demanded single combat. Adolf had lost his helmet earlier in the maul, and faced Albert bareheaded. After angry words, Albert speared his adversary through his exposed cheek and levered him from his horse. Once the Count of Nassau was pinned to the ground, his enemy jumped from his horse and finished the task with his ballock-knife. There was none of the restrained dignity and apparent regret that Rudolf had shown to the fallen Ottokar: Albert slaughtered his opponent as he would have dispatched a fallen steer, rising from the ground with his surcoat soaked with the blood of his enemy.

On 23 June 1298 the electors unenthusiastically chose Albert as the new King of the Romans. Their doubts and fears proved amply justified, for once in office, he seemed set to fulfil the role of the biblical King Rehoboam, who declared to his people, 'My father hath chastised you with whips, but I will chastise you with scorpions.' He was crowned in the chapel of Charlemagne at Aachen, and in August held his first Diet of the Empire at Nuremberg, with, it was said, 'a splendour that exceeded all previous examples'. He aimed to take the Empire to new heights and over the next decade steadily built up the power of the German Empire, Habsburg-led, until it seemed set to become the dominant force in Europe. The urge to acquire new territories seemed insatiable. Whenever a fief fell vacant, as in the case of the patchwork of fiefs, large and small, that collectively made up the Low Countries, or Bohemia, Albert laid claim to it, usually with the intention of allocating it to one of his own lineage. The opposition to this ambitious policy grew steadily. The princes of the Empire refused to pre-elect Albert's son, another Rudolf, and then sought to frustrate his policy of reclamation, which threatened their interests in the same proportion that it advanced the power of the Habsburgs. But steadily and remorselessly, in campaign after campaign, Albert moved forward.

Nor were his enemies merely secular. He faced a pope, Boniface VIII, more masterful and determined than any of the popes with whom Rudolf had dealt. For a number of years Pope and Emperor traded insults and sparred for advantage, but eventually, like his father, Albert found the means to achieve a *modus vivendi*. He formally accepted the terms of Boniface's declaration known as *Unam Sanctam*, which asserted papal superiority over any earthly monarch, probably the most extensive statement of papal claims ever made. In addition he promised to become the Pope's paladin, defending him against all his many enemies, and directly acknowledging the absolute superiority of the spiritual to the temporal sphere. He calculated that with papal support he could more easily advance his policy of aggrandizement within the Empire, and even outside it. Albert had ambitions to control Hungary and Poland, to dominate the mountains and passes of Switzerland; even for a moment, he aspired to the throne of France, when Boniface VIII threatened to excommunicate King Philip the Fair and allocate his crown and kingdom to Albert.[36]

Then on May Day 1308, this glorious prospect vanished. Infuriated by the growing resistance of the rebellious Swiss, who had seized towns and castles under his rule, Albert determined to punish them. He summoned his knights to the Aargau and with his queen, his elder son Leopold and a number of his younger children set out for his family castle of the Habichtsburg. In his entourage was his nineteen-year-old nephew, John, the only son of his dead brother. Albert had refused repeatedly to relinquish the lands that John believed he had inherited by right from his father. On the way to Brugg, John asked again, with some vehemence, and Albert contemptuously dismissed his claim, some said by offering him a wreath of wild flowers, observing that it 'better became his years than the cares of government'. John, like his uncle a man of a sullen disposition and a violent nature, decided to avenge the public insult in blood. When Albert and his entourage reached the northern bank of the Reuss, within sight of their destination, the river was high, and so a boat was called to ferry the party across. John and four conspirators volunteered to go first and notify the castellan of their imminent arrival. Then Albert, impatient to reach the castle, crossed with a single attendant and their horses, and trotted ahead, leaving the rest of his party on the far bank. Then 'as he rode slowly through the fields, at the foot of the hills crowned by the castle of Hapsburgh,[37] familiarly conversing with his attendant, he was suddenly assailed by the conspirators, one of whom seized his bridle. His nephew exclaiming "Will you now restore my inheritance?" wounded him in the neck.' Then all the four conspirators hacked at him with swords and daggers. 'The king, falling from his horse, was left weltering in his blood. His son Leopold and his attendants were the terrified spectators of the atrocious deed, and when they had passed the river, found the king just expired in the arms of a poor woman who had hastened to his assistance.' The murderer, John of Habsburg, was known thereafter as John the Parricide; Habsburgs had long memories and it was the fifteenth century before the name John was borne again by a member of the family.

ᕲ ᕲ ᕲ

The murder of Albert was a catastrophe for the Habsburgs. Their hopes of founding an imperial dynasty were dashed. Two active and domineering Habsburg rulers had been enough,[38] and the electoral princes meeting in November selected not the Habsburg candidate, Frederick, the elder son of Albert, but Henry, Count of Luxemburg. It was 130 years before another Habsburg sat securely on the imperial throne, and although they remained great landed magnates, the boundless expansive vision of Albert and Rudolf was brought suddenly to a halt. Their first response was to take revenge on all those who had been involved in the murder of Albert. The four murderers had fled, but enforcing the old Germanic tradition of 'blood guilt', Albert's sons and daughters exterminated the entire lineage of John's associates. On a single day, Leopold and his sister Agnes sat on a dais and watched as sixty-three blameless members in the household of Baron Salm were brought before them and beheaded one by one; the corpses were arranged in long rows before them. As a head was severed and the blood spurted, Agnes was recorded as crying exultantly, 'I am bathed in May dew.' It was her own retainers who stopped her from throttling the baby son of another of the conspirators. More than a thousand died in this welter of Habsburg vengeance. But Albert's widow, Elisabeth, together with the bloodthirsty Agnes determined to build a more permanent monument to her murdered lord. This, the abbey of Königsfelden, played a crucial formative role in the development of Habsburg identity.[39]

Pushed out from the rule of a worldly empire, the Habsburgs

retreated into an empire of the imagination. Deprived of real power, they painstakingly constructed a central role for themselves in a new dimension – in images, in architecture, in stained-glass windows, in symbols and ideas.[40] In the creation of this myth, the role of Königsfelden was fundamental. Elisabeth and Agnes intended that Albert's body should be the focus of the church which they built as a memorial to his murder. By tradition, the high altar was set at the precise point where he expired. In fact it is likely that the site chosen was not exactly where he had died, but some distance away. Instead the church was constructed atop the foundations of the great Roman legionary fortress of Vindonissa. Remains of its gatehouses, fortifications and roads were all in evidence. The remaining walls lay almost on the surface: the vault which was excavated for the bones of Albert and for those of his wife and daughter was dug with some difficulty into these well-built Roman foundations, and through the surface stones of the roadway.

Why build at this spot? The hidden context of this particular site was a direct and physical link to the empire of Rome. Was the abbey built on this location despite the difficulties precisely because of its undeniably Roman origins? Those buried within the crypt were immured in a Roman past. The Habsburgs had been elected emperors but there was already a sense within the family that their election merely confirmed some pre-existent and natural right to the office. When a later Habsburg, Rudolf IV (1358–65), laid claim to a special status for his lineage within the Empire, part of his claim was based on certain grants that were supposed to have been given to the Habsburgs by their Roman ancestors, Julius Caesar and Nero.[41] His document, the *Privilegium maius*, simply manifested what had long been current in a family tradition, transmitted orally.[42] Such claims to grand descent are common in many families, and in the Habsburg case, it provided a plausible explanation for their rise and triumph under Rudolf and Albert. It was the loss of power in the real world, the shock of deprivation and the injustice of Albert's murder, that pressed the Habsburgs to retreat into this world of the imagination.

The memorial church at Königsfelden is very large, but simple in structure: a single broad nave centred on the steps down into the crypt. It loomed over the growing complex of abbey buildings around, looking like a capsized Noah's ark. It was a double foundation of monks and nuns, whose duty was to pray for the soul of Albert and his lineage. At the east end beyond the crypt was a small circular choir, where the altar was placed. Above and around the altar, lighting the choir with an extraordinary light, were eleven stained and painted windows, thought by many to be some of the greatest works of art of the central Middle Ages. In those windows the Habsburgs were embodied in the mysteries of the Church.[43] Members of the Habsburg family were depicted in the margins of the Passion story and in the lives of the saints. In the fourth window, the young Duke Albert, son of the murdered Emperor, and his wife, kneel with Saint Elisabeth of Thuringia; in the sixth, another son of Albert, Duke Henry. In the eighth, Duke Otto and his wife, and above them a succession of the Lions of Habsburg stand, one above the other, protectively on each side of St Francis. In the eleventh, Duke Leopold I kneels with his wife. The windows depicting the 'Habsburg passion' are next to those of Christ's Passion, a set of images which ring the altar in a semi-circle.

This group of windows was replete with the imagery associated with the Habsburgs. In the third window, the risen Christ shows his stigmata, as he steps across the threshold to the tomb. Sleeping below the threshold is a soldier, who bears on his shield the emblem of the sun. The risen Christ, the Son of God, is visually associated with the sun image that later Habsburgs were to make their own. It was by extension a Habsburg, *miles christianus*, who watched over the entombed Son of God, and was the passive supporter of his Resurrection. The message of Königsfelden was that Habsburgs were founders, supporters, protectors of Christendom, whose deepest mysteries were being enacted around them. The windows made clear the unique bond which existed between the family and the mysteries of the faith.

The slender lancet windows at Königsfelden are, I believe, the first visual documentation, in a most dramatic form, of the symbolic associations which the Habsburgs wished to perpetuate.[44] It became the focal point, the place to which they brought their honoured dead. So it was to this church that they carried the bodies of Duke Leopold and his knights. Most of the windows can be dated to around the period of his burial in the abbey. Until Sempach, the church had lacked its focal point. The murdered Albert was never buried in the place designed for him. His body, temporarily interred while Königsfelden was being built, was transferred not to Elisabeth's new abbey church, but to the cathedral of Speyer to join the other emperors. The martyr's church had lacked its martyr; Leopold provided it. With their bones lying in the abbey, the deaths of Leopold and his knights were commemorated in a succession of paintings that adorned both the walls of the church and of its treasure house. To the Swiss they were arrogant tyrants: here in the family shrine, they were presented as sacrifices in a godly cause.

Königsfelden was richly endowed and attracted many pilgrims, but essentially, it was the private shrine of family, dynastic identity.[45] So how did it function for the Habsburgs? Albert and his surrogate Leopold were sacrificial kings, honoured as martyrs in the service both of God and of their lineage. Around them in the windows were other martyrs, like St Catherine, and John the Baptist, both dying by the sword, like Albert and Leopold. The purpose of the memorial, the endless masses said for the souls of the departed, was to remind those who came after. Let me suggest what might seem a rather far-fetched parallel. I believe that the murder on the banks of the Reuss (in sight of his wife and children) and the events of Sempach functioned for the Habsburgs roughly as the martyrdom of Husain does for the Shia branch of Islam: the memory of their deaths provided a constant reinforcement for dynastic values, defined the ethos of the family against the world outside. Their stories were told and re-illustrated countless times over the centuries, the first was the *Königsfelder Cronik*. But the same essential qualities were always reiterated. Thus, the murderer of Albert was presented as a man physically disfigured by his deed. In truth, it was Albert the One-Eyed who was hideously deformed. Leopold and his knights, as presented at Königsfelden, embody the chivalric, Crusader virtues. Königsfelden also revealed another aspect of the Habsburgs: like Christ himself and the holy martyrs and saints, adversity sanctified them. They could triumph by faith, by belief in the mysteries of the Church and by retreating within the protective traditions of their family. This inner resilience was a key to their survival in the centuries that followed.[46]

2

Cosa Nostra (Our Cause)

1300—1400

The castle and the fortified town dominate our image of the Middle Ages. They appear everywhere, elaborately and highly detailed in manuscript illustrations (especially in the Swiss chronicles of their struggle with the Habsburgs), and more crudely in wood carvings, drawings and sketches and on every variety of decorated object. The simple rural towers, the fortified townships – *bastides* – of central France, the much more elaborate defences of cities like Basel and Paris, were all evidence of a dangerous world. All over Europe a strong tower or stout walls were often the only guarantee of survival. The effects of endemic warfare had stunted every aspect of human development.

War raged in the eleventh and twelfth centuries, separating couples and decimating families. It also wreaked havoc with the physical environment in which the aristocracy lived. Families were forced to crowd into towers with few windows, owing to fear of missiles fired from below or assaults by ladder. To impede access, ground-level doors were blocked up leaving only narrow entrances 18 to 26 feet above the ground, which had to be reached by climbing a removable ladder, or dangerous staircase.[1]

In wilder regions, on the borders of Hungary or Scotland, it long remained the normal pattern of life. But in most parts of the Continent by the fourteenth century, the humble towers like the Habsburg castle above Brugg were memorials to a crude and distant past.

Yet castles continued to proliferate, growing ever larger and more elaborate. The great fortresses like the defensive chain built by King Edward I in Wales, the 'castle town' of the Count of Soissons at Coucy-le-Château, or Richard I of England's huge stronghold at Château Gaillard in Normandy, were more than military buildings, for as Roberta Gilchrist has observed, 'Space determines how and when men and women meet, work and mingle. Space becomes a map in which personal identity and boundaries between social groups are expressed.'[2] Like the great churches and cathedrals, military architecture expressed the nature of social order. Indeed, by the fourteenth century its strictly military functions had become secondary.[3] Castles had become tokens of power rather than weapons of war. Their true deterrent capacity lay in the mind; however strong their walls, and massive the towers. There were few sieges because no ruler or magnate would willingly engage in them. If a castle fell, it was most often by subversion, betrayal and treachery.

Castle-building was a political act, a statement and claim of power. The fortress dominated the terrain for many miles around, as if an invisible palisade had been thrown up containing and controlling all the land that lay within. Yet by contrast with many great families the Habsburgs built few castles and the marks that they left upon the landscape were scanty. Leopold III's predecessor and elder brother, Rudolf IV, had been dubbed *The Founder*, for his rebuilding of the great church of St Stephen's in Vienna in the High Gothic style (and in securing for it the status of a cathedral); he also endowed the city with its university. Others of his line built monasteries and founded towns, and embellished their ducal seats – Innsbruck or Graz – to match their new status. But, otherwise, they left little visible evidence of their passing. Many other noble houses, certainly no richer than the Habsburgs, built on a prodigious scale, and the Emperor Charles IV, King of Bohemia, erected a new city at Prague to rival any of the urban centres of western Europe. The lack of activity on the Habsburgs' part, their seeming inertia, seems all the more remarkable by contrast. Had they been so traumatized by the sudden and shocking death of Emperor Albert I that they sank into a torpor, into a decline only arrested by the resolute and dramatic action of the young Emperor Maximilian at the very end of the fifteenth century? This picture, of the slow decay into insignificance arrested and then reversed into a meteoric, vertiginous, ascent, accorded very well with Maxmilian's own view of himself – the knight of true chivalry, quintessential Emperor.

∽   ∽   ∽

We now enter a shadow-world, one where the power of faith was omnipresent, where some monarchs were anointed with a holy oil touched, it was believed, directly by the hand of Christ,[4] a world in which the power of the imagination could outstrip the power of the sword. It is a mental gap almost impossible for the modern mind to bridge. To our eyes the Holy Lance, which contained a nail from the True Cross, looks like a broken old spearhead, bound with silver wire, and with its cracked and fractured parts held together by a leather sheath. The Holy Cloth that was reputed to have covered the face of the dead Christ resembles a piece of rough, stained, fabric. But the totemic power and authority of these relics was incalculable. The power of faith could work miracles: just to stand in the close proximity to a holy relic could transform the future lives of men and women. In such a world and in such a context, the steady building of the Habsburgs' invisible power had a clear purpose, for it gave them a matchless weapon, a Castle Dauntless that no enemy could conquer or subvert.

This intangible protection was constructed and extended in much the same way as 'real' defences were built. Indeed, if a castle was as much a force in the mind as on the ground, as many modern writers now suggest, then the parallel is exact. An *enceinte* was extended little by little, with new towers, walls, drawbridges, moats and the like. So, too, the Habsburgs slowly but surely embellished the mythology of their own origins and of the dukedom that they now occupied. It was an imaginative and historical task of some complexity, based partly on the traditions of the family and partly on the documents and traditions inherited from the Babenberg Dukes of Austria, who had been closely connected with the Hohenstaufen emperors. Gradually their new narrative emerged, suggesting that divine intervention had given the Empire to Rudolf as a *natural* and *predestined* recognition of his inherent qualities of sanctity. Albert's martyrdom, like the death of John the Baptist depicted at Königsfelden, presaged future greatness for his family. Rudolf and Albert had been true emperors, ennobling the role and position, just as 'their ancestor' *Saint* Charlemagne had done. Rudolf too was considered saintly[5] through his close association with the Holy Body of Christ. By slow but logical stages the family came to believe that the Empire had been theirs by right of superior virtue. When God willed it, the imperial throne would be restored to them.

As so often in the Middle Ages, theory collided with reality. Tales of Rudolf I's good works, Albert's martyr's crown, and latterly, the sacrifice of Duke Leopold at Sempach, provided the spiritual birthright and common patrimony of all Habsburgs, *domus Austriae* – the House of Austria. However, the Habsburgs' newly minted destiny lacked any recognition beyond their domain: the cults of Rudolf and even the more established veneration for the Babenberg Leopold the Good were local or even restricted to the Habsburgs and their households. Shifting this inward sense of destiny into the world of political reality was the problem that Rudolf IV the Founder addressed directly in issuing the *Privilegium maius* (greater privilege). Custom and memory might be acceptable in a court of law, but nothing was so potent as a written document. The founding charter of the Dukedom of Austria had been a set of special privileges called the *Privilegium minus*, granted by Emperor Frederick Barbarossa in 1156 to the Babenbergs. This provided a measure of independence for the dukedom, and was the source on which subsequent claims were based. For a document of such importance it, unusually, lacked the usual golden seal, or *bulla*, having only the more common wax version, and indeed when Rudolf's chancery tried to find it in the abbey of Klosterneuberg, where it was reputedly stored, they could find no trace of it. It was eventually discovered in the family archive of the Babenbergs in Vienna.

Perhaps this misplaced charter sowed the idea that if one important document had gone missing, maybe other equally vital material had also been lost. From such a thought it was a short step to 'replacing' a document which had been mislaid. Michael Clanchy recounts just such an incident in an English context where it was

not unknown for monasteries lacking a crucial deed or document
well attested by oral evidence to construct the appropriate document, thereby 'justifying the ways of God to Man'.[6] Rudolf's
Privilegium maius has always been regarded at best as a bold and
highly coloured embellishment of the fact, and at worst as a
transparent forgery. Such a judgement misses the point. In the
Privilegium the Habsburgs were not asking for new rights and
privileges. They were seeking the public and permanent recognition
of their unique position, as it already existed; in their eyes it needed
no sanction. When the Emperor Charles refused to promulgate the
decree as an imperial edict, this was a reverse, but it did not
invalidate the assertions that they had made. Their claim was, in
the language of the law, of right and not of grace. Thus the Dukes
of Austria behaved as if the *Privilegium* were already enshrined in
law. To take a single example, Rudolf had asserted his right to
wear a crown, plainly modelled on the imperial crown, as an
outward emblem that he and his successors stood apart from the
other princes of the empire. The Emperor had demanded that this
should not be displayed on coins and in public; there is no evidence
that Rudolf complied.[7]

Charles IV has been well treated by historians. His actions,
however questionable, have always been assumed to have stemmed
from the highest motives. In reality, his concerns were not very
different from those of the Habsburgs. However strong a family,
the imperial throne was elective, and the Luxemburg dynasty,
which had lost the imperial throne on more than one occasion,
feared that the further loss of the imperial title would put them at
the mercy of their enemies.[8] It was easier for an emperor to fortify
the power of his lineage than for a mere duke. In his Golden Bull of
1356, Charles IV was seeking, his admirers believed, to end the
perennial quarrels over which rulers were entitled to select the King
of the Romans. At the same time he fixed the duties and powers of
the various imperial office holders by creating a new statute for
imperial government. But above all else, he sought to protect his
family and their status. The position of his own kingdom of
Bohemia had frequently been called in question. Now, in the fourth
article of the Golden Bull, Bohemia was enshrined in the imperial
structure as an electoral principality. Henceforward the King of

Bohemia would sit at the Emperor's right hand, with precedence over all the other rulers of the Empire.[9] So in any future election, the Luxemburgs could not be excluded from the horse-trading. But while the Golden Bull enhanced the position of Bohemia, it ignored the claims of the Dukes of Austria. Worse still, it was unambiguous: the Dukes, and hence the Habsburgs, were to be permanently excluded from the inner circle, the senior princes of Germany.

Their position had always been uncertain. No Habsburg had previously been numbered among the lay Electors, nor had the Babenberg Dukes of Austria before them. But their position was no more anomalous than that of the Bohemian king, and their claims to recognition were as strong. They had provided two Emperors in recent history. More controversially they were able to emphasize a connection with the Hohenstaufen, which tapped a strong vein of German patriotism. Frederick Barbarossa, so legend had it, was still sleeping under his mountain, waiting to rise again and rescue Germany in her hour of need. The Golden Bull[10] threatened both their political position, casting them into the second rank of German rulers, and also frustrated the burgeoning sense of their own identity.[11]

Rudolf's motives and intentions can only be surmised. The documents exist – like the Golden Bull of Charles IV and the *Privilegium maius* – but we can only edge uncertainly towards their true meaning. The characters and attitudes of even the main actors, like Charles IV, and his son Sigismund, Rudolf IV, and his great nephews, Albert V and Frederick V, who reclaimed the imperial title for the Habsburgs, are shadowy. But even with this slender evidence some inferences seem reasonable. In particular, the whole episode of the *Privilegium maius* provides a unique point of entry into the mentality of the Habsburgs. For long mocked as a palpable forgery, insufficient study has been made of what the *Privilegium* actually demanded, and hence what can be inferred from it. The five decrees,[12] presented in different styles – and in the case of the last document, from Rudolf I to his two sons, in German rather than in Latin – sought to build a coherent and mutually supportive case. Whatever its true validity, it played a key role in the construction of a coherent Habsburg ideology.[13] Pushing the assertion of Habsburg right from the domain of private custom into public law was a bold, and in retrospect, almost a rash, move. Rudolf IV staked everything on this written declaration of the family's rightful claim to a unique rank.

What we know of his character suggests an adventurous and intrepid nature. Dead before he was twenty-seven, he was a bright star in what had become a less-than-stellar family. In a short life he achieved more than any of his family since his namesake, Rudolf I. He was knowledgeable and widely read,

a prince of high spirit, and aspiring mind, [who] derived a peculiar eccentricity of character from his enthusiastic admiration of heraldry and antiquities. He investigated the musty records of the ancient dukes of Austria, sedulously examined the archives of his family and formed the project of reviving all the privileges and titles possessed, or even claimed, by his predecessors. At an early stage he used seals with fanciful devices, hieroglyphics and occult characters.[14]

His true intentions or expectations we can only guess. However, the timing and the context of his decision are revealing. By the mid fourteenth century, Europe was on the cusp between a world in which the oral tradition predominated and one in which the written word carried the greater weight. The power of the spoken word as the transmitter of tradition and custom from generation to generation was still in full force. Evidence before a court of law had to be given orally even if read from a written text; it was the formal declaration, made before witnesses that gave the written word its formal sanction.[15] Conversely, a written text once sanctioned by oral or legal process carried a particular weight, for by its very existence it testified to the truth of the matter contained within it. As Jack Goody has observed, writing something down did much more than simply store the knowledge in a convenient and accessible form. 'Once committed to writing, "customs" cannot just fade away. So while writing greatly increases the amount of information held in store and in this sense enhances the potentialities of the human mind, it also makes the problem of erasure much more difficult; in other words, deletion represents the other side of the storage coin.'[16] Once the claim was attested, written down and sealed with the insignia of the Empire, it achieved a degree of permanence and, more important, exerted a power of sanction.

Once inscribed, it was more difficult to deny its truth and validity. Rudolf attempted to achieve this crucial transition, from the private to the public domain.

In the *Privilegium*, Rudolf – and it seems fair to credit him with its creation,[17] for he was steeped in the traditions and history of his ancestors – united the territorial traditions of the various lands of Austria, the connections and customs of the Babenberg dukes, and the family mythology of the Habsburg clan outlined above. He sought to transmute all three from the realm of oral tradition into the domain of the formal, written legal document. It was in the process of weaving these proofs into a coherent form that other claims of a more speculative nature – grants made by Julius Caesar and Nero and enjoyed by the Habsburgs as their lineal descendants – were added.[18] This was already an established form of political argument. The novelty of Rudolf's approach was that he channelled this affinity directly into the Habsburg family, making them a cocktail of Roman antecedents, Christian virtue, and the true inheritance from the great German emperors of the past. Rudolf presented himself as the embodiment of this complex heritage. Jacob Fugger in his *Ehrenspiegel* noted that Rudolf had used a man with multiple faces as his personal emblem. This was the traditional depiction of the Roman god Janus, whom the Hohenstaufen imperial propagandists had characterized as the grandson of Noah. At a stroke Rudolf took his antecedents back to the dawn of history, following a path already well trodden by earlier imperialists. The chaplain of Frederick Barbarossa, Godfried of Viterbo, in his *Speculum regium*, had proved to his own satisfaction that 'Romans and Germans are of one seed . . . Romans and Germans as if one populace'. Charlemagne was the first embodiment of this dual ancestry, Roman and German, and so the Habsburgs stood in a direct line of succession to the founder of the Holy Roman Empire.[19]

'The Founder' also claimed – or reclaimed – titles that had been vacant, and his claim to the Duchy of Swabia had some legitimacy. This was a rank which the younger son of Emperor Rudolf I had borne, as had his son John the Parricide. But after John's murder of the Emperor Albert, no subsequent Habsburg had claimed this tainted name or the title associated with it.[20] Accordingly, in the fifth article of the Golden Bull, Charles IV had assigned the right to

control the lands of the Duke of Swabia to the Count of the
Palatinate. That is, he did not deny that the titles and their rights
existed, merely that they were in abeyance. So it was not implausible
for the Habsburgs – as a Swabian family of great antiquity, one
which had once held the title, as members of a lineage descending
from the great emperor Frederick[21] – to reclaim the right to the
duchy. By doing so he was making much more than a feudal claim
over lands in the valley of the Rhine. He was proclaiming that the
Habsburgs were the heirs not merely to the domain of Frederick
Barbarossa, but to the tradition of German greatness that he had
embodied. This was evident in the other titles that he had annexed.
The office of 'Master of the Imperial Hunt' had been granted under
the Hohenstaufens, but had died with them. Now Rudolf proclaimed that he was the heir to this title by custom and law, to a
rank that would allow him to sit at the right hand of the Emperor
(the very position Charles IV had allocated in the Golden Bull of
1356 to his own family as the Kings of Bohemia).

Rudolf's programme was so far-reaching that any ruler should
have balked at it. The Emperor's powers would have been drastically pruned under the terms of the *Privilegium maius*. He would
be prohibited from interfering in any fashion with the Duchy of
Austria. The dukes could rule their domain responsible only to
God for its good government. The Emperor would have to come
within the borders of the duchy to invest the duke with his title,
rather than the duke attend the Emperor at his court like a more
humble vassal. Equally the duke's duties to the Empire would be
sharply reduced. His contribution to the imperial army in time of
war, already limited by the earlier *Privilegium minus* of 1156,
would become purely nominal. Even the act of conveying the fief
was turned into a formality, for the duke was 'elected' Duke in
Carinthia prior to his sanction by the Emperor.

In one sense Rudolf simply mirrored the clauses of the Golden
Bull, and at each point demanded similar rights for the Habsburgs
to those allocated to the electoral princes. Although he did not
claim any role in the election of the Emperor, he asserted that in
every other respect the Habsburgs were the equal of the princes.
Or, indeed, their superiors. Through the 'grants' from Julius Caesar
and Nero, Rudolf was proclaiming publicly that the Habsburgs and

the Dukes of Austria had a longer and more honourable pedigree
than any of the other German rulers. Only the imperial office itself
had hitherto been held to descend directly from the Emperors of
Rome. Now this primacy was challenged as Rudolf claimed that he
was both lineally and politically descended from the Empire of
Rome, the heir of the Caesars, and of Charlemagne himself. This
by implication was a lineage much grander than that of Charles IV.
Of course, these wider claims are implicit and not explicit, but this
deeper meaning cannot have been opaque to his readers, schooled
in a century of imperialist and papal propaganda. The only plausible
alternative to this line of thought is to accept the view of Alphons
Lhotsky, in his study of the *Privilegium*, that this was merely an
example of Rudolf's 'vanity', but if so, he was only reflecting a set
of beliefs already widely held within the family.[22]

The ancient traditions and distant origins, both of the family and
the duchy, were largely an oral tradition, but none the less they
carried great weight. The Habsburgs made great play of their status
as Dukes of Austria. The duchy was of relatively recent vintage,
created by imperial decree in 1156, but it had inherited rights and
traditions from the earlier March of Austria, which had been a
bulwark against barbarian invasion from the east. This process of
claiming and creating rights by descent, almost by some sort of
osmosis, or sympathetic magic, was not new. The Habsburgs
embraced, by marriage, inheritance, by land right, or simple assumption, the multitudinous claims and traditions of other families.
Their gradual elision with their predecessors as Dukes of Austria,
the Babenberg dynasty, makes the point precisely.[23] It was only
after the Habsburgs took over the vacant Duchy of Austria that
the traditional Babenberg names of *Leopold* and *Frederick* began to be
widely used within the Habsburg family. But from that point
forward, they were among the most frequently used of all names
within the family. The purpose was clear: by this process of
naming, the Habsburgs bound themselves close to a family from
whom they had only the most vestigial descent.[24] Progressively,
over the years they became not merely the successors to the Babenberg lands, but incorporated them into their structure of kinship.
The Babenbergs became quasi-Habsburgs. Their dukes were frequently included in the tally of the Habsburg descent and later

generations of the family regarded the Babenberg Saint Leopold as 'our ancestor', in the same way as 'Saint' Rudolf,[25] who was unquestionably a Habsburg. This process, of claiming, colonizing and absorbing had been in play since the first Rudolf.

∽ ∽ ∽

All these claims and assertions – including the presumption of the Habsburgs' Roman origin, and the assumption of long-vacant titles – need to be considered in two aspects. First, the Habsburgs' belief in their special election by God did not stand or fall by their Roman descent or the range and extent of their titles. Their sense of identity had developed organically from this conviction of divine choice, and all the proofs and evidence simply reinforced their foreordained destiny. The argument was an additive and not a linear process. Take away imperial power, success in war and government, remove land and wealth, and still the Habsburg mission remained, complete and undamaged. While a single member of the family lived, even a child, he (or she) embodied the essence of the 'House of Austria' in every particular. A weak vessel – and there were many – could still transmit the heritage unalloyed to succeeding generations. This medieval mode of argument, fundamentally scholastic, underpinned the Habsburgs through all their succeeding centuries. Their doctrine of election was shaped in the speculative world of the fourteenth and fifteenth centuries, when questions such as the nature of sovereign power were being debated with a new vigour.[26]

But, like the papal claims to universal authority which had been proclaimed by Gregory VII, Innocent III and Boniface VIII, the Habsburgs' programme had to survive in a harsh and testing political environment. Innocent III, who reigned as Pope from 1198 to 1216, had stated the papal claim in its starkest form: 'You see then who is this servant set up over the household, truly the vicar of Christ, successor of Peter, anointed of the Lord, a God of Pharaoh, set between God and man, lower than God but higher than man, who judges all and is judged by no one.'[27] But his successors, even if they claimed as much, could achieve less. In his great bull *Unam Sanctam* Boniface had also proclaimed the awful power of his office, claiming the right to depose kings and oversee all the princes of the earth. But he had ended his days a fugitive, a refugee from Rome, for his opponent, Philip Augustus of France, could muster arguments just as potent for the rights of kings, and moreover, he had armed might on his side. For the Habsburgs, their reliance on this statement of independence was a speculative and highly risky venture, which could easily rebound on them.

Did Rudolf believe that the Emperor Charles IV, whose vaunting sense of his own status and that of his family was legendary, would be willing to sanction so profound a derogation of his powers? In retrospect what was unique about Rudolf IV's claims was not their novelty so much as their reckless adventurism. He risked bringing down the wrath of the Emperor upon his head just as surely as if he had set about turning the Habichtsburg or any of his many possessions into a fortified stronghold. The message of the *Privilegium maius* was: We, the house of Austria, are independent of your sovereign power . . . No Emperor could cheerfully accept such a derogation.[28] Perhaps it was only Charles's affection for Rudolf that caused him to stay his hand from more drastic action. But he threatened to deprive his son-in-law of his rights in the Tyrol, under an agreement that required imperial sanction, and demanded that he immediately abandon any use of the pretended titles and the use of the 'royal' crown, under the sanction that then he would be outlawed.

Four years later, in 1365, Rudolf was dead, while engaged in a new adventure in Italy as he sought to make a marriage alliance with the powerful Visconti family of Milan. With his death, and especially without a son or daughter to carry forward his concerns, these elaborate fantasies of the Habsburg mission rested. None of his younger brothers, who jointly became his heirs under the edict of Albert the Lame, had the will or the desire to pursue the claims made in the *Privilegium maius*. Not for the last time, the spirit of Habsburg mysticism skipped a generation, only to surface again among his nephews and great-nephews, in Albert V, who became Emperor Albert II, and in his cousin Frederick V, who became Emperor Frederick III. Frederick indeed completed the work of Rudolf IV by recognizing the *Privilegium maius* as true and authentic under the law of the Empire.

ဢ   ဢ   ဢ

The first Habsburg Emperor, Rudolf I, had been chosen at a time when the Empire had fallen into a state of incipient anarchy. The Habsburgs returned to the imperial throne when matters were far worse, and the whole structure of an ordered world was under challenge. In the half-century before Albert V, Duke of Austria, took the imperial throne in 1437 as Emperor Albert II the old mould of religious and civil society had been shattered. After him no one other than a Habsburg was to hold the title for the next three hundred years, and it was in their hands that the concept of empire was reformed, redirected and massively extended. Certainly Albert and his immediate successors inherited the shards of the old order, and it is in terms of that ambiguous legacy that their success or failure must be measured. But their succeeding generations, from the Emperor Maximilian onwards, amplified those ideas to such an extent that their echo may still be heard.

The Habsburgs' inheritance from their Luxemburg predecessors was a poisoned chalice. Charles IV, who had seemed like a new Charlemagne (Maximilian was later to call him the 'stepfather of the Empire'), died in 1378. His two sons, the elder Wenceslaus, who ruled from his father's death in 1378, until he was deposed by the German princes for ineptitude in 1400, and his half-brother, Sigismund, who was elected in 1411 and died in 1437, between them spanned almost half a century on the imperial throne. In their hands Charles's inheritance crumbled. Sigismund was unquestionably a more energetic and determined character than his sibling, but few of his complex and subtle strategies ever came to full fruition. Contemporaries marked him only as an intriguer and plotter, and we can see him in his portrait now displayed in the Kunsthistorisches Museum in Vienna. Under a huge fur hat, his pale etiolated features, thin lips, long nose, and a long wispy brown beard project saintliness rather than authority. He lacked either the assured regality of his father, or the earthy energy of his successor, Albert of Habsburg. He confronted a set of problems that were perhaps insoluble, a crisis of authority in society, and a rising tide of criticism levelled against the Church. The papacy had over the centuries more or less successfully claimed vast powers in human society. Now those claims were being challenged from every direction.

In October 1347, a galley entered the harbour of Messina, to the horrified eyes of bystanders a ship from hell. The vessel stank of corruption, and about its deck lay dead and dying sailors, oozing pus and blood. Even the few living fell ill and died within a few days.[29] Then from other points of contact with the east there were similar tales of a pestilence which spread with astonishing speed. In ten years perhaps as much as a third of the population of Europe died, and a chronicler of Sienna, Agnolo di Tura, provided an epitaph which had a universal application: 'Nobody wept no matter what his loss because almost all expected death . . . and people said and believed "This is the end of the world."' Tura himself buried his five children with his own hands. To this ravaging of the world, by what later came to be called the Black Death, the Church could provide no answers and was reluctant to accept the popular view that it was caused by the wrath of God,[30] inflicted on a wicked and corrupt world. Scapegoats were quickly found, especially the Jews, who were massacred wherever they could be found. Many were killed by the wandering bands of flagellants, who roamed the roads of Germany and France beating sin from themselves, and then, by killing the Jews, becoming the scourge of God, cleansing the world.

The pestilence threatened the stability of society in two senses. First, it destroyed the economic basis for agricultural and urban life. In much of Europe, where land was already marginal, the fields were simply abandoned when there were no hands to tend them. Second, the papal power had always stood between God and man, a necessary intermediary. Now that God had intervened so directly with his people, did the old superstructure of Holy Church have any validity, especially since the Church had become riven by factionalism and doctrinal disputes? Indeed, perhaps it was that very corruption within the Church, stinking to high heaven, that had brought down the foul and appropriate penalty upon God's people for allowing such an obscenity to persist. The clergy 'take no care at all of us, they live scandalous lives, they tread upon our heads . . . The common people make everything and deliver everything and still cannot live without being tormented and driven to ruin by these clergy . . . the prelates are raging wolves.'[31]

The old theories of papal supremacy, of a pure and powerful

Church leading humanity towards the fulfilment of divine will, had been transmuted into a reality of rapacious and corrupt ecclesiastics battening on civil society. This decay and degradation was evident to all. Yet popular faith, expressed through the building of churches and chapels, or participating in the proliferation of the new Marian cults – or the Corpus Christi celebrations – was as strong as ever. People's expectations of their pastors had risen and to many within and without the Church, the wealth of churchmen, garnered from the faithful over the centuries, was obscene. The whole engine of papal power was directed against these subversive doctrines of spiritual poverty. The old linkage of the papacy with the city of Rome had been broken in 1309; thereafter the Pope of Rome ruled not from the Eternal City but from the enclave of Avignon in the heart of France. There he was manifestly under the physical domination of the French king. This 'Babylonian captivity' lasted until 1377, and the Avignon popes resolutely denied all the insistent pressures within the Church for change and reform.

When finally in 1377 the Babylonian captivity was ended and Pope Gregory XI returned to Rome it seemed that at last the Church would reform itself. But when Gregory died in the following year and the college of cardinals elected the Bishop of Bari as Urban VI, the French cardinals fled from the city of Rome and declared that they had only elected Urban in fear of their lives from the volatile Roman population. They deposed Urban and dutifully elected the cousin of the King of France as Clement VII. Urban refused to accept his removal, and Christendom faced the problem of two popes, both claiming the plenitude of papal power. The only way for the dispute to be settled, according to the papal theory, was for the two popes themselves to resolve their differences, and for one to yield the 'Keys of St Peter' to the other. The dispute was prolonged for more than thirty years as neither the popes of Rome nor the popes of Avignon (successors to Urban and Clement were elected after the first actors in this Great Schism died) were willing to sacrifice their position. Meanwhile the discontent, both lay and ecclesiastical, at this impasse was rising, and in 1409 cardinals who had abandoned both Gregory XII in Rome and Benedict XIII in Avignon met at Pisa, to declare both the existing popes deposed for heresy. They immediately elected a new pope as Alexander V. But if Avignon and Rome could agree on little else, they were in unison on the illegality of Alexander's election. Thus by 1410, Christendom had three popes, three sets of cardinals, three claims to universal rule and no rational means to eradicate the anomaly. However, a solution was proposed, which was for the whole of Christendom to meet and resolve the issue, in a great General Council of the Church, as had been done in the early days of the Christian faith to settle matters of doctrine and practice. Exceptional circumstances called for exceptional measures:

The pope can be removed by a general council celebrated without his consent and against his will. Normally a council is not legally ... celebrated without papal calling and approval`. . . But as in grammar and morals, general rules have exceptions − and especially when the infinite number of special circumstances surrounding a special case has been taken into account. Because of this a superior law has been ordained to interpret the law.[32]

The strong tide of anti-clericalism was not so much against the Church as an institution, but against its corruption and the failure to fulfil its duty.[33] Such notions were anathema to adherents of the doctrine of papal supremacy. Throughout western society there was a new sense that the woes of the world demanded a new and reformed Church. As Steven Ozment has observed, 'Peter was commissioned by God to "feed my sheep", not to run them over a cliff. "God has given no status, no degree of dignity, no ministry of any kind," Gerson wrote, "except in order to serve the common benefit of all."'[34]

If there was no valid Pope to summon a General Council of the Church, who then could do so? The only claimant to such a universal power, who stood next to the Pope even in the strictest of papalist doctrines, was the Emperor, also ordained by God for the good of Christendom. Potentially, the weakening of case for papal power should have strengthened the authority of the imperial office. Sigismund was seen to be the hope of Christendom, yearning for reform and renewal. The *Reformatio Sigismundi* (The Reformation of the Emperor Sigismund), a tract which first appeared in the late 1430s, shows the fears and anticipation of the times.

Almighty God [it begins], Your anger is upon us; your wrath has seized us; we are as sheep without a shepherd.

> Obedience is dead
> Justice is grievously abused
> Nothing stands in its proper order.

Therefore God has withdrawn His Grace from us. We ignore His commandments. What He has ordered we do only if it pleases us. We practise obedience without righteousness.

But we ought to realize: matters cannot continue like this. We must undertake a proper ordering of spiritual and secular affairs.

It was the good Emperor Sigismund, it continued, who had summoned the Councils of the Church to Constance and to Basel to begin the process of recovery, and the secular princes and the princes of the Church who had frustrated his desire for reformation.

The Council's decrees told the highest personages what needed to be accomplished and what they should do and what they should leave off doing. But are they concerned? Not at all. They show (forgive the expression) their arse to the Council and wish no reformation.

The rulers and the Church have deserted God's people: only a true Emperor can bring justice to the world: 'The hour will come for all faithful Christians to witness the promulgation of the rightful order. Let everyone join the ranks of the pious who will pledge themselves to observe it. It is plain that the Holy Father the Pope and all our princes have abandoned the tasks set them by God. It may be that God has appointed a man to set things right.'[35]

One great fear subtly underlies all the others. In the *Reformatio*, there is a dialogue between a Christian knight and a Turk. The knight said: 'You are a wise man . . . you should see that our Christian faith is a noble faith. All things are well ordered with us and you will not find anything amiss. Why not be baptized and become a Christian?' The Turk replied:

I see that according to your Bible Christ has redeemed you with His death and chosen you for eternal life. But observing your actions I also see that not one of you truly loves Christ nor do you desire to live by His word. In fact, you deny Him. You take away your neighbour's goods and wealth; you destroy your fellow man's dignity; you even claim his person for your own. Is this done according to your Saviour's word and command? Now you plan to come across the sea and wage war upon us and gain eternal life by vanquishing us. But you deceive yourselves. It would be a far better deed were you to remain at home and do battle with false Christians in your midst, showing them the way to righteousness.

The author remarks, 'Such are the sentiments which we must hear from the infidels'. And he concludes the tale: 'The Turk also said: "If only you had changed your ways, turned to your God and kept your old laws, you would have defeated us long ago."'

This unlikely dialogue between Christian and Turk was not some convenient literary device, but an echo of a grim reality. It was not necessary to cross the sea to find the Turk. Like the plague of the Black Death, they were already present, ready to ravage God's people. Sigismund was King of Hungary, where he had spent much of his youth and where he had married Mary, the sole heir of Louis of Anjou, King of Hungary. A decade before he led the Christian world as Emperor, he had sought to mount a crusade against a new menace, the Turks, who had begun to advance into the Balkans in the 1340s. In 1389, they had destroyed the empire of the Serbs on the battlefield of Kossovo. In a single day, the nobility of the greatest Christian power in the Balkans were slaughtered, and were left to rot on what was known thereafter as the Field of the Crows, from the carrion eaters who feasted on the bodies of the thousands who had died. Within a year those same Turkish warriors were raiding Sigismund's Hungarian lands. He threw back their advance guard in 1393, but knew they would come again in force. He conceived the idea of a great crusade, under his leadership, that would unite the princes of Christendom and perhaps after destroying the Turkish power, go forward to achieve the Holy Grail, of recovering Jerusalem.[36]

The crusade might also be a means to reunite Christendom across the divide of the Great Schism. The idea of a holy war caught the imagination of the rulers and nobility of western Europe. Both Boniface XI in Rome and Benedict XIII in Avignon proclaimed the crusade. The enthusiasm, especially in France and Burgundy, was extraordinary, and preparations began on a scale unparalleled in earlier ventures. The army of France, led by the eldest son of the Duke of Burgundy, the Count of Nevers, amounted to 1,000 knights and their retinues. Twenty-four carts were needed to transport their rich dark-green velvet tents, all embroidered in Cypriote gold thread with the arms of the Count of Nevers. The accoutrements of the knights, with saddles and harness decorated with gold, silver and ivory, were all provided by the French exchequer; the sumptuous splendour made it appear a parade or tournament rather than an army gathering for war. But this was an illusion: knights and foot-soldiers were all fired with a zeal for the holy war, and a belief that they could emulate the deeds of their ancestors. The German lands, not to be outdone, sent contingents from all over the Empire, not so splendidly furnished as the French, but probably equal to them in numbers, giving a force of between 10,000 and 20,000 men.

The army assembled through the summer of 1396, marching along the line of the Danube to Vienna, where they were welcomed by Leopold, Duke of Austria, with a week of splendid festivities and tournaments. Nevers took the opportunity of borrowing 100,000 ducats from his host (and brother-in-law). The temptation to linger in that welcoming environment was powerful and it was well into July before all the elements of the western army had moved on down the line of the Danube into Hungary, towards the rallying-point for all the contingents from east and west at Buda. Here the knights from the Empire and France were united with the knights from Bohemia and Poland, and with contingents from the knights of the military orders of Rhodes and Malta and the knights from Italy who had accompanied Enguerrand de Coucy, Count of Soissons, from Lombardy. Here Sigismund welcomed the crusaders, and advised a slow and cautious advance. This was contemptuously disregarded, for, led by the Count of Soissons, the crusaders declared they came 'to conquer the whole of Turkey and to march into the Empire of Persia ... the Kingdoms of Syria and the Holy Land.' Some, including the intrepid count, did indeed come to Turkey, but not as conquerors ...

By now a vast and unwieldy body, the army divided into two parts, one on the north and the other on the south bank that moved more slowly forward. Their advance was marked by acts of rape, robbery and pillage on an epic scale, and all within the lands of Catholic Hungary. When they crossed the boundary into the Orthodox Balkans, they 'carried their excesses to the utmost extreme'. By September the army had passed the Iron Gates, marking the upper from the lower Danube, and met the galleys from Venice and Genoa, and the ships of the Knights Hospitallers. By September 1396, they had arrived at Rachowa, the first substantial town held by the Turks. Here the advance guard of French and Burgundian knights attempted a sudden assault, only to be thrown back with many casualties. It took the full force to overcome the garrison, and in the aftermath of the battle the Christians went mad with blood lust, slaughtering Orthodox Christian townspeople and Turkish garrison alike. Their next objective was the town of Nicopolis, a much more difficult obstacle. Set high on cliffs above the Danube, with a steep slope in front of the city to the south, and the gorge of the river Osma to the east, it was a site designed by nature for defence. Man had added a fortification of great strength and complexity, with multiple protective walls and high towers. The Turkish garrison was well equipped, with plentiful food and water, and they had sent the Christian inhabitants out of the city so they would not have useless mouths to feed. The crusaders decided to starve the city into submission, and camped in a wide circle around it, while their galleys cut it off from the river side. As at Vienna and Buda, the time was characterized by feasts and tourneys, while the foot-soldiers dug a leisurely sap towards the great walls.

Late in September, the crusaders had news that the Turkish Sultan Bayazid was advancing on them from the south with his army. A detachment led by the Count of Soissons advanced to meet them and achieved complete victory in a set of skirmishes. Emboldened, he returned to camp, to the chagrin of the other crusaders who yearned to come to grips with the hated infidel. The ease of his victory decided the western leaders of the crusade to place the flower of the army, the French knights, in the first line of attack. Sigismund urged them to follow the Turkish model and hold their best troops in reserve, but he was overruled, since the French custom was for the knights to ride in the van, a tactic which had already brought them to disaster at Crécy in 1346. The Count of Soissons argued for the King of Hungary's plan, but could not sway his fellow countrymen. Sigismund then decided to form his own battle-line, behind the French advance. Meanwhile, the Turks, whose scouts have given them full details of the lie of the land – and Bayazid himself knew the ground well – planned to resist the crusaders' advance. They grouped their men on the rise of a steep hill, so that the crusaders would have to approach from below. In the front line they placed their auxiliaries, the *akinjis*, grouped behind a forest of sloping and sharpened stakes hammered deep into the ground. Behind them at a distance were the infantry and archers, and just behind the crest of the hill, the main body of the Turkish army, the feudal cavalry, *sipahis*.

Early in the morning of 26 September, the great mass of French knights gathered at the foot of the slope. Above them waved three hundred silken pennons embroidered with silver, and at the front, four knights carrying the banners emblazoned with the image of the Virgin Mary. The advance halted and a number of esquires knelt down to be dubbed knight on the field of battle. For them a place of honour was reserved in the front rank. Then with a great cry of 'Vive St Denis' and 'Vive St Georges' the whole armoured body convulsed, and then lurched forward, first to a walking pace, then a trot, and then, against the slope, to a full gallop. As they approached the Turkish lines, they were showered with arrows, a great number finding their mark and causing many casualties to men and horses. The horses balked at the forest of sharpened stakes, and a few, unlucky, were forced on to the points by the press behind. The French commander called for a halt and a brief withdrawal, then they advanced again, this time at a walking pace, so as to find their path through the line of stakes and the mass of *akinjis* behind.[37] Once into the mass of men, the superior arms and equipment of the crusaders began to tell, and the heaps of Turkish dead began to grow. But by now the crusaders were becoming tired, under the hot sun, and they still had not engaged the main body of the Turks under the direct command of the sultan. The first knights reached the top of the hill, and shouted their battle-cries in exultation, before they noticed the huge mass of Turkish horse – perhaps 40,000 of them – standing silently on the reverse slope. Bayazid gave the order to charge, and the long Turkish line, their green-and-black standards before them, crying '*Allah hu akbar*', 'God is great', surged over the hilltop and on to the Christian knights below. The coherence of the French line vanished in a moment, and all that were left were little clusters of men, some, like the Admiral of France, defending one of the banners of the Virgin, or others, grouped around the leaders of the French army. As the Turks approached, the young Count of Nevers surrendered, and all over the field, the French submitted to the enemy.

Behind the broken remnants of the flower of French chivalry, the army of Sigismund was drawn up in silence with its back to the town of Nicopolis. As the *akinjis* had blunted the French advance, so too the battle with the knights, and their surrender, had disturbed the momentum of the Turkish attack. Despite the desertion of some of his allies, the King of Hungary gave orders for an immediate advance to the aid of the Count of Nevers, and furious hand-to-hand fighting ensued, with the Turks being slowly driven back. But 5,000 fresh horse, Christian allies of the Turks, arrived on the battlefield, and Sigismund was lost. With a few of his commanders, he embarked on one of the galleys at anchor in the Danube, and rowed off at high speed under a shower of Turkish arrows.

The carnage of the day had been great on both sides, but worse was to follow on the following morning. The sultan had ordered that all the thousands of prisoners be stripped naked and tightly bound. The leaders having been set aside for ransom, the remainder, including members of some of the oldest families of France, Burgundy and the Empire, were dragged before him in groups. Asked to abjure their faith, all refused, and were instantly beheaded, the heads being piled neatly before the sultan, and the torsos dragged away. Group after group were pulled forward and met the same fate, and soon the cairns of heads multiplied: grisly mounds covered the field. Only towards nightfall did Bayazid call a halt, his desire for vengeance slaked. Between three and ten thousand Christians died on that day, many more than had fallen on the battlefield the day before.

Sigismund sailed down the Danube, through the Black Sea to Constantinople, and returned to Hungary by way of Rhodes and Ragusa in the Adriatic. The whole episode revealed the strengths and flaws of his character. His plan for the crusade was well founded, but he lacked authority to command the wayward crusaders when they arrived. Before Nicopolis, his caution was justified, and so too was his decision to attack. But once again he failed to achieve his objective, through a fatal lack of determination. As Edward Gibbon succinctly put it: 'The battle of Nicopolis would not have been lost if the French had obeyed the prudence of the Hungarians; but it might have been gloriously won had the Hungarians imitated the valour of the French.'[38] The same lack of resolution defeated the other great initiative for which he was responsible, reform in the Church.

 ↶   ↶   ↶

Finally elected Emperor in 1411, Sigismund's deep concern for the rift in Christendom made him determined to seek a resolution by means of a General Council. He travelled to Italy and persuaded the (Pisan) Pope John XXIII to summon a General Council of the Church to the imperial city of Constance in November 1414, under the protection and in the presence of the Emperor himself. Over the winter of 1414, the roads to Constance were clogged with the wagons and horses of the princes of the Church, the doctors of theology and law from the universities of Europe, and an army of camp-followers. Over the three years of the sessions in Constance, twenty-nine cardinals, three patriarchs, thirty-three archbishops and a hundred doctors of theology met to resolve the pressing problems of Christian belief and practice, and to establish true government for the whole of Christ's people. In addition, the chronicler of Constance, Ulrich Ricenthal, also counted 1,700 trumpeters, musicians and fifers, 1,400 merchants, innkeepers and tradesmen, and 700 prostitutes, all required to service the needs of the great assembly.[39]

Among those summoned to Constance was the Czech preacher and reformer Jan Hus, held by many to be a heretic and a dangerous threat to the stability of Christendom. He had reluctantly obeyed the summons, although he knew that he was putting himself into the hands of his enemies. But with the promise of an imperial passport guaranteeing full protection, he travelled south early in November 1414. The Bishop of Constance ignored the imperial passport and placed the Czech reformer under house arrest, while preparing to charge him with heresy. When Sigismund arrived at the council, he did not demur at Hus's trial, even if his safe conduct had been flouted. After he had seen the evidence against him, he was convinced that the Czech was a flagrant heretic and privately advised that he should never be allowed to return home. Those remarks, uttered in confidence, soon came to the ears of the Czechs and were to cost him dearly.

At his last trial Hus was shouted down when he attempted to answer his accusers, and finally gave up the attempt, saying, 'In such a council as this I had expected to find more propriety, piety and order.' He was judged guilty, and for four weeks he resisted the most fearsome pressure to make him recant his heresies; but he adamantly refused. Finally, he was declared an incorrigible heretic who had condemned himself out of his own mouth, and was 'relinquished to the secular arm'. On 6 July, he was taken to the market-place of Constance, bound to a stake atop a vast pyre of tar-soaked wood and burned alive. His last recorded words on the way to the scaffold were: 'In the truth of that Gospel which before now I have written, taught and preached, I now joyfully die.'[40] As the flames rose, he could be heard chanting the words of the 'Kyrie eleison' before the smoke stifled him.

After the execution of Hus the council settled down to tackle the central issues of government and authority. Its achievements were nothing like as great as Christendom had come to expect. Certainly, the central issue of the Great Schism was settled. All three 'popes', in Bologna, Rome and Avignon, were put aside, and in 1417 the council elected a new leader, who took the name Martin V. But when the council ended its sessions in the following year, nothing had been done about the reform of the Church, which was to be debated and resolved at some later council.[41] At Constance the imperial star was in the ascendant. Sigismund had asserted an authority in the Church that many of his predecessors would have envied. In doing so he was fulfilling a need for the chosen emperor of the German people to act effectively, righting the wrongs of the world. There was a popular demand for a Universal Emperor, and scholars like Marsilius of Padua had also called for a secular monarch with wide powers. Sigismund's success was short-lived, and the moment of a revived imperialism quickly passed. On one side it seemed that the authority of the Emperor had been enhanced, but on the other he revealed that his power was chimerical. His incapacity showed itself even more starkly in his attempt to humble the Habsburgs.[42]

The Luxemburgs and the Habsburgs were closely intertwined by marriage, but Sigismund regarded the connection with fear and suspicion, quite unlike the amity which his father had shown. Perhaps this was because they had stood aside from the crusade to Nicopolis; the 100,000 ducats so lavishly promised by Leopold were never paid. Perhaps, too, the issue of the *Privilegium* rankled. Nor was it an antipathy to all Habsburgs, because his son-in-law, Albert V, who was to marry his only daughter and sole direct heir, was treated like his own son. But given the opportunity to humble his potential rivals, he made the most of it. Unwisely, in 1415, the nephew of Rudolf IV, Frederick, who held the Duchy of Tyrol, entered the complex debate between the Empire and the contestants for the papal throne. He backed one of the three concurrent 'popes',[43] John XXIII, against the wishes of the Emperor Sigismund.[44] He met the Pope at Merano, and accepted a papal title of Standard-Bearer to the Holy See and a pension of 6,000 ducats; in return he agreed to protect and support him. He accompanied the Pope to the council with a retinue of 500 heavily armed men.

When Sigismund arrived he demanded that Frederick should disband his retinue and formally swear allegiance. Reluctantly, Frederick obeyed. However, he feared that the Emperor would use the occasion of the council to work against him, and thus he supported the Pope in his desire to close the proceedings. John XXIII, who had hoped to be confirmed as sole Pope, now saw that the Emperor favoured a more radical solution, and that he would be deposed. By withdrawing he hoped to withdraw his sanction from the council and that it would collapse. On 21 March 1415, Frederick gave a tournament to which the Emperor and all the notables of the council were invited; while it was at its height, the Pope escaped from the city in disguise, to take refuge in one of Frederick's castles nearby. As soon as the tournament was ended, he himself left the city with all his men and declared his open opposition to the council.

However the council, backed by the authority of the Emperor, would not be forced into dissolution. On 15 April, it passed a decree entitled *Sacrosancta*, which declared it to be independent of the power of any of the popes. The council in full session declared that it was lawfully assembled 'in the Holy Spirit' and that it held its authority immediately from Christ. And it declared, directly threatening Frederick and any like him who supported one of the existing popes against its decrees: 'Anyone, of any rank and condition, who shall contumaciously refuse to obey the orders, decrees, statutes or instructions, made or to be made by this holy council ... shall unless he come to his right mind, be subject to fitting penance and punished appropriately.'

A further thesis circulated at the council suggested that 'the vicar of Christ is bound even more than an inferior to follow Christ', and that he could be summarily condemned for failing to meet this high standard. The weight of opinion at the council was so great that John XXIII suffered summary deposition (for, among other offences, heresy, simony, murder, sodomy and fornication) and for Frederick, excommunication, and a decree making him an outlaw within the Empire. This meant that anyone could take possession of his territories and other property without fear of punishment. All the neighbouring rulers took this opportunity to seize his lands and castles. The Swiss, absolved from their feudal duties, gathered in the remaining Habsburg lands south of the Rhine, including the Castle of the Habichtsburg, an eloquent symbol of Frederick's plight. Faced with the loss of all his possessions or submitting to the decision of the council and to his enemy Sigismund, he chose the latter and surrendered himself at Constance as a penitent to await his punishment.

A day was set for the Duke of Tyrol's ritual and theatrical humiliation.

No prince of the empire ever submitted to such indignities or experienced such degradation as Frederick.[45] To grace and witness his triumph, Sigismund summoned the most considerable princes of the empire and the ambassadors of the Italian states, with the chief fathers of the Council [of Constance] into the refectory of the Franciscan convent at Constance [Jan Hus was also tried and condemned in this same chamber]. The emperor having seated himself on his throne, Frederick entered, accompanied by his nephew, the burgrave of Nuremberg, and by his brother-in-law Louis of Bavaria, and thrice prostrated himself. The eyes of the whole assembly were fixed on the unfortunate prince, and a dead silence prevailed, till Sigismund demanded, 'What is your desire?' The burgrave replied, 'Most mighty king, this is duke Frederick of Austria, my uncle; at his desire I implore your royal pardon, and that of the council, for his offences against you and the Church; he surrenders himself and all his possessions to your mercy and pleasure ...' The emperor, raising his voice asked, 'Duke Frederick, do you engage to fulfil these promises?' and the duke in faltering accents, answered 'I do, and humbly implore your royal mercy.'

Frederick then surrendered all his fiefs and agreed to hold only what the Emperor chose out of favour to grant him. Sigismund came down from his throne, and raised him to his feet, and, taking his hand and holding it high, announced to all present, 'You all know, reverent fathers, the power and consequence of the dukes of Austria; learn by this example what a king of the Germans can accomplish.'[46] Not since Henry IV had humbled himself, barefoot and in a hairshirt, in the snow at Canossa in January 1076 before Pope Gregory VII had a ruler been so ritually and publicly degraded. With this dramatic stroke the Emperor had reasserted his authority.

But he failed to sustain his advantage. The response of other, less supine members of the Habsburg clan was immediate and suggests how far the self-protective and collective sense of the family, of *domus Austriae*, had developed. Frederick's brother Ernest, appropriately nicknamed The Iron, ruled the eastern domains of Styria and Carinthia as his share of his father's patrimony. These were rich provinces, with a flourishing agriculture, a thriving iron industry and strong connections with Italy on the other side of the Alpine range. He might well have been called the Iron-Willed; Ernest had the energy and determination to make his cadet branch of the family the dominant force among the Habsburgs. He occupied the Tyrol and simply challenged the Emperor to remove him by force. Not for the first time, Sigismund backed away from the challenge and relinquished his claim. At Nicopolis he had failed to assert his authority at the crucial moment over the other leaders of the crusade and had withdrawn to pursue his own course. At the height of the battle, when resolution would have brought him victory, he left the field. In the more tranquil context of Constance, he betrayed the same weakness. Faced with a challenge, he withdrew. He failed to force through the issue of reform and he failed to humble the Habsburgs. Other rulers became fascinated with alchemy and sought to turn lead into gold. Sigismund seemingly had the capacity to turn his golden opportunities into the base metal of failure.

Constance was a wasted opportunity, but the remainder of his reign was a catalogue of disaster. His behaviour towards Hus reaped a bitter harvest. Four hundred and fifty-two of the leading figures of the Czech nation had sent a manifesto to Sigismund denouncing the reformer's judicial murder. The Emperor was reported as saying that soon all heretics would be 'washed away'. The Czech nation rose in protest against Sigismund's authority, and when the King of Bohemia, his half-brother Wenceslaus, died in 1419, the Czechs refused to accept him as the rightful heir. The renunciation of the Luxemburgs spanned all the classes and social groups within Bohemia, and the ensuing 'Hussite Revolution' meant that for seventeen years Sigismund was excluded from his new kingdom. His authority in Hungary and in the Empire dwindled. The Council of Basel summoned in 1431 did not produce the reforms promised at Constance, and reversed many of the processes set in train during 1414–17. Once there had been rival popes: now there were rival General Councils. Sigismund, assailed by his enemies on every side, chronically short of money, proved powerless to take the lead.

The only reliable ally he found in all his difficulties was the young Duke of Austria, Albert V. He provided troops for Sigismund's campaigns against both the Turks and the Hussites, and in 1422 the alliance was cemented by the marriage of Albert to Sigismund's only daughter, Elizabeth of Luxemburg, and the Emperor declared that Albert would be heir to all his estates and titles after his death, supporting him as the future king of Bohemia and of Hungary. Whatever successes were achieved by Sigismund in his last years may be attributed to Albert's tireless energy. His reward was to be the title and authority that his family had known was theirs by right since the murder of his namesake a hundred and thirty years before. In December 1437, Sigismund knowing that his

end was near, called the nobility of both his kingdoms before him
to the town of Znaim in Moravia. He addressed them thus:

At this moment my only anxiety arises from an earnest desire to prevent
the dissensions and bloodshed which may overwhelm my kingdoms after
my decease. It is praiseworthy for a prince to govern well but it is not less
praiseworthy to provide for his people a successor better than himself . . .
a king may commend himself to posterity when he leaves behind him a
successor who will eclipse his own action . . . Ye all know Albert duke of
Austria to whom in preference to all other princes I gave my daughter in
marriage, and adopted him as my own son . . . I recommend him to you
as my successor; I leave you a king pious, honourable, wise and brave. I
leave him my kingdom rather I give to him my kingdoms, to whom I can
give or wish nothing better. Truly, ye belong to him, in consideration of
his wife, the hereditary princess of Hungary and Bohemia . . . I again
repeat I do not act thus solely from love to Albert and my daughter, but
from a desire, in my last moments to promote the true welfare of my
people.[47]

He withdrew, exhausted from the great council and told his body
servants to bring him the full imperial robes of state, with the
crowns and other regalia by his side. Slowly they dressed him in the
chasuble, cope and mantle, and set the crown on his head. Then the
last of the Luxemburgs sat down, surrounded by the emblems of power
he had wielded so inadequately, to await death. That he could not
even die in his capital city of Prague (once more in rebellion against
him) in the palace built by his father was the culminating irony of
his troubled life.

The young Duke of Austria was duly crowned king of Hungary
on the 1 January 1438, and on the 18th of March he was elected as
Albert II, King of the Romans, unopposed in the Diet of the Empire
at Frankfurt (he was also elected King of Bohemia in May, but he
still had to fight to secure that kingdom). There were high hopes of
this energetic and forceful ruler, who united in his person the
crowns of Hungary and Bohemia and the dukedom of Austria, a
man at the peak of his powers. 'I cherish the hope', wrote Wernher
of Mainz, 'that the empire has acquired a powerful ruler, who will
restore peace and law and will recall the princes and other selfish
magnates to their duties. Albert is a mighty lord, practised in war,

of untiring energy, and well provided with people and money.'⁴⁸
Where Sigismund was a ruler whose chosen domain was the council
chamber or the chancery, Albert radiated action and activity. Tall,
powerfully built, with a bull-neck and a full black moustache, the
new ruler looked what he was: a soldier. He inherited the dukedom
in his eighth year and he had been in the field since he was
seventeen. He had led his troops east into the border lands of
Hungary against the Turks, and latterly, in 1420–21, north against
the rebellious Czechs.

His reign, like that of his great-uncle Rudolf IV, was short but
full of achievement. He took a commanding stance in the disputes
that were once more paralysing the Church; and he began to reform the legal code of the Empire. But where Rudolf had had seven
years Albert had barely two. Early in 1439, he received news that
the Turks were again advancing into Hungary, and he gathered an
army, with some difficulty, to repulse them. He set up his banner
at Buda and then advanced through the swampy plain of Bácska
to cut off the advancing enemy on the line of the Danube. But it
never came to a battle. Both armies were laid low by dysentery
and the Turks retreated. In the imperial army one of the victims was
Albert himself. He reached Buda on horseback but was then too
weak to ride any further. He demanded that he should be carried in
a litter back to Vienna, and to his wife who was expecting their
fourth child. He was reputed to have told his entourage: 'I shall
recover if I can only once more behold the walls of Vienna.' He
died, still within the borders of Hungary, on 17 October 1439.

There is a bizarre sense of symmetry in Habsburg affairs. The
first Albert murdered at Brugg was cut down in his prime; his
successor, Frederick the Fair, who had claimed the imperial throne
as Frederick III, was incapable of being a worthy successor. With
the second Albert the evidence of promise is there and a little of its
fulfilment, but in his case also the Frederick who succeeded him
lacked the power, will and energy of his predecessor. But there the
parallel ends. Frederick III was elected King of the Romans by the
German people, and became the first and last Habsburg to be
crowned Holy Roman Emperor by the Pope in Rome. Some saw
him as a failure like his namesake, but more properly he should be
seen as the progenitor of Habsburg greatness.

3

Universal Empire

1400–1500

Frederick II, King of Sicily, Holy Roman Emperor, King of Jerusalem, protector of the Holy Places, *Stupor Mundi*, the Wonder of the World, died on 13 December 1250, and his body was buried in a vast tomb at the heart of the cathedral of Palermo. Or was the tomb, like that of the risen Christ, an empty sepulchre? For, according to some believers, he was not dead but only sleeping, and awaited the hour of Germany's need before he returned as her salvation, ushering in a golden age of peace. The same stories had been told of his grandfather, Frederick I, Barbarossa, who had died returning from the Holy Land, and whose last resting-place was never found. He too, it was said, still sat on his throne under the Kyffhauser Mountain in Thuringia, awaiting the moment of release. The legends merged into a composite, archetypal emperor, who bore the glorious name of *Frederick*.

> Hail Lord of the World
> Hail our Caesar . . .
> First among the princes of the earth
> Caesar Frederick . . .
> No sensible man doubts that
> Through God's power
> you rule above all other kings[1]

Within a generation of *Stupor Mundi*'s death he had reappeared on earth. In 1284, Germany was roused against Rudolf of Habsburg by a young man who claimed to be the returned Frederick, and the Emperor had to besiege the town of Wetzlar, capture the impostor, and burn him publicly as a heretic and sorcerer before the agitation died down. But the legend mutated in response: new stories suggested that Prester John, the mysterious Christian ruler of Abyssinia, had protected 'Frederick' with a mantle proof against the hottest fire and he had escaped the flames. In the fourteenth century, amid the horrors of the great pestilence (the Black Death), the mystical Frederick repeatedly walked the land:

... there appears by God's will the Emperor Frederick, so noble and so gentle ... Peace reigns in all the land. Fortresses threaten no longer, there is no need to fear force any more. Nobody opposes the crusade to the withered tree. When the Emperor hangs his shield upon it, the tree puts forth new leaf and blossom. The Holy Sepulchre is freed, from now on no sword needs to be drawn on its behalf. The noble Emperor restores the same law for all men ... All heathen realms do homage to the Emperor.[2]

Many believed that this returning Emperor would be the ruler of the last day of the world, of which pestilence, earthquake and famine were but the precursors. They were driven by a zealous hatred for the rich and the powerful; but even the rulers and nobility were not free from the powerful lure of the Frederickian mysteries. In the *Reformatio Sigismundi* (see page 54 above) the Emperor Sigismund was admonished, on Ascension Day 1403, by a voice from Heaven, which called to him: 'Sigismund, arise, profess God and prepare the way for the Divine Order. Law and justice languish neglected and scorned. You yourself are not destined to accomplish the great renewal, but you will prepare the way for him who will come after you.' (The saviour was identified as a priest Frederick of Lantnaw, possibly the author of the *Reformatio*.) This news did not please Sigismund, who was 'grievously saddened'. But, soon, he came to terms with his destiny and declared that

upon reflection we understood that we had been chosen to prepare a way for the new order ... from the day on which we became the Empire's servant we have striven to maintain the right order in the Church and empire. We have reunited the papacy, convoked a council and brought order into the estate of the Church. But nothing can be accomplished until he arises whom God has chosen for the task.

Of Frederick of Lantnaw, nothing more was heard. But the prophecy of the coming Emperor who would right the wrongs of the world had aroused enormous expectation. Had Sigismund been preparing the way for his successor, Albert II, who fulfilled all the criteria save one, and might by his qualities be recognized as 'true Frederick' despite his lack of the miraculous name? Then, with his sudden and mysterious death, the clear stream of destiny muddied and only gradually did the infinite wisdom of God once again become clear. As the Electors hunted for a new Emperor, the obvious candidate *was* a Frederick, Duke of Styria, the eldest son of Ernest the Iron. There were many fragments of evidence to suggest that this Frederick was the predestined leader for Christendom. First, he was the son of a Christian warrior. Ernest had made the dangerous pilgrimage to the Holy Land, and after his return had done battle with the Turkish infidel. The new Frederick had also made the journey to Jerusalem, following the path of his father and of both his namesakes, Frederick Barbarossa and Frederick II. Second, and perhaps this was a more important omen, he had been born exactly two hundred years after Frederick II had been crowned in Charlemagne's church at Aachen.

The search for precedents and hidden meanings created its own momentum. Frederick was rumoured to be reluctant to accept the offer of the imperial throne. But had not Christ himself been unwilling to accept his mission, and could not Frederick's unwillingness actually be seen to confirm his election? Even if the Electors were not credulous believers in the legends of the last Emperor, they could hardly be ignorant of the Frederickian myths or immune to their siren call. The Duke of Styria's greatest asset was that name, with all the expectations and trust that went with it. But he also inherited powerful Habsburg traditions, an unassuageable conviction that *domus Austriae* was God's chosen instrument. He and his brother Albert were the only living male heirs of the marriage of Ernest the Iron and Cymberga of Masovia, from whom he inherited his most striking characteristic, a fat and pendulous lower lip.[3] Both his parents radiated a physical energy and power; of his mother it was said she could crack nuts between her fingers and hammer nails into oak boards with her clenched fist. His father matched her: a powerful figure usually depicted in full black armour, carrying a huge double-handed sword. He seemed the warrior incarnate. Frederick too was tall and massively built, but there the resemblance ended. He was pale, with a very long, bony Roman nose, heavy jowls and small deeply set eyes, entirely lacking that animal vitality which characterized his parents. Even in his youth he was described as 'dignified', which was perhaps a benign gloss on his ponderous and slow-moving gait – characteristics that became more pronounced as he grew older, for he was voracious for food to fuel his massive frame. It was said that he died from greed, a consequence of eating too many melons on a hot summer's day.[4] Frederick was the antithesis of his athletic predecessor, Albert II. As a recent historian of the Holy Roman Empire, Friedrich Heer, remarked, 'He was Frederick the Fat, who matched not at all the dream figure of Frederick the Third for whom many men had yearned as the successor of the Hohenstaufen; he was deficient in all the qualities proper to an apocalyptical emperor, prince of world peace and saviour king.'[5] Yet no human being could fulfil all the expectations of the True Frederick, and he alone possessed both the name and the heredity. The ways of God could never fully be understood by frail and sinful humanity, but Frederick seemed his chosen vessel.

Of course, Heer was correct in that he could achieve very little in the real world, and he was reviled for it. He lost his lands to his neighbours, even his capital Vienna falling to his enemy the King of Hungary. He quarrelled with his brother Albert, a more active and engaging character. Coxe, in one of his characteristically confident and engaging pen-portraits, draws the contrast very clearly. 'Frederick was cold, phlegmatic and parsimonious; Albert of a frank, convivial and lively disposition; affable and courteous in his manner and liberal even to profusion. Ardent for military glory, he sought and despised fatigues and dangers; while Frederick explored the secrets of nature, or was absorbed in the pursuit of learning, Albert graced the dance and the revel, or triumphed in the tournament.'[6] He mistrusted his son Maximilian for much the same reason that he despised his brother's political and military exploits. Yet in other respects his family life was warm and content: his 'political' marriage to Leonora of Portugal became a union of love,[7] and his court at Wiener Neustadt,[8] across the Semmering Pass from his early home and ducal capital at Graz, was one of the most cultivated and stimulating of eastern Europe, a miniature version of the Prague of Charles IV. Here, and at his summer residence at Linz, he could indulge in his passion for gardening: one contemporary writer remarked that he 'often seemed more concerned to protect his plants from the frost than his domains from these barbarous invaders (the Turks)'. It has become customary to dismiss Frederick as an entr'acte – admittedly a long one for he was ruler for fifty-eight years – between Albert II and Maximilian, two men of a very similar active nature. His contribution was that, although he lost on every side, he never conceded to his enemies; in Rilke's words, catching very much the essence of the Habsburg spirit, 'Who is talking of victories? All that matters is to survive.'[9]

Yet it is possible to see him differently. Within that flaccid, bovine frame was an active intelligence, a supple and visionary mind and, like his father and mother, he was possessed of an iron will. He was probably more aware of the legendary and mystical antecedents of his house than any of his predecessors, except perhaps Rudolf IV, the Founder. He visited the ancient shrines of his ancestors: 'In his progress through the Aargau, he indulged his feelings with contemplating the remains of the citadel of Baden; he offered up his devotions at the tombs of his ancestors who reposed at Königsfelden and as he rode over the adjacent plain, he cast a melancholy eye on the dismantled turrets of the castle of Hapsburgh, the cradle of his illustrious family.'[10] He sought to construct a system of alliances that would allow him to rebuild the family domain in the Aargau and along the Rhine. Aeneas Sylvius Piccolomini, the future Pope Pius II, who entered Frederick's service as his secretary in 1442 and wrote his life, made much of his pilgrimage and its connection to the mission of the Habsburgs:

The princes of the sublime house of Austria, which ranks among its members many kings and emperors, deemed themselves secure of success only when they served the Supreme Being with fidelity and constancy. Frederick, following their example, was no sooner delivered from the care of his guardians, than despising the dangers and tempests of the deep, he repaired to Jerusalem, anxious to kiss the earth sanctified by the footsteps of our blessed Redeemer.[11]

The future Emperor was very aware of the symbolic importance of his role, and the rights which attached to it. Frederick's fascination with the mystical, sublime aspects of rulership fed voraciously on the legends and symbolism attached to the imperial title. Few of his predecessors had been much concerned with the deeper meaning of coronation and the regalia that symbolized his role as Holy Roman Emperor. One of his first acts once he had been crowned Holy Roman Emperor by Pope Nicholas V in Rome in 1452 was to confirm the *Privilegium maius* under the seal of the Empire.[12] Under the *Privilegium*, he decreed that the Duke of Austria (who was, he declared, entitled to call himself a king although none of his successors did so) should wear a prince's mantle and a crown,[13] 'surmounted by gables over a ducal hat'. This contained two symbolic elements, the hat (which took the form of a set of triangular spires surrounding a velvet cap, which was the emblem of the ducal title), and the single arch and a cross borrowed from the imperial crown, which was the essence of royal power.[14] After Frederick, each reigning archduke of the house of Habsburg was solemnly inaugurated with a ceremony that mirrored a royal or an imperial coronation. For his own imperial inauguration, the new Emperor showed a fanatical attention to the detail of the ceremony. Over the centuries, the procedures had become lax or corrupt, and many elements which once formed part of the ceremonial had been forgotten or abandoned. Frederick rebuilt the ceremonial architecture of imperial coronation, rediscovering (or inventing) new layers and structures of symbolic meaning.

Traditionally, the elements which had featured in earlier imperial coronations in Aachen included the Crown of Charlemagne[15] and various other items, such as an orb and sceptre; and a number of holy relics such as the Holy Lance and the Holy Cloth. When he was crowned at Aachen, the audience witnessed a ceremony that had become more elaborate and portentous, more 'imperial'. For example, when the orb was handed to him, it was with the words: 'Take the holy apple of thy majesty so that thou mayest rule over the whole world in the name of the Holy Trinity.' The robes worn by an Emperor were modelled on those of a bishop or a pope, and emphasized that the Emperor was sanctified by God, and was both king and priest . . .[16] Since early times, and most recently with the Luxemburgs, the Pope had crowned the new Emperor during the ceremony in Rome with a bishop's mitre which was worn, rather clumsily, inside the crown.[17] This 'mitration' was just one of the ways in which the papacy had sought to show the dependency of the Emperor upon the Holy See, just as centuries before the Pope had sent kings and emperors their crowns. Gradually, the secular powers had learned to avoid this sign of dependence and in 1442 Frederick took this process of emancipation a stage further. He did not wait for the Pope to grant him the bishop's mitre, but assumed it for himself. Frederick had a new crown made for him by the goldsmiths of Nuremberg,[18] a massive affair in which the bishop's mitre was incorporated, and decorated with the image of Christ in silver gilt, displayed in glory above an image of the Gospels. At the same time, he ordered new and elaborate reliquaries for the precious imperial treasures – the Holy Tablecloth, the Holy Apron and the Holy Lance.

He also began to redefine the role and authority of the Emperor. The new King of the Romans was the last of the holders of the title to be crowned by the Pope in Rome, and when he set out in 1453 across the Alps for his coronation, he carried with him all the elaborate paraphernalia of imperial coronation that had been used at Aachen. The intention was to dazzle and amaze the Italians. Frederick planned the coronation and his nuptials in Rome with astonishing care. He took the advice of astrologers as to when the coronation and the marriage should take place with the most auspicious portents in the heavens.[19] He must also have been aware of the wild prophecies circulating in Germany that the reborn Frederick would be crowned in Rome and unite Christendom once more, possibly even absorbing the role of the Pope into his own office. Late in the winter of 1451, Frederick, with his brother Albert, his ward Ladislaus, the posthumous son of the previous emperor, Albert II, and an entourage of German nobles, knights and ecclesiastics set off across the Alps to Verona, and thence to Padua and Ferrara.

At every stage he was received with elaborate ceremonial, each town competing to greet the Emperor most lavishly. Sienna, where he was to meet his intended bride, Leonora, the daughter of the king of Portugal, for the first time, provided the most splendid reception prior to his arrival at Rome itself. As his long caravan of retainers and supporters approached the city on 4 February 1452 they found 200 young men of the city, from the best families, waiting for them four miles from the city walls. At their head were three gloriously caparisoned *gonfalonieri* (standard-bearers), the one in the centre flourishing a huge imperial flag, with an eagle embroidered in gold on a black silk ground, while the smaller banners to each side bore the arms of Sienna. The standard-bearers rode forward, and offered the imperial banner to Frederick, who grasped the wooden shaft and, to loud cheers, formally took possession. Then the procession re-formed and, led by the *gonfalonieri* and with the Emperor surrounded by his new escort, moved towards the gates of Sienna. Beneath the gaze of thousands lining the walls and crowding the city gate, he was received by the leading citizens, the clergy and the doctors and students of the university, all of whom sang the ancient hymn, *Veni, creator spiritus*, as the chief magistrate of the city handed the town keys to Frederick, symbolizing their submission. Through his interpreter, Aenius Silvius (from whose account these details are taken),[20] the cavalcade, now joined by the citizens of Sienna, moved through the streets of the city, which were bedecked with silken banners, innumerable blazing torches, and decorative arches, to the cathedral. This joyous reception and heady pageantry seemed to echo the great Palm Sunday procession celebrating the entry of Christ the King into Jerusalem. As he approached the cathedral, there was a general roar, 'Long live the Emperor', from every side. Two days later, the Emperor was once more at the gates of the city, this time to receive his intended bride with an equally elaborate ceremonial.[21]

After Sienna each city-state vied more frantically with the next to receive the imperial pair with greater splendour, but Frederick, mindful of the Pope's fears that he had come to sweep away the temporal rule, issued a public oath of fidelity to the office and person of the Pope as he entered the papal domain.[22] This oath has been read as a submission to the power of the Pope, as antithetical to German dignity. But Frederick made no such mistake, for he was expert in the skills of the chancery and diplomacy. He wrote the document carefully and the oath was one of *concession* and not of *duty*; he promised to exalt the Pope and the holy Church, not because he was bound to do so, but because, as Emperor, he chose to do so. He was aware of the submissions made by both Rudolf and Albert I to the Holy See, and he was careful that at no point did he promise to obey the Pope as they had done.

It was, politically, a well-turned manoeuvre, conceding little and marking out possible advantage for the future. Frederick had skilfully elevated the role of the Emperor above that of the Pope and the Church. Or so it would have seemed had it been written in 1250 rather than 1453; by the fifteenth century, in a world where humanity had been ravaged by the great pestilence, and the Church, which had barely survived the Babylonian captivity and the Great Schism, was wrestling with the issues of heresy and reform, it was an anachronism. It also illustrates both the strengths and weaknesses of Frederick, and suggests why posterity has judged him so harshly. With his preoccupation with coronation, regalia, astrology, with relics, with the *Privilegium* and the universe of symbolic power, Frederick revealed his detachment from the real and pressing issues of his day. But was this, in his own eyes, a weakness? It was, I suggest, entirely in the Habsburg tradition – and within that mirror-world of transcendental, totemic, power, Frederick was not the abject failure seen by many historians, but the great artificer of the Habsburgs' future authority.[23]

Finally, after a tumultuous reception at Viterbo, the imperial party, now swollen to enormous size, came to their destination. At the third milestone from Rome the triumphant Emperor, like some victorious Caesar, was met by the entire college of cardinals, who escorted him to a lavish silk-hung pavilion just outside the walls of Rome where he spent the night before his triumphal entry into the Eternal City. Early in the morning, he passed through the city gates, riding through the streets to the square in front of St Peter's, where the slight figure of the Pope sat motionless on an ivory throne. Frederick approached, knelt, and kissed the

hand and then the head of the Pope, to be followed by his brother
and his ward, and then the whole throng of German, Austrian and
Italian dignitaries. The actual ceremonies of coronation and investiture were spread over a number of days. On 16 March 1452 he
received the Iron Crown of Lombardy from the hands of the Pope
and three days later was crowned with the Crown of Charlemagne
and was married to Leonora in the same ceremony. At the coronation mass, an eyewitness, the imperial minister Kaspar Enenkel
remarked 'that the Emperor attended the coronation clothed with
the Holy Robes of the Emperor Charlemagne, which had happened
to no emperor for many hundreds of years and which were all
treasured for the great honour and especial mercy of God'. Then,
still wearing the crown, he rode down to the bridge over the river
Tiber where he knighted his ward and his brother and three
hundred other 'persons of distinction'.

No comparable exaltation of imperial power had been seen since
the days of the first Fredericks. After his coronation he went south
to the kingdom of Naples, where it was said that he consummated
his marriage for the first time. Legend has it that he was reluctant
because he feared that any child conceived of this union might
resemble the Italians; a more likely origin of the legend was his
preoccupation with astrology, with the conjunctures of the stars at
the child's birth.[24] He need not have been concerned, for, however
warm his marital ardour, his first child did not appear until 1455.
After this dalliance in Naples, he retraced his path by slow stages
through Italy, handing out fiefs, titles and largesse as he went. The
royal party ended their Italian journey at Venice, where after ten
days of celebrations they finally moved north to Graz.

Had the reign of Frederick ended in 1453, or little thereafter, he
might have been regarded as a great imperialist visionary, who
painstakingly rebuilt the edifice of imperial power. In his own eyes
that was precisely what he achieved. He achieved peace between
the papacy and the Empire, especially after Aeneas Silvius was
elected Pope as Pius II in 1458. He had achieved the 'breakthrough'
– re-established the right of the Habsburgs to the imperial title.[25]
But the achievements of his reign peter out and it might seem
legitimate to conclude, that 'the reign of Frederick III is the longest
and dullest of all German history ... the unphilosophic mind

cannot descry anything of lasting interest, and the most careful inspection can reveal only a few things that are worth remembering'.[26] There is a dangerous tendency to read history backwards. It was impossible to 'restore the Empire' after Europe had been sundered by the Reformation and counter-Reformation of the sixteenth century; thus the last years before the breach, the late fifteenth century, seemed the final, and wasted, opportunity for such a universalist revival. It was certainly what many contemporary voices insistently demanded. Pamphlets circulated in Austria that called Frederick the 'Arch Night-cap'[27] of the Holy Roman Empire, while another from the late 1480s said that Frederick squandered his time at Linz collecting mouse droppings and catching flies. Others mocked his gouty leg, unfairly because by the spring of 1493, thanks to the incompetence of his surgeons, it had turned septic and smelled so rank that he was reduced to hiding coins in his apartment to attract his servants, who would otherwise have left him entirely to his own devices.[28] Regardless of any personal tendency towards lethargy and inaction, Frederick did not have the means to promote the crusade or to behave as the 'universal emperor'.

For all the high titles, Frederick was effectively in control only of his Duchy of Styria, and he had to share the revenues of those lands with his brother Albert. The remainder of Austrian lands, plus any claims to the crowns of Hungary and Bohemia, belonged to his ward, Ladislaus. Yet another branch of the family, his young cousin Duke Sigismund, enjoyed the revenues from the Tyrol. As the Emperor Sigismund had found, the Empire was an office not of profit but of ruinous costs, and Frederick did not have the resources to sustain an active role. He did not even have the resources to pay for his costly expedition to Italy for his coronation: the bills were met by the Pope. The death of Ladislaus in 1457 simply brought the opposition between the two brothers, Albert and Frederick, out into the open. From Ladislaus's death until Albert's in 1463, the brothers were at war, with their respective partisans ravaging the lands of the other; more dangerous still, and entirely against the traditions of the house of Austria, Albert VI had formed an alliance with an outsider, the powerful Bohemian warlord and future king, George of Podiebrad. Together they laid siege to the royal castle in

Vienna, where Frederick's queen and young son were trapped. Only Albert's sudden death and the arrival of a large detachment of loyal Styrian knights and retainers raised the siege. So weak did Frederick appear, and so bound up with his family quarrels, that there was a move to deprive him of the imperial title, a plot which failed only because no suitable replacement could be found.

Even Albert's death, although it removed the immediate challenge, did not allow Frederick quiet possession of his lands. To the east was the active and ambitious ruler of Hungary, Matthias Hunyadi, 'Corvinus'.[29] From 1463 to 1480, Frederick held his Austrian estates without challenge, largely by making a series of territorial and political concessions to Matthias, but in 1481 Matthias Corvinus found a pretext to enter the Austrian lands he had long coveted.[30] Thereafter, year by year, he eroded the territory still under Frederick's control. The Hungarian army, reinforced by mercenaries and hardened by years of warfare on the frontier with the Turks, was probably the superior to any other force in Europe, and the Emperor had nothing with which to match it. He lost Vienna in 1485 after a long siege by the Hungarians, and Frederick's own favourite residence, Wiener Neustadt, in the following year. Thereafter Frederick, with a retinue of 800 loyal knights, moved west, to Linz, and tried to rouse support against this affront to imperial dignity. It was only the death of Matthias in 1489 and the military skills of his son Maximilian that allowed him to recover his estates.

Frustrated, therefore, on every side, Frederick expressed himself content with minimizing his losses. One of his well known catchphrases was 'Happiness is to forget what cannot be recovered,'[31] and the catalogue of reverses over more than a half-century of rule disguises the skill with which he manipulated the slender political, financial and moral resources he enjoyed. It is clear from the records of his patrimony that he administered his resources with a close, even miserly attention to detail. The contrast between the crabbed Frederick of the accounts books and the visionary Frederick claiming universal power is hard to accommodate or to understand. Was it mere vanity or vainglory that lured this 'half duke' into claiming that his duchy or his lineage would rule the world? It has become conventional to assume that his dabbling with slogans, symbols and even necromancy were to compensate for his failure in the world of affairs. But we now know that he had these beliefs and aspirations before the world showed its sour face to him. The story is essentially a simple one. It was customary for rulers to choose a slogan or motto that would in some way encapsulate the nature of their rule. (Maximilian's chosen phrase, very true to his nature, was 'Hold the measure and look to the end'.)[32] Frederick, so his diary for 1437 records, discovered the mysterious acronym of all the vowels, AEIOU, for whose meaning there have been many suggestions. The seventeenth-century court librarian Peter Lambecius recorded some forty possible meanings,[33] ranging from the ingenious *Aquila Electa Iovis Omnia Vincit* ('The chosen eagle conquers all things') to the more prosaic *Austria Erit In Orbe Ultima* ('Austria will be the last in the world'). Shortly before his death, Frederick revealed that it denoted 'The whole world is subject to Austria,'[34] in its German version *Alles Erdreich Ist Österreich Untertan*. The monogram was emblazoned everywhere – on the books in his library, on his buildings, on coins and medals. But they were not the only devices with which he toyed. He chose visual emblems as well: one was a hand holding a sword resting upon an open book, with the motto, 'This rules, that defends,'[35] indicating perhaps how he regarded war as an inferior and subsidiary activity. Another was a tower, with bolts of lightning and thunder roaring above. This mystified his courtiers, and they asked him how it should be interpreted. Frederick replied: 'Do you not know that a prince is placed as a mark for the arrow, as lightning strikes at the high tower and does not touch the humble roof.' Perhaps this was the equivalent of 'collecting mouse droppings', just a bizarre and aimless antiquarianism. The alternative is that this was a new and potent technique of myth-making.

Aviad Rabin, writing on the complex meanings bound up in the Corpus Christi rituals, has observed: 'Knowledge is continually culled from ritual moments packed and rich with symbols, which convey meanings embedded in the particular structure ... So symbols convey knowledge, they are emotionally packed. They communicate information and induce moods which cannot always be expressed by words. Inasmuch as people communicate and interact they reckon to understand each other through the use of shared symbols.' I have argued that the Habsburgs were from the beginning alert to the multiplicity of meanings implicit in any act or event: the legend of Rudolf and the priest, the transmutation of Albert into martyr, and Leopold into a 'sacrificial king',[36] are all examples of this process at work. Frederick III pushed the whole process forward by a giant step, claiming for the Habsburgs a new idiom and source of symbolic and magical power. But this new empire, the universal rule of the house of Austria, would be achieved not by Frederick, but by his successors; he like John the Baptist was only a voice crying in the wilderness, 'Make straight the path of the Lord.'

In happier days, Leonora and Frederick had dreamed of a new and renewed Christendom led by the children of their union. Both seem to have been embroiled in this mystical notion, a *folie à deux*. Leonora preferred to be known as Helena, after the mother of the Roman Emperor Constantine, and when she was pregnant with her second child in 1458, both parents were convinced that this child would be both male and a ruler to lead the Christian world. They toyed with the names of Constantine, of George (Frederick had a passionate interest in the cult of St George), but in the end he was called 'Maximilian', probably after a more recent but obscure Balkan saint, Maximilian of Cilli. The names they chose for their other children were equally unusual within a Habsburg context. Their first-born son, named Christopher,[37] and their third, named John, died in infancy.[38] Of their two daughters, only one, Cunegunde, survived to maturity. Thus after 1467, when Leonora died and Frederick refused to consider a second marriage, the whole fate of the Habsburgs hung on three lives, Maximilian and his sister, or a distant cousin, Sigismund, Duke of Tyrol. Why Frederick did not remarry and attempt, heroically, to refill the genetic pool, rather as Ferdinand of Aragón roused himself in his last years, can never be known. But perhaps the long and bruising struggle with his own brother for the rights to their patrimony may have had an influence. The intensity of his parents' belief in Maximilian coloured the whole of his childhood at Wiener Neustadt. Lithe and athletic, with his father's long nose and the physical strength of his paternal grandparents, he seemed to have been born in the saddle. Even as a young child he played games of chivalry – mock jousts on little ponies, games of war, or Turks and Christians – outside the main gate of his father's castle, or in the courtyard by the church of St George.

The defining event of Maximilian's early years, indeed even before his birth, was the capture of Constantinople by the Turks. It was Frederick's dearest wish to mount a crusade against the ravishers of Christendom, but a lack of money or support from other rulers made it impossible. Instead, his response was characteristic. He created a new order of chivalry, the knights of St George, at Wiener Neustadt. In the same year he visited Rome for the second time, and on the first of January 1469 at a ceremony in the church of St John Lateran, Pope Paul II delivered the bull creating the new order under papal protection. Maximilian was dedicated as a knight of this new order, and committed to restoring the unity and strength of Christendom. The writer Grünpeck[39] in his joint life of Frederick and Maximilian shows that from childhood Maximilian was taught that he was a *Wunderkind*, chosen by God to accomplish great deeds. From the moment of his birth, miraculous tales were told. The new-born infant was so strong, so Grünpeck averred, that he could stand up in the bath being used to wash him clean of the blood and fluids from his coming into the world. The naked infant was depicted as an archduke of the house of Habsburg, wearing the archducal hat; in later years this child was transmuted into the 'German Hercules' of popular prints.[40] His early years were lived in conditions of honest simplicity, and he grew strong on plain and simple food. His favourite pastimes were swordplay, archery and jousting; and we are told that he learned to speak German, the local dialects and Latin (at which he never excelled) at an early age. Later he was to boast that he could speak seven languages, although probably only French and Flemish with any competence.

Physically he was much like his father, with the same reddish-gold hair worn long and the same long nose, but Maximilian was muscular where Frederick was simply obese. They shared some of the same bodily weaknesses: Maximilian eventually suffered the same agonizing gout as had marred Frederick's last years, and both became 'choleric' as a consequence. A double-portrait medal of 1490 shows them side by side, the old Emperor wearing his imperial crown and mantle, Maximilian a rakish hat and the collar of the

Order of the Golden Fleece. The profiles are striking in their similarity. Yet in character and behaviour they were quite different: Frederick, static and sedentary, happiest watching his flowers and vegetables grow; Maximilian restless and intensely active. For many years it was rare for him to spend more than a few days or weeks in the same place. He complained of a life spent 'rushing about hither and thither', but this sense of movement, of ceaseless, often contradictory activity pervaded the whole of his life. If he was enslaved to movement and activity, then that servitude came willingly and naturally. His personality was presented as the stuff of romance, the Arthurian legend of chivalry made real. He was the 'last knight', and delighted in the title.

Maximilian, alone of the whole Habsburg line, has been the hero of several novels. One such, by popular writer Charlotte M. Yonge, became a best seller when first published early in the twentieth century. So potent was this romantic image, so seductive Maximilian's personality, and so determined his attempt to write his own legend, that it is hard to view him dispassionately. Here was, indeed, the embodiment of all the hopes and fears of the past, a true *Frederick*, the *miles christianus*, a scholar, a visionary, an author, a politician, a man equally of strong human appetites and deep religious sensibility. Who else but Maximilian in his old age could think of becoming both Pope and Emperor; for whom else was such a desire even remotely within the bounds of possibility? With Maximilian, the Habsburgs had generated (from the unlikely loins of Frederick the Fat)[41] a Universal Hero. For the first time, we can have a clear sense of a Habsburg as an individual, rather than as a type or cipher. With Frederick III, this was possible to a degree, but with his predecessors scarcely at all. There are two reasons for this. In the first place, the art of portraiture had been moving from the depiction of category – 'king' or 'pope' – to the presentation of the individual, and, secondly, Maximilian delighted in seeing his own image, whether on coins and medals, in paintings or line engravings. The image of no earlier monarch was so widely known or so familiar. Even so, it is often difficult to say what was a true likeness for he presented himself in many guises. Some were flattering, others more naturalistic; only one, his death mask at Wels, an exact reproduction of the physical reality.

But Maximilian was adept at replacing reality with image, and before we are wholly entrapped in the web of his weaving, it would be wise to look at the reality of his achievement. On the surface, his record is remarkable. He recovered the Habsburg lands lost to the Hungarians, and in 1477 married the only daughter and heiress of the Duke of Burgundy, the Croesus of his day, thereby becoming reigning duke of the Low Countries. He fought for and defended those possessions on behalf of their children after the death of his wife. He was elected King of the Romans in 1486 (and declared himself Elected Emperor in 1508). He reformed the administration of the Empire, and restored peace and justice to Germany. In 1496 he married his son to the daughter of the Catholic Kings, Ferdinand and Isabella of Aragón and Castile, and in the following year his daughter to their son, the heir to the thrones of Spain; of his grandsons, one, Charles, succeeded him to the imperial throne in 1519 as a ruler whose lands spanned the Old and the New Worlds, the other, Ferdinand, was elected King of the Romans in 1531, governing the Austrian and the German lands; and securing the thrones of Hungary and Bohemia in 1526.[42] His rule was more benign than it was oppressive, and he died of a choleric fury brought on by the refusal of the tradesmen of Innsbruck to extend his credit. For the true achievement of Maximilian, like his father before him, was to achieve so much with so little money, and most of that borrowed.

The basis of all his future success, the Burgundian marriage, was accomplished on credit. In 1473 Charles the Bold, Duke of Burgundy, a man whose limitless and rampant ambition might have been a model for Maximilian's own career, was anxious to raise his dukedom to a kingdom, which its wealth and extent amply justified. He ruled a mosaic of territories, some held as fiefs of his cousins, the Kings of France, others as territories of the Holy Roman Empire which formed a great arc around the French kingdom, from the Mâconnais to the Hook of Holland. The magnificence of the Burgundian court outshone all others in Europe, and yet he was merely a duke. Only the Emperor could elevate his status, and he proposed that by a marriage alliance between his only daughter and Frederick's son, the fourteen-year-old Maximilian, and by making his duchy into a kingdom, the interests of both their houses would be served. The children of the union of Mary of Burgundy and Maximilian of Austria would be Kings of Burgundy, Archdukes of Austria and most probably, emperors as well. Frederick borrowed money and mortgaged estates to equip a party of sufficient distinction to meet the Duke of Burgundy at Trier. There the Austrian party still looked dowdy by comparison with Burgundian splendour, but the agreement was struck. However, at the last minute Frederick balked at creating a Kingdom of Burgundy, fearing (probably correctly) that once a king Charles would set his sights still higher, on the imperial throne. The arrangements broke down. But within three years Charles the Bold was dead in a ditch outside Nancy, his head sliced open by a Swiss halberd; Mary, now his heir, was determined to marry Maximilian, although richer and more powerful candidates presented themselves. It seems clear that Maximilian had made a powerful impression upon her when they met at Trier and she, the richest heiress in Europe, would accept no one else. Thus, if Frederick's diplomacy had provided the opportunity, it was his son's own force of personality that carried the day.

The death of Mary of Burgundy in March 1482 was both a personal and a political catastrophe for Maximilian. Self-willed, determined – as in her utter devotion to Maximilian – she died as she had lived. Mary had the Burgundian passion for hunting, especially falconry; so passionate, indeed, was she for her hawks that she had had them brought into her bedroom within a few days of their marriage.[43] Maximilian, great hunter though he was, considered that enthusiasm a little excessive. Nothing would keep her from the chase and although quite advanced in her third pregnancy, she went out with her hawks. Her horse, moving at some speed, stumbled and she was thrown heavily against a tree; picked up barely conscious, and bleeding from internal injuries, she was carried back to Bruges where she died. Maximilian had ruled the Burgundian inheritance only by right of marriage, and now only as the regent for his infant son Philip;[44] yet he had no territories of his own.

Only gradually was he able to recover the Austrian lands lost to Matthias Corvinus, and more usefully to secure the succession to his cousin Sigismund, Duke of Tyrol, in 1490. The mines and other assets of Tyrol made him a richer man than his father, and he made

Innsbruck his capital. It remained his favourite residence throughout his life, and he extended and rebuilt the ramshackle court over many years. Innsbruck rapidly outshone Frederick's dismal court in exile in Linz, as the relationship between father and son steadily worsened. In 1486, Maximilian was elected King of the Romans in his father's lifetime. Some authorities say that this was against Frederick's wishes, and that he worked to frustrate the election. This seems unlikely, for although the Emperor had little respect for his only son, his sense of dynasty and continuity was overwhelming. Once elected, Maximilian quarrelled more fiercely with his father than before, although Maximilian was careful to edit the harsher episodes from Grünpeck's *Life* before he allowed it to go forward for publication. Frederick's twilight years were filled with a deep gloom, and his mind turned more strongly towards astrology, alchemy and necromancy. Finally in his seventy-ninth year, in constant pain from his sores and ulcers, he died in August 1493, Maximilian succeeding him without challenge.

Maximilian's career as Holy Roman Emperor has been interpreted in two distinct and divergent ways.[45] In one, he was the great reformer, reorganizing and restructuring the Empire, putting it on a new and better administrative and structural basis. In the other, the great planner and coordinator fades away, replaced by Maximilian the pragmatic, the eternal, restless improviser. However, the two images are not inherently contradictory: what united them was his perennial poverty.[46] His attempts at imperial reform in the mid-1490s (mostly frustrated) were dictated by his desire to make the imperial institutions as effective and lucrative as those of Burgundy. His failure can be largely put down to the German princes, who did not want to see a more powerful or self-sufficient Emperor. But his administrative activity was enormous, a whirlwind of decrees, letters, charters and correspondence. Gerhard Benecke in his presentation of Maximilian's 'practical politics' remarked that in his Austrian domains no hunting castle was complete without the writing-desk in his personal chambers, however sparse the rest of the furnishings. He described 'Max.'[47] at work.

Correspondence was conducted in German, Latin and French, although Maximilian did most of his own writing and annotation in German.

Diplomata were formal agreements on parchment. Secondly there were *Patents* concerning feudal matter . . . then *Instructions* and *Papal Letters*. The most time-consuming and probably exhausting for Maximilian was his correspondence dealing with administration and finance . . . and also *Drafts*, which were usually loose sheets with large margins, often corrected in Maximilian's own, forcefully chunky, upright hand.

Benecke presents a picture of an active man forced unwillingly into a world of paper.

Although he was loyally served by a quite bewildering array of chancellors, treasurers, courtiers, envoys, secretaries, scribes and domestic servants, both peripatetic, like himself, or fixed in one town or the castle at Innsbruck, Maximilian spent most of his working life composing and checking through drafts . . . the character of the man is most immediately captured in his fleeting comments on the draft letters . . . The basic point is that Maximilian was a politician with many schemes, always impatient, always in a hurry, generally over-ambitious. Hence his archives have a breathless, chaotic and unexpected charm of their very own, more suited perhaps to the speed with which modern politicians have to react to pressure groups and their media than to an earlier epoch.

However, his inclination was to structure and good order, and his own direct involvement in the detail of administration anticipated his successor Charles V, and Charles's son, Philip II of Spain, whose capacity for good order was much greater than Maximilian's. His ability to plan for the long term, and his patient vision of the future, crystallizes not in the partial restructuring of the imperial institutions, but in his vision of Habsburg power buttressed and solidified by dynastic connection. There his successes are unalloyed. The dual Spanish marriages for his daughter and son to the heir to the thrones of Spain and his sister were undoubtedly a masterstroke, for it seemed to ensure that a grandchild of Maximilian would sit on the throne of the Spanish kingdoms. But matters did not turn out quite as planned. The Infante of Spain, Don Juan, Maximilian's son-in-law, was dead within six months of the marriage, worn out it was suggested by sexual excess, despite which his wife Margaret gave no signs of pregnancy. The line of succession passed to his elder sister, the Queen of Portugal and her son, and Maximilian's grand hopes faded. But mortality struck again, this time to the advantage of the Habsburgs. By 1500, all the male heirs of the Spanish monarchs had died and the inheritance descended to Juana of Castile and thence ultimately to her sons, Charles and Ferdinand. Charles was born at Ghent on St Matthias Day, 1500, and his brother Ferdinand at Alcalá de Henares in March 1503; they were brought up half a continent apart. Charles, born the Duke of Burgundy, grew up in his duchy, and Ferdinand, latterly under the protection of his grandfather and namesake, Ferdinand of Aragón, in Spain. They were not to meet until 1518. In these two boys and their sisters, the future hopes of the Habsburgs were concentrated.

The future of noble houses often hung by the thread of a single human life. Maximilian had but a single son and daughter, and his second marriage, to Bianca Sforza in 1494, which aimed to increase his progeny and fill his coffers,[48] failed on both counts. Bianca proved both barren[49] and wildly extravagant: the marriage was a disaster. The union of Philip and Juana ended with his unexpected death in 1506, which unhinged her completely. Their years of marriage had been marked by her passion for him, her wild jealousies of anyone on whom his wandering eye had settled (she slashed one young woman with a pair of scissors) and her nervous collapse after his death. She refused to allow his burial, taking his coffin with her as she moved from castle to castle, and daily inspected his body (only partially embalmed) for signs of renewed life. Only the direct intervention of her father finally forced her to allow his burial, and he arranged for her to be confined within the castle of Tordesillas with a small court and her youngest daughter Catherine for company.[50]

After the death of his son in 1506 Maximilian, as head of the house of Habsburg, had oversight of his grandchildren's future, and ever the good general, he deployed his forces effectively. The double betrothal of his grandson Ferdinand to Anne Jagellon, sister of the King of Hungary, and his granddaughter Mary to the King of Hungary himself, repeated the 'Spanish strategy'. But the difficulties that at times confronted him in his manoeuvres towards that goal sometimes seemed insurmountable. The stakes were high. No Duke of Austria could afford to be indifferent to the crowns of either Hungary or Bohemia; Maximilian himself had had to reconquer the Habsburg lands from Hungarian occupation barely fifteen years before. True security would come only when the Habsburgs also ruled in Hungary and Bohemia, as they had, fleetingly, under Emperor Albert II.[51]

Maximilian's strategy evolved over almost two decades, coming to fruition only after his death. He used whatever opportunities came to hand. Learning that the Queen of Hungary was expecting a child in 1506, he promised his infant granddaughter Mary to the still-unborn 'son' of the Hungarian king, who by good fortune indeed turned out to be a boy, Lajos. In the following year, he further agreed that the young Princess Anna of Hungary would marry one or other of his grandsons, Charles and Ferdinand, while Mary would complete her match with Lajos. But such pre-contracts could be broken,[52] and a formal ceremony and exchange of vows before witnesses provided a much stronger form of agreement. Accordingly, in 1515, he arranged for the seven-year-old Mary to be sent to him at Innsbruck from Malines where the children of Philip and Juana (save for Ferdinand and Catherine) were being brought up at the court of his daughter Margaret. With his grandsons, he faced an impediment. Charles had come of age and would decide on his own marriage,[53] especially since he would inherit the thrones of Spain. Ferdinand was far away in Spain, where his guardian, Ferdinand of Aragón, would not agree to the espousal.[54]

As a consequence, in St Stephen's Cathedral on 22 July 1515 it was Maximilian himself who knelt beside the twelve-year-old Hungarian princess, Anna, whom he then promised to marry in their behalf, while in the same ceremony her brother Lajos and his granddaughter Mary had affirmed their own agreement to their betrothal. But only two days before, on 20 July 1515, he formally adopted Lajos of Bohemia, the only son and heir of Ladislaus of Hungary, as his own son and asserted that he would ask the Electors to choose him as King of the Romans. The negotiations with the representatives of Hungary and Bohemia were tortuous and often ill-humoured. It was finally agreed that if neither of his grandsons completed the contract within a year, then Maximilian himself would consummate the marriage and make her his Empress. But the death of Ferdinand of Aragón in 1516 removed the impediment and his young grandson (whom he had never seen) dutifully acceded. It was 1521 before Ferdinand arrived in Vienna and the marriage was finally accomplished.

The canonical implications – in that Mary and Lajos technically became uncle and niece – were not considered, for it was a characteristic piece of Maximilian's improvisation, indicative of his desperate concern to secure his eastern flank at all costs. But, as in the case of the Spanish marriages, matters turned out more fortunately than he could ever have anticipated. No one could have foreseen that the young and healthy Lajos of Hungary would meet his end drowned in a stream after the battle of Mohács against the Turks in 1526, leaving no heir save his sister and his brother-in-law, Ferdinand, to whom the reversion of his kingdoms had been promised. In this, as in so much else, good luck followed the Habsburgs. Matthias Corvinus had already remarked, in respect of the Burgundian union, that while others waged war, the Habsburgs married their way to power and honour;[55] to that a later generation might have added that the Habsburgs' gain was another's misfortune. Maximilian's marriage politics was, undeniably, shrewd and deftly executed, but he should not, *post hoc, ergo propter hoc*, take credit for the blind workings of Fate.

How did Maximilian see himself and how did he want posterity to view him? In both cases we can speak with some authority, for he spent a good part of his life securing his eternal reputation. Many of the images we have of him are in civil dress, and in intimate rather than formal poses. There is the famous family portrait by Bernard Striegel, of Maximilian, with his wife Mary (long dead),[56] her eyes cast up to heaven, his son Philip (long dead) and his grandsons, Ferdinand and Charles. His hand protectively enfolds the younger child's, who holds his sleeve, while the elder Charles has his hand protectively on the arm of the young Lajos of Bohemia, his adopted brother, future King of Hungary, and prospective brother-in-law. Nothing about this picture is what it seems. Maximilian had never seen his young grandson Ferdinand, born and brought up in Spain, and named after his Spanish grandfather; Charles at the time the picture was painted was far away in the Netherlands. Maximilian, Philip and Charles all wear the heavy collar and golden ram of the Order of the Golden Fleece, the Burgundian order of chivalry. They are presented as Habsburg rulers, in profile, while Mary, Ferdinand and Lajos appear full face. Its subject is dynasty, with Maximilian at the head of *domus Austriae*, with his posterity; but it was intended for his personal use, perhaps as a reminder of the wife he had – undoubtedly – loved, of the son he had lost, and of the grandsons, though absent, whom he cherished.

The official face of Maximilian was different. For his tomb in Innsbruck, a matter that preoccupied him in his later years, he had his favourite engraver Hans Burckmaier engrave him a number of portraits, mounted on his war-horse in full armour.[57] This is Maximilian prepared for war or a tournament, lance at the ready. Jousting had been the passion of his youth, and he excelled at all the chivalric arts; his armour still exists, which is why we know he was a powerfully built, barrel-chested man, tall for the epoch, although not quite so tall as his father. Burckmaier prepared a number of engravings on the same theme, and he also made an engraving of his studio with the artist at work on a drawing, while the Emperor peered over his shoulder, no doubt advising on the fine points to be depicted. Maximilian left nothing to chance when it came to the presentation of his image to future generations.

However, the young Maximilian was never painted from life[58] by an artist of the stature of Titian, who was to be the court painter for both his grandson Charles and his great-grandson, Philip II of Spain. Ironically, more than a century after his death he was painted by an artist who presented Maximilian as he had seen himself. Peter Paul Rubens's portrait is a work of imagination, drawn from earlier studies, rather like Striegel's family portrait. But Rubens has caught the essential quality of Maximilian the soldier. We could link it to a specific event. At the first battle of Guinegate in 1479,[59] the army of France had overrun his cavalry and all that remained were his infantry, German *Landesknechts*, with their long pikes, a steel helmet on their heads and a breastplate. Maximilian, looking very like Rubens's image of him, had climbed down from his horse to stand in the front ranks, joking with them in a rough dialect, and made them straighten the lines of their phalanx, steeling them to face the oncoming enemy. In a moment he had steadied them to receive the full weight of the French charge. They withstood the first shock and he called them to move forward, leading the way himself. Catching the enemy off balance, the *Landesknechts* plunged their pikes into their midst, then with their short swords and knives, came to close quarters. Some using halberds in the Swiss manner knocked the French horsemen to the ground. Maximilian, despite the weight of his armour, was always at the front of the advance. What had seemed a certain defeat earlier in the day ended in victory, and he had preserved his wife's inheritance.

Rubens's Maximilian is a fighting man, for we can see his face framed by the open front of his sallet (helmet) but he is also something more. On the breastplate is the blazing sun, emblem of empire. This is Maximilian the Christian knight, as he portrayed himself in the great cycle of publications which marked a unique contribution to building the image and fortune of the house of Habsburg. No ruler has ever possessed so sure a sense of propaganda, and created so much of it for himself. Louis XIV of France was deeply conscious of the image that should be presented of his luminous monarchy; but he left the execution and direction to others. Maximilian both defined the programme and, as the engraving by Burckmaier wryly observes, intervened constantly in its production and presentation. In 1450, Johannes Gutenberg of Mainz had perfected a machine, modelled on a wine press, that allowed the production of multiple copies of texts made from movable type, that is, letters that could be arranged and rearranged to produce new texts. This element of mass production was not entirely new: *scriptoria*, or copying workshops[60] – almost factories – of scribes had produced multiple copies of copied texts in earlier periods. It had also been possible to produce single images from a primitive form of woodcut earlier in the fifteenth century. Gutenberg's invention, which spread rapidly through Germany and Italy, quickly allowed the mass production of written texts, and within a few years the production of texts that contained both words and images.

How early Maximilian became aware of this new technology is hard to say.[61] By 1500, he was correcting the proof pages of Grünpeck's *Life*; by 1510 he was preparing his first volume of autobiography and by 1512 he had a programme of a dozen publications planned or in progress.[62] His motive was outlined straightforwardly in *Weisskunig* (The Lord's Anointed):

When a man dies his works do not follow him, and whosoever does not build himself a memorial in his lifetime has no memorial after his death and is forgotten with the bells [that toll at his funeral]. And therefore the money that I spend in this way building my memorial is not lost.[63]

In classic Habsburg fashion this plethora of activity reflected a lack of progress or success in the 'real' world of politics and affairs. The early years of the sixteenth century were full of frustration for Maximilian. He desired above all else to be crowned Emperor in Rome as his father had been; yet continual political setbacks and rivalries in Italy made it impossible. When he declared himself Elected Emperor in 1508 this was a poor substitute, and in practical terms, it still left him open to challenge, especially from the ambitious kings of France, first Charles VIII, then Louis XII and Francis I. Perhaps age and increasing ill health also had a part to play. Yet his programme of public presentation went far beyond the temporary exigencies of politics or saturnine gloom.[64] Maximilian aimed to establish the Habsburg claim to world power in the public domain, not just in the courts and chanceries of Europe.

Maximilian's historical consciousness and understanding of his station in life is reflected in all of his writing. It therefore comes as no surprise that he sought to incorporate into his genealogy figures of classical and pagan antiquity. The need to organize his public image and to lend authority to his most cherished and ambitious strategies made such use imperative. It was valid because he could count on the broad acceptance of these assumptions by his subjects, whether learned or ignorant, noble or non noble. His passion to combine the word with the image to bring together imagination and representation in his works testifies to his desire to reach an intimate understanding of the past and to represent his person and his time as in tune with the past, thus establishing at the same time a rapport between himself and the future.[65]

Maximilian saw himself as the epitome of the Habsburg mission and by harnessing the power of knowledge and research to achieve his own immortality, he secured the future position of his lineage. Consistent themes run through all his major works, those published and the others merely projected. In an age fascinated by the stars, he constructed what can only be considered a new cosmography. At the heart of the universe was the Holy Trinity of Father, Son and Holy Ghost. But next to them, both servant and intermediary with sinful mankind, was Maximilian, king and priest, and the house of Austria, chosen by God to carry the divine presence into the world.[66] Maximilian and his team of humanist researchers discovered that more than a hundred saints featured in his ancestry. More than that, they discovered that 'among his ancestors were Jewish kings, Trojan princes and Roman emperors, the saintly Charlemagne, to say nothing of Roman and Greek divinities and the bizarre godheads of Ancient Egypt'.[67] Maximilian created a network of scholars, artists, engravers and printers, some of whom were engaged for almost two decades on his great project.[68]

The life and career of Maximilian, rather like the life of Christ, provided the necessary lessons for human salvation. The first element was the life of Maximilian considered as allegory. He planned to recount his autobiography in three volumes. Only the first, *Theuerdank*, was published in his lifetime; the second, *Weisskunig*, languished in manuscript until it was published in the eighteenth century, and the third, entitled *Freydal*, remained unpublished until the 1880s. All were by him, dictated or written by himself; for the most part he would edit and correct the scripts taken down orally by his secretaries. Some episodes would be written or revised in his own hand; but the structure and ordering of the books seem to have been settled between Maximilian and his secretaries, Markus Treitzsauerwein and Melchior Pfinzing, who cut and edited the work. But Maximilian supervised the images and engravings used to illustrate the books, commissioning and briefing the artists and viewing their rough drafts.[69]

Theuerdank is the story of Maximilian's wooing and courtship of Mary of Burgundy, and his journey to win his bride. It is written in verse, each of the 118 verses accompanied by an engraving portraying a different episode in his journey. The allegory is so complicated and so dense that Melchior Pfinzing included a key to the action and the characters when the book (which was completed about 1506) was first published in 1517. Maximilian becomes Prince Theuerdank (Precious thanks), who has to conquer three enemies on his journey to claim his bride, Ehrenreich (Rich-in-honour). The wanderings of Theuerdank, very like those of the Grail knights in the Arthurian cycle, culminate in a great tournament, in which the prince triumphs. Afterwards, his enemies Fürwittig (Too-clever-by-half), Unfalo (Clumsy and accident-prone) and Neidelhart (Jealousy and envy) are killed – one beheaded, another hanged, and the last thrown from the walls of Ehrenreich's castle. These were the human flaws in Theuerdank/Maximilian's own character that he has so triumphantly overcome, so that he can now go on crusade and restore a shattered Christendom. But the message of *Theuerdank*, enveloped in a complex literary and allusive form, is anything but clear, and his political message is obscure. His next volume, *Weisskunig*, is much more straightforwardly didactic. Here the miraculous conception, birth and early life of the White (and Wise) King,[70] the Lord's Anointed, followed by his struggles and eventual triumph provide a model for a troubled world seeking guidance.

From the moment of conception the hero is marked for a greatness that would transcend all measure, and which could only be compared . . . to the knights and martyrs of the past. Maximilian's ardent wish [was] that . . . all people should understand that his just claims to greatness prompted him to illuminate the meaning of *Weisskunig* with many accompanying woodcuts so that the common man might understand the message without fail.[71]

Maximilian increasingly came to rate the power of the image more highly than the power of words. In a world where literacy was limited, and Germany lacked a common language or dialect across all regions and classes,[72] this was a prudent strategy. But it also posed problems. It was a lack of appropriate woodcuts[73] that delayed the production of *Weisskunig*. And these problems were compounded with vast works that were composed almost entirely of images. If *Theuerdank* was obscure, the *form* of the two great visual works was familiar to all. The first, the Triumphal Arch, was reminiscent of the temporary arches (often made of wood and canvas) erected for the festivals that were such a prominent part of public life. Often these processions and arches, like those for Frederick's entry into Sienna and Rome, or the sumptuous *joyeuses entrées* popular in Maximilian's Burgundian duchy, were crudely reproduced in pamphlet form. Maximilian took this common idiom and made it into a narrative of his life and achievements. The Triumphal Arch had deeper and more literary roots. It echoed the stone arches erected by Roman emperors, some still to be seen in the Eternal City. The historian Johannes Stabius, who masterminded the whole complex operation, involving draughtsmen, artists, printers, and a host of scholars, said that it was 'The same shape as, of yore, the Arcus Triumphales erected to the Roman Emperors in the City of Rome'. It consisted of three open arches or portals – the Portal of Fame, the Portal of Honour and Power, and the Portal of Nobility, all topics that were, in Stabius's courtly phrase, 'often traversed by His Majesty's Imperial mind'. But it is an archway only in a notional sense: it is merely the conceptual framework for a series of tableaux and scenes, some from the life of Maximilian, others genealogical or mystical icons. In its purpose and effect it was analogous to the chapel of St George in Wiener Neustadt, where the statue of Frederick III stands surrounded by the hatchments of his (and Maximilian's) lineage.

This was a 'paper building' never to be built. The 'architecture' is a conceit only providing a structure and order for the enactment of the Habsburg myth. Some 200 copies of this Arch were published before Maximilian's death and 500 afterwards at the order of his grandson Ferdinand; the woodblocks – or many of them – still survive. To this day, it is the largest engraving ever made – covering more than ten square metres, made up of over 190 single sheets, glued together, and standing more than three metres high. Standing in front of it, it is impossible even for the sharpest eyes to read or perceive the fine detail in the topmost towers: why then was it produced in this form? The ancient historian Paul Veyne considered a similar problem, posed by Trajan's column in Rome, where the topmost panels are virtually invisible even with aid of a powerful telescope.[74] He concluded that the structure did not need to be 'read' in the conventional sense: all who saw it knew that it was meant as an exaltation of the imperial power of the Emperor Trajan, a public and permanent declaration of his conquests and triumphs. So too, with Maximilian's Arch, the fact that it existed, that its inner logic and argument had been presented to the world, was sufficient.

The complexity and convolutions of that argument almost defy description. It employs all known devices of glorification from the simple recording of historical events to cryptic emblematical allusions. On twenty-four panels above the two side portals his victories and political triumphs, including the succession of dynastic marriages, were presented. His more personal achievements – as a patron of the arts, his prowess as a huntsman and his skills as a linguist – together with his quasi-religious accomplishments – sustaining the Order of St George, discovering a holy relic at Trier – appear on the turrets; and on the pedestals of the columns are Maximilian's ancestors, real and imagined. These include the emperors from Julius Caesar to Rudolf I, and the kings of Spain and England; saints associated with the Habsburgs, like St Leopold (for whom Frederick III had secured canonization), and others annexed, like St Arnulf, the legendary founder of the Carolingians. And atop the columns are the four Habsburg Emperors, Rudolf I, Albert I, Albert II, and Frederick III.

Pride of place on the central front is given over to Maximilian's family tree, which hints at a Trojan origin, but actually begins with Clovis and the Merovingians. Flanking the main descent on each side are the lineages of Castile and Aragón and the Babenbergs, all 'colonized' by the Habsburgs. On the top of the tree sits Maximilian enthroned, worshipped by twenty-two figures of Victory, and honoured by his son Philip and his daughter Margaret. At the very top of the central portal, under a cupola, sits the iconic figure of Maximilian, surrounded by a mass of symbolic details, drawn from the 'new science' of Egyptian hieroglyphs. This and many other details require a key, which was provided by Stabius. He notes that where two archdukes appear on the pedestal of the central portal, they symbolize strict order and justice. Sirens, hanged by the neck, denote 'the ordinary adversities of the world which yet have done no damage to this noble Arch of Honour [that is, to Maximilian and his house], and God willing, will never be able to do so'. Each image echoes and praises its creator. Even the pomegranate, which was a common symbol of fertility and unity, had, we are told, 'been adopted by the Emperor in his youth because it struck him as an image of his own self: "Though the pomegranate lacks a particularly handsome skin, yet its interior is full of noble munificence and shapely seeds."' Stabius concludes that 'much could be written about the many other ornaments, but may every beholder explain and interpret them himself'.

Erwin Panofsky has summed up the intricate complexities of the Triumphal Arch in a lapidary sentence: 'It demands to be read like a book, decoded like a cryptogram and yet enjoyed like a collection of quaint and sparkling jewellery.'[75] The Arch was, equally, a form of public theatre, its columns, towers, belvederes, garrets, peopled with the ever-growing cast of *domus Austriae*. The researches of Maximilian's genealogists,[76] plus his own deep passion for the topic, had widened the range of possible ancestors and appendages. The volume of Habsburg genealogy was completed but never published, but the knowledge amassed in its writing underpinned both the Arch and the final project, the Triumphal Procession. This was to Maximilian's own design, drawn up about 1512, and much more straightforward in its concept than the elaborate intellectual fantasy of the Triumphal Arch. It involved many of the same artists and engravers – including Dürer and Burgkmair, with Altdorfer, Huber and Schäufflin all contributing a number of engravings. Work on the images was not completed until 1518, and at Maximilian's death in 1519 it was still incomplete.

As with the Arch, it was on a substantial scale. The 'procession' extended like a paper frieze to more than sixty yards; in Maximilian's plan it was to have been even longer and more elaborate. Even in its attenuated form, fantasy and whimsy play equal roles. Led by a griffin, drummers, flute players, falconers and huntsmen, a fantastical pageant unrolls. Elaborately decorated carts pulled by oxen, deer, horses and mules, even camels, carry tableaux of Maximilian's life and triumphs. A whole army of jesters, *Landesknechts*, knights, Turks, Hungarians, Bohemian flailmen march in front and behind the tableaux. Then come the knights armed for the tourney, followed by a string of riders carrying banners representing the towns or cities of Maximilian's domain, his wars and victories. Then, a change of mood and pace: a wagon bears 'the bold emperors, kings, archdukes and dukes, whose coat of arms and name Emperor Maximilian bears and whose lands he rules'. To the traditional

Habsburg ancestors have now been added: King Arthur, Charlemagne, Clovis, Godfrey of Bouillon, King of Jerusalem, Duke
Philip of Burgundy, Odobert, King of Provence. These were but a
selection of the new recruits to the house of Austria. Hans Burgkmair produced engravings for seventy-seven such ancestors, while
Leonhard Beck prepared another, larger, set for 'The Saints of the
House of Habsburg'.[77]

The procession continues with the imperial banner and sword,
and then the princes, counts and barons of the Empire. At the very
end of the procession, just before the baggage train, are what are
called 'the people of Calicut, some mounted on an elephant, others
wearing feathers and carrying bows'. The legend reads,

> The Emperor in his warlike pride
> Conquering nations far and wide
> Has brought beneath our empire's yoke
> The far off calcutish-folk
> therefore we pledge him with our oath
> Lasting obedience and troth.[78]

Here for the first time is a suggestion that the Habsburg mission
extends beyond Europe to the whole world. But the procession
lacks its centrepiece. Dürer had not completed his work on the
Triumphal Car that was to carry the Emperor and all his family
before Maximilian died, though his first sketch is dated 1512. It is
for a simple carriage, with the Emperor enthroned at the back and
his children and grandchildren on benches before him. In the
version as published in 1522, all the other members of his family
have disappeared and the Car now represents the apotheosis of
Maximilian. Every aspect of it has acquired symbolic meaning. For
example, the wheels of the car are labelled 'Dignity, glory', 'Magnificence, honour', meaning that these are the forces that have carried
the Emperor throughout his life, while the horse's bridles are
shown as 'Nobility' and 'Power,' which were the qualities of his
rule. Atop the car Maximilian now sits in solitary state, under the
image of a blazing sun, and above him a banner states: 'As the sun
is to heaven so Caesar is on earth.'[79]

The difficulty with this sacralizing vision of Maximilian is that it accords so ill with the totality of the man. He was, certainly, obsessed with lineage and genealogy, with death and survival, but these were predominantly passions of his old age. They were but the final resort of his energy and unrelenting curiosity. Maximilian was a warm-blooded creature. He loved dancing and plays, and as he wrote himself: 'I have danced and tilted lances and enjoyed carnivals. I have paid court to the ladies and earned great thanks; for the most part I have laughed heartily.'[80] The evidence of his animal passions is the long list of his bastards (from the years of his loveless marriage to Bianca Sforza), whom he provided with bishoprics or honourable marriages once they reached maturity. Passion seems to have been a hereditary trait. His son Philip, once he had seen his future wife Juana of Castile for the first time, demanded that the bishop marry them that very afternoon so that they could consummate the marriage without delay. And his sister Margaret roused (and reciprocated) enormous and devouring passions in her young husband . . .

But Maximilian was also devout, for who else but a true Christian could have discovered, as he did in 1512, 'the seamless coat of Christ', taken from Him before the Crucifixion, miraculously hidden below the altar of Trier cathedral. According to the popular legend, an angel came to him and told him to ride to Trier. There in the cathedral fifteen candles were mysteriously burning on the altar in the empty church; Maximilian ordered the altar to be moved and there beneath it he found the Holy Coat, together with the dice that those who had crucified him had used to cast lots for his raiment.[81] Like Rudolf I before him, who had protected the Holy Sacrament, Maximilian was well on the way to becoming another Habsburg 'saint', showing once again that the Habsburgs, by divine choice, were the protectors of the True Faith.

It is hard to understand the mystical power of lineage, for it only worked so long as its rules were honoured and obeyed. Once the bonds of credence were broken, then it had no force or value. In his last years, Maximilian's mind focused on death, and he wanted to build for himself a more tangible memorial. Innsbruck had for more than twenty years been his favourite city, which he had made his personal residence. There he could hunt in the mountains and be at ease when he rested from his travels. He decided that he would lie in the cathedral at Innsbruck, where he began to build a tomb, commissioning statues and effigies, marble and bronze panels, from the finest sculptors north of the Alps. In form and meaning it would echo the Triumphal Arch and the Triumphal Procession: a double line of kings would stand guard over him, while he would lie in a vast stone vault, surrounded by the images of his victories and triumphs. In 1518, the tomb was still not complete in all its details (no scheme of Maximilian's ever was) but it was ready and waiting for its occupant.

In November Maximilian rode south to Innsbruck, half expecting it might be his last journey. When he arrived there the innkeepers of the town refused to accommodate his entourage until they were paid for earlier visits, while the town council refused to receive him officially. Roused to fury, perhaps to the point of a seizure, Maximilian departed in his litter, heading north to the Danube where he would take ship for Vienna. But at Wels on the Danube he realized that he was dying. His last weeks were spent with his favourite dogs by his bed and the caged birds that accompanied him everywhere, singing through the daylight hours. Above all he enjoyed listening to Joseph Mennel read to him from his history of *The Noble Deeds of the Habsburgs*. Finally he died quietly, on 12 January 1519. In Innsbruck his great tomb remains empty, for he instructed that he should be buried under the altar steps of the church of St George at Wiener Neustadt, the town where he had grown up, fought in his first tournament, and been made a knight of the order of St George. Where he was buried, he said, he would feel the priest stand on his chest when he raised the host during the mass. But his chest was an empty cavity, for his last command had been that his heart be embalmed, carried to Bruges, and reunited with the body of his first wife, Mary of Burgundy. Was he not Theuerdank, 'the last knight', who had finally come to the end of his long quest?

4

El Dorado (The Golden One)
1500–1550

In September 1548, Titian completed his equestrian portrait of the Emperor Charles V, to commemorate the great triumph at the battle of Mühlberg. It was traditional to present such studies of a Great Captain against a background of struggling armies, as Rubens later depicted Charles's great-grandson, the Cardinal Infante, at the battle of Nördlingen. But here, apart from the Emperor in half-armour, gilded and chased overall, the scene is one of peace. Charles, mounted on his charger, is riding in a tranquil parkland; even the sky, though shot with cloud, has the calm of twilight. War seems far away. The picture radiates a quiet confidence of coming victory. The Emperor, more saint than warrior, looks forward, his eyes unfocused deep in reverie; only his horse, pawing the ground, seems eager for action. What dominates the picture is the long slender spear that Charles carries in his right hand, running from left to right diagonally across the whole width of the scene. Titian painted his patron as the quintessence of chivalry and that spear is the key to its meaning. He has made Charles the eponymic Knight of the Golden Fleece, for around his neck are two silken cords, dyed deep vermilion, and from it, almost lost amid the elaborate gilding and chasing of his breastplate, a miniature ram's head and fleece, the insignia of the Order.

He saturated his painting with classical and religious allusions. In his right hand the Emperor carries not the baton of a general or the lance of a nobleman, but that long spear. This is no ordinary weapon, like the stubby hunting-spear or partisan which he actually carried on the battlefield, but an evocation of the Holy Lance that pierced the side of Christ at the Crucifixion. The Christian knight in Dürer's engraving carries just such a long lance over his shoulder and Titian echoes Dürer, displaying Charles as *miles christianus*. Here is a reborn Emperor Constantine,[1] or a new St George, who has gained a great victory over the forces of darkness and the dragon of heresy. In this case the unseen enemies are the Protestant princes of Germany. The dominant colour in a muted range of browns, blacks and golds is the deep crimson associated with majesty, from the harness and the cinnabar plume on the horse's head, to the gold-fringed general's sash tied over his left shoulder.[2] This was Charles the Majestic, Universal Emperor,[3] Crusader, but also a Prince of Peace. Titian's work delighted Charles, for it wordlessly embodied his own self-image. Twenty years before, his Chancellor Mercurino Gattinara had laid out the world at his feet: 'Sire, God has been very merciful to you: he has raised you above all the kings and princes of Christendom to a power such as no sovereign has enjoyed since your ancestor Charles the Great. He has set you on the way towards a world monarchy, towards the uniting of all Christendom under a single shepherd.'[4]

Many nations of his Empire regarded him as their own. But, by blood, Germany had the smallest claim upon him. His grandfather, Maximilian, had a Portuguese mother, his father Philip was the son of Mary, heiress to the riches of Burgundy. Charles was born at the Prinsenhof in Ghent, in his duchy of Burgundy; he was brought up with his sisters, Eleanor, Isabella and Mary, by his aunt Archduchess Margaret of Austria at Malines not far away from his birthplace. His first languages were French and Flemish and in a long life he visited the German lands only nine times. Spain had more claim upon him, both by descent and inclination. There he married his cousin Isabella of Portugal and his children were brought up as Spaniards; he was King of Spain before he was Holy Roman Emperor, and he died and was buried in his Spanish lands. After his twentieth year, he habitually spoke and wrote in Spanish.[5] Yet despite this, following Karl Brandi, we should think of him as neither German nor

Spaniard, but in his essence, as a Duke of Burgundy, whose emblem was the Golden Fleece that he carried around his neck.

Subsequent generations of Habsburg rulers were rarely portrayed without either this small golden ram (or lamb) or the massive golden collar of the order set upon their shoulders.[6] Within a generation it had become a badge or emblem of the house of Habsburg. This elision – between the Habsburgs and the Golden Fleece – is usually passed over as an inevitable development, but it was much more than some natural or ineluctable process. There were other orders of chivalry more truly 'Habsburg', like the Order of St George established by Frederick III, and honoured by Maximilian.[7] Nor was the Golden Fleece very much more ancient or, of itself, especially distinguished. The English Order of the Garter had the longest pedigree, except for the military crusading brotherhoods – The Hospitallers, the Order of St John, the German Order and the like. But the identification between Charles and the Golden Fleece was fundamental. He was still an infant when elected a knight, although this was strictly against the regulations of the order. When he grew old enough to read and understand, the history and aspirations of the order assumed an extraordinary importance for him. In his autobiography, Charles mentioned holding the meetings (the chapters) of the order in the same terms as he did the greatest matters of state. More than that, he showered honours and privileges on his fellow knights. He stifled his overweening sense of pride and accepted all the humble duties that knighthood laid upon him. When the order met, it was the duty of all the members to criticize and admonish their brothers, including the sovereign of the order, the Emperor himself. Twice Charles willingly endured this most searching assessment of his government from his fellow knights. Nor would he be swayed from his decision that only the order had the right to discipline its own members. This exaggerated, mystical reverence was peculiar to Charles and was not shared by his successors.

The Golden Fleece was Charles's birthright. It was founded in the Sainte Chapelle of the cathedral of Dijon[8] on 10 January 1430, in celebration of the marriage of Philip the Good, Duke of Burgundy, his great-great-grandfather, and Isabella of Portugal.

It was instituted, 'out of the Duke's love for chivalry and to protect
and propagate the Christian Faith', or as a contemporary poet
wrote:

> Not for amusement, nor for recreation
> But that above all God shall be praised
> And the good shall gain glory and high renown

Each of the knights wore a heavy scarlet mantle, lined with
sable, and embroidered with gold thread; and on their shoulders
they bore the heavy golden collar and the ram, emblem of their
confraternity. When they met in Chapter they sat in silence under
their banners and hatchments, listening to the chancellor of the
order praise or blame them for their conduct. They were enjoined
to be dignified, sober and always zealous for the honour of God
and their order. Reading the descriptions of their lavish banquets
and elaborate rituals, it is often hard to give credence to these high
motives. In 1454, with the loss of Constantinople fresh in the mind,
the duke wished to dedicate himself and his nobility to a crusade to
recover Christian honour in the east. Knights of the Golden Fleece
vied with each other to hold the most splendid feast to promote the
cause. At one celebration the Lord of Revestein appeared dressed in
white from head to foot, as Lohengrin, the Swan Knight, the
embodiment of chivalry. At successive banquets, the hosts competed
in a form of sumptuous potlatch. Rooms were decorated with
costly velvets, silks and brocades, hung with gold and silver bells,
which sounded when stirred; the guests, male and female, were
arrayed in fanciful costumes, under exotic furs and feather capes,
oversewn with pearls and precious stones.

The cooks redoubled their artifice as they sought to outdo the
previous triumph of the culinary arts. At Philip's own banquet, the
centrepiece was an edible tableau 'wonderfully wrought' of Jason
and the Golden Fleece. The walls of the great chamber were hung
with Flemish tapestries depicting the labours of Hercules, a suitable
backdrop for the ordeals by gastronomy his guests were to undergo.
Down the line of the room the long tables were covered with silken
damasks. A sense of heady ostentation prevailed: the plates before
each guest were of silver and gold, and to the duke's right a large
bronze statue of a naked woman was guarded by a rampant lion; at

the end of the tables, an ingenious cascade of water gushed from a jewelled grotto. Even the service of the food had taxed the ingenuity of the cooks and the chamberlains. Most of the courses were ceremonially borne in, to fanfares; others – the great dishes bearing the culinary *pièces de résistance* – were winched down from the darkness of the ceiling. Each dish became the opportunity for some new artifice: a fire-breathing dragon pursued by a heron, families of animals in lifelike poses, birds in flight. Finally, from the back of an elephant,[10] the assembled knights were exhorted: 'Dear son, draw thy sword / For the glory of God and thine own honour.' Then a live pheasant was brought into the hall, and carried before each man there, who placed his hand upon its plumage, and took the crusader's oath, by 'God, the Virgin Mary, his lady and the Pheasant'. The duke, as sovereign of the order of the Golden Fleece, additionally promised to challenge the Ottoman Sultan to settle the great issue of Jerusalem in a truly chivalric manner. The solemn matter ended, a comely young maiden came in, depicting 'God's Mercy', accompanied by 'Twelve Virtues', who curtseyed to the knights and exhorted them to keep the oath they had just sworn on the Pheasant. A short and pregnant pause ensued, then the musicians struck up again, and 'God's Mercy' and the 'Twelve Virtues' enthusiastically joined in the dancing to which the new crusaders now dedicated their remaining energies.[11]

But despite these saturnalia, the order was a serious attempt to reinvigorate the tarnished traditions of chivalry and knightly conduct. The regulations forbade a knight of the Golden Fleece to leave the battlefield once the banners had been flourished, that is, once it was indicated that it was to be a fight to the finish. In the battle of Anthon shortly after the order was established, two of its members did flee the mêlée. Both were held to have brought disgrace upon their fellows and expelled from the order; one of the pair, overcome by the dishonour, left immediately on a pilgrimage from which he did not return alive. Knights were required to wear the emblem of the golden lamb at all times and, in battle, to display the heavy gold collar on top of their armour. Any adversary should know that he faced a knight of the Golden Fleece. The sovereign of the order was responsible for replacing any collars that were lost in battle. Maximilian, to his great financial embarrassment, had to pay for four gold collars that vanished during the hand-to-hand fighting in the battle of Guinegate.

∽   ∽   ∽

The Golden Fleece was created at a time when, as Jan Huizinga has pointed out, there was not a prince or great noble who did not desire to have his own order. Orléans, Bourbon, Savoie, Hainaut–Bavière, Lusignan, Coucy, all eagerly exerted themselves in inventing bizarre emblems and extraordinary heraldic devices. The chain of Pierre de Lusignan's 'Order of the Sword' was made of gold 'SS' which denoted 'silence'. Louis of Orléans's 'Order of the Porcupine' threatened to impale its Burgundian rival on its quills. The wealth and power of Burgundy enabled Philip the Good to create an order of chivalry more splendid and flamboyant than any of the others. But behind its creation were deeper motives hard to disencumber from the surface glister of the feasting and ceremony. The idea of the crusade had bitten deep in Burgundy. It was his grandfather Philip *le Hardi* who first responded to the idea for a new fraternity of knights sworn to the crusade, to carry on the tradition of Burgundian chivalry. (The duke's son, the Count of Nevers, had been the ill-fated commander against the Turks at Nicopolis, and many Burgundian knights had died in that battle's fearsome aftermath.) 'The Soldiers of the Passion of Christ',[12] to be drawn from all the Christian nations, would be dedicated to uniting the whole of Christendom in repelling the Turks. Philip died before he could achieve this great goal and it was bequeathed to his grandson who, on 27 November 1431, summoned twenty-four knights to assemble in Lille for the first chapter of the Golden Fleece.

With the establishment of the Golden Fleece, Philip as the sovereign Grand Master of an order of chivalry now ranked with the kings of Europe. This did something to redress the sense of grievance that had become almost a hereditary attribute of the Burgundian line. In their eyes, Burgundy deserved a position greater than that of a mere dukedom. Earlier in history, a great Burgundian kingdom had ruled the land from the Mediterranean to the Alps. Later it became Lotharingia, the Middle Empire of the Carolingians. Not until the eleventh century was this Kingdom of Burgundy – or Arles – subsumed into the Holy Roman Empire, and its status lost.

The later dukes of Burgundy inherited all the traditions of that southern kingdom, which had once overshadowed Paris and the Île de France, and they aspired to restore it. None the less, for all their longings and posturing, Burgundy remained a mere dukedom, its rulers the vassals of both the French king and of the Holy Roman Emperor. In creating the Order of the Golden Fleece Philip the Good not only fulfilled the ambitions of his father and grandfather, and advanced the position of his house, but he also laid claim to a status greater than that of the kings of France and even of the Emperor himself.

It had at first been intended that the order should bear the name of Christ himself, but Philip called his brotherhood after the archetype of all the warrior bands, the brotherhood of the Golden Fleece, the legendary Argonauts led by Jason, who sailed to the ends of the earth to recover the legendary Golden Fleece from Colchis. The classic heroism and inspired daring of the Argonauts made a deep impression on Philip. Tapestries depicting their exploits covered the walls of his chamber in his favourite castle at Hesdin, and in his library he had amassed manuscripts that described the Trojan wars and the voyage of Jason. He ordered his chaplain to write for him a new history of the voyage and its deeper meanings. For in Philip's eyes, the voyage of the Argonauts was plainly a crusade. Was not Christ himself the Lamb of God, who takes away the sins of the world? Were not the Argonauts rescuing the Lamb of God, Christ, just as the crusaders, new Argonauts, would recover the holy city of Jerusalem? The two sets of images, Argonaut and Crusader, Jason and Philip, elided.

There was a further reason to make this identification, for Philip the Good could trace his roots, through Charlemagne back via Rome, to Troy and beyond. The legends said that Jason had burned Troy on his voyage to the east, thereby beginning the long chain of events that led to the voyage of Aeneas to found the new Troy, Rome, and thence down through the many generations to Philip himself. Trojan blood ran, he believed, in his veins. All these symbolic connections were not the product of chance or coincidence, but evidence of a divine logic gradually revealed. Huizinga has described this mental framework, a world that unfolds itself like a vast whole of symbols, like a cathedral of ideas. It is the most richly rhythmical conception of the world, a polyphonous expression of eternal harmony ... In the Middle Ages the symbolist attitude was much more in evidence than the causal or the genetic attitude ... From the causal point of view, symbolism appears as a sort of short cut of thought. Instead of looking for the relation between two things by following the hidden detours of their causal connexions, thought makes a leap and discovers their relation not in the connexion of cause and effects, but in a connexion of signification.[13]

The creation of the Order of the Golden Fleece was, for Philip, the fulfilment of both his personal and his familial destiny. On his tomb in the cathedral at Dijon, two lines were carved:

POUR MAINTENIR L'EGLISE QUI EST DE DIEU MAISON
J'AI MIS SUS LE NOBLE ORDRE QU'ON NOMME LA TOISON

(To sustain the holy church which is God's House,
I made the noble order called the Golden Fleece)

As only the true king could pull the sword from the stone in the legends of King Arthur, so too only a true descendant of the Argonauts could have created the noble order. The truth was self-evident, buttressed by the massing and concatenation of symbolic evidence.

Symbolist thought permits an infinity of relations between *things*. Each thing may denote a number of distinct ideas by its different special qualities, and a quality may have several symbolic meanings. The highest conceptions have symbols by the thousand. Nothing is too humble to represent and glory the sublime. The walnut signifies Christ: the sweet kernel is His divine nature, the green and pulpy outer peel is His humanity, the wooden shell between is the cross. Thus all things raise his thoughts to the eternal ... Every precious stone, besides its natural splendour sparkles with the brilliance of its symbolic values. The assimilation of roses and virginity is much more than a poetic comparison, for it reveals their common essence. As each notion arises in the mind the logic of symbolism creates an harmony of ideas.

Huizinga[14] shows how the medieval mind accepted a *symbolic assimilation* of ideas.

The emblem of the Golden Fleece was also a symbolic assimilation. The golden ram stood for the simple ideals of chivalry and presented them as an answer to the manifold exigencies of a chaotic world. The knights, like the Round Table of the Arthurian legend,[15] would reverse the spirit of discord, would begin to restore order to a world where the forces of the Antichrist were about to conquer. (Images of the Antichrist were now often depicted with the features of the Turk, seen as coarse and cruel.) These heroes, the new Argonauts, were to be the most selfless, loyal and dedicated men in Christendom and this new unifying power would emerge from the dukedom of Burgundy, always foremost in chivalry. Eventually the harmony of the order would bring peace to a troubled world.

It is impossible to know how seriously these claims were made or how many believed in the magic realism of such grand solutions to the travails of the world. Later generations, reading history backwards, dismissed the late medieval world as an era of extreme credulity, and used the idea of the 'Renaissance'[16] – a rebirth – to divide off the dying old world, looking backward, from the new, which looked forward toward the vision of human progress.[17] Others have been less convinced of the divide, and have warned that 'the inertia of mediaeval society was very strong. Religion was not overturned or undermined . . . Nor was the aristocratic structure of society submerged . . . As the old certainties slowly dissolved or grew more limited in application, curiosity took their place; of course, previous centuries had contained men of ample curiosity, but society had not encouraged its practice or inflamed its appetite.'[18] As the chronological boundaries of the Renaissance have been extended both backwards and forwards, and its geographical limits shifted from its Italian heartland to embrace the whole of Europe and then the known world, the confident delineation of a dividing line, between the old and the new, has faded. Magic, astrology and alchemy, all thoroughly medieval in their origin and mental structures,[19] flourished as never before, and were presented to a wider audience by the new technology of the printing press.[20] New techniques in art allowed more complex presentation of what was often a traditional message. In all the areas of propaganda and communication the Habsburgs were confident pioneers.

In 1515 Charles, who had been crowned as Duke in his eighth year, was finally declared of age. He stood before the assembled notables of the Burgundian lands in the Great Hall of his ducal palace in Brussels, and declared: 'Be good and loyal subjects and I shall be a good prince to you.' (It was in that same hall, forty years on, that, walking with difficulty and resting on the shoulder of his page, the young Prince of Orange, he took his leave of them.) In the following year he was elected as sovereign Grand Master of the Golden Fleece. At that ceremony, the young Charles was asked to declare his personal badge and emblem. He handed the chancellor of the Order an unusual device: two classical columns emerging from the sea with the phrase 'Plus Ultra' (still further). Many explanations have been given of the meaning for both the image and the slogan, which appeared in a number of different forms. In some the Habsburg eagle enfolds the columns with his wings, while the imperial crown surmounts them. In another the two columns actually intertwine like the caduceus, the wand of two serpents carried by the God Mercury. In a third Charles carries the two columns on his shoulders, with an inscription that likens him to Hercules.[21]

Implicit in all these images was the claim that Charles embodied the classical world, but then went beyond it; he was a ruler of the old world, but equally and uniquely of a new world beyond the oceans. All the images alluded to the newly discovered world beyond the seas, of which as King of Spain he was suzerain; they suggested that Charles had broken the boundaries of the medieval injunction *ne plus ultra* (no further), by passing the Pillars of Hercules. He scattered these images on coins, medals, on buildings and in written texts and documents, with an enthusiasm and profligacy that echoed his great-grandfather's use of the cryptic AEIOU monogram. But above all Plus Ultra proclaimed that nothing was beyond the capacity[22] of the Grand Master of the Golden Fleece, who was shortly to become the new Universal Emperor.

Historians[23] have pointed repeatedly to Charles's failures. A recent critic skewered him neatly:

By 1550 [after his victory at Mühlberg] he had reached the pinnacle of power . . . he spoke and behaved as if there was nothing he could not achieve if he set his mind to it. Perhaps he had come to believe his own propaganda. Immensely arrogant and grasping, Charles nevertheless appeared to epitomize chivalric notions of the warrior king to at least some of his contemporaries. They were often awed by his power, though seldom by his presence. He was capable of exuding *bonhomie* and his vices often put him on a level most common men could relate to. His gluttony was proverbial, his dislike of paperwork and preference for action both in the field and in the bedroom gave him a very human touch in younger days. But in the 1550s the darker side of his character predominated . . . Stubborn, unwilling to yield to advice that did not accord with his own preconceptions and desires, he still showed physical courage and determination not to let go of power, even if this led to greater destruction.[24]

He fell far short of his own ambitions, and expectations.[25]

At his birth his stars, by which contemporaries set so much store, with the sign Capricorn in the ascendant, presaged future greatness: 'Whoever has the ascendant in the first degree of Capricorn will be a king or emperor.'[26] It had been the sign of the Emperor Augustus, and some began to hail the new-born Charles as 'the New Augustus'. At his christening on 8 April 1500, his gifts suggested his future status. His father Philip made his infant son ruler of the duchy of Luxemburg, while his governor and chief tutor, William of Chièvres, had given him a suit of silver armour inlaid with gold with, on the breastplate, a large image of a phoenix.[27] When older, his attention wandered when his tutor, Adrian of Utrecht (later Pope Hadrian I), tried to lead him through the New and Old Testaments; his interest only revived when they came to the 'heroic' books full of war and victories (Judges, Kings and Maccabees); he kept a French translation of Thucydides' great *History of the Peloponnesian War* at his bedside, and carried it with him throughout his life. Deeds of chivalry filled his waking hours. He heard the stories of his grandfather's deeds in battle at Guinegate, and at the end of his life, in retirement in Spain, he turned his hand to translating Oliver de la Marche's *Le Chevalier Délibéré* (The dedicated knight), an allegorical poem in honour of the heroic deeds of the house of Burgundy, from French into Spanish. (It had been de la Marche who had ridden the elephant at the Feast of the Pheasant and called the knights of the Golden Fleece to arms.) If his aunt and guardian Margaret of Austria's palace at Malines was sober by comparison with Charles the Bold's castle at Hesdin, it was still pregnant with the Burgundian vision of honour and chivalry,[28] which he found in the many illustrated books and manuscripts, fine pictures and tapestries that she had accumulated.

Charles's delight was to escape from his enforced studies and to ride, hunt or practise knightly skills with his small group of chosen companions, all of which was pleasing to Maximilian, who saw his own nature echoed in his grandson. It was at his grandfather's insistence that he laboured dutifully at his languages under Adrian of Utrecht. French was his mother tongue, but in his ninth year Chièvres wrote to Maximilian that, 'in obedience to your Majesty's wishes, I shall take care that he shall learn the Brabantian [Flemish] language as soon as his tongue is sufficiently pliant for it, and he shall learn how to read it'. If he learned Spanish, it was with no great dedication,[29] for at the first meeting of the Castilian Cortes which he attended in 1518, one of the specific requests the Cortes made was that he should learn to speak Spanish, as befitted a King of Spain.[30] In later years, although he would speak in Spanish to his brother Ferdinand, born and brought up in Spain, when they wrote to each other, Ferdinand would write in Spanish and Charles would reply in French.

It was deeds of honour and chivalry to which Charles aspired. Since the death of his father in 1506, Charles, although still a minor, had been titular King of Castile; but his grandfather Ferdinand of Aragón had manipulated the regency to ensure that he would not come of age in Spain until he was twenty-five. But by the autumn of 1515, the health of Ferdinand of Aragón was visibly declining. Since his second marriage to the eighteen-year-old niece of Louis XII of France, Germaine de Foix, he had had one stillborn son, and many crudely suggested that Ferdinand had been drained by the effort to sire a male heir to Aragón, even if Castile was lost to the descendants of his daughter and Philip the Fair. He had dropsy, that made his legs and arms swell agonizingly, and found difficulty in breathing. But he still had the energy to hunt, and it was after a stag hunt near Palencia that it became clear that he was close to death. But even then he sought to avoid what was evident to all around him. At first he refused the attentions of his confessor, but as his condition steadily worsened, he accepted the inevitable and made his peace with God. In the evening of 22 January he signed his last will and testament and he died early the following morning. The following day what was now a cortège proceeded south, towards Granada, where he had asked that he be buried beside Isabella in the monastery of San Francisco in the Alhambra. It had been her wish that all subsequent kings of Spain should be buried in Granada, as a thank-offering to God for the great gift of the reconquest of Spain from the Moors.

Almost two months later, on 13 March 1516, Charles, now undoubted King of Spain, wrapped in a black mourning cloak, set out in procession with his fellow knights of the Golden Fleece from the ducal palace in Brussels to the cathedral of St Gudule to celebrate a requiem for a dead knight. Two thousand burghers lined the streets holding oil-soaked *flambeaux*, their shafts wrapped in black cloth, while in the cathedral, the interior was bright from innumerable candles and tapers. The elaborate tapestry wall-hangings and the rich cloth-of-gold frontals, the gilded side altars and the great high altar itself, all shimmered in the flickering light. The knights took their place under their banners, Charles closest to the pulpit. The chaplain of the order preached a sermon on the theme that 'This is a dance of death which all must tread, even kings and princes. This is the irrevocable law of life. Sceptres and crowns must fall. Let us not forget how swiftly joy and feasting may run to mourning and lamentation.' Then the heralds of the order twice issued the summons into the echoing silence of the church: 'Don Ferdinand!' Three times the answer came back, 'He is dead.' Then his banner was lowered to the ground, and the herald rose again calling loudly, 'Long live their catholic Majesties Queen Juana and King Charles!' Then Charles came forward, letting slip his mourning cloak and stood alone before the high altar. The Bishop of Badajoz took a short jewelled sword or dagger from the altar, where it had been blessed, and gave it to the new king. He raised it on high pointing to the four corners of the cathedral, signifying the world, and a great shout rang out from all parts, 'Vivat, Vivat, rex!'

How was the new king to govern his dominions – which extended from the south of Italy to the New World? Within two years he would also be Emperor Elect, and then his responsibilities would extend east to the perpetually threatening boundary with the world of Islam. The theory of universal monarchy provided nothing to cope with the problems of time and distance. Fernand Braudel calculated that on average it would take a week or two to cross the Mediterranean from north to south, and two or three months from east to west, barring natural and human hazards such as storms and pirates.[31] Communicating with the New World could take many months, the reality behind the conquistadors' ironic saying, 'If death came from Spain we should all be immortal.'[32] Nor were time and distance the only problems, for throughout Europe a profusion of petty jurisdictions defended their privileges and authority with a vigour largely lacking in their administration. Everything conspired to make the wheels of government turn slowly. Charles's apologists blame his failure on the scale of the problems he faced.

It was inevitable that the interests of the Universal Monarch and the King of France should conflict, for Charles had inherited his Burgundian grandfather's determination to restore the boundaries of his state to their traditional limits. That extension could only be carved from the lands of France. In the north, France aspired to advance her domains into the Netherlands, reinforcing an ancient rivalry. In Italy, the quarrel had many more dimensions, and many more participants, involving the territorial interests of the papacy and those of the Italian city-states, large and small. In Germany, the Universal Monarch was also the Archduke of Austria, and the other princes rightly saw that Habsburg interests would be advanced under the banner of Christendom. All those forces of opposition lay latent, like weeds in the soil. Charles was determined to disturb the *status quo* and resistance grew on every side. It did not require the vast additional threats – the growth of Protestantism and the advance of the Ottomans – to doom his efforts to failure. Seeking more, Plus Ultra, he achieved less.

In his own mind, the militant Protestants and the ravaging Ottomans had much in common. Both were malign forces, one destroying Christendom from within and the other assailing it from outside. With many of the issues – clerical abuses and the failings of the Church – Charles was himself a protester. Brought up in the reformist traditions of the Netherlands, with tutors who were friends or disciples of Erasmus, he sincerely believed in a reformed and purified Catholic Church. In his *Paraphrases of the Gospel of St Matthew*, which the Universal Savant, Erasmus of Rotterdam dedicated to Charles, the duties of the universal Emperor which he propounded were close to those which Charles (although never an Erasmian) had formulated for himself. The proper route to change was well mapped out in his mind: a general council of the church should be called, by the Pope or by the Emperor, and these conflicts resolved by the whole body of the faithful. Almost the first issue that he faced as Emperor was the challenge[33] posed by Martin Luther in the autumn of 1520. At first Luther believed that Charles was the best hope for reform. 'God has given us a young and noble ruler to reign over us and has thereby awakened our hearts once more to hope.' He never entirely lost the belief that somehow Charles could be won over to the cause of reform.

Yet when they stood face to face at Charles's first imperial Diet held in the city of Worms in the following year, the gulf that emerged between them was unbridgeable. Luther's fundamental position, which he stated in public before Charles on 18 April 1521, was that he would accept no ultimate authority other than the word of God: 'So long as I cannot be disproved by Holy Writ or clear reason, so long I neither can nor will withdraw anything, for it is both criminal and dangerous to act against conscience. So help me God, Amen.' Conscience made the individual the judge of last resort.

Charles, by contrast, on the next day, spoke for the accumulated wisdom of all Christians, but a wisdom focused through the special mission of the Habsburgs. His speech was first read in French, as he had written it, and was then translated into German, so it could be understood by the majority of the assembled princes and officials. He spoke as a Habsburg.

Ye know that I am born of the most Christian Emperors of the noble German nation, of the Catholic Kings of Spain, the Archdukes of Austria, the Dukes of Burgundy, who were all to the death true sons of the Roman Church, defenders of the Catholic Faith, of the sacred customs, decrees and usages of its worship, who have bequeathed all this to me as my heritage, and according to whose example I have hitherto lived. Thus I am determined to hold fast by all that has happened since the Council of Constance. For it is certain that a single monk must err if he stands against the opinion of all Christendom. Otherwise Christendom itself would have erred for more than a thousand years. Therefore I am determined to set my kingdoms and dominions, my friends, my body, my blood, my life, my soul upon it.

He told his listeners that they like him had heard what Luther had said the day before; now Charles declared: 'I regret that I have delayed so long to proceed against him. I will not hear him again: he has his safe-conduct. But from now on I regard him as a notorious heretic . . .'[34] No word of Rome, or of the authority of the Pope, which Luther had challenged, but an assertion of the rights of the Christian community to discipline its members. Over the remainder of Charles's reign, as the fissure grew between Catholic and Protestant, the primacy of conscience over authority was renounced by the Protestants as firmly as it had been by the young Emperor. In 1553, when the godly Protestants of Geneva burned the Spanish theologian Michael Servetus for denying the Holy Trinity, they triumphantly reasserted the authority of the Christian community to act as the ultimate earthly judge. In its essence, the dispute was not so much about doctrine, but about authority and power.[35]

In 1520 Charles had no intention of denying the mission with which he had been charged barely six months before. On 22 October 1520, he had ridden into Aachen for his coronation, in full armour with a gold and scarlet saddle-cloth (very like the image presented by Titian), preceded by Count Pappenheim, the hereditary Grand Marshal of the Empire, holding the Imperial Sword before him. Before and behind them marched a throng of horsemen and men-at-arms, followed by the town councillors of the city, the knights of the Golden Fleece, the electoral princes and their retinues, with the heralds of the imperial court at the rear. To each side of the column, horsemen scattered new coins with the Emperor's image on the face and Plus Ultra on the reverse over the crowds, which scrambled for his largesse: the applause and shouting was tumultuous. Early on the following morning, clad in the simple white garment of a penitent, he swore the imperial oath, was robed, and crowned. Each time, answering 'Volo' – I will – to the questions, he promised to preserve the Christian faith, the honour of the holy Church, to care for the weak, and to reverence the Pope. Then the Archbishop of Cologne, who traditionally crowned the Emperor, turned to the congregation, representing the people of the Empire, and asked if they would bear true allegiance to the lord Charles, 'after the command of the Apostle'. 'Fiat, Fiat' – let it be done – came back as an answering roar. Crowned and acclaimed, he climbed the shallow steps and sat enthroned on the stone seat of Charlemagne.

The German princes had elected him King of the Romans at the strong urging of the Emperor Maximilian, who had dispensed thousands of ducats on his behalf. It was wildly rumoured that more than two tons of Habsburg gold were scattered to outbid Francis I of France, the other contender. But there was no natural affection for any foreigner and the Burgundian Charles seemed as alien to many Germans as Francis. The only unifying bond was that of descent: in his essence, by the blood that ran in his veins, Charles *was* German. By his presence and by the immense prestige that attached both to his imperial title and to the ideology of power which was fashioned round him – Charles was likened to Augustus, and Jove[36] – he could hold the centrifugal forces of his Empire in check. His absence – and despite his endless travelling, his visits to any part of his domains were erratic or infrequent – had the opposite, laxating, effect. His chancellor, Gattinara, was a descendant of Dante, and heavily infused with the notions of universal authority embodied in *De monarchia* (considered so subversive by the papacy that it remained on the index of prohibited books until the twentieth century). But even the Italian Gattinara, who had served Margaret of Austria in Burgundy, was very aware of the tangle of local interests and sensitivities.[37] But recognition of diversity could not solve the fundamental political problem of the Emperor's absence.

Charles's grasp of imperial affairs was erratic, perhaps because his visits – nine in all – to Germany were so irregular. Much of his vast correspondence dealt with the affairs of the Empire, which more and more focused on the twin issues of the Turks and the Lutherans. Over the years, as he spent more time in either Spain or Italy, Charles responded instinctively to the nuances of Mediterranean politics, while he floundered in his dealings with the Germans. By contrast Ferdinand, born and educated as a Spaniard but appointed Charles's lieutenant in the Empire, developed a subtle responsiveness to the way in which his new German subjects thought and acted. Until Charles came to Spain in the autumn of 1517, they had never met. To Ferdinand, his elder brother, dressed in the (to Spanish eyes) outlandish Burgundian style, must have seemed an exotic and mysterious figure. We do not know how they communicated, since Charles spoke little or no Spanish and Ferdinand spoke only Spanish. (Perhaps a fractured Latin provided the means of interchange.) That first encounter, in a dusty little village called Mojadas, just to the west of Valladolid, set the tone for their future relationship. At the first meeting, they embraced (an engraving was later made of this touching occasion), then Ferdinand held his brother's stirrup as he dismounted, and gave him a towel so that he could wash off the dust of travel. On the following day, it was Charles's turn, and he handed his younger brother the heavy collar and insignia of the Golden Fleece.

That exchange – the formal submission of the younger, the benevolent condescension of the elder – established the tone of their relationship for the remainder of their lives. In the past centuries, strife between brothers (*Bruderzwist*) had at times paralysed the house of Habsburg, and Ferdinand like many younger brothers could find cause for grievance. But his support for Charles was absolute, and although they quarrelled, he never allowed himself to become a focus for the swirling tides of faction that eventually washed over Charles's monarchy. Together they entered Valladolid, Charles in full armour, a gilded man, for his armour seemed to some spectators (used to the more utilitarian equipment of the Spanish knights) to be made of solid gold.[38] At a little distance came Ferdinand, followed by a procession of Burgundian and Spanish notables, riding to the sound of drums and trumpets. Some months later, in February 1518, the grandees of Spain assembled to swear allegiance to their king, and Ferdinand was the first to make his submission.

Ferdinand's formal functions accomplished, Charles swiftly dispatched him to his aunt's court in the Netherlands, so that he could not be seen as a rival in Spanish eyes. His sudden departure, never to return to the land of his birth, was seen as an affront to both the kingdoms of Castile and Aragón, one of the few issues on which they spoke with a common voice. Ferdinand, born and brought up in Spain, named after their great king, they regarded as their own; Charles was, with his mother, their lawful king but not regarded with any affection. Charles's removal of his brother was prudent: when revolt did break out in Spain in May 1520, within days of him leaving Spain for his imperial coronation at Aachen, the rebels (*comuñeros*) sought to speak in the name of *their queen* 'imprisoned' in Tordesillas. In her befuddled state Juana even spoke in favour of the nation's rights and the rebels' desire to restore the traditions of her parents, the Catholic Kings, Ferdinand and Isabella; but she refused to sign any decree at their behest.[39] Ferdinand would have formed a perfect focus of discontent.

His future destiny lay in the north. At the Diet of Worms on 2 April, Ferdinand sat close to his brother during the debates with Luther. On 10 April, the marriage contract with Anne of Hungary was finally concluded, with the exchange of rings and vows by Ferdinand's proxy and by Anne herself, with the wedding to take place at Whitsuntide at Linz, on the Danube. Two weeks after they married, his sister Mary and Anne's brother Lajos, the other half of Maximilian's grand marriage strategy, were united in Prague. His vision, of the rulers of Austria, Bohemia and Hungary linked by their common Habsburg ancestry, was fulfilled. However, the negotiations over Ferdinand's rights and status were difficult to resolve. It was only a few days before the wedding that Charles had ceded him the Austrian Habsburg lands as his domain and the negotiations dragged on until early in 1522, for Ferdinand was being asked to sacrifice his rights to inheritance over both the Burgundian and the Spanish lands to which his birth entitled him. These were much more valuable than Austria, which by contrast, brought him only the major share of Maximilian's massive debts. Finally, in secret, on 7 February 1522, it was agreed that Ferdinand and his descendants should have an absolute right to inherit the Austrian lands, while Charles reserved the Burgundian and the Spanish territories for himself. But in public, Ferdinand was to act merely as his brother's regent in the Austrian lands and as his representative within the Empire. Charles also promised that once he was crowned as Emperor by the Pope, he would secure Ferdinand's election as King of the Romans. With that agreement in hand, he left for Spain, and was not to be seen again in the German lands for almost a decade.

The conundrum of the Universal Empire was that the Emperor ruled everywhere, but like any mortal he could only be in a single location. However, the Habsburgs developed the tradition of the regent into a political art form. The long traditions of the family provided a model.[40] But the Habsburg practice was more flexible – and adaptable – than the use of regency in other nations. Regents were common throughout medieval and renaissance society, used in all cases where minors or the insane could not act on their own account. In many areas women too were also considered 'incompetent', needing the governance and guidance of a responsible male. With royal or noble houses the practice was different. Women could and did hold the rights of regent over their own children and even over a male heir, but often in association with a single male co-regent or with a wider council of male supervision. The Habsburg practice had traditionally been more open, for the rights under the *Privilegium maius* were inherent in the blood and not restricted by gender. Thus, archduchesses enjoyed the same rights as their male siblings, and Maximilian's sister Cunegunde had trenchantly defended her rights as an 'archduke' in a dispute over inheritance. Where the Salic Law,[41] which operated in France and the imperial succession, restricted inheritance to males, the reverse was true in the traditional Habsburg domains, as well as in Burgundy and the Spanish lands, where women could both inherit land and rule in their own right.[42] The linking of these traditions was viewed by contemporaries as being significant. The poet Ariosto in *Orlando Furioso* hailed the empire of Charles as uniting the lines of Spain and Austria:

> I see the will of heav'n doth so incline
> The house of *Austria* and of *Arragon*
> Shall linke together in a happie line,

> And be by match united both in one:
> I see a branche grow by the bank of the Ryne,
> Out of this house, as like there hath bene none,
> Whose match (thus much to say I dare be bold)
> May not be found in writers new or old.[43]

The poet continues, lauding the personality of

> This wise Prince his deare anointed
> One shepheard and one flocke he hath appointed.

But two elements are in play here: the individual – the wise Prince – but also those sharing a common descent from that 'match united both in one'. Charles's brother Ferdinand, his elder sister Eleanor, and his younger sisters, Mary, Isabella and Catherine, as well as all Charles's and Ferdinand's own children, all shared that common heritage.

Felix Austria nube. The Habsburgs used their kin in the complex geometry of dynastic marriages with the skill born of long practice. Of Maximilian's grandchildren, Isabella was married off to the King of Denmark, whose nickname 'the Nero of the North' gives some indication as to his character, Mary was betrothed to Lajos of Hungary, and Catherine married the King of Portugal. Charles himself married Isabella of Portugal, as he confided to his brother, as the only sure way of securing stability in the Spanish kingdoms in his absence;[44] he married his widowed elder sister, Eleanor, to his great rival Francis I, partly to cement a political agreement between them, but also to provide a back-channel of communication when all others were blocked. However, Habsburg women were more than tokens in the marriage stakes.

The policy of using the Habsburg kin, both male and female, as regents has attracted little attention,[45] except to note the achievements of Charles's aunt, Margaret of Austria, and his sister, Mary of Savoy.[46] How and why the Habsburg family were used in this manner are the more pertinent questions. A viceroy, such as the viceroy of the Indies, or of Naples, could be anyone who 'acted in the name and with the authority of the supreme ruler'. A regent was of a higher order, and endowed with the quality of sovereignty, personally and not vicariously. There was a distinction 'between

"Princes who were not Regents or Soveraigns".' 'His Imperial
Majesty' was described as 'Regent Archduke' of Austria, setting
him apart from all those archdukes who were merely titular.[47] A
regent could, within the limits set by Charles, take the place of the
Universal Emperor better than any viceroy. Almost all who were
suitable were pressed into service in one form or another. Under
Charles, his brother acted for him as his representative in the
Empire, his aunt Margaret of Austria, and then his daughter Mary
of Savoy, in the Burgundian lands; his son Philip II in the lands of
the Spanish crowns, and his nephew Maximilian and his daughter
Mary, who took Philip's place in Spain from 1548 to 1550; and
latterly his daughter Juana, when Philip set out from Spain in 1554
for his marriage to the Queen of England. Subsequently his granddaughter Isabella and his great-nephew Albert also ruled in the
Netherlands.

This mobilization of the lineage depended on having sufficient
Habsburgs to deploy. While Charles's own blood line proved thin,
and his son Philip II from four marriages produced only five
children who survived past their childhood years, Ferdinand's
progeny were both more numerous and more robust. Thirteen of
his children survived, and his elder son Maximilian continued the
tradition, with nine. Such a profusion could prove almost as dangerous as a dearth of heirs, for it created enormous strains both
economically (with the need to provide estates or dowries),
or politically, as brothers and cousins vied for position. One solution to the former was the Church, which provided benefices or
monastic positions for many Habsburgs, both male and female.[48]
Nor was entering the Church any absolute bar to a secular career.
Albert–Ernest was a cardinal when he was called on to marry his
cousin Isabella, for them to become joint regents of the
Netherlands.[49]

Descent made every Habsburg a native of any part of the
domains. The Burgundian towns had rejected a duke of Savoy as
their *regent*, after Mary retired in 1555; they would only allow him
the title of 'lieutenant-general of the Netherlands'.[50] But they could
have no objection to any member of the house of Austria, who was
of direct descent from Charles the Bold ... If Charles could not
split himself, members of his own kindred standing for him were

the best substitute available. It is hard to think of any other royal or noble house that made such a practice of distributing power amongst members, secure in the knowledge that, like a paid official, they would relinquish office and estates upon command. For the larger part of Charles's reign using his own family in this fashion seemed an unqualified success. Both his aunt and his sister proved outstanding rulers of the complex Burgundian inheritance. His brother, who had to shoulder the defence of Europe against Turkish invasion with little support from the Emperor, manipulated the politics of the Empire with greater skill than Charles. All suffered, however, from the Emperor's endless demands for more and more money to sustain his succession of wars and a style of imperial grandeur that proved almost as ruinous.

For the peripatetic Emperor, using his kin in this fashion fulfilled two cardinal objectives: first, as Habsburgs they could provide an imperial simulacrum in his absence; but second, as regents all their decisions were subject to his final ratification, which allowed him to trim their policy to his own. On the other hand, it was difficult to dismiss or discipline a Habsburg, and any territory that had formerly been governed by a member of the dynasty considered it a slight to be ruled by anyone of lesser status. The pool of talent was not all that large. After Isabella's death in 1539, Charles was hamstrung for he could find no one to replace her effectively until his son Philip was old enough to take her place; but he would not countenance the appointment of any of his male kin whom he judged inadequate to the role, nor any female, he wrote to Philip, unless she was married, widowed or 'old enough to be widowed'.[51]

In many cases, his regents ruled more wisely and more effectively than Charles himself. Although the pressure of governing two continents forced him to govern by proxy or on paper (and he was served by a number of able secretaries and chancellors), he was never the natural and well-ordered bureaucrat that his son became. Impatient with the minutiae of government, his true passions were those of his youth: he craved honour and glory. Charles was thirty-five years of age before he commanded an army in battle, but the inner compulsion to defend Christendom always worked powerfully upon him. His character has been characterized as 'phlegmatic', but it disguised a more restless spirit, which craved decisive action. The victories in Italy, like the battle of Pavia in 1525 at which the French King Francis I was captured, were accomplished in his absence. A short-lived peace allowed him to claim what had been denied his grandfather, coronation as Holy Roman Emperor in Italy. But not in Rome, for his troops, hungry and unpaid, had sacked and plundered the Holy City in 1527. In the autumn of 1529 he travelled to Bologna with a large retinue, while preparations were made for his coronation with the Iron Crown of Lombardy and the Imperial Crown by the Pope at Bologna. The dates he selected for the double coronation were the twenty-second and twenty-fourth of February, the anniversaries of his birthday and of the victory at Pavia.

With the cheers of the crowds at Bologna barely stilled, Charles set out for Innsbruck, where he met Ferdinand and his sister Mary, a widow since the death of Lajos in 1526. He spent almost three years in Germany and his Burgundian lands. With the prestige of a crowned Emperor, he had little difficulty in securing Ferdinand's election as King of the Romans, and he appointed Mary to take their aunt Margaret's post (she had died in 1529) as regent of the Burgundian lands. He had less success with the issues of religion. Two Diets, at Augsburg in 1530 and at Regensburg, ended with the decision that only a General Council could resolve the issues, and as Charles's former confessor wrote to him from Rome, 'The pope and the cardinals would sooner see this council in Hell than on earth.' Faced with this impasse, Charles sought action in another dimension. There had been public declaration at the time of his coronation that with peace in Europe and a crowned Emperor to lead them, now was the time for the long-promised crusade. With ferocious energy, and calling forth the resources of all his lands, both military and financial, he gathered an army to defeat the Turks, advancing again on Vienna, which they had narrowly failed to capture in 1529. But Suleiman the Magnificent withdrew and deprived Charles of his personal crusade. However, there was an alternative field of glory, not along the line of the Danube but on the southern shore of the Mediterranean, where the Muslim world was exposed to Christian vengeance.[52]

In February 1495 the Pope had given the kings of Spain, recently triumphant in Granada, exclusive rights to the conquest of North

Africa, which would be a preparation for the recovery of the Holy Land. In her testament in 1504, Isabella referred to this papal concession, and called upon all her successors to continue the reconquest of Spain on the African shore. Charles cannot have been unaware of his grandmother's dying injunction, and was determined to attack the Muslim port cities of Tunis and Algiers,[53] which were being used by the corsairs who raided Christian shipping.[54] The Iberian kingdoms had already achieved footholds on the North African shore. Melilla had been taken by the Duke of Medina Sidonia in 1497, Oran and Mers el Kebir in 1509 and Tripoli in 1510, while Tangier had been held by the Portuguese since 1471. But an expedition into such a climate and terrain, so far from home, was risky, like any amphibious operation. The dangers became apparent a generation later when the King of Portugal, Sebastian, seeking to emulate his predecessors, was killed fighting in North Africa; his demise led inexorably to Portugal's forced unification with the Spanish crowns. The outspoken Cardinal Tavera echoed the fears of many when he wrote to Charles, 'Look how much depends on your person, and how you would leave your kingdoms, if for our sins, some disaster should befall you. God forbid! And if this should not move you, remember that Your Majesty's son is still a child.'[55]

Nothing would deflect Charles. By cajoling and threatening the nobles and towns of Spain (and receiving with gratitude a contingent from Portugal), he assembled an army of 30,000 men at Barcelona. Perhaps more important, he had the ships to carry them and the artillery necessary to undertake a siege. Meanwhile, the Spanish *tercios* serving in Germany, Italy and Sicily had been denuded to provide troops for the expedition, and two great fleets, including contingents from the Pope and the knights of the Order of St John at Malta, were to unite off Sardinia, when Charles would reveal their ultimate destination. More than 500 ships, crammed with more than 60,000 men, finally united off Cagliari, and at a council of war Charles announced that their destination was to be Tunis, built on the site of the ancient city of Carthage. Whether this factor weighed at all with Charles is not clear. But at least one of the artists who accompanied him presented the conquest of Tunis as the victory of Rome over the barbarians, with Charles clad in the short Roman tunic and his soldiers armed in the Roman style. When the huge fleet arrived off the port of Tunis, La Goleta, in June 1535, in good order and eager for action, the Christians had not won a major battle against the power of Islam since a ragtag army had defended Belgrade against Mahmud II in 1456. The garrison he confronted at La Goleta was Ottoman, and Kair-ed-Din (Barbarossa) was the sultan's Grand Admiral. Ottoman intelligence sources had suggested that Tunis was the likely target of the great expedition, and he had spent some months strengthening the fortifications at La Goleta, and called in all his reserves from Algiers and from the local princes, so that he had a force of 20,000 horsemen with a large number of infantry levies. His janissaries and trained troops, numbering about 6,000, were concentrated at La Goleta, under the command of an experienced soldier named Sinan. There they awaited the attack.

The campaign was handled in a masterly fashion. The fleet under the Grand Admiral, the Genoese Andrea Doria, and the army commanded by the Spanish Marqués del Vasto collaborated under the watchful eye of the Emperor. The guns from the fleet pounded the walls of the citadel daily, and although Sinan mounted night attacks on the encircling Christian lines, his defences were slowly being reduced to rubble. On the day of the first great assault, the guns battered the defenders for six hours, from first light. Then, as the guns fell silent, Charles, in full armour despite the searing heat, addressed his polyglot army, each contingent in their own language. They had fought, he said for the honour of God, with the blessing of the Pope and all Christians, and before their Emperor; they would now raise the cross of Christ over the walls of the citadel. He was answered with a crescendo of cheers, then the *tercios* began to move forward under a withering fire from the shattered walls. But nothing could stop them and they advanced slowly to a rhythmic drumbeat. Other columns approached La Goleta from all sides. Suddenly, as the columns reached the walls and began to scale the stone-filled breaches in them, the fire from the defence slackened and died, and the defenders burst out of the fortress, to retreat across the shallow waters of the bay towards the city of Tunis six miles distant. The Ottoman cavalry, always in evidence just out of gunshot, galloped forward to their relief.

Only after the fortress was taken did the scale of the Christian achievement become apparent. In the harbour were 87 galleys and galiots, and more than 300 brass cannon were mounted on the ramparts. The magazines were full of food, shot and powder. After allowing his men to rest for four days, Charles decided, despite the heat and the risk of being cut off from his fleet, to advance on the city of Tunis. Meanwhile Barbarossa had collected an army of about 50,000, but among whom there were few trained soldiers; only his few janissaries could equal the battle-hardened *tercios* and *Landesknechts* in Charles's ranks. The advance was opposed at every stage by the Ottoman forces, but they could not penetrate the pike wall, or resist the fire of his arquebusiers. Barbarossa fell back and prepared to defend the city. However, he received news that the Christian slaves, mostly from the galleys at La Goleta, who had been held in the citadel had seized the city. His first thought had been to slaughter them all as a precaution before the battle started (they numbered many thousands), but his commanders had dissuaded him, pointing out that without the galley slaves, his maritime power would be paralysed. Now faced with the eventuality which he had feared, sandwiched between Christians advancing from the shore and firing on him from the walls of the city, he ordered a general retreat.

The city elders came to Charles with the keys of the city, which he accepted,[56] but his troops would not be deprived of the rights to sack and pillage. Some no doubt had been present at the sack of Rome, but at Tunis, the carnage was much worse.

The soldiers fearing that they would be deprived of the booty which they expected, rushed suddenly and without orders into the town, and began to kill and plunder without distinction. It was too late to restrain their cruelty, their avarice, or their licentiousness. All the outrages of which soldiers are capable in the fury of a storm, all the excesses of which men can be guilty when their passions are heightened by the contempt and hatred of difference in manners and religion inspires, were committed. Above thirty thousand of the innocent inhabitants perished on that unhappy day and ten thousand were carried away as slaves . . . the emperor lamented the fatal accident which had stained the lustre of his victory.[57]

The Jews of the city were enslaved by the triumphant Christians and sold, 'both men and women, in the most diverse countries, but in Naples and Genoa, the Italian communities bought the freedom of many, may God remember them for it'. Some, less fortunate, ended in Spain, where they were compelled to abjure their God or suffer the attentions of the Holy Inquisition.[58]

Charles's triumph at Tunis now only merits a footnote in most texts, but its effect on contemporaries was considerable. On 5 April 1536, the victorious Emperor entered Rome 'with extraordinary pomp'.[59] A near-contemporary described it more exactly, 'he celebrated a Capitoline triumph according to the custom of the ancient Roman Emperors'.[60] He had marched up Italy from Naples with his entire army, and when they arrived within sight of Rome on 4 April, many Romans remembered the sack of the city only nine years before. But now the troops were under perfect discipline, and so many of them were there to parade through the city that some old buildings were cleared to allow the great mass to marshal. One of the structures destroyed was the ruin of an ancient temple dedicated to peace, and significant omens were read into its removal. It took the entire day for the Spanish *tercios*, Italian city contingents, German *Landesknechts*, Flemish crossbowmen and arquebusiers, to march through the city. They were followed by the horse, including Hungarian hussars, Spanish *jinetes*, and the more heavily armoured men at arms. Towards the rear there were carts loaded with treasure and booty, and it was said, some Moorish captives, in the true Roman style. Then a mass of freed slaves, who had been dressed and 'furnished with the means of returning to their own countries, displaying their benefactor's munificence'. They carried banners 'extolling his power and abilities with the exaggeration flowing from gratitude and admiration. In comparison with him, the other monarchs of Europe made an inconsiderable figure.'[61] Then came the nobility and dignitaries, preceding Charles, dressed simply in a suit of half-armour, who was followed by the college of cardinals in their scarlet robes. At the end of the procession came the imperial halberdiers, the Emperor's closest bodyguard. Charles came to lay the fruits of his victory before the Pope, Christ's vicar on earth.

It was Holy Week, the most sacred days in the calendar of the Church, the moment at which Christ was crucified and then rose

from the dead, to save a sinful world. Charles's crusading triumph
also represented a kind of resurrection and on Easter Monday he
asked to be received before the Pope, the entire college of cardinals,
the corps of diplomats, and the dignitaries of the city, as well as the
great nobles in the army. He spoke, in Spanish, with great passion
for an hour. He wanted only peace, he said, for he knew at first
hand the horrors of war. But all his attempts to preserve the peace
of Europe had been prevented by the French king, who had forsworn his solemn promises given in the Treaty of Madrid that
allowed him freedom. When he had made further promises in the
Peace of Cambrai (1529), he had broken those agreements as well,
and he was conspiring with heretics in Germany. Charles challenged
Francis (as he had before) to single combat. Addressing the Pope he
said, 'I promise your Holiness, before this Holy College and all the
knights here present, if the king of France wishes to face me in
personal combat in the field of honour, without armour but with a
sword and dagger, on land or sea, on a bridge, or on an island, in
private or with our two armies present – wherever and however he
decides, in accordance with the code of honour, I will accept.'[62]
This he delivered with 'an elevated voice, a haughty tone, and the
greatest vehemence of expression and gesture. The French ambassadors, who did not fully comprehend his meaning, as he spake in the
Spanish tongue, were totally disconcerted ... When one of them
began to vindicate his master's conduct, Charles interposed abruptly
and would not permit him to proceed.' The meeting began to
disperse in silence, led by the Pope and the cardinals. There was the
'greatest astonishment of the extraordinary scene which had been
exhibited. In no other part of his conduct did Charles ever deviate
from his general character.' By the following day he had recovered
himself, and told the French ambassadors that he had not meant to
issue a personal challenge to Francis, but was simply seeking a
means to prevent war between Christians. The moment was then
largely forgotten, taking its place among the long catalogue of
Charles's chivalric gestures.

Tunis stands at roughly the mid-point of his active career, and in
retrospect it seems like its apogee. At no later point was his sense of
triumph so unalloyed by doubt or subsequent disaster. This is the
Charles portrayed by Leone in his bronze statue of the Emperor in

a heroic pose, 'Subduing Fury'. He stands calm and at rest, clasping a long Roman spear (very like the spear in Titian's equestrian portrait). His stance suggests self-possession, his gesture 'indicative of boldness or control – and therefore of the self-defined masculine role, at once protective and controlling'.[63] He was both shield and governor of Christendom, and it was from Tunis onwards that there was a concerted attempt to portray Charles in this fashion. The imagery of Tunis became crucial in the presentation of the triumphant Emperor. Numerous pamphlets circulated describing the Emperor's moment of glory, and a series of engravings by Martin van Heemskerck celebrated his prowess. The artists who had accompanied him to Tunis produced their work, notably the Haarlem artist J. C. Vermeyen, the court painter to the regents Margaret of Austria and Mary of Savoy, who had sketched the entire campaign, from the summoning of the host to Barcelona to its triumphant conclusion. From these sketches, almost ten years later, he prepared cartoons from which were woven a set of twelve huge tapestries, which were finally completed in 1554.[64] Other artists who had been nowhere near Tunis produced work invoking the same triumphalist themes.

The elements of the Tunisian victory became almost synonymous with Charles. In Francisco Terzi's engravings of the great men of the House of Austria, Charles is presented as a conqueror of cities (represented as a female figure with 'a mural crown') and trophies of captured Ottoman weapons.[65] But Vermeyen's tapestries had the key role in the iconography of Charles's rule. With the set of eight tapestries designed by Bernard van Orley on the subject of the battle of Pavia, they established a new set of conventions for presenting the glory of the Habsburgs in a new medium, more portable and flexible than Maximilian's paper Triumphs.

As a consequence of his peripatetic style of rule, Charles never established a permanent ceremonial headquarters. The problem of creating a portable Hall of Princely Virtue [a room or set of rooms used to glorify the superior moral and physical qualities of the ruler] was solved by an ingenious expedient. A portable decoration was created in the form of tapestries which could be easily rolled up and packed to accompany Charles on his travels ... The tapestries were so heavily used by Charles and later by Philip, that a copy needed to be made to save the original. Both the old and the new sets, as they are called in the inventories, found their way to Spain where they acquired an almost iconic status and continued to be used on all manner of state occasions.[66]

But they were not the first tapestries used to glorify the Habsburgs in this fashion: the sequence entitled 'Los Honores', woven to celebrate Charles's election as Holy Roman Emperor in 1519, established the model.[67] Work began in 1520 and they were displayed at Philip's baptism in 1527. They 'comprise a didactic allegory through which the newly elected king could learn which virtues to practice to reach Honor, the highest reward of kings.' Vermeyen's sequence completed the cycle, presenting Charles, at the peak of his career, achieving a crusader's honour. But the pursuit of honour was a treadmill. Charles and later Philip were both warned: 'As soon as a prince loses but one grade of reputation, friends will become mistrustful, enemies will be encouraged, and in the natural course of events, he will be reduced to the lowest grade.'[68] The glorification of the ruler by all means at his disposal was a process that required constant attention and development, a cultural politics of ostentation and display that was to prove both ruinously costly and ultimately fruitless.

ᘯ   ᘯ   ᘯ

In Charles's case the struggle ended twenty years on in the same Great Hall in Brussels where, barely past boyhood, he had first made his pact with his Burgundian subjects. In his retirement he was not renouncing the world; much nonsense has been written of his intention of becoming a monk in his retirement in the Hieronymite monastery at Yuste, not far from Palencia in Spain. But he was retiring from the field of honour, abandoning the ceaseless chase for the bubble of 'reputation'. He 'retired' in the military and not the modern sense, leaving the field of conflict undefeated. Quite what he intended and expected is not clear, and it is likely that his intentions shifted over the years that he had planned his retirement. Some said that he had had this withdrawal in mind from his childhood, or from immediately after his victory at Tunis and his triumph in Rome. Perhaps his model was the Emperor Diocletian, who abandoned the cares of office for a more tranquil and retired life in his vast palace at Split. Charles's departure was as theatrical as his arrival on the stage of empire in the cathedral of Aachen.

On 25 October 1555, he sat for the last time on the chair of state. Three days before he had, in an emotional ceremony, ceded his title as Grand Master of the Golden Fleece to Philip. When he rose to speak he leaned on the shoulder of the young prince of Orange, and spoke with a loud, firm, voice, speaking from the notes he held in his hand. He told his audience that from his seventeenth year 'he dedicated his life to public objects, reserving no portion of his time for the indulgence of his ease and very little for the enjoyment of private pleasure'. He recounted his endless journeys, and told his audience that only illness compelled him to leave them; but 'instead of a sovereign worn out with disease and scarce half-alive, he gave them one in the prime of life, accustomed already to govern, and who added to the vigour of youth all the attention and sagacity of maturer years'. Then he spoke directly to his son Philip,

If I had left you by my death this rich inheritance, to which I have made such large additions, some regard would have been due to my memory on that account; but now when I voluntarily resign to you what I might have still retained, I may well expect the warmest expression of thanks on your part. With these however I dispense, and shall consider your concern for the welfare of your subjects as the best and most acceptable testimony of your gratitude to me . . . and if the time should ever come when you shall wish to enjoy the tranquillity of private life, may you have a son so endowed with such qualities as you can resign your sceptre to him, with as much satisfaction as I give up mine to you.[69]

Then he sank back into his seat exhausted, to receive the homage of his son and the plaudits of his ministers and nobles. In a later ceremony he resigned the crown of Spain to Philip, and eventually, after difficult negotiations with the Electors, the Empire to his brother Ferdinand. It was finished: Charles had set in train the process by which he would became a private gentleman. Pope Julius III thought his resignation 'the strangest thing ever to happen'.[70]

There had been few moments in the near-forty years of Charles's maturity when his human qualities had broken through his mask of command, undermining his public composure. He was given to neither anger nor elation: the word usually used was 'phlegmatic', a studied calm. This calm, patrician *gravitas* became the model to which all his successors aspired. It was said of his son Philip in his maturity that he 'says nothing nor does anything except with the decorum and majesty proper to a king';[71] the pattern, in this as in much else, was his father's conduct. Yet we know that the inner man harboured deep emotions. Faced with crisis after crisis in his last years as Emperor, he more than once fell into a deep and sullen depression, incapable of action or decision. We know that his love for his wife Isabella, from whom he was constantly parted, was profound and unfeigned. When she died, suddenly of fever on May Day 1539, his public response was formulaic: 'The merciful God has decided to take her to Him. Her death is a great sorrow to all, and especially the Emperor.'

But in private, writing to his sister Mary on the day after her death, he confessed his desolation: 'I feel the anguish and sorrow that you can imagine at so great and extreme a loss . . . nothing can console me except to reflect on her goodness, her exemplary life as a Catholic and her edifying death.'[72] Alonso de Santa Cruz, who was close to Charles, recorded that 'to describe the sadness which his majesty feels at her tragic death will take many pages'. He begged his sister to scour Margaret of Austria's picture collection for any portraits of the dead queen; any she could find should be sent to him with all speed, packed with the greatest care for the journey, lest they suffer any damage. At the end of his life, he took a number of Isabella's likenesses with him to his retirement, and in Titian's *Gloria*, which shows Charles in his shroud, gazing up at God the Father and Christ in majesty, it is Isabella who stands just behind him. *This* was the picture that delighted him perhaps more than any other. And in a mulberry-coloured silk bag 'three cased miniatures of the empress, painted in her youthful beauty, and soon after the honeymoon in the Alhambra, kept alive Charles' recollection of the wife whom he had lost'. We have no knowledge of any sexual disloyalty, despite their long absences; all the Emperor's bastard children were born either before his marriage or in his lonely years as a widower. He never seriously contemplated remarriage.

Only after Charles had laid down the last of his official roles and was a private citizen did the sense of the individual emerge, partly perhaps because for the first time in his life he was not perpetually in motion. Symbolically he chose a new crest that combined the arms of Burgundy with those of an archduke of Austria, to which he had been born. At Yuste he could tend his garden, for

he had ever been a lover of nature and a cherisher of birds and flowers. In one of his campaigns, the story was told, that a swallow having built her nest and hatched her young upon his tent, he would not allow the tent to be struck when the army resumed its march, but left it standing for the sake of the mother and brood. From Tunis he is said to have brought not only the best of his laurels, but the pretty flower called the Indian pink, sending it from the African shore to his gardens in Spain, whence in time, it won its way into every cottage garden in Europe. Yuste was a very paradise for these simple tastes and harmless pleasures.

At last he could indulge his passion for clocks and other mechanisms, and he delighted in tinkering with them. Visitors were surprised at the plainness of his rooms.

For the hangings of his bedroom he preferred sombre black cloth to gayer arras; but he had brought with him from Flanders suits of rich tapestry, wrought with figures, landscapes or flowers, more than sufficient to hang the rest of his apartments; the supply of cushions, eiderdown quilts and linen, was luxuriously ample; his friends sat on chairs covered with black velvet, and he himself reposed himself either on a chair with wheels, or in an easy chair to which six cushions and a footstool belonged.

Even in the dry climate of Yuste he could not escape the pains of gout. Perhaps this was why at times he seemed selfish and crabbed, as when his two elderly sisters, who came to visit him, were denied a room for the night, 'nor would he even offer them a dinner'.[73] Yet his affection for them, his childhood companions, was very deep. With his sisters, especially Mary and also Eleanor, with whom he had grown up there was a remarkable ease and openness. They would often wrangle and disagree, but the love and mutual loyalty that bound them together was apparent. Charles would listen to Mary when no on else could persuade him, or move him from his obduracy.

In retirement he lived much as he had before, but without the cares of state. He wore plain and simple clothes, including perhaps the burnouses from Tunis, which are recorded in the inventory of his possessions after his death. He lived unostentatiously and in private, but everything was of the finest quality. Even the water with which he washed his hands was poured from silver ewers into gold or silver basins, and his table was set with plates of gold and silver, with cellars and other tableware by Tobbia and Cellini. It was calculated that he had more than 13,000 ounces of gold and silver plate at Yuste. He continued to indulge his taste for rich food, and in the morning he went straight from mass to the table, as the saying was, in Italian, *dalla messa, alla mensa*. He lacked all restraint in eating – part perhaps of his Burgundian heritage, although he loved some of the rough and spicy Spanish dishes: 'His appetite was voracious; his hands were so disabled with gout that carving, which he nevertheless insisted on doing for himself, was a tedious process; and even mastication was slow and difficult.' Despite this he bolted his food, and finding it hard to chew, often swallowed it whole. At the end of the day was another large meal, 'consisting frequently of pickled salmon and other unwholesome dishes'. It is now believed that he may have suffered from diabetes in his later years, which fuelled his appetite, and then contributed to his other disorders, gout and chronic indigestion. Overeating certainly exacerbated the gout which afflicted him ever more painfully in his later years, to the extent that in his last campaigns, in 1546–8, he could not use a stirrup but had his leg supported in a canvas sling. The pain, as he rode over rough ground, is hard to imagine. But apart from in the single outburst in Rome, he succeeded in presenting himself a calm and distant figure, imbued with that *gravitas* that was becoming to a ruler, especially the Universal Emperor.

Obduracy was Charles's strongest and least attractive characteristic, and there too the pangs in his limbs worsened his temper and made him even more stubborn. Where his brother Ferdinand proved able to trim and adjust his course as the exigencies of circumstance demanded, Charles was always immovable on the Protestant issue as on so many others. In his autobiography, the challenge of the Protestants looms larger than all the other issues; and his horror of heresy filled his last years. When a small group of Lutherans was discovered in Spain, he declared that after he had spent a 'lifetime fighting heretics', now his final resting-place was to be 'defiled' by their presence. He urged the authorities to dispense with the niceties of justice and condemn them to the fires without delay.[74] He could concede a certain nobility to the Ottomans – the Protestants, by contrast, were the enemy within. The Turks had provided him with his crusade, the chance to carry war into the infidel domains. Perhaps the war against the Protestants was also a species of crusade, and at the battle of Mühlberg, the battle-cries on the Catholic side had been crusaders' shouts of 'Santiago' and 'Sankt Georg', respectively St James the Moorslayer (*Matamoros*) and St George the Dragonslayer, revered by the Habsburgs.

He was a long time dying. In August 1558 he began to take cold baths, for he said, 'I would rather have a slight fever than suffer this perpetual itching.' The fever turned out to be more serious, and each day he was carried out in his wheeled chair to sit in the sunshine under the loggia that ran around his house. One day he asked to have a portrait of Isabella brought to him and he sat staring at it for some time. Then he asked for a sketch of the Titian *Gloria*, to set alongside it; the original had been placed behind the high altar in the monastery chapel, into which he could see from a window constructed so that he could look on the altar from his bed. For two weeks he fought back against what now seems to have been malaria. By 19 September, he felt death was close and he asked for extreme unction. On the following day he revived, and asked to take mass. His confessor said it was unnecessary, as he was already in a state of grace. Charles, with a wry smile, replied, 'It may not be necessary, but it is good company for so long a journey.' He weakened through the day, and by the evening he seemed to have only an hour or two left to live. Still he hung on, until, past midnight, it was St Matthew's Day, 21 September. Speaking quietly the archbishop of Toledo told him that he had been born on the feast of St Matthias the apostle, and he was about to die on the feast of St Matthew, who for Christ's sake had forsaken wealth, as Charles had forsaken imperial power. The Emperor interrupted him. 'The time has come. Bring me the candles and the crucifix.' The candles were ranged around his bed and the crucifix which Isabella had held in her dying moments was handed to him; Philip, too, was to die with it in his hands. Charles held it at arm's length, focusing on the little figure on the cross, then he clasped it to his chest. Then firmly, he said in Spanish, 'Ya, voy, Señor' (Now, I am going, Lord), and his fingers relaxed, loosing the crucifix, and the archbishop held it to Charles's dry lips, and then before his dimming eyes. Suddenly, he roused himself, shouted, '¡Ay Jesús!' and died, just as the clock was striking two. It was, all agreed, a most Christian death, of one who was 'the greatest man that had ever lived, or ever would live, in the world'.[75]

That morning his body was embalmed and encased in a lead coffin, inside a case of chestnut wood, and lowered from the window of his bedroom into the church below. There covered with a black velvet pall, the monks prepared to bury Charles as he had instructed, like his grandfather Maximilian in the church of St George in Wiener Neustadt, under the altar, so that a priest saying mass would tread on his head and chest. But he knew that this was only a temporary resting-place, for the Universal Monarch could not remain in a tiny chapel in the Spanish wilderness. Years before, he had planned that a chapel should be created in the new cathedral in Granada, so that it could provide a mausoleum for himself and his descendants, following the injunction of Isabella that Granada should be the last resting-place of the kings of Spain. But as with so many of Charles's schemes, it was never completed. Although a sanctuary was created for the Habsburg tombs, in front of a special altar where the Holy Sacrament would stand before them, honouring that long Habsburg connection that went back to the first Rudolf, it remained empty. Instead, he wrote to Philip that his body should lie at Yuste, until his son made the appropriate arrangements.[76] He lay beneath the altar for sixteen years until the new burial place was ready in another but infinitely grander Hieronymite cloister, the great monastery palace of St Lorenzo del Escorial, which Philip had built in the mountains to the north of Madrid.

But, Charles's apotheosis was delayed a little longer, until 1593, when the chapel of the Escorial was completed. There, for the Gospel side of the altar, Leone's son Pompeio had created in bronze, at full life-size, the old Emperor's family at prayer, Charles kneeling at the front, with his wife and sisters behind. Almost eighty years before when the Spaniards had first seen him as he rode through the streets of Valladolid as a young man of eighteen, they thought he was encased in gold from head to foot, and called him *el dorado*, the golden one. Now, Pompeio Leone, at Philip's command, had covered the raw bronze of all the figures with a deep and lustrous gold leaf. Charles was a golden man indeed, for all eternity.

5

A War to the Last Extremity

1550–1660

The Habsburgs ruled in Spain for close to a century and a half after Charles's abdication, a long episode in a longer history. But it marked – or distorted – the future history of the Habsburgs irrevocably, and long after Habsburg rule had ended in Spain, its memory maintained a shadowy half-life in the customs and attitudes of the court in Vienna. In that context it was often referred to as the 'Spanish ceremonial', meaning the stiff, unbending rituals that were thought to have been *de rigueur* at the court of Philip II and his successors. But in practice the true Spanish ceremonials, the heavy 'Spanish mantle', a form of elaborate cloak, the court hat,[1] the measured paces backwards and forwards dictated by the rules of precedence, were swept away by the Emperor Joseph II in the eighteenth century. The musty court ceremonials of the last Habsburgs were newly minted under Joseph's nephew Francis and his successors. They may have been Spanish in their aspirations, but very few of them, in their detail, predated the French Revolution. But they referred back to a period of Habsburg supremacy, when divine favour shone upon the Habsburgs, making them the rulers of two worlds, on both sides of the Atlantic, and far east into the Pacific. In the history and literature of Spain it is still referred to as the Golden Age – *el Siglo de Oro* – and that is how it was regarded by generations of Habsburgs to come.

At his resignation, Charles's inheritance had been split, although he had wanted his only son Philip II to succeed to the imperial dignity after the death of his brother Ferdinand, as well as possessing the lands of Spain in Italy, the Netherlands and the Americas. But the notion of a *division* is a misnomer. In Charles's eyes, and in accord with the evolving practice of the family, whoever ruled in any of his territories did so more as a 'regent', than as a 'sole possessor'. The Habsburg inheritance was a collective possession.

Even Philip II, hailed as a 'new Apollo' and Lord of the World, held the lands in trust for future generations of his lineage. Although the family was divided into two branches, one centred on Austria and the other on Spain, and the antagonism between the two houses could be visceral, common interest dictated that the Habsburgs should stand together. They did so for as long as the Habsburgs ruled in Spain.[2] Philip II and his sons were the senior line, and with the riches of the Netherlands and the gold and silver of the Americas, incomparably the richer. While Ferdinand and his successors held the imperial *title*, the kings of Spain promoted an imperial *style*, a grandeur that outstripped their cousins. Earlier generations of the family had built castles and even palaces in the Netherlands and the Austrian lands. But these were not grand and ostentatious buildings. The courts at Graz and Innsbruck, as well as the new apartments in the Hofburg in Vienna, did not promote a sense of display. Even the turrets and great chambers of Margaret of Austria's château at Binche, which possessed a sumptuous interior, were rich in the Burgundian style, with fine objects and furnishings set in a plain frame. There was nothing on the grandiloquent scale of the Habsburg buildings in Spain.

The first great Habsburg palace was the building in the Roman manner, constructed at Granada to the orders of Charles V by the Toledan architect Diego Machuca. It was never occupied, since Charles did not return, as he had intended, for the long stay in Granada where he had passed the happy days of his honeymoon with Isabella. The palace, however, existed as a symbol of his rule as the 'New Augustus'. Its structure, a perfect square surrounding a geometrically exact circular courtyard, encircled by a double portico of doric columns, echoed Charles's claim to be the ruler of the round world.[3] Its walls were decorated with the scenes of his triumphs, like the great marble frieze that commemorated his victory at

Mühlberg. But his endless journeying (and perhaps his temperament) did not allow him to establish a single centre of his rule. He restored the *alcázares* of Madrid, Toledo and Segovia, a process which his son Philip continued. Philip also built new hunting-lodges at Aranjuez and at El Pardo, close to Madrid. Unlike his father, Philip sought a static, centred style of rule. His choice of Madrid as his capital city, which was geographically the epicentre of his kingdom, seemed unusual to contemporaries,[4] who had expected him to settle on Valladolid or Toledo as his capital. But others recognized the lure of a point symbolizing his centrality. 'It was right', his biographer Cabrera de Córdoba wrote in 1876, 'that so great a monarchy should have a city fulfilling the function of a heart, located in the middle of the body, to minister to all its states in peace and war.'[5] Perhaps a further attraction was that Madrid and its desiccated plain at the foot of the Sierra de Guadarrama had comparatively so little history, so little entanglement with the past of either Castile or Aragón. Madrid and its pendant jewel, Philip's supreme achievement, the palace monastery of El Escorial, had no antecedents.

The Escorial was, by any measure, the greatest monument of the age.[6] He himself chose its location, thirty miles north-west of Madrid, and there is a spot on the hills high above the building where folklore has it that he used to sit for hours watching its construction. Geoffrey Parker, whose short biography of Philip II gets closer to the man than any of the alternatives,[7] writes:

To begin with it was to be one more monastic foundation, like the Parral at Segovia or Saint Jerome in Granada,[8] or Our Lady at Guadalupe, all founded by Philip's predecessors. Like these three, the monastery was to be staffed by members of the Hieronymite order, for whom the royal family had a particular respect . . . But there was more to Escorial than that. From the first the king intended it to be a royal mausoleum, and there were regular funeral processions to the monastery whenever a member of the royal family died. Philip had the remains of his father brought there from Yuste in 1568 and he wanted to bring the Catholic Kings from Granada, but the bodies were far too decomposed (instead he had special lead sarcophagi made for them, so their mortal remains would be better protected).[9]

The Escorial was more a city than a single building. A huge granite rectangle, more than two hundred yards along the longer side, it embraced a palace, a church, monastery, seminary and a school, laboratories and distillation equipment for the king's chemical experiments and astronomical observations and the greatest library in the world. Philip had instructed his architects, 'Above all ... simplicity in the construction, severity in the whole; nobility without arrogance; majesty without ostentation.'

Where the palace of Charles V had invoked the twin principles of the circle and the square, the Escorial imposed a grid, a rectilinear absolute, upon the world. Its architects, first Juan Bautista de Toledo and after his death, his assistant, Juan de Herrara, working under the critical gaze of his royal master, achieved a monument without many precedents and certainly no imitators.[10] The Escorial was dedicated to St Lawrence, on whose day, 10 August, Philip had won his only military victory,[11] at St Quentin in 1557: the palace-monastery was his thank-offering for the victory. The instrument of St Lawrence's martyrdom was an iron grid, heated to the point of incandescence, and it neatly provided the inspiration for a succession of sixteen courtyards, buildings within the building,[12] all aligned on the central axis of the Church of St Lawrence of the Victory, with its dome soaring three hundred feet above the sanctuary of the church below. The high altar was the heart and focus of the entire building, rising to fill the whole wall – some eighty-six feet in height, of multicoloured marbles, with paintings, entablatures and bronze statues ... On either side of the altar, in perpetual worship, were the royal Habsburgs, on one side Charles V, his wife and daughters, on the other Philip II and three of his wives, and the ill-fated Don Carlos, his eldest son. Beneath these life-size kneeling bronzes was the sepulchre.[13] 'At the very bottom of the foundation, under the great altar,' wrote Fray Francisco de los Santos, visiting the church in 1650, 'was constructed a spacious church of circular form.' Here were placed the coffins of the Habsburg ancestors,[14] the first of more than 6,000 holy relics that were brought to the Escorial, making it, by its accumulation, the greatest shrine in Christendom.

Philip's contemporaries tried to find an analogy or a model for El Escorial. His amanuensis and librarian, Padre Luis de Sigüenza was convinced that it was Solomon's Temple rebuilt:

Here, as in Noah's ark, many souls will be saved ... Here as in the tabernaculum of Moses, God is present ... Here as in the other Temple of Solomon which ... Philip II was imitating ... the divine psalms are sung day and night, sacrifice is continuously offered, incense always burns and the flame is never extinguished ... before the divine presence, and below the altars rest the ashes and bones of those who were sacrificed for Christ.[15]

Whether any such plan existed outside the vivid imagination of the Habsburg genealogists we can only guess, but Philip plainly regarded the Escorial as the heart not only of the Spanish empire but of the Christian world. All the Roman imagery which had been evoked for Charles V was redoubled for his son: Philip adopted the Sun Chariot of Apollo for his emblem and the motto, *Iam illustrabit omnia* (Now he will illuminate everything), where the Divine Light and Philip's own radiance were inextricably enmeshed. Another contemporary, the Venetian Girolomo Ruscelli, wrote of the Spanish king in his *Le impresse ilustri* in 1566,

The King intends to ... illuminate this shadowy world with the holy light of God; this is communicated by the motto ... In order that the King ... may illuminate every heresy with his splendid light, God has imbued his mind with the sun's rays ... and inspired this emblem which is an oracle or prophecy that the whole world will soon be illumined with divine light through the universal conversion of the infidel to the true Catholic Faith.[16]

The power of the Escorial was amplified by the cumulative sanctity of its relics. By his last years, Philip had secured pieces of the True Cross and one of its nails, a hair from Christ's beard, a thorn from the Crown of Thorns, and part of the handkerchief used by the Virgin Mary at the foot of the Cross and still stained with her tears. Whole bodies and 103 heads were shipped to the Escorial, including St Maurice, whose martyrdom El Greco had painted for the king. Among the heads was that of St Jerome, described in the inventory as 'a healthy, mature and solemn head' that Philip had rescued from the iconoclasts in Cologne. Most of the smaller relics, each of them in a jewelled or decorated reliquary, were kept in a locked chamber behind the High Altar. Once the great presses were opened rows of relics were visible, ranged along the shelves, each sacred object in a casket in the shape of a head, in gold, enamel, and precious metals.[17] The king would frequently visit this collection, sometimes with his children. Padre Sigüenza described how Philip would ask to be shown a particular treasure: 'He would ask me to show him such and such a relic. When I took it in my hands, before I could wrap it in silk or linen, the very pious king would genuflect, taking off his hat or cap, and kiss it in his very hands . . . His children would imitate him. This happened to us alone and in secret in the room.'

In later royal palaces, the alignment was upon the life and daily itinerary of the monarch: in the Escorial, the monarch stood to one side, to the greater glory of God.[18] The building and all its contents were designed as an engine of faith, a weapon against heresy, corruption and disbelief. All its elements were, in Philip's eyes, part of a composite whole. It was 'the eternal home of the kings of Spain, the eighth wonder of the world'.[19] The building work began on 23 April 1563, with the prior of a new monastic order laying the first stone in the presence of the king, and took twenty-one years to complete. The culmination was the consecration of the church on 9 August 1584, on the Eve of St Lawrence. Philip's own rooms were completed in the first few years and he spent more and more time there after the late 1570s, especially during Holy Week and other great festivals of the Church. The whole complex of the royal apartments occupied about one-third of the whole building, but Philip's own rooms took up little more than ninety square yards, three near-monastic cells, with whitewashed walls above blue tiles from Talavera and terracotta floors that made the rooms cool in the summer. From his simple bed Philip could look down into the Church; as Sigüenza described it: 'The alcove where he slept was filled on both sides with small images of saints so that no matter which way he turned in bed he received consolation in beholding such excellent company.' He did not impose this austerity on others: his daughter Isabella's rooms close by were much more comfortable and regally decorated.

One of the Venetian ambassadors to the court of Spain, Paolo Tiepolo, wisely wrote to the Doge and Senate in 1563, 'One can never be sure . . . about the inner natures and impulses of other men. With the passage of time, their personalities change, they develop new habits and they come to hate what they once delighted in.'[20] Philip was no exception. If he did not, as a young man, like to drink and carouse like his Austrian cousins, he enjoyed the other lusts of the flesh. He had his passions apart from religion. He had a true connoisseur's eye in art and sculpture, and a taste for reading, although, speaking only Spanish and poor Latin, he was excluded from much of the material in his library. Tiepolo portrayed Philip as 'slight of stature and round faced, with very pale blue eyes, somewhat prominent lips and pink skin, but his overall appearance is very attractive'. In private, he had a wry sense of humour quite unlike the famed 'Spanish composure' he was required to maintain in public.

As he grew older and suffered the death of those close to him, disasters in war and politics, and the creeping fear of advancing Protestant heresy, his attitudes and expression grew harsher. Like his father and grandfather, his health was poor. Tiepolo's predecessor, Michele Suriano, noted that: 'His Majesty's health is very delicate, and so he regulates his life carefully. He usually eats very nourishing food, and avoids fish, fruit and other things that give rise to evil humours. He sleeps a lot and takes little exercise and his amusements are all tranquil ones.' Work, if not a passion, was a necessity, given that he was determined not to concede control in any area to his subordinates or advisers. His father's advice had been: 'Trust no one, listen to everyone, decide alone.' In his later years 'The Escorial' came to represent Philip's system of government, a court and government detached from the traditions of urban and civic life, a place of work and worship. The structure developed quite slowly but was there in embryo from his early years on the Spanish throne.

The Escorial had a central complex at its heart – the cathedral, the seminary-monastery and the library. In Philip's eyes these functions were not to be distinguished. The edifice glorified God but also the house of Habsburg. He evolved slowly towards a system of government that transformed the monarch from a ceaseless, restless mobility to a static and sedentary state. For the last twenty years of his life, if not before, he spent more and more time at the Escorial while his ministers and officials remained in Madrid, and he told his son in the last year of his life[21] that for a monarch travel was pointless, and he would do well to remain a fixed and meridional point within his kingdoms. This change in style had many manifestations. Where once, with Maximilian and Charles, there had been many folk-tales of some peasant unknowingly meeting his monarch on a journey and telling him some home truths, there are no such narratives of Philip. He was often strongly criticized for his desire for isolation. His almoner told him: 'God did not give kings authority over men so that they could withdraw to their study to read and write, nor even to meditate and tell their rosaries, mainly so that Your Majesty can have a better excuse for getting away from people.'[22] He began the process of separating the ruler from the people, creating a sanctuary, a sacred space within which he functioned like an archbishop within the core of his cathedral.

At the Escorial, the sacred space embodied a cathedral within its walls – indeed the whole complex of buildings was centred upon the church, into which Philip could look from his own rooms, as his father had done at Yuste. But he created another space, not sacred precisely, but dedicated to the divinely ordained business of government. The paper produced by Philip's style of rule was prodigious, and in its bundles, files and folders was a bureaucratic and administrative system that became a model for later members of Philip's lineage. He ordered that the castle of Simancas in Castile should become the central archive for the papers of state, and further decreed that the provincial chancelleries, such as at Granada, should be developed and improved.[23]

In all this it is easy to lose sight of Philip as an individual, to make him either a desiccated bureaucrat made of paper (rather in the manner of Giuseppe Archimboldo's 'puzzle portrait' of the Austrian imperial librarian, Wolfgang Lazius, who was composed entirely of papers and books) or the monster of the Black Legend created by those who opposed his rule, notably the Dutch who rebelled against Spanish dominion.[24] His letters to daughters Catalina and Isabella reveal a man with a deep love for his children, with an ease and delight in the minutiae of their lives that is the reverse of *gravitas*. He rejoiced at their birth and sorrowed at the too-frequent deaths in infancy. Outwardly, he would put it down to God's will, but inwardly, he suffered. When Catalina, by then duchess of Savoy, died in 1597, he broke down completely, as his father had done after he watched his wife Isabella die.[25] Philip's daughter, Isabella, who stayed with him until his death, was the sole remaining comfort of his life.

Philip approached government with the same sense of method that he followed in his religious observances: system was all. A series of fourteen councils and committees advised the king, but all decisions were taken by Philip personally: there was no delegation of authority. Communication was mainly in writing rather than orally: minutes were submitted to Philip who read them and annotated them with his instructions for further action. In time the pressure of business (one council which had produced only three bundles of papers per year in the 1560s was generating over thirty by the 1590s)[26] meant that experienced ministers and secretaries undertook more routine administration on their own account, but only with the direct and formal approval of the king. Sometimes Philip would read and approve several hundred documents in a single day, and his memory, although prodigious, could prove fallible. The problems of exercising central control on territories so widely spread and various could not be resolved, but Philip compounded his father's tendency to undertake policies beyond his strength and purse. It is perhaps a negative tribute to the strength of the system he created that it did not collapse entirely under the pressures to which he subjected it.

Philip waged war constantly,[27] and it brought his state to bankruptcy and near-catastrophe on numerous occasions. But for the most part these were not wars of aggrandizement but of defence, a counter-offensive against those forces that sought to challenge and destroy his inheritance. He conceived that inheritance in religious terms, and his wars as crusades. He carried the Cross against the Ottomans in the Mediterranean, against Protestant heresy in the Netherlands, against lapses back into Islam by the Moriscos (Muslims forcibly converted to Christianity) in Granada, against paganism and unbelief in the New World. His implacable determination to achieve his objectives whatever the cost in fact brought him some success.

The internal war in Granada has been largely forgotten, or overshadowed by the conflict with the Dutch or with the Turks. In Granada, there was no victory like Lepanto which saved

Christendom from the Turk and which could be celebrated with *Te Deums* sung in rejoicing throughout his realms. It did not even have the merit of the seemingly endless conflict in the Netherlands, which at least was fought over the richest province of his empire, and against the plague of heresy. Granada had been at peace since 1501, when its people had first risen against their new Christian overlords. In theory, the Moorish population was thereafter required to abandon Arabic, to change their distinctive style of dress and customs, and adopt the practices of the dominant Castilian culture.[28] But a succession of royal captains-general, with the agreement of Charles V after his stay in Granada in 1526, had tempered the rigour of the regulations, to the extent that they became virtually a dead letter. Philip, therefore, faced a population, nominally Christian but in every other way Islamic, controlling the southern access to Spain at a time when Turkish power was rising to a peak in the Mediterranean.

The archives of the captain-general in Granada reveal the extent of contact which the Moriscos of Granada maintained with their co-religionists in North Africa,[29] and they also show that the Ottomans had both spies and small detachments of troops in the mountains of the province. Against this evidence was the advice of the military authorities in the province that the threat was more imaginary than real, and that a harsher policy towards the Moriscos would push them unnecessarily into revolt. But in November 1566 Philip signed a decree enforcing all the old ordinances that was to come into effect on 1 January 1567, and for almost a year the Moriscos experienced the full rigour of Christian militancy. On Christmas Day 1568 the long-expected revolt broke out.

From all over the kingdom came reports of Moriscos taking up arms. At the village of Cadiar, a knight of the order of Santiago travelling with fifty armed men had been ambushed and all were killed. The news reached Granada early on Christmas morning, and patrols in the city were redoubled. In the churches, the celebrations were tinged by fear as the rumours of a general rising spread from congregation to congregation. On the night of the day after Christmas, the Feast of St Stephen, it was bitterly cold and snowing heavily; the soldiers, now discounting the rumours of an uprising, stayed in their barracks. Although the city wall was well built, there was one point where an old entry point had been blocked with a simple mud wall. Here about 800 armed men from the surrounding villages and the mountains silently assembled, and quickly opened the blocked gate. Their leader, Aben Farax, told the elders of the communities in the city that the people of the Alpujarras, the core of Morisco resistance, were in open revolt and he called upon them to seize the city. They scornfully told him that they had expected an army of 8,000, not a frozen band of 800 renegades, and refused him their help and the support of the Moriscos in the city. Aben Farax led his men through the city, attacking a church, and ransacking the shop of an unpopular apothecary. Then he drew his men up around the gate to the Alcazaba, and summoned all good Muslims to join him. None came, and he left with his men through the hole in the wall by which they had entered.

From this point onward, the revolt was doomed, although it required two years of the most savage fighting finally to crush the last vestiges of resistance. Sir William Stirling Maxwell, writing of the Alpujarra mountains, the heartland of the Moriscos to the south-east of the city of Granada, in his life of Don John of Austria, explained why. Don John, who was placed in command of the royal army after the local commanders failed to suppress the revolt, faced a considerable task.

The country was admirably suited for that petty warfare for which Spain has always been famous. The greater valleys are for the most part of their length extremely narrow, and bounded by precipitous hills, and they branched into glens so numerous and intricate, and so like each other in character, that it was a hopeless task for a stranger to pilot his course through their endless ramifications. Even those parts of the country which seem comparatively open prove on closer inspection to be furrowed with hidden ravines ... The winding tracks which traversed the country at every turn were commanded by some beetling brow or tuft or brushwood, from whence a musket or a crossbow could securely dispose of an approaching foe.

In each village the people took their vengeance on the Christian authorities who lived among them. The first thing to be destroyed was the church, the symbol of their oppression. Then they killed the priests and the mayor.

The Christian Alguazil and the village curate ... became victims of tortures like those inflicted in the dungeons of the Inquisition. Their feet and legs were roasted over fires of charcoal; tied by their wrist to the top of towers, they were let fall time after time on the pavement below until their lower limbs were beaten to a jelly; their eyes and tongues were torn out; their ears and noses cut off; their joints were hacked asunder, from their extremities upwards; their mouths were filled with gunpowder which was then ignited; their heads were beaten to pieces with hatchets; and their mangled carcasses were sometimes sewed up in the carcasses of swine and burned, sometimes exposed on the hillside to feed the fox and the wolf. More than one Morisco, fiercer than his fellows, tore out and devoured the quivering heart of the enemy.[30]

When the Christian troops discovered the remains of these atrocities, they repaid in kind, and with interest. There was no more savage war in the course of the century, and had the Ottomans provided more aid to the rebels the chances of success were high. Failing that support, the rebels were doomed. The last Moriscos defended their homes and villages until they were driven out by a 'scorched-earth' policy adopted by the Spaniards as they moved relentlessly from village to village. Many fled across the sea to Africa, providing a focus of hatred for Spain that the Ottomans used to good effect.[31] In the end Granada was purged[32] and Philip rejoiced that he had at last completed the work begun by his great-grandparents, Ferdinand and Isabella.

Philip's solution to his defeated subjects was draconi n. He was implacably determined to remove – by death or deportation – all those of Moorish extraction from Granada.[33] Between 80,000 and 100,000 were deported from the cities and towns of the kingdom to be distributed to Christian towns in Castile and Aragon. In his victory, however, he had a higher goal. His ultimate aim was to win the souls of the Moriscos for Christ. In their new enclaves, surrounded by Christians, the displaced Moriscos were to be converted. This work began immediately, if slowly, but the king pursued the policy of winning the Moriscos for Christ with a steady consistency. In 1596 the province of Valencia, which had a large number of Moriscos, both native to the province and those expelled from Granada, was finally given a Committee for the Religious Instruction of the Valencian Moriscos, which was to engage in the sustained work of conversion, with a team of Arabic-speaking missionaries, 'led by a friar experienced in the conversion of the Indians'.[34] This was a lesson not lost on the Dutch, also in rebellion against Philip's rule. Roughly at the same time that the Morisco issue was coming to a head, Philip was sending his renowned infantry, the *tercios*, under his most accomplished commander the Duke of Alva, to bring the Dutch to heel.

When Philip had first visited the Netherlands as Charles's heir a decade before, he had felt no affinity for this, the heart of his inheritance, at least in terms of money. Speaking no Flemish or French he had seemed a foreigner to all the inhabitants of the Netherlands. When he returned to Spain, he left behind him Spanish troops, whose unpopularity quickly united the disparate peoples of his domain. Some also (rightly) suspected that he eventually intended to introduce the Inquisition into the north, making it as powerful as it was in his southern kingdom. Philip was appalled by the spread of Protestantism that he had observed in the Netherlands, which he equated, not without reason, with political treason. The Netherlands had always been suspicious of a strong central authority: Charles had dealt gently with them through the persons of his aunt and sister; Philip treated them as he would Spaniards. His approach was invariably harsh. 'In matters of religion do not temporize, but punish with the utmost rigour and severity,' Philip wrote to Cardinal Granvelle, who was his representative in the north.[35]

Both politics and religion dictated the nature of opposition to Philip; the same cities that had opposed his great-grandfather Maximilian now came out against him; while the lords who had supported his father now resisted him. The young Prince of Orange, on whom Charles had leaned during his abdication speech, was to be found at the heart of the noble opposition to Philip's political and religious innovations. In December 1565 Philip dashed any hope of compromise with the people of the Netherlands by issuing new and harsher instructions to his governors, ordering them not to be more accommodating to the people, as the leading Netherlanders had hoped, but to behave more harshly. In Prescott's rolling phrases,

Whatever doubts had been entertained were dispelled by these last dispatches, which came like a hurricane, sweeping away the mists that had so long blinded the eyes of men, and laying open the policy of the crown, clear as day to the dullest apprehension. The people passed to the extremity of despair. The Spanish Inquisition, with its trail of horrors, seemed to be already in the midst of them. They called to mind all the tales of woe they heard of it. They recounted the atrocities perpetrated by the Spaniards in the New World, which, however, erroneously, they charged upon the Holy Office. 'Do they expect', they cried, 'that we shall wait tamely here, like wretched Indians, to be slaughtered by millions.' Men were seen gathering in knots, in the streets and public squares, discussing the conduct of the government, and gloomily talking of secret associations and foreign alliances.

Within a year, public revulsion had forced the king to retreat, and relax his decrees. The near-immediate consequence, so it seemed, was a frenzy of iconoclasm. The great cathedral of Antwerp was sacked, and all the relics, paintings and stained glass were destroyed.[36]

A considerable number of the reformed party entered the building and were allowed to remain when the congregation had withdrawn . . . Left in possession, they burst into one of the Psalms of David. The sound of their own voices seemed to rouse them to fury. Before the chant had died away, they . . . broke open the doors of the chapel and dragged forth the image of the Virgin . . . Others tore off her embroidered robes and rolled the dumb idol in the dust, amidst the shouts of the spectators.

This was the signal for havoc . . . The rioters dispersed in all directions on their work of destruction. Nothing escaped their rage. High above the great altar was an image of the Saviour, curiously carved in wood, and placed between the effigies of the two thieves crucified with him. The mob contrived to get a rope around the neck of the statue of Christ and dragged it to the ground. Then they fell upon it with hatchets and hammers, and it was soon broken into a hundred fragments. The two thieves were spared, as if to preside over the work of rapine below.[37]

Everything else was destroyed. Priceless works of art were hacked to pieces and more than seventy altars stripped and plundered. The sacramental wafers were trodden under foot; the rioters drank the consecrated wine out of golden chalices, and rubbed the holy oil into their shoes or feet. Every image, all the carved or decorated woodwork, every stone curlicue, was hacked or smashed to pieces. Within hours, the floor of the church, almost the same size as St Peter's in Rome, was littered with decapitated marble and stone statues, tapestries and altar cloths that had been used for obscene purposes.

On that first day of destruction, the only part of the cathedral that was spared was the chapel of the Golden Fleece, with the banners and escutcheons of the knights left intact. After three days spent ravaging all the churches and chapels of the city and the vicinity, the rioters decided to return to complete their work. As they began the work of destruction, tearing the banners from the walls and hacking at the heraldic shields, while smashing the elaborately carved stalls, a small party of knights of the Golden Fleece entered the cathedral, in armour, with swords and spears and followed by a small band of their retainers. Although massively outnumbered, they pushed through the mob into the chapel. There they warned the rioters to leave the chapel in peace. They were ignored, and the work of destruction continued. Incredulous that the low-born mob should ignore them, the knights dragged the ringleader from the stalls down on to the floor. He pleaded for mercy, but infuriated they stabbed him through the throat, and then hacked at his body. As the crowd thinned in terror, the knights saw the destruction that had already taken place in their private sanctum, and burning with rage slaughtered one or two more of those rioters to hand. Then seizing another dozen or so close by, they took them outside and lynched them, taunting them as they died, all the while slashing at them with their swords and spears.

For Philip, the obscenity of the iconoclasm was exceeded only by their treatment of the Host. On the first day they had ground it underfoot; later they became more inventive.

The deeds of violence perpetrated by the iconoclasts were accompanied by such indignities as might express their contempt for the ancient faith.

They snatched the wafer, says an eyewitness, from the altar and put it into the mouth of a parrot. Some gathered the images of the saints together and set them on fire, or covered them with bits of armour, and tilted rudely against them. Some put on the vestments stolen from the churches and ran about the streets with them in mockery. Some basted the books with butter, that they might burn more easily ... It answered their purpose to judge by the number of volumes consumed.[38]

Faced with the prospect of social and religious chaos, the Knights of the Golden Fleece and other leaders of the Netherlands advised caution. The Count of Egmont told the regent, Philip's sister, Margaret of Parma, 'First let us provide for the security of the state. It will be time enough then to think of religion.' Margaret spoke as a true Habsburg, 'No, the service of God demands our first care; for the ruin of religion would be a greater evil than the loss of the country.'[39] To her brother, she denounced the disloyalty of those like Egmont and Hoorn, who had advised her to treat with the rebels. When Philip heard of the desecration, he said, in 'the most violent fit of anger, some said tearing at his beard in rage and frustration, "It shall cost them dear; by the soul of my father, I swear it, it shall cost them dear."' If this outburst took place – as seems plausible even though some denied it happened at all – Philip soon reassumed his habitual icy reserve.

His determination to come to a reckoning with the rebels was implacable. He wrote to the Pope in August 1566 that he would try to do so without taking up arms; in any event he would go himself to bring them to heel. But, he warned, 'neither danger [to myself] nor ruin of these states, nor of all the others that are left to me will prevent me from doing what a Christian prince fearing God ought to do in his service [and for] the preservation of the Catholic faith and the honour of the apostolic see.'[40] Circumstances prevented his coming in person to put down the rebellion, but the Duke of Alva, who marched up the long 'Spanish Road' from Italy to the Netherlands in 1567, with, like Xenophon, his *ten thousand*, gave him the instrument of his revenge. Alva was urged on by Philip, even to executing his fellow knights of the Golden Fleece, Egmont and Hoorn, whom he was sworn to accuse only before a chapter of the order. Philip harried him and demanded their deaths. The new captain-general of the Netherlands had the power to enforce an iron rule that Margaret of Parma had never possessed. On Ash Wednesday, 1568, he arrested 500 citizens, who were quickly tried and executed. 'Five hundred were taken . . . I have sent them all to their just deserts.'[41] Deliberately, he humiliated the natural leaders of the Netherlands who had strayed from loyalty or orthodoxy. 'It was common, says an old chronicler, to see thirty or forty persons arrested at once. The wealthier burghers might be seen with their arms pinioned behind them, dragged at a horse's tail to the place of execution.'[42] The ordinary folk were simply hanged without the formality of a trial. The tribunal 'of Blood' proceeded according to set policies. 'Persons of Condition' were beheaded, others hanged, gibbeted or broken on the wheel. Routinely, those who had been involved in the iconoclasm were burned alive.

There were some protests. The Emperor Maximilian II, who had succeeded his father Ferdinand four years before, wrote to his cousin in March 1568, before the great spate of executions, suggesting that a milder policy might be more suitable and in accordance with tradition. Philip rebuffed him, replying that what he was doing

has been for the repose of the provinces, and for the defence of the Catholic faith. If I had respected justice less, I should have dispatched the whole business in a single day. No one acquainted with the state of affairs will find reason to censure my severity. Nor would I do otherwise than I have done, though I should risk the sovereignty of the Netherlands, not though the world should fall in ruins around me.[43]

The executions of Counts Egmont and Hoorn were the clearest sign of this implacable will. Philip wanted their deaths, and instructed Alva to accept no opposition. He provided a letter suspending their right of appeal to the knights of the Golden Fleece, which was widely held to be illegal. On the day of his execution, Egmont dressed in a crimson damask robe over which he wore a black Spanish mantle fringed with gold, black silk breeches and a black hat, with black and white plumes. From his prison, the Maison du Roi, overlooking the market-place of Brussels, he had watched the scaffold being covered with a black cloth. On it stood a small table, also shrouded with a black cloth, on top of which rested a silver crucifix and in front of it two crimson cushions, on which the victims would kneel. After the deed was done, the executioner would bear the severed heads ceremoniously to the corners of the platform where there were two pointed stakes, with steel tips, like crude lances, to receive them.

Egmont received absolution, and knelt on the cushion, then removed his robe and mantle, so that he was now clad all in black. From his pocket, he pulled a black silk cap with which he covered his eyes; behind him the executioner, specially selected for this great event, appeared, with his long heavy sword over his shoulder. The crowd fell silent. The executioner measured his distance, swung his sword and with practised ease took off the head with a single blow. The head 'leaped' from the body, and Egmont fell forward, while the executioner picked up the rolling head, and spiked it on the stake, so that it stared out sightlessly over the crowd. Then he turned and dragged the body to one side of the platform, where it was covered with a cloth.

It was afternoon before the second victim, Count Hoorn appeared, walking slowly through the thousands of soldiers guarding the ritual sacrifice. He was dressed more soberly than Egmont, in a plain black suit, with a 'Milanese cap' on his head. When he climbed on the scaffold he saw the bloodstained shroud and asked if that was the body of Egmont. He seems to have ignored the head on its pole, but he knelt and, within a few minutes, his head was spiked on the other pole. For three hours, the heads were left on display, and then the heads and the bodies were placed in lead coffins and taken to rest in local churches and then to the family estates for burial. The effect of these two executions was precisely what Philip had intended. He was glad, he told Alva that he was 'well pleased that the two lords had made so good and Catholic an end', but to the duke's regrets, he had none: 'No man may shrink from his duty.' The Netherlands were shocked and cowed, and perhaps one measure of the success of Alva's 'Council of Blood', was that tax revenue rose sixfold.[44] The work of God and the good of the king and his house thus came together.

The Dutch quickly saw the connections – and coherence – of Philip's plans. But they also witnessed the failure of those grand schemes. Later, in *A Vision of the Fall of Castile*,[45] they presented an elaborate allegory of the tower (Castle) of Castile (presciently!) battered by the Swedish ram, and at the same time undermined by the Moriscos of Granada, who were depicted as hares and rabbits; by the Turks, Moors and Portuguese rebels who appear as mice; and by the Dutch, as geese. The Habsburg eagles fly from the defeat of the Spanish armada. Arranged around this complex narrative image like a strip cartoon are much simpler examples of the universal wickedness of Spain. They begin with the execution of Egmont and Hoorn, then various murders in the Netherlands, burning Indians in the New World, Indians slaughtered and thrown in pits, burned alive, or eaten by dogs. Many of the images suggest a strong tinge of sexual sadism in the Spanish mentality: naked women, often pregnant, feature in many of the scenes of torture. The Inquisition is shown at its grisly work, then the capture of Lisbon in 1580, the war against the Moriscos, the murder of Don Carlos, and atrocities in Catalonia. The Spanish solution, it suggested, to every problem, had been torture and annihilation, for the Moriscos as much as for the people of the Netherlands. The parallel – and the Dutch perception of a Spanish 'grand plan' – is revealing. Various solutions to the Morisco problem (as to the issues of heresy in the Netherlands) had been proposed. At one point it was suggested that all the Moriscos be embarked on ships, which would then be taken to sea and sunk, thus drowning the entire nation. Another proposal from one Gómez Dávila suggested in 1598 that Philip emulate the French in the Massacre of St Bartholomew, and order that each community should kill the Moriscos in their midst. Others pointed to the Ottoman model and suggested that all the children should be taken and brought up as Christians, while all male Moriscos should be castrated to bring an end to the problem.[46]

In the end, in 1609, after Philip's death, a final but more humane solution was devised, and the entirety of the Morisco population was uprooted and moved to the ports, whence they were transhipped to the shore of North Africa, where they were left to fend for themselves.[47] The humanity of the decision was relative to the severity of the other solutions, but in Spanish eyes its attraction was that it radically excised the corruption inherent in the Moriscos from the land of Spain. Philip II's attitude to heresy and rebellion in the Netherlands was not very different: he was as determined to extirpate the Protestant contagion in the north as he was to remove the taint of Islam and Judaism from the land of Spain. In 1556, he had noted on his confirmation of a law banning all those of 'impure blood' from holding Church office in Castile, that 'all the heresies which have existed in Germany and France . . . have been sown by descendants of the Jews'.[48] Born in Spain, speaking only Spanish, not surprisingly he viewed the rest of the world through the distorting lens of Spain's experience. The consequences of this astigmatic viewpoint were profound.

∽   ∽   ∽

In old maps Spain stands at the extremity of Europe, and separated by the Pyrenees from the rest of the continent. The Iberian peninsula had over many centuries diverged from the paths followed by the rest of western Christendom. Uniquely, Spain and Portugal had experienced centuries of Islamic occupation, not border raiding but constant contact with a vibrant and active Muslim culture. Córdoba, the seat of the Spanish caliphate, and Seville were at one time larger than any of the Christian cities of Europe, and although the Islamic occupation had been slowly eroded in the centuries of reconquest, the frontiers, both political and social, had been permeable. There were many Muslims who adopted Christianity, known as *Mudejares*, and a number of Christians, including members of the royal family itself, who were rumoured to have Moorish – or Jewish – blood running in their veins. The Jews had for centuries coexisted, despite occasional persecution, with both Muslims and Christians in the peninsula. Many had also accepted Christianity and were called *Marranos* or *conversos*. In practice, if not in theory, all three cultures had mixed and interpenetrated.

The avowed aim of the Catholic Reconquest, accomplished by Ferdinand and Isabella, had been to capture the whole of the Spanish lands for Christianity. Their first act after the conquest of Granada in 1492 was to purge their kingdoms of all alien and non-Christian elements. On 30 March 1492, they decreed that all Jews must leave their kingdoms or convert to Christianity. Up to 150,000 left, many to the more benign lands of Italy or to the Ottoman empire, which welcomed their wealth and industrial skills. This concern for 'One nation, one faith' was not a novelty in Spanish society. In Toledo in 1449, after riots against the Jews of the city, the town council had decreed that no one of Jewish ancestry could ever hold public office in the city. Only those of 'pure and untainted blood' (*limpieza de sangre*) could be full citizens of the city.

Pure blood became a Spanish obsession. All the nations of western Europe had regarded Jews as little better than animals, and the horrors inflicted upon the Jewish communities of Germany and Austria are among the most sordid annals of an age that took public pleasure in such cruelty.[49] Christians both feared and despised the Jews, so obviously an alien race, and, the church proclaimed them collectively the murderers of Christ. But they were also imbued with mystical and magic powers. Fear and hatred combined to create fantasies of Jewish ritual murder and atrocity, in which innocent children would be kidnapped, tortured, bled white and killed. A noted Catholic scholar, Johannes Eck, a doughty opponent of Luther, wrote a pamphlet cataloguing the terrifying practices of Jews.

'Blood is central to Jewish magic ... Its very nature is demonic: Jews need Christian blood to anoint their rabbis; Jewish babies are born with two tiny fingers attached to the skin of their forehead (the very image of the devil himself), and without Christian blood it is very difficult to remove these fingers without harming the child; above all Jews need Christian blood to wash away the blood stain inflicted on them by God because they had crucified Christ. 'It is no wonder [Eck concludes] that the Jews now buy the blood of innocent children, just as their fathers had bought the innocent blood of Christ from Judas with thirty pennies.'[50]

The mystic power and force of blood was recognized by many societies, and in medieval Europe it was regarded as the essence of life. Illnesses were ascribed to bad or corrupted blood, and the removal of excess or dead blood by leeches and cupping was a standard medical procedure.

Blood was recognized as one of the most potent of all magical forces; blood's power for evil was held almost as great as its power for good. Just the right blood, properly used, could bring strength and good fortune, the wrong blood – or blood improperly used – could bring disaster. So almost from the outset of man's attempt to influence his environment, there arose the laws of forbidden blood – the deep-rooted complex of blood taboos.[51]

Blood was the essence of life, and if blood escaped from the body, it could both corrupt and be corrupted. Menstrual blood or the blood of childbirth was especially malevolent. Powerful charms were used to staunch the flow:

> Blood, stay in yourself, just as Christ is in himself
> Blood, stay in your veins, just as Christ is in his pain
> Blood, stay fixed, just as Christ was to his crucifix.[52]

The Church had declared that the body and blood of Christ were not merely symbolized by the wafer and wine of the Eucharist. They truly and physically became the corporal body and the real blood of Christ. Jews were then accused of stealing the Host and then torturing (for the second time) the actual body of Christ. The iconoclasts in the Netherlands had also been guilty of the same unpardonable offence. Some of the most popular shrines and festivals in late medieval and early modern Europe were those that reverenced the blood of Christ and of the saints. Devotees worshipped the anguished figures on the Cross, contemplated the agony of St Sebastian, pierced with arrows, celebrated the Transfiguration of Christ, imagined Christ's wounds, and in some cases, worshippers actually experienced (by the power of auto-suggestion) the bleeding stigmata on their hands and feet. Spain was a fertile ground for these sanguinary cults. In Spain, Jews were not so much the takers of Christian blood but the givers of corrupt blood, through sexual congress and the birth of children of mixed marriages who were 'infected' with this hereditary taint or stain. That is, the belief in the corruption and danger of the Jews was no different in Spain from that held elsewhere in western Europe; but because Jews had become more integrated into Spanish society, they could use the power of sex to inveigle Christians into contaminating themselves. This was the Spanish terror, of the enemy in their midst, of an outwardly conforming Christian, who nevertheless carried bad blood in his (or more often her) veins.

What was true of the Marranos was also true of the Moriscos,

1. The imagined Maximilian I in 1518 as the embodiment of
knightly virtue, by Rubens

CLEOPHAS · FRATER · CARNALIS · IO=
SEPHI · MARITI · DIVAE · VIRG · MARIE

IACOBVS · MINOR · EPVS · MARIA · CLEOPHÆ · SOROR
HIEROSOLIMITANVS · VIRG · MAR · PVTATIVA · MA
TERTERA · D · N

IOSEPH · IVSTVS · SIMON · ZELOTES · COBSO
BRINVS · DNI · NRI ·

2. The family of Maximilian I (1459–1519): an imaginary portrait by
Bernhard Striegel. There is another copy in Spain, by a lesser artist.
Two of those portrayed were already dead and the artist had only ever
seen two of the other subjects

3. Philip II (1527–98), with the emblem of the Golden Fleece and holding his rosary, by Sofonisba Anguiscola

4. The Emperor Rudolf II in 1593, by Lucas van Valckenborch

5. Charles VI, wearing the mantle of the Grand Master of the Golden
Fleece, points to his several crowns, *c*.1730, by Johann-Gottfried Auerbach

6. (*Above*) A family Christmas with Maria Theresa and Francis Stephen, painted by their daughter, the Archduchess Maria Christina

7. (*Left*) Archduchess as artist. All Maria Theresa's children had to learn a practical skill. Maria Christina became an accomplished artist. Self-portrait in her own room at Schönbrunn, 1776

8. The Empress Maria Theresa (1717–80), by Martin van Meytens the Younger

9. The family of Leopold II (1747–92), like the image at the top of the
painting a fountain of fecundity, by Johann Zoffany

10. The return of Emperor Francis I of Austria from the Diet at Pressburg, being greeted by the ecstatic people of Vienna. One of a series of murals by Johann Peter Krafft (1780–1856)

11. Emperor Ferdinand I of Austria, Apostolic King of Hungary and the last crowned King of Bohemia (1793–1875), by Friedrich von Amerling

12. (*Left*) Emperor Franz Joseph I of Austria (1830–1916), by Francis Xavier Winterhalter

13. (*Bottom left*) Franz Joseph's favourite portrait of his wife, the Empress Elisabeth: Winterhalter at his most romantic

14. (*Bottom right*) Katharina Schratt, the intimate friend of Emperor Franz Joseph I. She bears a striking resemblance to the Empress Elisabeth when young. By an anonymous artist, 1880

15. Maria Luisa de Bourbon (d. 1792), the wife of Emperor
Leopold II, and the mother of sixteen children

16. Emperor Francis I at his desk, 1806

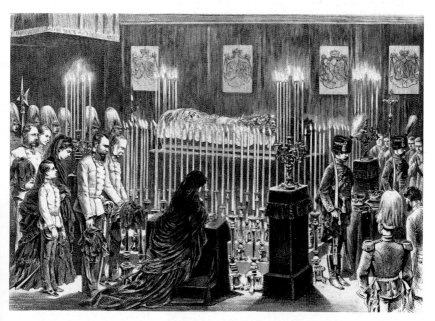

17. The traditional exequies for Archduchess Sophie, mother of Emperor Franz
Joseph I, in 1872 in the Hofburg Chapel, Vienna

18. Crown Prince Rudolf
with his wife and daughter,
1888

19. Archduke Franz
Ferdinand, heir presumptive
to the throne of Austria, and
his wife, the Duchess of
Hohenberg, in 1914

20. Emperor Franz Joseph I in hunting clothes, 1908

21. Karl I of Austria, his wife Zita and their children in
exile at the Château de Hertenstein, Switzerland, *c.*1922

22. Dr Otto von Habsburg with his family in 1966,
on the balcony of their house at Pöcking

who were also 'New Christians'. There were many accusations of Moorish blood entering and corrupting Christian stock. The book *La Tizón de la Nobleza*, issued by Cardinal Francisco Mendoza y Bobadilla in 1560, claimed to expose those noble families in Castile that had contaminated blood, by either a Jewish or a Moorish taint. The Mendozas, he proudly asserted, were one of the few families without any such a stain on their escutcheon. A similar title published in Aragón, the *Libro Verde*, was banned by Charles V and later by Philip II (it asserted that their Trastámara ancestors were doubly corrupt, having married Moors and consorted with Jews); but it circulated in secret. Every Marrano or Morisco was suspect; Morisca midwives or wet nurses were thought to represent one way, other than by sexual union, by which Christian blood could be corrupted, especially since milk was believed to be of the same essential substance as blood.[53] Philip's decision to distribute the Granadine Moriscos throughout Spain meant that sources of possible contagion, even if nominally Christianized – which few believed – were broadcast through all the Christian communities. The only weapon against so mortal a danger was the Holy Inquisition, which waged a ceaseless war against the forces that undermined Christian faith.

Those forces – impure blood, or Protestant heresy – gradually elided, conceptually speaking, as the century proceeded. The laws of *limpieza de sangre*[54] covered all the Spanish dominions, and prohibited those of tainted blood from holding any office, position or title. In time, the taint included Moorish or Jewish blood, condemnation for heresy, or even being the subject of a prosecution by the Inquisition for a lesser offence. It has been calculated that probably about 35,000 cases of religious deviation came before the Inquisition during Philip's reign[55] and almost no family was secure against their investigations. The effects on Spanish society were omnipresent. The leading authority on the statutes of *limpieza de sangre* has written that

Spain's obsession with blood purity in the sixteenth and seventeenth century led to considerable social turmoil. As the generations passed and memory of the conversos faded, efforts were redoubled to unearth the traces of long forgotten 'impure forefathers . . .' Communities used to vie with each other in the security of their pure blood statutes. The old college of Saint Bartolemew in Salamanca, the source of Spain's most important leaders, took pride in refusing admittance to anyone even rumoured to be of Jewish descent. Hearsay evidence and words spoken in anger to the effect that someone was a Jew or a descendant of Jews, sufficed to disqualify a man, a kind of 'civil death' understandably feared by Spaniards. As investigation into ancestors ranged ever further back into the distant past, until 'time immemorial' as some put it, even families considered Old Christian lived in constant fear lest some long forgotten 'stain' be brought to light or a hostile rumourmonger destroyed a reputation.[56]

In this case Jew, Marrano or *converso* can be taken to include Morisco or heretic. It was not until 1865 that the final distinctions between Old and New Christians were finally abolished – although to gain some kind of perspective, the civil disabilities of Roman Catholics in England were only ended in 1829, and the universities of Oxford and Cambridge stood out even longer.

Spaniards became experts on racial distinction, as a consequence of this preoccupation with pure blood. In Spain a poor man of 'untainted' blood was the superior of the greatest noble,[57] even the king himself, who had even the tiniest alien corpuscle. Sancho Panza, in Cervantes's picaresque novel *Don Quijote*, boasted that he was 'free from any admixture of Jew or Moor' and hence the inferior of no man.[58] Across the Atlantic, the Spanish created a vocabulary of racial distinction, with *bozales, ladinos, lobos, limpios, mestizos, pardos* – no less than eighty-two terms which described the precise degree and type of ethnic mixture.[59] Some of this same terminology entered English, providing the structure of racial specification for the slave south of the United States of America – with the *quadroons, octoroons, maroons* and the like.

∽   ∽   ∽

It was in this Spain, under Philip II and his successors, that the male children of the house of Austria were brought up. Maximilian II, Ferdinand's son and heir, and all of Maximilian's four sons grew to maturity at the Spanish court, while the daughters of Philip II and his son Philip III made the journey north from Spain to marry their Austrian cousins. The increasingly diffuse family was not always harmonious – Ferdinand's grandsons were notoriously at loggerheads – and the political interests of Vienna and Madrid often diverged. But self-interest dictated that an ever closer union was desirable. The impact of this Spanish fixation with blood and race on the Habsburgs remains conjectural. But their marriage patterns in the century and a half of the 'Madrid–Vienna axis' are unique in the history of western Europe. 'Happy Austria marries'; and it is a matter of record that the Habsburgs had gained their patchwork of lands by marriage alliances and inheritance rather than by war. This focus on marriage and alliance underestimates the intense military activity undertaken, especially in Italy to sustain and consolidate their holdings. It also, wrongly, suggests that other families did not use marriage in the same way to cement or consolidate political alliances. But what distinguished the Habsburgs' marriage strategy, especially after the death of Charles V, was its inventiveness and capacity to adapt to new circumstances. No other royal house had developed so coherent a notion of 'the power of the blood'.

Since the late nineteenth century, the marriages of the Habsburgs in the period from 1550 to 1700 have been considered a genetic disaster, with cousins and even closer relatives marrying and then replicating the same incestuous patterns generation after generation. But as the anthropologist William Rivers wisely observed more than eighty years ago,[60] 'the nature of systems of relationship depends on forms of social structure rather than on differences of race'. The Habsburgs were accustomed to thinking of themselves as a group above and beyond the rules which applied to others; their unusual and distinctive marriage patterns are further evidence of this special election. Thus, to marry 'in', conserving the blood, was good; to marry 'out' could lead to disaster,[61] both economic and political.

The standards by which consanguinity was measured varied over the centuries, but under even the most generous definitions, the marriage of uncle to niece was prohibited both biblically and by Rome.[62] The Church had gradually extended the degrees of prohibited marriages, with the intention, so the Protestant reformers averred, of making money by dispensing individuals from the wider prohibitions of the canon law and permitting marriage within the prohibited degrees.[63] But in taking this stand, the Church was reflecting a wider social belief. The repugnance for such close unions was general. No other noble or royal house in Europe united such close relatives. Montaigne believed that close connections between kin were harmful for another reason, as they would unnecessarily inflame the sexual passions. 'There is a danger that the affection that one has for such a woman may be immoderate, for if marital affection exists there entire and perfect, as it should do, and one overburdens this further with the affection that one owes to one's kinfolk, there is no doubt that this addition will transport such a husband beyond the bounds of reason.'[64] These matters demand the close attention of a comparative anthropologist, and none seems to have ventured into this field.[65] But some of the patterns identified by Claude Lévi-Strauss,[66] certainly prevailed among the Habsburgs. There was a presumption between 1550 and 1700 that the most *desirable* and *appropriate* marriage was between members of the Habsburg lineage.[67] An exchange of marriage partners between the Spanish and the Austrian branches of the family was the most acceptable of all.

Endogamy became the rule, and taking only the immediate descendants of Ferdinand and Charles V, and of their children, the repeated pattern of intermarriage is striking. Philip II married four times, twice to his own kindred. His elder daughter Isabella married her cousin. His son and heir, Philip III, also married an Austrian cousin. Of Philip III's five children who survived to adulthood, two went into the Church and two married their Austrian cousins. The second marriage of Philip IV was to his Austrian cousin, a daughter of Emperor Ferdinand III. One of their daughters completed the circle and married her uncle, the younger son of Ferdinand III, the Emperor Leopold I. But according to Lévi-Strauss's terminology, the Austrian Habsburgs were 'wife takers' more than they were 'wife givers'. Of the thirteen children of Ferdinand I who survived to marriageable age, only two, his elder son Maximilian and his daughter Anne, married their kindred. Of Maximilian and Mary's ten surviving children, three married 'in' to the family.[68] The pattern followed through to subsequent generations, until the Spanish line ended with Carlos the Bewitched. His parents were cousins, and all his grandparents were Habsburgs. Infertility finally brought the practice to its end: there were no more Spanish brides for Austrian brothers.

To contemporary eyes, there were some practical and theoretical reasons that underpinned the Habsburg practice. It was widely believed that the blood of royalty had an almost sacramental quality, and royal blood should not be diluted. Joachim de Bellay wrote in 1560 that the King of France would certainly not permit misalliances: 'He will not permit a noble blood to become adulterated with a weaker blood.'[69] The Habsburgs had a limited choice of Catholic[70] marriage partners of equal rank and status, and often where there was no social or religious impediment, politics got in the way. France, the arch-rival, was often ruled out on this account. A family union resolved all these problems, and perhaps we should look no further than convenience to explain many of these couplings. There were fourteen Spanish Habsburg marriages, male and female, between 1643 and 1679.[71] Six were to other Habsburgs, four were to France, one each to England and Portugal, one to Savoy, and the last to a daughter of the Elector Palatine. Within the Austrian branch of the family, there were eighteen marriages in the same generations. Six were to other Habsburgs, three each to Poland, Tuscany and Bavaria, and one each to France, Mantua and Transylvania. For the Habsburgs, marrying 'in' both preserved the territorial patrimony and reinforced this most precious and purest of bloodlines. But in Spanish eyes, there was an additional, perhaps paramount, benefit. It ensured that the strict purity of the lineage was preserved. In marrying even another royal house there was a risk of tainted blood, especially since the contamination could extend over so many generations. Sometimes reasons of state took priority, as when the French marriage was preferred to the Austrian with the union that was to produce Louis XIV of France.

To suggest that a 'Spanish vocabulary' of taint and corruption permeated northern Europe in the era of the Counter-Reformation ignores local tendencies in the same direction. But Spain was the strongest force in mounting a counter-offensive to the spread of Protestantism, both doctrinally and in military terms. Indeed, the two cannot truly be separated. The war for faith and doctrine had to be fought to the last extremity. The chilling logic of the Jesuit Luis de Molina was a far remove from the code of the Golden Fleece. He recommends that the godless should be exterminated:

If from [the killing] there is some usefulness for the Church, and even for the guilty ones. For example, when dealing with gentiles, those who can hardly be expected to convert or abandon their sinful life. In that case it would be without doubt holy and legitimate to kill them all, or at least as many as would be considered necessary ... such an execution would be just in itself, and a manifestation, also, of the love of God and neighbour. It would serve the good of the Church and ... even of the executed ones themselves, for death would impede them from continuing accumulating sin on top of sin. They would suffer less punishment in the eternal flames than if they had continued to live in this world.[72]

The Protestant 'black legend' of Philip II attributes to him and his 'creatures', especially the Duke of Alva,[73] a lust for the most unspeakable cruelty and an inexhaustible capacity for deceit and duplicity. Political concerns were often dressed up in the garments of religion, and Philip used the defence of the faith as an excuse for acts of pure *realpolitik*. His insistence on the execution of Egmont and Hoorn had had nothing to do with religion, and much more with his desire to bring his rebellious Dutch subjects to heel. Yet many of those subjects were heretics, and heresy and disloyalty went hand in hand. The whole nature of heresy had changed through the century, as Protestantism acquired a solid political and military standing, and as Catholicism purified itself of the excesses that had engendered Luther in the first place. For sincere Catholics heresy seemed like a contagion. Whereas at the Diet of Worms heresy had been a matter of argument and doctrine, and Charles had condemned him for his refusal to withdraw his words, by the end of the century, heresy was more generalized. It was widely described as a 'taint' or a 'contagion', both words used, equally, in the cases of *limpieza de sangre*.

Philip has often been accused of indecision and many historians have suggested this was a characteristically Habsburg flaw.[74] In Spanish he was known as the 'cautious' king, *el rey prudente*, but in reality Philip exhibited the reverse of indecision. Even in matters that came close to him personally, he would not be turned from the path that he deemed just and right. The dark story of Don Carlos, Philip's first son, born in 1545, has become the material for opera and drama, and contributed to the malign legend of Philip. From his youth, Carlos was physically handicapped, but he was also apparently mentally unstable. How much this was due to heredity and how much to the circumstances of his childhood is not clear. His mother only survived his birth by four days, and his father's long absences left him in the hands of servants and officials. Philip had asked his father to take an interest in Don Carlos when he retired to Spain, but Charles found his grandson disagreeable and would have nothing to do with the boy after their first meeting. In 1562, Carlos fell down a flight of stairs at the University of Alcalá de Henares, where he had been sent to study, and his life was only saved by a trepanning operation carried out by the great Flemish anatomist Vesalius. Thereafter, his personality altered for the worse.

Never an appealing individual, thereafter he was given to the most fearful and savage rages. He threw a page out of a window and attacked the Duke of Alva with a knife. His horses' flanks were always lacerated by the sharp rowels of his spurs, for they could never gallop fast enough for him. His sexual appetite was prodigious. But until the year before his death he remained on reasonable terms with his father. Then on 18 January 1568, quite unexpectedly Philip burst into his son's room in full armour and with a drawn sword; he ordered his guards to place his son and heir under close arrest. Don Carlos was placed in confinement and his appointed keeper was the son of the official who had been responsible for his great-grandmother Juana in her long and harsh detention at Tordesillas. His imprisonment did not last long; and the sudden death of Don Carlos from self-starvation on 24 July was attributed to Philip's cruel malevolence, the same cruelty that had sent his fellow knights of the Golden Fleece, the Counts of Egmont and Hoorn, to the scaffold in the Netherlands barely a month before.

This stubborn fixity of purpose was much more of a constant in the house of Habsburg than indecision. There were many examples of this trait at work. Closest to Philip in his interests, although most distant in time, was the Emperor Ferdinand II, who unlike his father and uncles never lived in Spain, yet exhibited the Castilian traits much more clearly than they did. Ferdinand knelt in prayer for their immortal souls as the men he had condemned to die on 8 November 1620, in the great square of Prague, were beheaded or strangled, and their heads set on spikes. In this he echoed Philip himself, who was reputed to have answered a condemned noble at an *auto de fé* in 1559, who demanded of the king how he could permit such a thing to happen to his loyal servant; Philip was said to have replied that he would himself have carried the wood to the pyre if it were necessary to root out heresy. From the generation of Charles V and his brother Ferdinand, through Ferdinand's son Maximilian II and his grandsons Rudolf and Matthias, who inherited the imperial throne, and his other sons, Charles and Ferdinand, who governed the Austrian elements of his patrimony, all displayed the same determination and almost obsessive determination upon their chosen objectives. It took different forms. Maximilian II would not be swayed from his refusal to accept the strict demands of post-Tridentine conformity. At his death he refused the Catholic sacrament, on the grounds that to take the holy wafer alone would offend his conscience, while to take both wafer and wine would offend his family; he died, as he had lived, a Christian but not formally a Catholic or a Protestant. As Emperor, Maximilian had zealously pursued his multitudinous interests.

Characteristic of Maximilian [observed R. J. W. Evans] was a broad curiosity combining the rediscovered learning of classical antiquity with a new concern for observation and comparative analysis. The Emperor evinced a particular interest in botany. He loved to frequent the gardens of his residences beautified with the latest horticultural skills. Busbeq [his envoy] brought back tulips, stocks and lilacs from Constantinople, and Marteoli, Doedens and especially Clasius achieved work of lasting importance in plant identification and classification.[75]

Many of these concerns were sustained by his eldest son Rudolf, who matched Maximilian's wide interests with a driving determination to create a great court and collection of art at Prague. But what had been a breadth of intellectual interest in his father, all of a part with his many languages, became an obsession with Rudolf. Where his father had been an accomplished soldier and an effective ruler, Rudolf followed his passions entirely, leaving the affairs of state to wither. His brother and eventual successor, Matthias, seems to have been no less obsessive, but focused exclusively on hatred of his imperial brother:[76] but once he finally achieved the imperial power he had craved, in 1612, he appeared to have no end in view. Equally, their uncles had each pursued their own courses with remorseless determination. Ferdinand, who ruled the Tyrol, married a commoner, Philippina Welser, in 1557 against implacable opposition from both his father and his brothers. Nothing would sway him from this most un-Habsburg course of action. Like his nephew Rudolf, Ferdinand was principally preoccupied with amassing a great collection of art and mystical objects, at his Schloss Ambras, close to Innsbruck. None of these Habsburgs was *indecisive*, even if the objects of their obsessive attention seemed bizarre or worthless to later generations.

Only Ferdinand I has attracted solid admiration from modern scholars,[77] and he seemed to have passed on his political sense and sensitivity only to his elder son, Maximilian. In one degree or another his other sons and grandsons neglected the skills of government. Their concerns were ideological rather than organizational or administrative; yet in this, they were more in the mainstream of the Habsburg tradition than Ferdinand I. If we seek a parallel for his style and approach – and such analogies are always fraught with peril – then it is to be found not in the Austrian lands, but in the Spain of his grandfather, Ferdinand the Catholic, who was his guardian and mentor. The encomium delivered on Ferdinand the Catholic by one of his biographers fits his grandson almost as well, saluting 'his sobriety and moderation, the decorum and respect for religion which he maintained among his subjects, the industry which he promoted by wholesome laws and his own example; his consummate sagacity which crowned all his enterprises with brilliant success, and made him the oracle of the princes of the age.'[78] The strength and effectiveness of Ferdinand's government, from the first years of his acceptance of the Austrian domains in the 1520s through to his death in 1564, were marked by an easy pragmatism and tolerance, quite unlike the rigidity of his brother Charles V. Consequently his star has been rising while that of his brother and his successors has been waning. One reason is that it is difficult for

the twentieth century to appreciate the religious zealotry of Ferdinand II (and of his son Ferdinand III and grandson Leopold I) or
the elaborate cultural politics of Philip II, and his grandson Philip
IV of Spain. The interests and preoccupations of the 'mad' Emperor
Rudolf II in his castle fastness at Prague at one time seemed
completely beyond rational understanding.[79]

❦   ❦   ❦

Although the personalities in Madrid were very different from
those of Vienna, Innsbruck and Prague, close parallels emerged.
The artistic capital which the Habsburgs gathered so assiduously
had many common elements. They often bought the work of the
same artists and demanded much the same iconography. Philip II
and Rudolf both sought works by Breughel and Dürer, and if the
exuberant fleshiness of Rudolf's favourite artists was not so often
found on the walls of the Escorial or the Prado, Philip also
appreciated a fine nude and dwelt on the complex mysteries in
Bosch's work, of which he owned thirty-three by 1574. The Austrians had an equal passion for the work of the Milanese, Giuseppe
Archimboldo, who was first brought to the court of Vienna by
Ferdinand I and worked for Maximilian II and for Rudolf II.[80] His
intricate composite portraits were a form of still life, uniting the
limitless diversity of the natural world to the human form. Arcimboldo's portraits suggested that the human and the natural worlds
were but twin aspects of the same cosmic harmony, that all life
shared the same essence and common nature.[81] This syncretism had
little in common with the exclusivity of the Catholic zealots, who
were increasingly denying the possibility of including anything that
fell outside the strict rules of orthodoxy. It is perhaps not surprising
that Archimboldo, like Bosch, had no successors: the time for such
work was rapidly coming to an end.

The classical rhetoric ('conscious virtuosity, irregular composi-
tion, dramatic devices, allusiveness')[82] of Bartholomeus Spranger,
also popular at Rudolf's court, was more easily adapted to the
pursuit of an imperial grandeur that was consonant with the
demands of Catholic purity. So, alongside Spranger's erotic master-
pieces,[83] produced to suit the inventive tastes of his imperial master,
were works that could have dignified the walls of a Counter-Refor-

mation abbey. His *Triumph of Wisdom*, painted in 1595, sported only a pair of exposed nipples, while his *Bellona* of 1600 seemed positively androgynous. Spranger also turned out a highly acceptable *Adoration of the Shepherds*, 1600, which would have satisfied the most ascetic celibate. To Rudolf's raddled eye, however, the Virgin Mary might have seemed to share the physique of the Psyche whom Spranger had depicted six years before, but with her clothes on. The elision of classical idiom with a Christian context (on occasions laced with a tincture of sex and sadistic violence) became the matrix for portraying Habsburg imperial grandeur for the century to come.

The vocabulary of images – the incessant glorification of the house of Habsburg – was common to both Madrid and Prague, and where Philip scoured Europe for the fingers of saints and scraps of holy cloth, Rudolf was equally resolute in his pursuit of rare jewels and exotic contrivances. So too was his uncle Ferdinand in Schloss Ambras. But both the Escorial and the Hradčany palace were inverted, closed places which enshrined the monarch and his objects, and if Rudolf did not shut himself away to tell his rosary, like Philip II, he certainly withdrew to his laboratory or library, invisible from his people or even his court. Philip's extraordinary diligence and his bureaucratic love for paper certainly had no parallel in his cousin, nor indeed in his own son and grandson.[84] But they inherited his 'iconographic programme', and all the ideological claims that it embodied: Philip IV, the 'Planet King', in his palace of the Buen Retiro created a public forum for the Habsburg iconography that had hitherto been hidden within the walls of the Escorial.

Building a palace-as-showcase was the principal means by which Philip IV's minister the Conde-Duque de Olivares sought to glorify his master. The exterior of the new palace of the Buen Retiro was plain and sober with a stylistic austerity that followed the pattern of the Escorial. But it was essentially 'a pleasure pavilion set in an enormous park of formal flower gardens, secluded groves, little pavilions and hermitages, and long avenues set about with statuary'.[85] The real action was taking place within the walls. 'Theatrical' certainly describes the activity on the little stage and auditorium where 'entranced audiences watched breathless as gods and

goddesses descended from the clouds in triumphal chariots and
Circe transformed Ulysses' followers into swine with a swirl of her
magic wand'.[86] But the overall effect of the Buen Retiro was of
visual excess, of saturation with images. Within it, in winter the
walls were covered with tapestries and in summer with a huge
number of pictures. There were fourteen galleries in the public part
of the palace plus many smaller rooms and suites. The painting
inventory of 1636 listed 885 canvases, and by Philip's death in 1664,
it extended to more than 1,500.[87] The effect was best described by a
contemporary French visitor just after Philip's death in 1664: 'In the
palace we were surprised by the quantity of pictures. I do not know
how it is adorned in other seasons, but when we were there we saw
more pictures than walls. The galleries and staircases were full of
them, as well as the bedrooms and salons. I can assure you, sir, that
there were more than in all of Paris.'[88]

The core of the palace was the Hall of the Realms, the temple to
the Habsburg dynasty, a long gallery more than 110 feet in length
with a high, vaulted ceiling. Along the north and south walls,
above the twenty windows, were the coats of arms of the twenty-
four kingdoms that made up the Spanish empire. Under them were
twelve large battle paintings, celebrating the military glories
achieved by the armies of Philip IV, and separating the battle scenes
were ten scenes from the life of Hercules by Zurbarán (Philip had
already been hailed as a new Hercules Hispanicus), and around the
doors five great equestrian portraits of the royal family by
Velázquez. Each of the battle paintings was a narrative of Habsburg
triumph, leading the eye to the royal gallery of Philip III, Philip IV,
his heir Balthasar Carlos and the queens of Spain: the associations
were unambiguous. The Spanish kings wrestled like Hercules with
danger, discord and the forces of nature; like Hercules, they (or
their armies) were everywhere victorious. In one the victorious
general pointed to a tapestry portrait of Philip, in armour, being
crowned with a victor's laurels by the goddess Minerva and the
Conde-Duque himself. Before this portrait, the artist had depicted
'the people' kneeling down in adoration.

The Hall of Realms celebrated a largely illusory glory. If Spanish
arms had been triumphant, Spain was also heading towards political
and economic collapse. In 1640, Portugal reclaimed its independence

and Catalonia came out in open revolt; three years later the 'invincible' Spanish *tercios* were beaten at the battle of Rocroi. Perhaps too much has been made of this defeat as an emblem of Spanish decay. The reality was that a Spanish army, starved of supplies and new equipment, unwisely laid siege to the French town of Rocroi, just over the border from the Netherlands. Confronted by a much larger relieving force under the Duc d'Enghien (better known to history by his later title of the Great Condé), the Spanish fought with their traditional skill, twice repulsing the ferocious French assaults. Under fire for hours, they finally asked for terms of surrender, which Enghien was prepared to grant; but when the French commander and his staff advanced, some of the Spanish (thinking it was a new attack) fired on him. Enraged, he ordered his artillery to smash the Spanish squares and then used his infantry to destroy the residue. More than 8,000 Spaniards were killed and 7,000 captured; only about 3,000 crossed the border to safety. Spanish power was not ended by Rocroi as has been suggested, but it is true that: 'The Spanish infantry never regained the prestige they lost at Rocroi, which was to the army of Spain what the defeat of the Armada was to her navy.'[89] Thereafter, the offensive power of the famous Army of Flanders, which Alva had first brought north seventy-five years before,[90] was blunted. There were no more victories that would have dignified the Hall of Realms.

Worse disasters were to follow. In October 1646, the heir to the throne, Balthasar Carlos, died, just before his seventeenth birthday. Three years later Philip IV married again, to the intended bride of his son, Maria Anna of Austria, daughter of his cousin the Emperor Ferdinand III, and set about the wearisome business of breeding a new heir. Their first daughter married her uncle Leopold I, then three children died at birth or in early infancy. Their third son, who seemed unlikely to survive, did so, against all the odds, to succeed his father as Carlos II in 1665. But for the last nineteen years of Philip IV's reign his successor was in doubt, or the throne of Spain rested on the uncertain life of a child. In such circumstances, the expectation of his Austrian cousins was that one or another of them might yet reunite the heritage of Charles V.

I have deliberately not differentiated between the branches of the Habsburg lineage, but it is more normal practice to treat the

'Spanish' and 'Austrian' Habsburgs as separate entities. Adam
Wandruszka has drawn attention to the difference in style between
the Spanish and the Austrian Habsburg courts. He cites the Venetian
ambassadors, who detected a 'certain hauteur, be it in walking, be
it in every bodily movement, which makes them [Rudolf and his
brother Ernest] . . . hated. For in every respect this runs contrary to
the local custom here, which demands of a sovereign a certain
familiar manner of speech, and is regarded as an attribute imported
from Spain, which is considered bad or detestable, and when they
had come from Spain, his Majesty noted this and drew their
attention to it.' What Spain provided was a mask or demeanour for
monarchs. 'The type of sovereign represented by Charles V and his
son remained the model for the German Habsburg line from
Maximilian II's sons, who were educated at Philip II's court, down
to Leopold I and Charles VI.'[91] Yet when their younger brothers
Matthias, Maximilian and Albert spent their years at the Spanish
court, their Austrian ease of manner (*Gemütlichkeit*) apparently
survived the experience. But they were younger sons, and perhaps
under less pressure to conform. In practice, it is almost impossible
to identify or isolate wholly 'Spanish' or 'Austro-Burgundian' traits
in the Habsburg lineage. Like the famous 'Spanish ceremonial' it
was an amalgam of different, and often parallel, traditions. But, by
some curious process of reversal, the next generation of 'Austrians'
seemed to have inherited the religious fervour of Philip II, although
Ferdinand II, unlike his uncles and his own father, Charles of
Styria, was not educated in Spain but at the Jesuit University of
Ingolstadt in Bavaria. With his own sons, Ferdinand and Leopold-
William, and his grandsons, the Spanish connection was reinforced.

Ferdinand I had an abundant quiverful of children of both
genders, as did Maximilian II and his brother Charles of Styria.
(Maximilian's sons added little to the genetic pool save a fair
number of talented but illegitimate children.)[92] But of Charles's six
sons all save one had a string of daughters[93] and his eldest son,
Ferdinand II, had only two boys, one of whom (Leopold William)
made his career in the Church. Ferdinand III dutifully produced a
total of eleven children, but only two sons who survived infancy.
The death of his elder son, Ferdinand, from the universal scourge
of smallpox in 1654 brought the younger brother Leopold to the

fore, as the senior surviving male in the Austrian branch of the house of Habsburg. After 1665, he was the only surviving male member of his immediate lineage. Thus despite all this prodigious begetting, the twin Habsburg thrones (in the male line) depended on two sickly cousins, Leopold and Carlos. Although much has been made of the dire genetic effects of inbreeding, much more dangerous for the Habsburgs was the devastating rate of infant mortality, and the prevalence of epidemic disease in the close confines of the courts, in Madrid and in Vienna, Graz and Innsbruck. Numerically, the Habsburgs seemed to produce a great many more daughters than sons, and these daughters tended to survive longer than their seemingly more vulnerable brothers. Of course, the life expectancy of Habsburg women was drastically reduced by early marriage, repeated pregnancies, and death in childbirth or from puerperal fevers.

When so many died, survival itself seemed the result of divine choice, and Ferdinand II and his successors concluded that God had saved them to fulfil his work. Like the first Rudolf, they should take up the Cross and make it their badge, become Christian warriors in a war that had to be fought to the last extremity. There could be no compromise with heresy and unbelief. Ferdinand II received his instructions at first hand; on one occasion, much celebrated thereafter in engravings and popular ballads, the divine voice spoke to him directly. He had been chosen as the designated heir to succeed Matthias although the strict logic of primogeniture would have given the succession to one of his elderly uncles. The Habsburgs recognized that they needed youth and energy if the house, and Holy Church, were to survive.[94] Ferdinand has always been portrayed as a fanatic, determined to restore his domains to the Church. His critics pointed to his successful campaign against the Protestants in his duchy of Styria; but under the accepted doctrine (in Protestant as well as Catholic states) that the prince determined the religion of his people, he was within his rights. As King of Bohemia, he reluctantly swore to uphold the decree of toleration (the Letter of Majesty) that Rudolf had been forced to concede. There is no evidence that he intended to break his word:[95] the initiative came from the other direction. The imperial government in Prague may have been 'unpopular' and 'overthrown by a well-timed Protestant rising'[96] – but legitimacy was on Ferdinand's side. The now well-worn story of the Defenestration of Prague does not require a further airing[97] – but the unexpected survival of Ferdinand's representatives (which they attributed to the personal intervention of the Virgin Mary) was held to be a miraculous omen. It confirmed Ferdinand's sense of boundless confidence and optimism even in the face of disaster; like Philip II he *knew* that Christ and his saints would not desert him.

For a time it seemed that he was alone. Frederick, the Protestant Elector Palatine, was elected as a more congenial king by the Bohemians, and he set about creating a coalition against Ferdinand. In August 1619 an army of (mostly) Hungarian Protestants under the Prince of Transylvania, Bethlen Gabor, with a great mass of raiders out for plunder, marched on Vienna, while the Bohemians advanced from the north. It was then that the divine voice spoke from the altar, 'Ferdinand, I will not desert you.' On this occasion, salvation was provided by his brother Leopold who sent 400 armed troopers from Tyrol. Ferdinand had taken as his motto *Legitime certantibus corona* (To those fighting the just fight goes the Crown), and while he realized the possibility of defeat he had an inner conviction that God would not allow him to fail. In the shadow of the Bohemian crisis, he told his confessor, 'I have weighed the dangers that approach from all sides and since I know of no further human aid, I asked the Lord for his help. But if it should be the will of God that I go under in this struggle, so be it.'[98]

His fortunes indeed turned and he was elected Emperor in 1619, as the Catholic states banded together to create an army under the command of the Netherlander, Tilly, one of the most accomplished soldiers of the age. At the battle of the White Mountain, a chalky plateau just outside Prague, on 8 November, the greater skill and daring of Tilly routed the Protestant army, which fled back to the city, and then in panic west towards the German border. The Protestant King and his family barely had time to collect their possessions before they were hurried away. On the following day, the imperial forces entered the city, at their head a portrait of the Virgin which was solemnly carried into the cathedral of St Vitus; Ferdinand made the Holy Virgin the captain-general of all his armies, in the Spanish fashion. But it was summer before the full weight of Ferdinand's implacable determination was felt by the people of the Czech lands. The Letter of Majesty was rescinded, the imperial seal torn from it: Ferdinand was determined to bring the country back to the true faith after almost two centuries of heresy. He began with what was the equivalent of an *auto de fé*. On the evening of 6 June, twenty-seven of the most eminent men of the Czech lands who had supported the rebellion suffered the penalty of treason. A low platform was erected in the open square in front of the town hall. A popular print depicted the grisly events, how some were hanged, one had his tongue cut out, another had his tongue nailed to the gallows, for both had blasphemed. Outside the city there was a charnel-house, where the bodies were hacked apart, so that the limbs could be sent to notable points through the kingdom. By morning twelve heads were spiked on the Bridge Gate of the city. His triumph in Bohemia – and he took no pleasure in the gruesome events of Prague – convinced Ferdinand that it was his duty to prosecute the war against unbelief to the utmost extent.

From that decision, the continuance of what later became known as the Thirty Years War was assured. Spain and Austria had the greatest of incentives to strike back against the forces of Protestantism. Although the war devastated Germany, and transformed the shape of Europe, the decision did not seem flawed in Habsburg eyes. As the philosopher Leibniz later put it: 'When the empire began to sink, God awakened a new power in Austria.'[99] The sense of divine favour seemed to infuse the whole life of Ferdinand, and certainly the legend that was made of him after his death. In this his confessor William Lamormaini's book of the *Virtues* of Ferdinand, published in 1638,[100] was instrumental in reinforcing the old sense of Habsburg election, and drawing the conclusion that divine favour had fallen upon Ferdinand since his birth, and would flow out to his successors, loyal and true sons of the Church. Where Habsburg piety in Spain had been allied with grandeur, in Austria it took a more modest but more compelling form. The profusion of shrines, of local saints – St Leopold, St Florian, St Notburga and 'Saint' John Nepomuk, formally canonized in 1729 – was matched by an increase in the number of wayside shrines and of statues of the Virgin, who now increasingly wore a version of the Habsburg imperial crown rather than the traditional Marian diadem. The traditions of the Habsburg burial developed and ramified. In 1618 the church of the Capuchins in Vienna, a 'new' order renowned for its asceticism and evangelizing fervour, was selected as the last resting-place for the bodies of the Habsburgs. However, their viscera and hearts were the perquisites of other foundations. The hearts were placed in silver caskets, rather like the Canopic jars of the Pharaohs, and presented to the church of the Augustinian order, where they were kept like Philip II's relics in rows in a large press behind the high altar. The entrails, the seat of the emotions, were the right of the cathedral of St Stephen's, where they were received with due reverence in their silver caskets.

Under Ferdinand III, the first Emperor to be buried in the Capuchin crypt (the Kapuzinergruft), the traditions of the family 'saints', especially 'St Rudolf' with his close associations with the Host, were revived and promoted; but by this new tradition of burial and reverence for the dead emperors, with the sacralizing of their bodies,[101] they provided a fresh supply of family saints, more tangible and real than their predecessors. The Spanish Habsburgs had their own traditions of burial and memorial, described by Stephen Orso,[102] but they followed much more closely the traditional 'exequies' created for Charles V and Philip II. The new ceremonials formulated and developed in Vienna, like the Corpus Christi procession and Holy Week celebrations, in which the Emperor, imitating Christ's humility, washed the feet of his people, focused on the head of the house of Habsburg in an almost sacerdotal role. The greatest ruler on earth came as a penitent sinner before the King of Kings ... The evening before an imperial burial, the body was displayed in the Rittersaal of the Hofburg,[103] 'on a dais covered with cloth of gold edged in black and under a canopy of black velvet. The room and all the rooms of the palace were draped with black mourning crape ... the corpse ... was dressed in the Spanish style, hat on head, the mantle on the dead Emperor's shoulder, his sword at his side and a silver crucifix in his hands.' Great silver candlesticks, which were lit night and day, were around the body, which was guarded by eight members of his former household while teams of Augustinian monks prayed continuously for the perpetual rest of his soul. On the morning of the burial, all the bells of the city sounded a low and continual dirge. The coffin was preceded by a long procession led by the Emperor's household, followed by his 'family', then the religious orders, the city officials, and representatives of the estates of Austria, each bearing a white candle; the knights of the Golden Fleece followed, in the full robes and collar of the order, leading the imperial musicians and choir. Then came the coffin itself, carried by twenty-four gentlemen of the Golden Key. On top of the coffin was the imperial crown, the orb and sceptre, and his collar as a knight of the Golden Fleece. The crowns of Bohemia and Hungary rested at a lower level on two cushions.

Following the bier were the foreign dignitaries and diplomats, and the imperial family, led by the new Emperor. Finally came the Life Guards and the garrison of the city, with their arms reversed and their drums muffled, beating a slow single drumbeat that united with the monotone of the bells. At the little church of the Capuchins, there was room for only the most eminent of the great throng and after prayers were said for the soul of the departed Emperor, the coffin was carried down the narrow stairs into the crypt below. As the coffin of the dead Emperor approached the doors of the vault, they were closed and barred. The procession halted, in complete silence. Then the court chamberlain knocked three times loudly on the door; from within a voice asked in Latin: 'Who comes?' The chamberlain replied, 'His Imperial Majesty.' The reply was: 'I know him not.' The chamberlain tapped lightly on the door three times. The words were repeated: 'Who comes?' The chamberlain replied: 'A poor and miserable sinner.' The doors were opened and the prior of the Capuchins welcomed the last remains of the lord of the world.

Death was their last victory, and the elaborate tombs created in the Kapuzinergruft echo that sense of triumph. Each of the Habsburgs buried in the vault had contributed to the advance of militant Catholicism. In this sense, the war to the last extremity against heresy had been won. Only one obstacle remained. The court preacher at the court of Leopold I, Abraham a Sancta Clara, who abominated Jews and heretics, hated Muslims most of all. 'What is a Turk?' he asked in one of his sermons before Leopold:

You Christians, don't answer before you are informed. He is the replica of the Antichrist; he is a vain piece of a tyrant; he is an insatiable tiger; he is a damned world-stormer; he is a cruel 'never enough', he is a vengeful beast, he is a thief of crowns without conscience; he is a murderous falcon, a dissatisfied damned bag of a wretch; he is oriental dragon poison; he is a chainless hell hound; he is an Epicurean piece of excrement, he is a tyrannic monster.[104]

His views on the Prophet Muhammad were even less generous. For almost a generation, from the most favourable peace granted to the Ottomans after their defeat at the battle of St Gotthard, the Turkish menace had been quiescent, secured by a treaty. The advance of the Ottomans on Vienna in 1683 was not unexpected, as it had been when Suleiman the Lawgiver camped around the walls in 1529. Rudolf had 'fought' a war against Islam, in which he was depicted, with Matthias, as the bringer of victory. But although the Ottomans had been active in the Balkans and in the Hungarian plain, for much of the later sixteenth century they had never seemed so mortal a threat as the Sultan's fleets had appeared to the kings of Spain. But the scale and power of the Ottoman advance in 1683 created a terror on the Spanish scale. For generations afterwards, mothers in Graz frightened children with tales that the Turks would get them.

The Ottoman siege and the subsequent salvation of Vienna on 12 September 1683 were followed by a sense of relief and rejoicing throughout Europe. The city was saved by the troops of many Christian states, but without the presence of Leopold. Two days after his capital was secured, he returned to the city from the safety of Linz. He had first received the news when a line of beacons was lit along the line of hills that stretched west from the Wienerwald along the Danube. At first the whole credit was rightly enjoyed by the victors at Vienna; John Sobieski, the King of Poland, sent captured Ottoman trophies to the Pope and to the Doge of Venice. But on his arrival Leopold demanded the limelight, and much of the credit for the city's safe deliverance. Above the main gate of the city he had inscribed in golden letters in Latin a long text that included these words:

By the Sanctity and Liberality of Pope Innocent the XI
By the Counsel and Industry of the August Emperor Leopold I

· · ·

With the Help of JESUS Christ
Without the Help of the Most Christian Monarch
Against the Most Unchristian Monarch
VIENNA Stands Freed.
The Turkish Power Totters.
Rebellion Fails.

· · ·

Happy AUSTRIA (for Which GOD Always Doth Wonders against the
Turks and the French
Arises from Her Ashes, and after Devastation TRIUMPHS.
You, Therefore, That are Enemies Fear GOD, Fighting for Leopold
You That are Subjects, Love Leopold, Fighting for GOD

· · ·

For Though the Powers of the Air, Earth and Hell be Moved, at Last
The Christian Cause Will Triumph

Thus Leopold fought for God and God fought for Leopold, and together, in this mystical union, they defeated the last enemy.

6

Felix Austria – the Happy State

1660–1790

Simplicity was the true mark of the Habsburgs. Philip II in his austere black clothes, relieved only by the glint of the Golden Fleece, was far removed from the gaudy display of other contemporary courts.[1] Yet when young, the Habsburgs dressed fashionably and with a sense of courtly style; it was only Habsburg rulers in their maturity who abandoned their youthful splendour for the drab, almost monastic, black habitually worn by all of them from Philip II to Leopold I. This was 'the Spanish tradition' and at first it handicapped the Habsburgs in fulfilling the more theatrical demands of a baroque monarchy. Philip IV, for all the fine pictures and furnishings of the Buen Retiro, could not compare with the systematic acquisition of glory by the court of his cousin, Louis XIV.

The apogee of traditional *Spanish* display had been the great masque presented on Palm Sunday, 1623, 'notable not only for its beauty, its ingenuity and costly garments, and the high nobles and gentlemen who took part ... The best horses that Andalucia could breed or the world could see were brought out for that day, with glittering trappings and harness liveries, devices and accoutrements, richer than had ever been beheld.' By Spanish standards, perhaps, but not by the more sophisticated judgements of the French or English courts.

First twelve drummers, thirty trumpeters and eight minstrels, all on

horseback and dressed in white and black velvet; after them came the
pioneers on foot and then the royal grooms and thirty-six splendidly
caparisoned horses covered with housings of crimson velvet fringed with
gold, bearing upon each a crown of cloth of gold, and a cipher of 'Philip
IV'. They were led by thirty-six lackeys, some in black and some in
crimson, their garments being trimmed with frizzed velvet-like embroidery.
The farriers came next, distinguished from the lackeys by wearing caps
instead of hats. Thirty-six postilions followed, dressed like slaves in
silvered plush on a black ground, with hats to match.[2]

Louis XIV moved far beyond matching hats and frizzed velvet.

Almost forty years later the young King of France organized a
carousel, 'a kind of equestrian ballet', a mounted masque in the
great open space in front of the palace of the Tuileries. In this
seventeenth-century equivalent of the tournament, held before a
vast and admiring crowd, Louis appeared as the Emperor of the
Romans, and in competition with his nobles, wheeled and caracoled
his horse in a masterly demonstration of the arts of horsemanship.
The courtiers were organized in teams and all dressed in equally
fantastical costumes, supposedly epitomizing the qualities of the
Romans, the Persians, the Turks, the Indians and the Americans.[3]
The 'Americans', with their appearance suggestive of trees and wild
animals, led by the Duc de Guise, must have been considerably
hampered in their complicated evolutions by their towering (and
perilously tottering) headresses.[4]

This was the 'first entertainment of real splendour'[5] organized by
the Sun King, and was the prototype of many more. Upon his
shield Louis bore the device of the blazing sun and the motto 'As I
saw, I conquered' (*Ut vidi vici*).[6] By this means he gave notice that
he intended to challenge for the symbolic primacy which the
Habsburgs had always claimed as their own. From the accession of
Louis XIV in 1660 and of his cousin, Leopold I, as the Emperor
only three years before, the relationship of intense rivalry deepened
and became more rancorous. The Austrian Habsburgs saw Louis and
his successors as their nemesis, an antagonism that lasted, reciproc-
ally, right to the French Revolution (and beyond). The French
people's contempt for Marie Antoinette, wife of Louis XVI, was
the greater because she was a Habsburg princess, '*l'Autrichienne*'.

At times the Habsburgs and the Bourbons were in alliance politically, but this did not remove the underlying sense of intense competition that underpinned the relationship between the two.

The Habsburgs had developed the old Burgundian traditions of public ceremonial into an art form. When the young Emperor Leopold I returned in triumph to his capital, Vienna, after his election on 1 December 1658, he was met at the city gates by the Bürgermeister, carrying the keys of the city and prepared to deliver a lengthy panegyric. The Emperor rode slowly in procession through the streets to the cathedral of St Stephen, where the bishop greeted him and a sung Te Deum celebrated his safe return. Then the whole assembly re-formed outside the cathedral and processed through the city, under great arches decorated in the red-and-white colours of Austria, and with elaborate scenes depicting the historic triumphs of the house of Habsburg. The noise, according to eye-witnesses, was cacophonous, with the peals of trumpets, the beating of drums, the cheers of the people, and the constant firing of the cannon from the city walls.

The recipient of this adulation, tiny under his full black wig, presented a stark contrast with the heroic postures of his ancestors beneath whose images he had just passed. Leopold had never been expected to succeed, for his elder brother was both the favourite of Ferdinand III, and a much more obviously imperial figure. He had been elected King of the Romans in 1653, but died suddenly and unexpectedly in the following year. Leopold had been educated to be a Prince of the Church, and martial dignity, which later portrait painters foisted upon him, sat ill on his shoulders. Archdeacon Coxe, his near-contemporary, presented an accurate and unforgettable impression: 'He was of a weak and sickly constitution, low in stature, of a saturnine complexion, ordinary in countenance and distinguished with an unusual portion of the Austrian lip.' On public occasions,

His gait was stately, slow and deliberate; his air pensive, his address awkward, his manner uncouth, his disposition cold and phlegmatic ... Leopold possessed all the private and domestic virtues; he was pure in his morals, faithful to the marriage bed, a good father and a kind master. Though reserved in public and with strangers, he was open and facetious with those who formed his private society; and he delighted in the tricks of buffoons and dwarfs, who according to the custom of the times formed part of his establishment.

An Italian visitor, the Abbé Pacicicelli, who observed him during the 1670s, concurred.

The Emperor is of small stature and delicate complexion: the hanging lip peculiar to the House of Habsburg, is so marked in him that the eye teeth protrude, which somewhat impedes his speech. He is dressed in the Spanish fashion – red stockings and shoes, a red or black plume in his hat, and round his neck the great collar of the Golden Fleece, which is sometimes covered by his mantle . . . when the court was in mourning the Emperor would allow his beard to grow for six weeks . . . His Majesty every day hears three masses in succession, at which he remains constantly on his knees, never raising his eyes from the many books which are spread before him on the floor.

During Lent there were some eighty services, which the officials and diplomats had to attend, which was the cause of much grumbling and discontent.

Leopold's education by the Jesuits had a profound influence upon him and he showed the order great favour, although he did not allow them the same role in respect of his elder son. But

to them he owed the acquisition of multifarious knowledge, and such an intimate acquaintance with theology, jurisprudence, metaphysics and the speculative sciences that he was called the most learned prince of his age . . . [he] displayed rather the virtues of a recluse and the acquirements of a professor than the qualifications of a prince. He was minute in acts of devotion, much addicted to astrology and alchemy, and proud of displaying his knowledge of Latin style. He wrote epigrams, anagrams, inscriptions and fables; he possessed great judgement in painting, was distinguished both as performer and a composer of music, and considering the scantiness of his revenues, may be ranked among the most liberal patrons of the arts and sciences.[7]

Coxe also suggests that so great was his Catholic devotion and good works that 'he was deemed worthy of canonisation by Pope Innocent XI and a Spanish priest in Rome actually dedicated a chapel to his honour'. There is a more negative picture, one that was assiduously promoted by the French and by his other enemies. To Protestants Leopold was a narrow Catholic bigot, obsessively devoted to the interest of the Church, who persecuted the reformed Churches as fervently as his grandfather Ferdinand II, who like Ferdinand was determined to bring his people firmly under his autocratic control. He was depicted as casuistical and deceitful, a man who first took money from the Jews to enlarge his palace and then sold their land to the vengeful burghers of Vienna, who immediately expelled them.[8] Above all, it was claimed he suffered from the characteristic Habsburg vice of indecision.

∽   ∽   ∽

Louis's splendid carousel at the Tuileries in 1662 was echoed five years later when Leopold prepared a whole winter of festivities in Vienna to celebrate his marriage to Margareta Maria Theresa, daughter of Philip IV. 'The entry of the Infanta into Vienna took place on the 5th of December with a pomp that afforded the court historians of the time a most fruitful theme for gorgeous details. In an old woodcut, Leopold appears in a mantle and plumed hat, wearing a flowing wig à la Fontagne with collar and frill point of lace à la Van Dyke and moustache and beard on the chin à la Henry IV.' The bride and groom rode in a golden carriage drawn by six cream-coloured stallions with long white manes, in a procession that took three hours to pass through the city to the church of the Augustinian order. The bridal pair alighted there to pray at the shrine of St Maria de Loretto, and then proceeded to the high altar of the church where the papal nuncio proclaimed the nuptial benediction. A week later, there was a great fireworks display, accompanied by a 'grand mythologico-symbolic representation' in front of the bastion by the Hofburg.

Two artificial 'mountains' sixty feet tall had been erected. One was Vulcan's forge and the other Parnassus, complete with nine muses in flowing wigs and hoop petticoats, and with a winged figure of Pegasus perched on the summit. The scaffolding for the pyrotechnics joined the two mountains, and in the background was a Temple of Marriage surmounted by the imperial eagle. The Emperor himself used the first torch to ignite the fireworks, whereupon 500 fires were lit, symbolically representing 'the universal blaze of triumph of the whole world'. Scenery was wheeled on and off throughout the evening as the pageant unrolled. At one point,

on the right is seen the archducal house of Austria as a strong tower; on the left the Spanish castle, in allusion to the arms of Spain. From each of these large towers, surmounted by the letters V.A., V.H. (Vivat Austria, Vivat Hispania) a thousand rockets rise; and on each side a hundred salutes are fired from small mortars. The fire balls shot from the mortars explode in the air with several thousand reports after which the letters V.L, V.M (Vivat Leopoldus, Vivat Margareta) are seen. Flourish of trumpets and roll of kettledrums.

In the final display of the evening, 'from all the pillars, pyramids, statues of the Hymeneal Temple there rise 73,000 lights, with at least 300 rockets charged with three pounds of powder. The letters A.E.I.O.U. (Austria erit in omne Ultimum) float in the air.'

The whole of Vienna was given over to these pageants and spectacles. On 24 January 1667, after many rehearsals, there was a four-hour equestrian ballet. Duke Charles of Lorraine led the 'squadrons of the air', General Montecuccoli the 'squadrons of fire'; Prince Dietrichstein and the Graf von Sulzbach marshalled the troops of Earth and of Flora. Leopold took the central role, under the admiring eyes of his bride, wearing a set of costumes even more elaborate than that worn by Louis, while Margareta Maria and his mother watched from the windows of the Hofburg, which had been draped in cloth of gold. At a mid-point in the long performance,

there appeared in sight a star-spangled globe and over it Immortality sitting on a rainbow ... the globe then opened and displayed the Temple of Immortality, with the figures of the fifteen deceased Emperors of the House of Austria, all of them mounted on stately horses and arrayed in gorgeous robes, these figures approached the temple preceding the car of Glory, which was in the shape of a silver shell, with a magnificent colossal pearl lying in it [this was an allusion to the pearl of great price, the new Empress]. The shell besides exhibited the portrait of the Emperor Leopold as the sixteenth Caesar of the House of Austria. The car was followed by three others with captive Indians, Tartars and Moors.[9]

The same, consistent, themes were presented in all the ingeniously contrived entertainments, not merely lauding the bridal pair, but stressing the continuity and antiquity of the house of Habsburg.

The anthropologist Clifford Geertz has introduced the concept of the 'theatre state' to describe the priorities of the kingdom of Bali in the late nineteenth century.[10] It is relevant to the Habsburgs. Leopold seems consciously to have moved beyond the old Habsburg ceremonial structures – the street theatre of the *joyeuses entrées*, the court ceremonials like the Golden Fleece – to more public and literally *theatrical* events. He mounted more than four hundred of them.[11] The first major building of his reign, after the extension to his palace of the Hofburg (the Leopoldinertrakt), was a huge wooden theatre designed by Giovanni Burnacci, which backed on to the fortifications behind the Hofburg. This seated up to 1,500 people, with three tiers of galleries, and an extraordinary *trompe-l'œil* ceiling painted to represent the soaring vault of a baroque church. Here Leopold's own musical interludes, arias and accompaniments, were performed – over 100 completed works of considerable quality survive – and he took the leading role in a number of elaborate productions. In one of the first masques, he and the young Empress took the parts of *Acis and Galatea* in an entertainment of the same name, and were painted by Jan Thomas in the gold, silver and scarlet costumes that they wore for the occasion, and late in 1667, Leopold took the initiative in presenting a much more didactic drama.

Theatrical productions, including masques and operas, were a device frequently used to combine pleasure with a hidden moral or political undertone. At the Stuart courts under James I and Charles I and in both Italy and in Spain, the masque (and the opera) were enormously popular. In Madrid, the little theatre of the Buen Retiro was so successful that it was used for public performances as well as those open only to the courtiers. The skill with which the Habsburgs used the graphic and pictorial arts to present their dynastic mission has been the theme of earlier chapters. Under Leopold, the arts of the theatre and music (and the highly developed skills of baroque stage management) were pressed into service to present the same Habsburg motifs of dynasty, divine election and continuity in a new manner. In the opera *Il pomo d'oro* (The

Golden Apple) (of discord), written by the court poet Francesco
Sbarra with music by Marc Antonio Cesti and numerous arias by
Leopold himself, the apple for the most beautiful of all women was
presented (after five and a half hours) not to one of the contending
goddesses, as in the classical myth, but to the young Empress. The
final scene, recorded in a set of engravings published and widely
distributed, was *The Court of Austrian Glory*, which taxed the
ingenuity of the stage designers to the utmost.

The curtain rose on a stage where the mounted figure of the
Emperor in armour was revealed, dead centre, posed atop a pile of
Turkish armour, swords, banners and spears; above him two
winged putti held a vast victor's circlet made of laurel leaves. To
left and right was a soaring classical colonnade, improbably decorated with vines, trophies of arms and yet more Ottoman impedi-
menta. (The Ottoman theme commemorated the Austrian victory
over the Turks at St Gotthard in 1664.) On each column sat more
winged putti, wreathed in laurels. High above the figure of Leopold,
in the sky, a crowned figure rode a winged horse, with attendant
divinities resting on their clouds. Encircling the stage were the
personifications of the many lands and cities over which the
Habsburgs ruled, both in Europe as well as one dusky, befeathered
figure representing the Indies.

Up to this point the whole confection was no different from any
number of similar entertainments at the French or other courts. But
Austrian Glory resided in figures of Leopold's ancestors, mounted
and in armour standing on bronze columns painted with the
emblems of their victories. This tradition of presenting the whole
Habsburg lineage, an animated genealogy, can be traced back at
least as far as to Maximilian I. He had intended that his tomb at
Innsbruck should become a temple of the dynasty, ranging the
bronze statues of his ancestors, real and imagined, around him. In
an exercise akin to that of Philip II collecting his relics in the
Escorial, Maximilian amassed a hundred or more 'saints' which he
claimed belonged to the House of Habsburg, and which were
drawn for him by Hans Burgkmair.

The depiction of Leopold as the epitome of Habsburg triumph
became a constant theme. In another many-layered allegory on the
same theme painted by Gerard van Horst in 1670, Leopold becomes

a rather improbable Hercules, in full Roman armour and a court wig, carrying a huge club almost as tall as himself.[12] He stands outside a temple on the three-headed hydra he has just slain. This certainly represents the Ottomans, but also the other enemies, Heresy and Rebellion. Despite the classical framework the iconography is Christian. At his feet sits the Virgin Mary and the Infant Christ, wrapped in a cloak of deep bright, Marian blue, which is the dominant hue in the whole image. Crosses pervade the picture – as crucifixes, sword hilts, even the crosspiece of an anchor.[13] The defeated Turks prostrate themselves under the watchful eye of the Goddesses of War, while a bare-breasted figure of Fame places the victor's wreath on Leopold's head. Another angel, with a Habsburg eagle as her head-dress presents a submissive female figure representing the defeated Hungarian allies of the Turks. At the foot of the temple steps the triumphant Emperor's pet spaniel stares adoringly up at him, beside the Crown of St Stephen, again emphasizing Leopold's victory over Discord.

The construction of Louis XIV's iconography of glory, as the Sun King, was paralleled by its mirror image, the glorification of Leopold and the Habsburgs. But against the individual, solitary glory of Louis XIV, the Habsburgs ranged the traditions of their long lineage. A very similar image to that presented by Van Horst was of Louis XIV alone in his coronation robes, with his foot on the two-headed hell-hound, Cerberus, and a stave representing Hercules' club, being crowned by Victory. This was a statue some thirteen feet tall, designed for the Place des Victoires in the heart of Paris. A contemporary described it as 'A vast winged woman close behind his back, holding forth a laurel crown over the king's head . . .' The statue bore the dedication 'to the immortal man' (viro immortali) and the marble pedestal carried an inscription listing ten major achievements of the reign. Around it were grouped four bronze captives, six bas-reliefs depicting Louis's triumphs and four torchères, which were lit every night. The statue was unveiled in 1686 with great ceremony, with music, fireworks and cannon salvos. Even the king himself came to view his new likeness.[14]

Despite surface similarities, the approaches and intentions of Leopold I and Louis XIV were very different. Peter Burke in his highly original study of Louis's struggle to take the primacy of Europe, writes:

In the course of the reign, the king distanced himself from [the traditional emblems and symbols of regality] without abandoning them altogether. Unlike medieval rulers, he did not often wear a crown, or hold a sceptre or a main de justice (a staff surmounted by a hand). Louis did not often sit on a throne. Among the rare occasions on which he did so were audiences [to] Algerian and Siamese envoys ... One is therefore left with the impression that a throne had come to be regarded as an archaic survival, so exotic that it was used simply to impress Orientals. Even the representation of the king shifted away from the traditional regalia, and often showed him in ordinary clothes, sitting on a chair and holding a baton rather than a sceptre to demonstrate his authority.[15]

Burke goes on to point out that in the most famous portrait of Louis, by Hyacinthe Rigaud, he holds a sceptre, but upside down, leaning on it rather in the manner of a prop, while his ordinary clothes are visible under the royal mantle. The sword of state was half concealed, and there was no orb. Elsewhere he points out that the king often appeared in a solitary splendour. The Habsburg practice was different in every respect, and the gulf widened. Almost as if to draw themselves apart from the new French model of monarchy, the Habsburgs began to stress the traditional and atavistic elements of their rule. Where Charles V and Philip II (and, similarly, Philip III and Philip IV) might have been portrayed without the emblems of the Habsburg mission, their successors found (it seems) a greater need for accoutrements.

Leopold I was almost invariably festooned with the trappings of regality, or displayed amid a parade of his ancestors. Like his grandfather Ferdinand III and his more distant ancestor Rudolf II, he had a deep interest in the practices of alchemy. When the Augustinian monk (and alchemical fraud), Wenzel Seiler, wished to impress Leopold with his skill, he transmuted a large medallion from silver into gold on St Leopold's Day in 1677. On the face of the medallion he cast the busts of all forty-one emperors, going back to Pharamond, king of the Franks, and finishing with Leopold as the large central figure of the medallion. The medallion and the day of its creation were held to be symbolic of the new Leopoldine Golden Age.

Leopold intended that the Golden Age should continue under his son Joseph. He succeeded in arranging his election as the King of the Romans in 1690, and when the new king returned to Vienna, the arches under which he passed outstripped anything previously seen in the Habsburg lands – and equalled or exceeded those erected in France. Two vast columns *à la Charles V* framed the Gate of Honour, designed by Fischer von Erlach the Elder. Above the central arch was a globe, held up on the shoulders of two lithesome giants. In the centre of the globe sat the new Sun King, Joseph, holding high the sceptre of his authority, the effulgent rays of his presence radiating in every direction. Atop the globe a proud father and mother sat side by side on the wings of an imperial eagle. Banners, angel trumpeters, figures of Hercules, and nubile Muses completed the cast; a whole succession of such arches stood along the route into the city.

Later generations persisted in the same style of emblematic association. Maria Theresa, kept by her gender from the imperial throne, frequently posed with the crowns of the kingdoms that she ruled, as in the famous portrait by Martin van Meytens the Younger, where her index finger (resting on the sceptre the head of which is a miniature of the globe) points suggestively down towards her three crowns on a plush red cushion. Her grandson Francis, the last Holy Roman Emperor and the first Emperor of Austria, was painted by Friedrich von Amerling in the 'coronation robes' that he never wore, with the crown on his head, a massive sceptre in his hand, the sword of state prominently exposed, and his neck festooned with a jumble of military and civil orders. The orb is prominently in view. In the case of Francis the reference is not only to the earlier images of his ancestors, but to Gérard's depiction of Francis's upstart and unwelcome son-in-law, Napoleon Bonaparte, in his velvet-and-ermine coronation robes, with a great staff topped by the imperial Eagle of France, no crown but an orb prominently displayed by his side,[16] and on his head not a crown, but the victor's laurels, in gold. Every aspect of Napoleon's Empire was proclaimed in his newly minted sovereignty, through this concocted imagery and symbolism. By contrast Francis, whose title of 'Emperor of Austria' was as much a novelty as Napoleon's (and some said, possessed an even smaller claim to legality), presented an image of the centuries-old continuity of the Habsburgs.

∽   ∽   ∽

The old tradition of propaganda by publication, which had languished since the days of Maximilian, was revived. Under Ferdinand III, and more particularly under his son Leopold I, there was an ever growing flood of panegyrics on the Habsburgs and their antecedents. Many old texts in manuscript were issued for the first time or long-forgotten volumes republished, like the great popular history of the dynasty by J. J. Fugger, written almost a century before but not printed until 1682. Some of these volumes were funded by the court, but many more were produced speculatively, knowing that they would find a receptive readership. Thus, during the second half of the century the output of genealogies, and legal treatises advancing the ancient claims of Habsburgs, appeared in hitherto-unequalled numbers. One view is that it was a sign of insecurity among the Habsburgs, that for the first time they needed to bolster their prestige and position by this form of advertisement. However, these volumes, large and small, also celebrated the capacity and willingness of the Habsburgs to absorb the celestial radiance; Leopold in particular was almost invariably bathed in the light of Divine Favour. But equally, he stood *for* and on behalf *of* a family renowned for its sanctity. In image after image he was depicted as the scion of a noble race, and this style of presentation persisted well into the following century. The Habsburgs, after Ferdinand II, displayed a confidence and determination that had all but lapsed in the days of Rudolf and Matthias. It was the ebullient assurance of the baroque, through which Ferdinand III, and more especially his son, became the focus of a cult of regal divinity.

Leopold was an active participant in this myth-making. He has, rightly, been called the greatest bibliophile among European rulers of the seventeenth century; but his was more than a mere collecting passion. As Rudolf had sensed the power of images, and of his 'magic', Leopold was aware of the power of the written form.[17] He used the resources of his library in Vienna, almost the rival of the

Escorial, to manifest the range, extent and antiquity of Habsburg power. In this he was heir to the earlier tradition of Maximilian I, Charles V and Philip II. Like them Leopold was a Sun King, but the light that shone upon him was the light of Christ. The extent of his aspirations can be seen in the plan for a huge programme of publication – twenty-five volumes – drawn from the manuscripts and other treasures in the library. Only eight volumes appeared,[18] but they are sufficient to give a sense of the whole project. Peter Lambecius, his librarian, selected materials which focused attention on the antiquity and power of the Habsburg lineage. The choice of material published in the volumes, their arrangement and juxtaposition, the choice of illustrations, these were no accident. Other projects on a smaller scale told very much the same story: Leopold was the worthy vessel for God's favour, and through him and the house of Austria, light and goodness would be brought into the world.

Many of the images of Leopold were produced as prints and images intended for popular sale. The tradition of the pictorial frontispiece to books, with a strongly dynastic theme, was a peculiarly Austrian development.[19] This provided a visual synecdoche of the more elaborate themes and intention of the work. An author would write an elaborate dedicatory essay, as in 'The Study of Laws Relating to the Imperial House of Austria' by Don Juan Felipe de Inazaghi, Baron de Kymburg, which he dedicated 'To Leopold, the Prince of Peace, The Best and Greatest of Princes, May He Live and Triumph'. To this act of adulation his brother Don Antonio had added 'A Poem on the Theme of Leopold's Greatness', while a frontispiece had been prepared to illustrate the higher meaning of the work.[20] The text, which is in Latin, is a conventional reiteration of the antique genealogy of the Habsburgs. The image is much more dense, complex and original. On the left hand side of the image is a bust of Leopold, his eyes turned up to heaven, and crowned with laurel. The bust rests on an urn carried by two winged putti, and from the urn grows a living laurel tree, which encircles the bust (Leopold is, it suggests, *doubly* victorious).

Above him flies the double-headed imperial eagle clutching a cushion in its talons, on which rests the imperial crown and sceptre. A beam of light shines down from heaven emanating from the monogram of Christ, IHS (*In Hoc Signo*), and is thus the Divine Light. This Divine Light falls upon the ram of the Order of the Golden Fleece around Leopold's neck, which is immediately transformed into the monogram of Christ. This in turn beams the Divine Light on to the world below and also on to his own portrait, carried by two more putti. (So Leopold is *doubly* impregnated with the Divine Light.) Actually, triply, for to complete the scenario the Virgin Mary touches the transformed ram/IHS with her wand, while with her left hand she points up to heaven. From her breast a radiant light suffuses the Emperor.[21]

For contemporaries, the implicit meanings in these and similar images would have been immediately apparent;[22] three centuries on, and brought up in a largely secular world, many of these pictures are to us as mysterious as Egyptian hieroglyphics. This and many similar engravings display the seamless conjunction of Catholic and dynastic themes in a uniquely Habsburg use of visual communication. The complex and convoluted constructions corresponded to a reality actually visible in society. The images of the Counter-Reformation were omnipresent. They extended from the many manifestations of the Virgin Mary, so much favoured by the Emperor Ferdinand II and his descendants, through the new reverence for the 'national' Saints, like St John Nepomuk, canonized in 1729, to the astonishing profusion of new images and church ornament throughout the Habsburg lands. The festivals of the Church were celebrated with an unparalleled dedication and regularity. Leopold is presented as but one of a pantheon of Habsburg rulers, all bathed in the divine light. The underlying motives for his emphatic presentation of traditional regality can only be inferred, but it first developed as the Habsburgs faced new and much more dangerous challenges to their traditional values and practices.

The political problems that confronted Leopold were larger and more complex than the challenges faced by any of his predecessors since Ferdinand I. From the 1660s he was menaced by a twin threat from the east, of a revived and expansionist Ottoman empire, and a Hungarian 'nation' determined not to relinquish its independence and, in the case of Protestant Hungarians, their religious freedom as well. While the Bohemians had caved in after a single battle, the

Hungarians fought a long and bitter war, both in the open field and as a *guerrilla*. The larger part of Hungary was not Habsburg territory at all but under the suzerainty of the Turks, to whom the local Hungarian and Transylvanian rulers paid their homage and taxes. In the east, therefore, the three heads of the hydra – infidel Ottoman, Protestant heresy, and social disorder – were united in a single land.

To the west the prospect was not much better. The consequence of the Peace of Westphalia in 1648 was that the power of the Emperor was even more vestigial than it had been before, especially since Leopold had been forced to make numerous political concessions to ensure his election. He could only exercise influence in Germany through complex and fragile alliances with a number of independent states. The equivalent of the Turkish menace in the east was the ever-growing power of France in the west. If any nation could be said to have gained from the horrors and economic disaster of the Thirty Years War, it was France. For the most part, the war had not been fought on her territory, and entering the war after most of the other contenders had reached economic and military exhaustion, she was able to sweep the table of the choicest gains in the final settlement. For both the Austrian and Spanish Habsburgs, France's intentions overshadowed all other considerations, for Louis XIV was determined to become the great conqueror as befitted the heir of the Caesars. He claimed part of the Spanish Netherlands, on the specious grounds that his Spanish wife and not her younger half-brother Carlos II was true heir under the law of Flanders. He was resolute in his desire to 'reclaim' the Franche-Comté, and eventually Lorraine and the great strategic cities, like Strasbourg, a process euphemistically called 'reunification'.[23] Family loyalty gave Leopold concern for Spanish territories like the Netherlands and the Franche-Comté but also from the belief that these lands might soon form part of a reunited Habsburg domain, given the dubious prospects of his deformed and sickly cousin, Carlos II, King of Spain.

The confrontation with France moved along two linked but separate trajectories. The political struggle has been chronicled in many traditional histories. Analysing the struggle for superiority, expressed in cultural terms, has been left to the historians of art.[24]

They have frequently assumed that the Habsburgs simply followed the French lead; it is, after all, regarded as 'The Age of Louis XIV' and not, even in the former Habsburg lands, as 'The Age of Leopold the Great'. This denies the skill and ingenuity – and the originality – of Leopold's cultural politics. I would not want to claim too much. The element of emulation, of looking-over-the-shoulder to the culture of Paris and, latterly, Versailles, was ever-present. Ernst Wangermann noted that Johann Fischer von Erlach's first (and unbuilt) project of 1688 was for a gigantic palace to replace the old hunting lodge at Schönbrunn, which was to be erected on top of the hill (where the Gloriette now stands) so that the huge edifice could be seen from every direction, with below, grottoes, cascades, pools, *allées* and vast formal gardens. The architect was 'recalling but at the same time overshadowing Versailles . . . clearly intended to symbolize Habsburg primacy over the upstart Louis XIV'.[25] Probably the best description of this phantasm is Edward Crankshaw's.

The building was still called an imperial hunting lodge, but it was a palace on a fabulous scale. The grand entrance from the city side was flanked by twin pylons [columns], with spiral reliefs, surmounted by imperial eagles. These broke the low line of the two-storied guard-houses, which enclosed a vast space for carrousels and other equestrian delights. Elaborate twin fountains with large circular basins gave relief to this immensity, which was bounded by still larger, curvilinear basins spouting more fountains and backed by rocky cascades.

On each side of this basin were walled gardens, and the whole divided the parade, or carrousel, ground from the approaches to the palace itself. Making use of the gentle hillside for further terracing, the next level was approached by two ramps overlooked by colonnaded retaining walls bristling with life-size statues. The ramps led to each side of an imposing parterre, with more basins and fountains and flower beds. And this parterre served as a sort of pediment for the palace itself, approached now by two more ramps, this time centring on a great circular space broken by the largest basin of all, which was encircled by the carriageway passing before the main entrance, a classical portico on a powerful scale, with wings curving forward to form a semicircle half enclosing the carriageway, and then thrown out on each side to make a great façade. The whole was pierced by 150 windows on two floors, and the skyline was broken by statues surmounting each vertical piercing. Two large pavilions, domed and cruciform, flanked the main façade.[26]

Some sense of the power and effect of such a building can be gained in today's Vienna, by walking up from the Lower to the Upper Belvedere, the palaces designed for Prince Eugene. It was, by comparison with the first Schönbrunn, on a miniature scale, but the skilful use of landscape features has created much the same impact.

ᗧ   ᗧ   ᗧ

Leopold faced problems in every dimension. First, and most important, he had no male heir until the birth of Joseph, as the fruit of his third marriage, in 1678. By the time of his first marriage, in 1666, he was the last remaining male Habsburg out of all the prolific Austrian lines, for death had culled his half-brother and cousins. Only Leopold and the sickly Carlos II of Spain stood to carry on the name of Habsburg. Leopold's excitement when his first child, born in September 1667, was a son was cut short when the infant died in his sixth month. The first daughter of Leopold and Margareta, Maria Antonia, survived to maturity, but a son, Johann Leopold, born in 1670 died in the first days of life, not long after an epidemic disease threatened Leopold's own life. Finally, his cup of sorrow overflowed when his wife died on 12 March 1673. He poured out his heart to his old friend Graf Pötting, who was his envoy to the Spanish court in Madrid, and who had conducted the complex negotiations behind their marriage. Writing in his curious pidgin, part German, part-Spanish and Latin, with the occasional dash of Italian, Leopold told him that now he knew the sorrows of Job, for his 'most loved but sadly no-longer-wife' had died, after eight days of fever; and after she died it was discovered she was carrying a healthy son. In his diary, he wrote: 'My heart breaks . . . but always may Your Will be done.'[27]

Within months his courtiers were tactfully suggesting that he should consider remarriage, if only to ensure the security of the state. Leopold refused even to discuss the matter, turning his mind instead to composing a Mass for the Dead in his wife's memory.

Many Habsburg marriages seemed despite their political origins to have turned into genuine love-matches, and the anguish that Habsburg parents felt at the death of their children, even as tiny infants, also seems unfeigned, even if expressed in terms of a dutiful resignation to the divine will. But Leopold's obduracy in the matter of remarriage was overcome and six months later he married another Habsburg, Claudia Felicitas, daughter of Ferdinand Carl of the Tyrol. She was young and attractive, and aware of the honour offered to her. But for Leopold she was 'not like my only Margareta'. Two and a half years later, still without a male heir, he buried his second wife and, within a few months, he was married for the third time. Eleonora of Pfalz Neuburg not only outlived him but bore him ten children, of whom six survived to maturity. Their first-born was a son, Joseph, born 1678, but a second son, Leopold Joseph, died of smallpox in 1684. Their third child, Charles, was born in the following year. Both Joseph and Charles succeeded their father as Holy Roman Emperor, while most of their daughters, all of whom bore the name Maria (both their parents had an extraordinary veneration for the cults of the Virgin), survived their brothers.

Leopold had fulfilled his first duty, to provide heirs, but the Habsburg tendency to produce more daughters than sons, and for those females to be more robust than Habsburg males, carried through into the next generation. Both Joseph and Charles's sons died in infancy, and the family faced the fate which Leopold had so dreaded, that the long line of male Habsburgs, father succeeding son, or brother following brother, would come to an end. By the late seventeenth century, there were great fears that European population was in terminal decline, a particular theme in Spain and in the countries that had experienced the destruction of the Thirty Years War and subsequent conflicts. The words of the sixteenth-century philosopher Giovanni Botero, 'if Spain is accounted a barren land this is not due to any deficiency of the soil but to the sparseness of the inhabitants',[28] seemed prophetic. The failure of royal houses to produce healthy heirs or to lose children as infants or from epidemic disease was not a problem restricted to the Habsburgs. Even the royal house of France suffered terribly from infant death and epidemic disease, so that Louis XIV was succeeded by his great-grandson.

The focus of all Europe was on the succession to the throne of Spain. Carlos II, whose life had been expected to end abruptly ever since his birth, but who survived for thirty-five years. French ambassadors to the court of Spain were at pains to stress his physical decay and mental decrepitude; Habsburg diplomats, like von Pötting and the more accomplished Franz von Lisola, were more inclined to stress the vital signs. Carlos was not quite the imbecile portrayed in most histories. He did not lack shrewdness and an obstinate will of his own. When he came of age in November 1675 (he had been king since his fourth year) he refused to sign a document that would have prolonged the regency of his mother; plainly, he was capable of understanding and signing decrees, of following arguments and making political judgements. He found it hard to walk, was virtually illiterate, but he also possessed many of the traits that can be recognized in other members of his ancestry. He was as stubborn as his namesake, the Emperor Charles V, and as pious as his cousin Emperor Leopold I. He had the proprietorial feeling of all the Habsburgs for the Host, and was delighted to be painted kneeling before the monstrance. But he also had the iron discipline required of a Spanish king. At the long *auto de fé* in the Plaza Mayor of Madrid to celebrate his marriage to the niece of Louis XIV, Marie Louise of France, he sat for fourteen hours watching the interminable and gruesome spectacle, with only a single quarter of an hour to answer the 'pressing needs of nature'.

Despite his physical limitations, he was plainly highly sexed, if the discreet commentaries of his doctors are to be believed. A French diplomat called Rébenac sought to get to the truth by asking the queen herself. He reported to Louis XIV:

She was anxious to confide in me something she had never wanted to tell anyone, namely that she was not really a virgin any longer, but that as far as she could figure things, believed she would never have children. Her modesty prevented her explaining any more fully, and my respect prevented me asking questions, but I gathered from what she said that there was a natural debility which was attributed to too much vivacity on the King's part, and finally, Sire, that the coction, as the doctors call it, was not perfect.[29]

Spaniards believed either that the king and queen were bewitched, or that the King of France, to prevent the birth of an heir to the Spanish dominions, was supplying abortifacients which prevented the Queen producing the long-desired heir. With no heir, the Bourbons could claim the throne of Spain by right of descent from Louis XIV's Spanish mother, a daughter of Philip III. His son the Dauphin was 'incontestably heir presumptive and the only legitimate heir'.[30] When Marie Louise died in 1689 (some said, of poison), there was great pressure to find a new wife, and to produce an heir to the Spanish throne. The chosen candidate, Maria Anna, sister of the Empress, had no more luck than her predecessor.

Carlos's metabolism was unstable. One month he might be as the English ambassador, Stanhope, reported him in 1697:

His constitution is so very weak and broken much beyond his age that it is generally feared what may be the success of such another attack. They cut his hair off in his sickness, which the decay of nature had almost done before, all his crown being bald. He has a ravenous stomach, and swallows all he eats whole, for his nether jaw stands so much out, that his two rows of teeth cannot meet; to compensate which, he has a prodigious wide throat, so that a gizzard or liver of a hen passes down whole, and his weak stomach not being able to digest it, he voids in the same manner.

Yet within days he could be completely recovered. This pattern continued year by year. In the summer of 1699, Stanhope was writing again.

His Catholic Majesty grows every day sensibly worse and worse. Thursday they made him walk in the public solemn procession of Corpus which was much shortened for his sake. However, he performed it so feebly that all who saw him said he could not make one straight step, but staggered all the way; nor could it be otherwise expected, after he had had two falls a day or two before, walking in his own lodgings, when his legs doubled up under him by mere weakness. In one of them he hurt one eye, which appeared to be much swelled, and black and blue in the procession; the other being quite sunk into his head; the nerves they say being contracted by his paralytic distemper.

Within weeks, on August 17, he was writing a corrective. 'His

Catholic Majesty is well again, almost by a miracle. So far as I can judge . . . he has the very same looks as I remember him in the time of his best health.'[31]

In the intermissions between his physical collapses – and almost all of the accounts refer to his physical rather than his mental condition – Carlos was pressed to resolve the question of the succession. His prime concern was to avoid the dismemberment of the Spanish dominions, but the other European states, notably England and the Dutch Republic, were unwilling to see any solution that either gave France the Spanish lands entire, or restored the Habsburg Empire to the extent it had enjoyed under Charles V. Leopold, by contrast, was determined that his younger son Charles should succeed to the Spanish lands, while Joseph took his rightful place as Emperor. Failing that, he was prepared to accept the son of his eldest daughter, Maria Antonia, and Max Emanuel of Bavaria, who was half a Habsburg. Unfortunately, the six-year-old Bavarian prince, who was an ideal compromise candidate, died suddenly in 1699, making a confrontation between Habsburg and Bourbon inevitable.

By October 1700, Carlos was plainly in a terminal decline. On 2 October, he ordered a will indicating his intentions to be drawn up, but leaving the names blank; then on the following day, in the presence of the Cardinal Portocarrero and a notary, the vital names were inserted. He left his kingdoms entire to the second son of the Dauphin, the Duc d'Anjou, and failing him, to his elder brother, the Duc de Berry; and failing either of the two French candidates, to the Archduke Charles. But, he declared, the inheritor must inherit the whole of his domains 'without allowing the least dismemberment nor diminishing of the Monarchy founded with such glory by my ancestors'. The effort was almost too much for him, and he developed an enteric fever. On 8 October, his doctor reported he was almost dead, with a terrible flux, and 'almost 250 motions in nineteen days'. But again he rallied, and made what seemed an almost miraculous recovery. His last attempt to secure peace was made by adding a codicil to his will whereby he hoped that the Duc d'Anjou might marry a Habsburg archduchess, thereby uniting the two contending houses. The effort drained him, and Carlos collapsed again; for a week the queen dutifully fed him from a spoon with *milk of pearls* (milk with pearls dissolved into it) but he declined further, becoming stone deaf.

His doctors laboured heroically to save him. They ordered that essence of cantharides, better known as Spanish fly, which was a stimulant, should be painted on to his feet, while the warm bodies of freshly killed pigeons were laid on his head to attract the morbid humours, and prevent vertigo. Still he lost heat, so on the night of 29 October, they covered his trunk with the entrails of freshly killed animals in an effort to restore his vital energy; by this point he could no longer speak and reject their further ministrations. Finally they ordained that he should be bathed with large quantities of an astringent remedy called Agua de la Vida (water of life), which had the effect of making him break into a great sweat for four hours that was regarded as a most hopeful sign. His condition improved, and he was able to speak again; celebrations were prepared for yet another divinely ordained recovery. The chills and fever seemed to have passed, and the king began to sleep. But in the early hours of the morning of 1 November, he began to sink fast, and at 2.49 he died.

On the following morning, Cardinal Portocarrero ordered the publication of the will signed on 3 October, and sent messengers to Versailles. When the news reached Vienna, Leopold tried to strengthen his position for the war that he now believed inevitable. He sent his troops, commanded by the young Prince Eugene of Savoy, victor over the Turks at the battle of Zenta in 1697, to secure the links between his Austrian lands and Italy, and awaited developments in Germany. He did not have long to wait. The War of the Spanish Succession occupied the rest of his life, and the life of his son Joseph I, and reawakened many of the fears that had dominated the early years of Leopold's reign.

The Bavarian allies of France invaded the Tyrol just as the Hungarians reopened their revolt against Habsburg authority, with French funds and arms to support them. All that was lacking was a new Ottoman assault, and even that was threatened. But the Habsburgs, in alliance with the English and the Dutch, fought back. The rebellion in Hungary was crushed, the Turks never materialized, and most remarkably, Austrian armies began to acquire a European reputation. Years of victory in battles with the

Turks did not count for much, since this was classed as war with primitive forces; and it is true that technologically the Ottomans were at least half a century behind European developments. However, they were fearsome and skilful fighters. The 'Turkish generals' like Louis Margrave of Baden had a great reputation in Austria, but little acclaim beyond her borders. The Emperor's army was insignificant in terms of numbers by comparison with that of France. In 1683, Leopold's troops were unable to prevent the siege of Vienna, and it required the combined forces of Germany and Poland to save the city. But this perception of Austrian weakness changed when Leopold's chosen commander, Prince Eugene, and the English general Marlborough won a series of stunning victories over the French armies, at Blenheim, Ramillies, Malplaquet and Oudenarde – for the first time the Austrians were seen to be a major military power, occupying the pivotal role once fulfilled by the Spanish *tercios*.

The consequences of this new-found prowess were immediately visible. The territory ruled by Leopold in 1700 was almost double the extent he had inherited in 1657. Instead of a thin strip of Habsburg Hungary, with the threat of Ottoman advance to the walls of Vienna and beyond, the Turks had been thrown back beyond Belgrade; the threat, however, was not entirely removed and the Ottomans still showed astonishing power and resilience. The Hungarians would never be the most tractable of subjects, and before the end of Leopold's reign, they were in revolt again, wiping out all the gains of earlier years. But despite the continuance of war or the threat of uprisings, the eastward advance of the Habsburgs was irreversible, altering the political and economic balance of the Empire.

On 5 May 1705, Leopold died quietly in his sixty-fifth year. On 17 April 1705, the grand chamberlain Count Harrach wrote that the Emperor had cancelled his normal visit to Laxenburg on the advice of his doctors. Then he seemed to suffer from a series of mild heart attacks. He was purged and appeared dramatically better, even energetically accompanying the Italian singer Angelo Grimaldi. But three days later he had a relapse, and summoned his confessor. For the last few weeks of his life, the Empress never left his suite, and in the last week never left his side or changed her dress. On 26 April, he signed his last testament, and handed over all his offices to Joseph. About midday, on 5 May, he said farewell to all his family and early in the afternoon, when he felt his last moments upon him, he ordered his musicians to be brought into his chamber, and there by the light of the funeral candles they lulled him into death to the sounds of his own composing. The elaborate ceremonials of his burial I have already outlined in the last chapter and the death of Leopold after almost half a century on the throne caused little stir, because he had organized the transition to take place without incident. The Jesuit order habitually referred to him as Leopold the Great, while the famous philosopher Gottfried Wilhelm Leibniz wrote elegiacally:

> Habsburg,
> To thy eternal glory, Leopold
> Thou hast shown us how to be holy and great:
> Continue to be both[32]

It was a hope not capable of fulfilment, at least not immediately. Neither Joseph nor Charles adhered to the austere moral standards of their father. Both followed what was delicately called the 'French style of gallantry'. Joseph was constantly at odds with his father, partly for personal reasons but mostly on political grounds. He took after his mother rather than his father, being taller than Leopold, fair where his father was dark, with blue eyes, and a restless, hectic nature quite different from that of either of his parents. When he married Amalia of Hanover in 1699, his father-in-law was advised not to include any ladies in waiting 'of conspicuous personal attractions' among her attendants. A pamphlet was even published in Rome, with papal acquiescence, which dwelt at some length on his amorous adventures,[33] while the Duchess of Orleans, writing in May 1705, noted the common belief: 'That the present Emperor is *galant à l'outrance* is no secret, the whole world speaks of it.'[34]

In politics he was seen as a modernizer, impatient with the old ways, which occasioned many disputes with Leopold, who became more fixed in his habits and attitudes as the years advanced. But the ageing Emperor was shrewd enough to see that the war with France could not be carried out in the old style and he allowed considerable latitude to Joseph and his supporters. The second Joseph, the son of Maria Theresa, looked back on his great uncle and namesake with awe and respect, and saw him as a prototype for his own passion to change and reform; by extension he equated his mother with the traditionalism of Leopold I. In a new study of Joseph I Charles Ingrao has shown that Joseph I did indeed have a coherent and reforming plan for the Empire, but it bore little resemblance in detail to the aspirations of Joseph II.[35]

A tense relationship between ruler and heir, as between Leopold I and Joseph I, between Maria Theresa and Joseph II, and later, between Franz Joseph and Rudolf (and, latterly, between Franz Joseph and Franz Ferdinand) was perhaps an inevitable consequence of the new structure of primogeniture. Of the remaining Habsburgs, only Francis II (I) had a good understanding with his heir, Ferdinand, but that was based on a relationship between a dominant and powerful father and a slow-witted and dutiful son.[36] Other royal families suffered similar problems, but in the case of the Habsburgs, it was perhaps a new form of an old tension. The *Bruderzwist* – strife *within* a generation – was replaced by strife *between* the generations. In September 1703, Leopold fixed the structure of succession in a manner which had never previously been attempted. In the first of a series of family statutes, which continued to be enacted up to the twentieth century, he restricted the succession to his sons, and then to the daughters of the last male in his direct line. This cut out the descendants of his daughters, a decision conditioned by his experience in the convoluted succession to the Spanish throne. Although he had two sons, thereafter the only heirs were Joseph's two daughters, for Charles was still unmarried. This narrowing of the line of possible claimants, preferring a close female heir to a more distant male successor, was taken still further when Charles VI, succeeding his brother, refused to accept his father's statute and created his own, giving an absolute preference to his own immediate lineage.

If Joseph was considered an incipient reformer in some fields (although an arch conservative in others), his younger brother is universally looked upon as a throwback to his grandfather's generation; neither judgement is correct. Joseph's death from smallpox, in his thirty-fifth year, came as a complete surprise. It was a disease that ravaged rich and poor alike. In the eighteenth century, two empresses, six archdukes and archduchesses, the Elector of Saxony and the last Elector of Bavaria all fell victim to this virulent contagion. The treatment advised by his doctors was ineffectual. They insisted that he should be shut in a sealed room, without draughts or ventilation, and wrapped him tightly in a band of English flannel almost twenty yards in length. Joseph had no confidence in the remedy, and just before his seclusion and swaddling, he (according to the Hanoverian secretary Robothon) sent back all their letters to his mistresses, sought the Empress's forgiveness for his infidelities, and made his confession. On 17 April 1711, he died. His brother and heir was still far away in Barcelona, sustaining his claim to the Spanish throne. It was September before he was able to take ship for Italy, leaving his wife Elisabeth of Brunswick-Wolfen-büttel to follow him when it was safe to do so. It was two years before she was able to rejoin him in Vienna.

In appearance, Charles united the features of both his parents. One eyewitness who saw him at dinner in 1703 as he was leaving to take up the throne of Spain, described him as:

Of middle stature, of slight frame and thin legs; has large brown beady eyes and eyebrows of the same colour; a long and nearly straight nose; and somewhat flabby cheeks, and hanging underlip. The expression of his features rather stern and melancholy, and he seems of an impatient temper; for whenever he seized anything or cut up his meat or pushed away his plate, he always did it with a certain abruptness, which could not escape notice.[37]

Charles had travelled more widely than any of his predecessors since Charles V. He visited England on his way to Spain, was received by Queen Anne and made much of by the ladies of the court, whom the Queen had specially selected for their charms in a desire to impress her visitor. After dinner, he played cards with the queen, and was escorted to his chamber by the bevy of English beauties, after bidding the Queen good-night and receiving a present of jewels to the value of £50,000. However, he found the English too boisterous, and avoided an invitation to return. He arrived at Barcelona after a long sea voyage in August 1705, and spent the next six years in rather desultory campaigning for his new kingdom.

The summons to return, albeit as the new Emperor, was unwel-come. He had been away from Vienna for almost eight years, and had met his Spanish mistress, the Duchess of Pignatelli-Belriguardo, then aged eighteen, shortly after he arrived in Spain; when his wife arrived in Barcelona in 1708, he married the duchess to his imperial chamberlain, Count Althann. Althann was his master of horse and had apartments close to Charles; he and the new Countess Althann met every day at the same hour. She accompanied him to Vienna while his wife remained in Barcelona.

In most accounts of Charles VI it is suggested that he imposed a rigid Spanish etiquette, as if he had never lost his longing for his lost kingdom.[38] But the Spanish tradition was already well estab-lished in Vienna, and he did little by way of innovation. Nor was it so much a 'Spanish' style as a Habsburg style, a conscious rejection of the dominant French model. The most obvious difference was the remarkable piety of the Austrian court. The Duc de Richelieu, more used to the relaxed standards of the French court, wrote to Cardinal Polignac after a particularly trying Lent in 1726.

I have led a pious life here during Lent, which has not left me free for a quarter of an hour; and I avow that if I had known the life that an ambassador leads here, nothing in this world would have determined me to accept this embassy ... Only a Capuchin with the most robust health could endure this life during Lent. In order to give your Eminence some idea, I have spent altogether, between Palm Sunday and Easter Wednesday, 100 hours at church with the Emperor.

In the streets outside there were crowds of people beating themselves with whips, while on their chests they carried notices listing their sins; others dragged heavy chains through the streets in penance or carried massive crosses on their backs. Most if not all were masked. A great many Viennese joined in the processions and the public penances, although some observers noted that the release from the normal social restraints on public displays of emotion, the masks and concealment, allowed 'a good deal of profane love making'. These fervent displays of public sorrow echoed Holy Week as celebrated in Spain (which can still be seen to this day) rather than anything native to the city. For the court as for the citizens, the Lenten season culminated on Maundy Thursday, when the Emperor received twelve ancient paupers at the Hofburg, and formally washed their feet, in imitation of Christ, and on Good Friday, the court went to each of the city churches in turn to pray at the sepulchres. Easter came as a blessed relief.

Immediately after Easter, the court went to the little Gothic palace at Laxenburg, set in the middle of a lake and with good hawking. The whole court moved *en masse*, but the little castle was so small that only the imperial family and their immediate entourage stayed within its walls. There they would relax, with a great informality; at night there would be billiard contests (a particular passion of the Emperor and Empress) with the family and chosen courtiers. In July the court moved to the new Favorita palace, on the outskirts of the city, which had been built at Leopold's orders to replace an earlier building burned by the Turks in 1683. The Favorita was in good hunting country, and billiards were replaced by shooting contests as the prime distraction – both Charles and Eleonora, and their daughters, were expert shots. The Emperor also liked to spend whole days in the woods with his rifle, shooting birds and small animals. There were rules of behaviour at both Laxenburg and the Favorita, but the atmosphere was relaxed and cheerful. The return to the city and the discomfort of the Hofburg in October cannot have been welcomed by any of them.

In this regular patterning of the year, the Habsburgs simply observed the passage of the seasons in the same fashion as many of the noble and ruling houses of Europe. Town manners and country manners were very different, and as Charles VI put off the Spanish mantle and his court etiquette when he left the Hofburg, so too his daughters, with relief, relinquished their court dresses and tight corsets for riding habits[39] and comfortable hunting clothes. The universal impression, that Habsburg courts were frozen into an antique immobility, governed by an unbreakable ceremonial, was partly true, but it was also a legend largely of their own making.

The appearance and official style of the court became ever more self-consciously different from the French pattern, a distinction which became a matter of patriotic duty. As under Leopold I, court dress and accoutrements followed the Spanish model. Dr Vehse, who had read almost all the diaries and first-hand accounts of the period, characterized it precisely.

In the interior of the Hofburg the most strictly measured *grandezza* reigned paramount. It was a strange medley of Olympian revelry, of Spanish monastic severity, and the rigorous discipline of a barrack . . . The court costume was Spanish, the predominant hue being black; the imperial livery, according to the armorial colours [a double-headed eagle, always black on a golden-yellow background]. The head coachman alone always wore the yellow velvet pelisse with a yellow velvet cap with a white plume on it. All the court carriages were black; the Emperor only drove in his red 'body coach'. The Emperor and all his courtiers wore the Spanish dress, with short Spanish cloaks, all black, with point lace . . . On gala days his Majesty wore a gold brocade or scarlet and gold embroidered dress . . . The only article of dress borrowed from France was the powdered flowing wig, which Leopold I already wore in his time.

However, the life of the courtier was not all *grandezza* and genuflection. Charles's passion for hunting and for the simpler country life caused him to escape from the constraints of the court as often as possible, if only for a few hours or days. The Hofburg itself, apart from the new wing constructed by Leopold, had few attractions. A visitor in 1704 described it:

Within the apartments of the Emperor; the walls thick and ponderous, like a city wall; the staircases dark, without any ornament; the rooms low and narrow, the flooring of common deal, meaner than which could not be found in the house of the humblest citizen. All is as plain as if it were built for poor friars. On a small spot called the Paradise Garden, fenced in with walls, under the windows of the apartments of the Empress, some flowers and shrubs drag on a stunted existence.

He as well as the courtiers were bound and restrained by the rules of behaviour. But in the 'country palaces' – the Favorita, Laxenburg – the Emperor and the courtiers dressed more informally, in the German style, and in general 'there was greater liberty'.

The prohibition on French influences was absolute.

In the French dress – especially the white stockings [the Habsburgs always wore red, with red shoes] – even during the time of Charles VI no one dared to show himself at the Hofburg. The Emperor, as often as he saw anyone attired in that way, would at once cry out 'Here is one of those confounded Frenchmen.'[40]

The antagonism to the French lessened under Maria Theresa, with her French-speaking husband, Francis Stephen of Lorraine, when the old regulations for the Spanish styles were progressively relaxed until they were abolished under Joseph II. Prussia, at least for Maria Theresa, replaced France as The Enemy.

Charles VI's new Empire was outwardly more successful and prosperous than any of its predecessors – if it were to be judged by his lavish building programme.[41] His ambitions paralleled those of Louis XIV and Louis XV. He intended to build the temple of the dynasty in the most holy of Habsburg shrines, the abbey surrounding the burial place of St Leopold at Klosterneuburg on the hills just outside the city, overlooking the Danube. It was to be the equivalent of the Escorial, which had been lost for ever to the Bourbons. The knowledge that his ancestors were now buried in an alien soil was horrific to him, and this may have encouraged his daughter in her later campaign to recover the bones of her more distant ancestors in Switzerland and to rebury them in securely Habsburg and Catholic soil. The motive behind the creation of such a shrine has been suggested by Friedrich Heer. Talking of the great baroque monasteries, he wrote,

The baroque revival of monasteries is remarkable as an attempt at restoring the union . . . between the Empire and the Kingdom of God . . . The baroque houses of Austria aspired to this selfsame harmony . . . Church, cloister, 'imperial salon', library, art collections, 'cabinets of natural objects', formed an indivisible whole. The great staircases found in these houses are often an unfurled escutcheon, proclaiming this last western communion between the separated spheres: at Göttweig, for example the emperor enthroned in the heavens as a Sun God, is surrounded by allegorical figures of the arts and the sciences. These are both monasteries and imperial palaces, the cloister is a mansion. The different spheres – imperial and sacred, religious and political, scientific and artistic – intersect. Melk merges into its cliffs, Göttweig into its mountain – dazzling monstrances built into the rock of the victorious empire (the empire conceived as an imperial church).[42]

The plans for Klosterneuburg were designed by Daniel Gran, the architect of the imperial library, in the form of a modified grid, like the Escorial, but with twelve great towers; six were capped by huge stone crowns, each one different and representing one of the Habsburg lands; one tower above the staircase well had the double eagle of the Empire at its pinnacle, and the three towers of the chapel were marked by the doubled cross of Lorraine. Inside, in the fresco for the imperial salon, Gran promised to display, 'the glory and majesty of the house of Austria, stemming from the Babenbergs, heightened by the Habsburgs and prolonged in the Lotharingians'. Charles's apotheosis in the imperial library is even more grandiloquent, and marks the curious conjuncture between the Habsburg sense of the written word as power, and the temple of dynastic identity.

This building mania rested on an uncertain foundation. By the late 1730s the dynasty certainly seemed likely to come to an end. Charles had no son, and unless his wife Elizabeth achieved a biblical miracle on a par with that of the mother of John the Baptist, he would have no male heir. Unless, that is, she died and he married a younger woman; this was not to be. Failing a male heir the Habsburg family, which had held the imperial throne continuously since Frederick III in the fourteenth century, would be excluded from the imperial title. In 1713, Charles VI had set aside the promise he had made ten years before, and created a new family statute that made his own rather than his brother's line the heirs to the Habsburg lands. Moreover, he established a strict principle of primogeniture, something that Habsburgs had toyed with since the sixteenth century but had always found inconsistent with the traditions of the family and uncertain in its effects. In 1713, Charles had no children, so that the declaration represented a future rather than a present intention. It was placed into public law as the Pragmatic Sanction,[43] and ratified by his Estates and the governments of Europe. Charles's first child was a son, Leopold John, born amid much rejoicing in April 1716, but he died on 4 November of the same year. Some said that his second name was unlucky for the Habsburgs. In the following year, his second child, born thirteen months after the first, was a daughter, Maria Theresa, who immediately became his heir under the terms of the Pragmatic Sanction. Another daughter, Maria Anna, appeared in equally short order in 1718. The final child of the imperial couple was Maria Amalia, born in 1724. She died in

1730 and there were no more young Habsburgs to fill the imperial nursery.

Increasingly, during the 1720s, it became the common assumption (although one which Charles VI himself would not tolerate) that his heir would be Maria Theresa, and the direct line of male succession, which could be traced back to the eleventh century, would be ended. In one sense, this posed less of a problem in the Habsburg lands than in a country like France, where a female could not rule; there was no such problem in the Habsburg lands and the women of the house had traditionally fulfilled political roles. Charles's own sister Maria Elisabeth governed the Spanish (or now, Austrian) Netherlands on her brother's behalf from 1725 to 1741, and was followed by his younger daughter. Maria Theresa could technically rule Hungary and Bohemia as their queen, and the Austrian lands as their archduchess. But she could not be elected to the seat of Charlemagne where the old Carolingian rules, commonly known as the Lex Salica, prohibited the election of any save a man. However, the Habsburgs, for good reason, remained fixated upon an empty title whose powers were increasingly theoretical, although the imperial legal and financial structures continued to exist and, after a fashion, to function.

Habsburg primacy and prestige was built around their imperial status. This they had buttressed and supported consistently since Charles V, in publications, public inscriptions, coinage and medals, and works of art. Two connected themes ran through all these activities. The first was the antiquity of the Habsburg line, their natural sanctity, and their imperial descent. The second was that these characteristics and qualities made them the natural and appropriate occupants of the imperial throne, the first family of Europe. The image of Charles V's twin columns Plus Ultra, like Frederick's AEIOU device, remained a popular motif in the house of Habsburg. The architect Johann Fischer von Erlach placed two vast columns, modelled on Trajan's Column in Rome but showing scenes from the life of St Carlo Borromeo, outside the new Karlskirche, dedicated in 1713. This was Charles VI's thankoffering for the end of the plague in the city; Fisher von Erlach had also worked as an assistant to the architect Burnacini on the Plague Column erected by Leopold I, a monument even more replete with complex dynastic

symbolism. His first design for Schönbrunn had sported two towering pillars as a grand entrance. But as any child knows, knock away
one of the columns supporting a house, and it will collapse. One of
the pillars of the House of Habsburg was the imperial title – and it
was questioned whether it could survive without it.

Charles VI was aware of the danger and he took what steps he
could to counteract it. Much of the Habsburg claim to primacy was
based on legend, like the one hundred 'saints' of the house of
Habsburg, or claims that they were descended from Noah or the
house of David. He summoned a scholarly Benedictine monk Marquard Herrgott, of the abbey of St Blasien in the Black Forest,
located in the few remaining territories that the Habsburgs still
possessed in Germany. The abbey was within a two-day journey of
the old castle at the Habichtsburg, and the monastery at Muri that
contained so many of the early charters of the family. Herrgott was
already known and trusted by the Emperor, who had used him
on numerous diplomatic missions, including a lengthy stay in Paris.
What he asked him to do was construct a fully documented and
historical record of the family's descent, abandoning the legend and
hearsay of the past, and creating a corpus of evidence that would
stand the critical inquisition of a court of law. In effect, Herrgott
was to construct a true history of the family from cases and
precedents of the past, to bring genealogy (on which so much of the
Habsburg claim depended) from the era of myth into the age of
science.

Truth in this context was a relative concept. Herrgott was to
judge and evaluate the evidence that he discovered, and by giving it
an appropriate context, to elevate those elements that advanced the
Habsburg cause, and to diminish those which did not tell the true
story. There were even suggestions that he doctored some of the
evidence but these claims were never proved. By creating such a
powerful body of evidence Herrgott and his master believed that
those who wished to diminish the status of the Habsburgs would
need to produce an equal body of evidence and research; here
again, the legal concept – the massing of evidence – was paramount.
Herrgott's work was to be printed and published but not so much
with the intention to communicate, for few could be expected to read
these dense volumes. They were intended to predetermine any legal

or political outcome by their very existence. While he was collecting and compiling his evidence, a further requirement was laid upon him. Maria Theresa seemed likely to marry Francis Stephen, the Duke of Lorraine, and Herrgott was made aware that it would be valuable to show the antiquity and legitimacy of such connections: the uniting of the two oldest houses of Europe. He adjusted his work accordingly. When the *Genealogia Diplomatica Augustae Gentis Habsburgicae*[44] was published in two large volumes in 1737, it precisely fulfilled the brief given by the Emperor. He showed his gratitude by giving Herrgott both a generous pension and the rights to the profits of the book, which was published under imperial privilege.

The work was described as a compilation of documents, but Herrgott had interpreted 'documents' very widely, and it included almost every possible kind of material – seals, flags, tombstones, plans, maps, engravings of buildings – to sustain the Habsburg claim. But most remarkable of all was the manner and style of presentation. Accompanying and framing the texts were a set of intricate and allusive images, very much like the frontispiece to Inazaghi's treatise,[45] that provided the hidden meaning and purpose of the huge work. The emblems associated with the Habsburgs, especially the sun, occur and recur through the engravings that introduce and conclude each section. Herrgott spent an enormous amount of time (and money) securing precisely the right images for his text, all of which were drawn and engraved specifically for the purpose. He expressed the central intention of the book on the first page. He showed a chariot drawn by lions, surrounded by putti carrying cornucopia, symbolizing plenty, and a putto bearing a Janus mask, strongly associated with the ancient Habsburg claims to empire. Above the chariot the sun is rising and in the chariot, driving the lions, is a woman with the swaddled figure of a crowned child. The title line reads 'Legitima Maiestas Habsburgica' (The lawful majesty of the Habsburgs). It requires no shift of the imagination to link the woman and the child with the true majesty of the Habsburgs, and to make the woman Maria Theresa and the child her future progeny.

It was indicative of Charles's cast of mind that so much effort was made to buttress the theoretical position of his daughter while at the same time neglecting the military and political resources that would allow her to defend her inheritance. When he died unexpectedly she inherited an army in decay and a near-empty treasury. The resources had been spent on his new library, on churches and other buildings, on the new palace at Schönbrunn and, at the lower end of the scale, in buying works of art, books and manuscripts, and on projects like Herrgott's *Genealogia*. But in 1740, Charles was still in vigorous good health and secretly hoping that he might remarry; Maria Theresa had married Francis Stephen in November 1736, and by the summer of 1740, the Emperor had three granddaughters but no grandson. Then, in June his eldest granddaughter died, but in the following month he learned that his prolific daughter was pregnant again, perhaps with a future archduke. In early October he set out from La Favorita to go hunting as usual, hoping for a good bag of duck on the Neusiedel Lake. The weather was atrocious, with a series of cold grey days of constant snow or sleet, but nothing would keep him from his favourite pastime. He had arrived at his hunting-lodge suffering from mild stomach pains and thought nothing of them. After several days of extreme cold, the pains worsened, but he continued.

On the evening of 10 October, his cook had prepared a stew of mushrooms, which the Emperor, always hungry after a day in the field, ate voraciously. He was violently sick in the night, and his companions hurried him back to Vienna, with Charles vomiting and fainting along the way. Once in bed and under the care of his doctor, he seemed much better, but on the following day he had a relapse and plainly whatever it was that ailed him seemed likely to prove fatal. His family gathered at his bedside, but he gave instructions that Maria Theresa was not to see him in his haggard state lest it bring on a miscarriage. Over the space of a week, he settled his affairs, gave his ministers their instructions, received the consolation of the faith, and prepared to die well, like all true Habsburgs. At two in the morning, his bed surrounded by the tapers due to an archduke, king and emperor,[46] and holding a crucifix, he died, the last of the male line of the Habsburgs. He was in his fifty-sixth year. Had he lived as long as his father, another nine years, the course of his family's history and that of Europe might have been very different.

He died leaving a twenty-three-year-old young woman as his heir. Despite the agreement of most of the European powers and his own Estates to the terms of inheritance under the Pragmatic Sanction, the weakness of Maria Theresa's position quickly became clear. The Elector Palatine addressed her as 'The Archduchess Maria Theresa' and the King of Spain referred to her, in strict logic, as 'The Grand Duchess of Tuscany' (Francis Stephen had, under pressure, exchanged the dukedom of Lorraine for a domain in Italy). Others, like the Duke of Bavaria, claimed that he was entitled to a portion of the Habsburg lands in the right of his mother, one of the daughters of Joseph I, under the agreement to which Charles had agreed in 1703 and forsworn in 1713, as well as by a direct but distant descent from a daughter of Ferdinand I. Frederick II of Prussia, not yet The Great, ordered his troops into Austria's Silesian duchies on the grounds that he thereby *prevented their occupation* by any other power. Within three months of her father's death Maria Theresa faced the immediate loss of large parts of her domains. In cartoon after cartoon, from England to Hungary,[47] she was displayed as being robbed of her clothing (her territories) by her lascivious neighbours. 'The Queen of Hungary stripp't' provided a good excuse for depicting Maria Theresa as a victim of a rape more literal than metaphoric, the French Cardinal Fleury taking the principal role. In one cartoon he is demanding 'Let me handle it', in a none-too-subtle *double entendre*, as his hands paw her youthful and near-naked form. In a Hungarian version, he is seen pulling away the hand with which she has modestly covered her pudenda. A spirit of chivalry was less evident than the misogynist feeling, coarsely expressed, that women have no place in government.

Her gender prevented her election as Holy Roman Emperor (and brought down on her a torrent of foul innuendo), but Maria Theresa transmuted this unalterable fact into her greatest asset. She appealed directly to the loyalty of the Hungarian nobles as their young queen, and legend has her carrying her young son in her arms, an event as mythically fertile as the legend of Rudolf I seizing the crucifix as his sceptre. She gained their support and adulation, and some troops. Myth and fact quickly separated, but it was the myth that persisted. Unable to be a traditional Habsburg monarch,

Maria Theresa became the mother of her country, *Landesmutter*, as well as the birth-mother of an ever increasing brood of healthy and attractive children. The elision of the young archduchess with an image of fecundity had begun (prophetically) with her birth. The back of the medal commemorating that event shows the new infant apparently emerging from a cornucopia, amid the fruits of the earth, both held in the arms of her mother, who was dressed in the style of an imperial Roman matron.[48] The legend of the medal reads 'Hope being reborn on earth'.[49] Later, the frontispiece to the *Histoire Générale de l'Auguste Maison d'Autriche*, by Jean Laurent Krafft,[50] published in its French edition in Brussels in 1744, shows a plainly pregnant Queen (Maria Theresa) on her throne embraced by a youthful prince (Francis Stephen). At the foot of the dais, the God and Goddess of War stand guard with shield and drawn sword; the index finger of Bellona points to the gravid empress, indicating where the future of the house of Habsburg lay in its moment of crisis.

With this young Queen of Hungary, the emphasis of the Habsburgs shifted, discreetly and slowly, from being encircled by the replicas of the dead ancestors to being surrounded by the image of the living future of the dynasty, of fertile motherhood, proud paternity and the joint fruit of their loins.[51] The portrait by Mytens of the sons and daughters of Maria Theresa in 1749 shows a painting filled with lively, beautiful children, the three boys dressed in Hungarian style, the four girls in the French style, with Joseph aged eight sitting elevated in the centre holding the collar of the Golden Fleece while his elder sister Maria Anna fondles the dangling ram.[52] The emphasis on the dynastic emblem (the Golden Fleece) and the Hungarian costume are the dominant themes. The assiduity with which Maria Theresa developed her role as Queen of Hungary was evident everywhere. Shortly after her coronation, the engraver Gottfried Bernhard Göz depicted her as Queen, with the caption 'A most devoted Hungary'. At her feet knelt a handsome hussar, his hand on his heart and his sword drawn to protect his queen.[53]

The sheer *profusion* of children dominates the numerous paintings of the families of Maria Theresa, Leopold II and Francis II (I).[54] The number of children was seen almost as a response to the death and decay of the old line with Charles VI; Joseph II wrote cheerfully to his brother Leopold that his exuberant activity in the marriage bed absolved him (Joseph) from the need to contribute his quiverful. 'Excellent populator, dear brother, how much I owe you! Your wife is pregnant yet again. As well as being a service which you render to the state, it imposes on me an eternal obligation. Continue, dear brother, and do not slacken your efforts. Boldly present as many children to the Monarchy as you can. If they are like you, there will never be too many of them.'[55]

The image of fecundity was everywhere. The traditional images — cornucopia, naked putti — acquired new meaning. If sexual licence was frowned upon in Maria Theresa's Austria, motherhood was very much favoured. She personally blessed Austria with thirteen children who survived into puberty, of whom five were still alive in 1800. Thirteen of Leopold II's sixteen children grew to adulthood, while his son Francis, the last Holy Roman Emperor and first Emperor of Austria (which gave him the bizarre designation Francis II (I)), did his duty to the extent of four marriages and siring thirteen children. Maternalism and family life became the dominant theme of the Habsburgs. The historian of population (or depopulation) in France, Carol Blum, has written eloquently of the fear of the decline in human numbers. There was

a curious misconception almost universally held throughout the century, that the human race was diminishing, its fertility nearly exhausted ... The world was experienced as depleted and the future as ominously headed towards the extinction of the human race. This idea, that there are fewer of us than there used to be, so antithetical to our contemporary sense of suffocation in pullulating humanity, extended to the rest of nature and to the earth itself, perceived as aged, infertile, and worn out. This *perception* that the world, and especially the kingdom [what she says here of France applies with equal or greater force to the Austrian domains] had become wasteland, had important consequences in the kinds of arguments brought against absolutism, arguments bolstered by an emotional logic accusing a withered despot of failing in his sacerdotal duty: to ensure the fertility of the land. In fact one might speculate that the declining fertility fallacy, although factually incorrect, was psychologically irresistible to disappointed subjects of a faltering monarchy.[56]

The reverse was also true, and the constant fecundity of Maria

Theresa gave strength and a sense of the future to the Habsburg domains. She was well known to have remarked immediately after the birth of Joseph, 'I wish I were already in the sixth month of a new pregnancy,'[57] which was seen as evidence of her implacable determination to defeat all her adversaries on the battlefield. She told her advisers who wanted to make peace with France and Prussia, two mortal enemies of the Habsburgs in alliance in 1741, that she would have none of it. The English ambassador, Robinson, described the scene. 'The ministers [on hearing of the Franco-Prussian alliance] fell back in their chairs white as corpses, one heart only remaining undaunted, that of the Queen.' Later, he reported, she remarked, 'I am only a poor queen, but I have the heart of a king.' He, if no one else present, would have recalled the words of Queen Elizabeth of England, speaking to her army at Tilbury, under threat of invasion by Maria Theresa's ancestor, Philip II, 'I know that I have the body of a weak and feeble woman, but I have the heart and stomach of a king, and of a king of England too.'[58] Even the palace of Schönbrunn reflected this sense of family, as Gordon Brook Shepherd observed, 'Unlike its great architectural and political rivals, Versailles and Potsdam, it remained also a home. Despite its size (there are no fewer than 1,441 rooms in the building) and the sumptuousness of its galleries and state apartments, something of this domestic aura clings even to the untenanted palace of today.'[59] Comparing the first design of Fischer von Erlach with his second design, as altered and reduced by Maria Theresa's architect, Pacassi, shows a building if still not on a domestic scale, far removed from the monster first envisaged in 1688.

Maria Theresa has come to be considered 'motherly' partly because of her heroic fertility, but also because she seemed to be so different, so human,[60] in comparison with the public reserve of her father and grandfather. In time, events brought the imperial throne back to the 'new' house of Habsburg-Lorraine, and her son accompanied by Francis Stephen was to be crowned King of the Romans. Goethe, who described the coronation, noted:

As her husband in his odd attire passed by on the way to the cathedral, exhibiting himself, so to speak as the ghost of Charles the Great, he jestingly raised both hands to draw her attention to the orb and sceptre and the quaint gloves he had on: whereupon she burst into uncontrollable laughter, to the great pleasure and edification of the watching crowd which was thus privileged to behold the wholesome and unaffected harmony prevailing between the foremost married couple in Christendom. But when the empress, in salutation to her husband, flourished her handkerchief and shouted her own 'Vivat', the enthusiasm and rapture of the crowd knew no bounds.[61]

Years later she once rushed into the Imperial theatre one night, dressed informally, to announce to the large audience in quivering tones of excitement: 'Our Leopold has had a son.' She spoke with a heavy Viennese accent, laced with argot, writing as forcefully and ungrammatically as she spoke. Francis Stephen never learned to speak German, so French became the language of the court. But his written French was so bad that his wife, no linguist herself, would correct his most glaring errors. In her ease and openness, Maria Theresa apparently anticipated the *natural* behaviour of the Romantic Age. Such appearances are deceptive, for she remained a traditional Habsburg in every respect.

She ruled her family with an expectation of absolute obedience.

She was a devoted but a highly self-conscious mother [Derek Beales has observed] and she did not forget that she was also a ruler and the head of her House. She drew up for each child, as it left the nest, elaborate instructions on religious observance, health precautions, diet and the duties of his or her station . . . Lent and other penitential seasons must be strictly kept, and Francis' death solemnly observed; confession and communion must be regular; only approved books are to be read, and decorous clothes worn; wives must obey their husbands; nudes in painting ought to be covered up.[62]

She wrote to all her children at least once a week, advising encouraging and cajoling. She was, as she said, 'insatiable in the matter of grandchildren' and she showered her daughters and daughters-in-law with constant advice on how to increase their tally if deficient, or how to care for those they had produced. She expected to be obeyed. All the little archdukes and archduchesses received training in some practical skill. Joseph was sent in 1756 to the court printer Joseph Trattner to learn the Black Art; the court connection did Trattner no harm, for within a decade he was a multimillionaire.[63] Some of her daughters became accomplished artists. But they had no choice in the matter: their mother continued to dictate every move in their lives, even after they had married. She told her youngest and most wayward daughter, Marie Antoinette, Queen of France, that she was *not allowed* to give up wearing corsets lest she ruin her figure, and she set spies on many of her children to ensure that they followed her commands. More of them than Marie Antoinette may have felt,[64] 'I love the empress, but, I'm afraid of her.'

The Queen-Empress revered her father's memory (if not his policies) and in many respects she persisted in his preoccupations. Marquard Herrgott was set to work producing an even more lavish set of volumes, dwarfing his *Genealogia*, extolling the antiquity of the House of Habsburg. The *Monumenta Augustae Domus Austriacae*[65] was a veritable encyclopedia of the house of Habsburg, in eight massive volumes, ending with a catalogue of all their tombs and mortal remains. Monumentality was evidently the order of the day. Her court librarian, Adam Kollar, reissued, in a much more elaborate and prestigious form, not only the entire eight volumes of his illustrious predecessor, Peter Lambecius's culling of the imperial library, published under the authority of Leopold I,[66] but prepared a shortened and more 'popular' version as well.[67] All these projects were funded by the court, but they served to create an interest in the Habsburg past. Archives and libraries were scoured for popular Habsburgica. The first printed edition of Maximilian's *Weisskunig* was also published as a successful commercial venture, in 1775, from the manuscript in the imperial library by Abbé Hoffstätter, with all Burgkmair's illustrations.[68]

One bizarre preoccupation which she inherited from her father concerned the exhumation of her distant ancestors. The early Habsburgs had rested in Basel cathedral and in Königsfelden for more than four hundred years. Certainly Königsfelden, which was being used as a barn, was not perhaps the most reverential atmosphere for the bones of the martyred Leopold, victim of the Swiss at Sempach. In 1739, Charles VI had arranged for the vault to be opened and its contents surveyed. His death prevented any further action. Thirty years later, his daughter carried matters to their conclusion. On 10 September 1770, Maria Theresa made a special request to the cantonal authorities of Bern to allow all the remains to be removed. After some haggling this was permitted, and they were taken in a cortège for reburial in a splendid new mausoleum at St Blasien in the midst of the Black Forest, in Habsburg territory. This was not the end of their journeying. Her grandson Francis II, concerned that the abbey was no longer in the domains of the Habsburgs, in 1807 arranged for the bones and all the records of the abbey to be removed to another Benedictine house of St Paul in Laventhal, in the heart of Austria; there the bones remain to this day, buried before the high altar.[69] This episode illustrates the ambivalence of Maria Theresa, in some aspects seeking to throw off the shackles of the past and in other areas, embracing them.

Her eldest son and heir, Joseph, had no doubts as to where he stood. He bitterly (and memorably) described his mother's court as

an assemblage of a dozen old married ladies, three or four old maids, and twenty young girls, who are known as the Ladies of the Court, seven archduchesses, an empress, two princes [and] an emperor co-regent under the same roof – and yet no Society at all, or at least none that is rational or agreeable, since they all keep themselves to themselves. The gossiping and squabbling between one old woman and another, lady and lady, archduchess and archduchess, kept everyone at home, and 'What will people say?' prevents the most innocent gatherings or parties ... The intelligent, bored to death with the stupid women, eventually find an outlet for their intelligence, and then use it in the most unsuitable ways, whereas if they had the opportunity to deploy it in good company they would never contemplate such follies.[70]

Joseph's energy, impatience, and his belief in the possibility of 'the rational' ordering of the world, was everywhere apparent. In many respects he was a mirror of his mother. Like her, he worked long hours, winter and summer. Like her he seemed inured to any sense of personal discomfort; the bracing cold of the Empress's rooms was the terror of less spartan souls. Both of them were impatient with the more fustian elements of the past. Count Kheven-hüller, bemoaning in 1765 the spirit of change and innovation, dated it from 1741. 'This unhappy spirit of innovation, which happened soon after the death of the late emperor Charles VI and has daily gained strength, seems under the present reign to gain complete control.' He lamented that at Easter, 'The washing of the feet, though already announced and although everything had been prepared according to the old usage, was suddenly abolished, and the chosen men and women received two ducats a head from charity.' Maria Theresa, 'could have prevented this questionable innovation; but partly, as is well known, she inclines in the same direction herself, and partly she often lacks the necessary courage and firmness.'[71]

Joseph's two periods of rule, jointly with his mother from the death of his father and in his own right from 1780 to 1792, were marked by a cascade of reforms. What drove him forward might be disguised as the exercise of pure logic, but it masked a characteristically Habsburg drive to overcome all obstacles regardless of the consequences. In his determination to sweep away the pointless vestiges of the past, he had the zeal (of Reason rather than the Divine Will) that had motivated his more potent ancestors. Joseph confronted by the recalcitrant Hungarians or the obstinate Netherlanders, unwilling to be set free, had the same utter certainty of a Philip II or a Ferdinand II that his cause and course was right. Joseph was a man driven by powerful emotions. The loss of his young wife, Isabella, in November 1763, from smallpox (the same disease that marred his own features) left him utterly devastated. They were married for three years. When seven years later, on 23 January 1770, his only daughter, the living evidence of their life together, died of pleurisy, after receiving her first and last communion, he had no one to whom he could pour out his grief. But in letters to her governess, he wrote not as an emperor, but a distraught father. 'I have ceased to be a father: it is more than I can bear. Despite being resigned to it, I cannot stop thinking, and saying every moment, "Oh my God, restore to me my daughter, restore her to me." I hear her voice, I see her. I was dazed when the terrible blow fell. Only when I had got back to my room did I feel the full horror of it, and I shall go on feeling it for all the rest of my life, since I miss her in everything.' He told the governess, the Marquise d'Herzelles, that she was to have his daughter's possessions, but he asked one favour. 'One thing that I would ask you to let me have is her white dimity dressing gown, embroidered with flowers, and some of her writings. I have her mother's, I shall keep them together.'[72] In some this would have passed for sentimentality, but in Joseph, as in his mother, it was a consequence of their deeply passionate and emotional natures. She, like the good mother, was determined to control and direct the future of her family – be it her progeny or her nations. She defended them all tigerishly against the ravages of external enemies like the arch-predator, Frederick II of Prussia, and she demanded loyalty and obedience in return. *Maternalism* in the style of Maria Theresa and *Paternalism* as practised by Joseph grew on the same stem.

Power came to him unexpectedly at the age of twenty-four. His father had grown very fat with good living, although he continued to ride and hunt and his health seemed good. In August 1765, the court had travelled to Innsbruck to celebrate the marriage of Leopold to the Infanta María Luisa of Spain. Francis Stephen had been suffering from pleurisy and the damp air of Innsbruck made it difficult for him to breathe. What fascinated him in the city was the tomb of Maximilian, which he visited again and again, taking both Joseph and Leopold with him. On 18 August, returning from the opera, two long and tedious performances, he collapsed by the door to his rooms in the old palace, falling into the arms of his eldest son. The seizure was massive, and although his doctors opened his vein and attempted to bleed him, he was already dead. Maria Theresa displayed the kind of grief that had once characterized her ancestor, Juana of Spain. She had to be taken forcibly from the room where he died, and back in Vienna she insisted on sewing his shroud herself. From that moment onwards she wore nothing but deepest mourning, while her apartments and carriages were all draped in black velvet. The rooms that she had shared with Francis Stephen on the first floor of the Hofburg were preserved and never used again; she moved her establishment to the third storey.

For the remainder of her life August was always spent in solitude and prayer, and the eighteenth day of every other month was set apart to his memory. She cut her hair short and seriously contemplated retiring to an order of nuns which she had founded in Innsbruck. In the years that followed her grief waned but never disappeared. She put aside memories of his infidelities and occasional boorishness, and remembered only his warmth and vivacity. The tomb that she had made for them both in the vault of the Capuchins has the effigies of Francis Stephen and Maria Theresa, looking for all the world like a loving couple on a rumpled bed.

Joseph found his father's will, written in his own handwriting, amid the chaotically organized papers in Francis Stephen's town house in Vienna. It revealed that his father's financial speculations had been enormously successful and he was the sole owner of a vast private fortune, no longer dependent on his mother for his income. Moreover, as King of the Romans, he automatically succeeded as the Holy Roman Emperor. But although his mother, a month after Francis Stephen's death, made him co-regent, she did so 'without surrendering the whole or any part of our personal sovereignty over our states, which will continue to be kept together and moreover without the least actual or apparent breach of the Pragmatic Sanction'.[73]

For fifteen years Joseph chafed under the constraints of this untidy arrangement. His authority was limited in some areas, less constrained in others. The army had notionally been his father's concern (although he was a notably unsuccessful soldier). Joseph longed for a military role and he was prepared to be more than a ceremonial general. In the 'Potato War' of 1777–9, in which the opposing armies manoeuvred in Bohemia and lived off the peasants' potatoes while the diplomats tried to resolve the question of the succession to the throne of Bavaria, Joseph stayed with his troops, and endured the same cold and deprivation. The campaign was a complete disaster. Ten years later, he had no more success, leading his armies to failure against the Turks in Serbia and Transylvania, and narrowly escaping capture. A new general brought them to victory. During that decade the cares of office had visibly taken their toll.

The man who had formerly been so vigorous and healthy showed the most unmistakable signs of rapidly failing strength. His eyes became weak and watery; he had sore legs [an inheritance from his mother and grandmother]; erysipelas in the head had obliged him, even as far back as 1783, to wear a wig; whilst before that he wore his beautiful fair hair, which had gradually assumed an auburn tinge . . . with two simple curls and pigtail. His complexion, once so clear, was now of a reddish-brown hue; the smallpox marks looked as if deepened, and his hanging cheeks added to the length of his face.[74]

To what end had he sacrificed his health and his happiness?

By his own lights, he sought the *good* of his people. Throughout his life he had sought to make *good arrangements* for which he received no thanks at all. In his last months, he wrote despairingly to his brother Leopold in Florence, 'I am unfortunate in everything I undertake . . . [and there is] the appalling ingratitude with which my good arrangements are received and I am treated – for there is now no conceivable insolence or curse that people do not allow themselves to utter about me publicly.'[75] This contrasts with the unswerving determination of his earlier years and his belief that energetic action would bring its just reward. His energy and the cascade of changes that he unleashed – the decrees and instruments alone are numbered in the thousands – were in the service of 'enlightened' ideals, although Joseph had read very little of the great philosophers and practitioners of 'Enlightenment'. He abolished serfdom, reduced censorship, restricted the rights and privileges of the nobility, instituted freedom of worship, and created a bureaucracy – of administrators and secret police to put his programme into effect. His former tutor Christian August Beck had written: 'Sovereigns must consider that it is their task to promote the security and welfare of their subjects. As true fathers of the fatherland they must never lose sight of the laws of justice and righteousness . . . As God's lieutenants on earth they must imitate humanity's lawgiver and never demand from us but what will be conducive to our own happiness.'[76] The young Joseph had given much the same thought a different twist in his *Reveries* (1763). His notion, he realized,

smacks of despotism, but without an absolute power . . . to be in a position to do all the good which one is prevented from doing by the rules, statutes and oaths which the provinces believe to be their *palladium*, and which, sanely considered, turn only to their disadvantage, it is not possible for a state to be happy, for a sovereign to be able to do great things . . . God keep me from wanting to break sworn oaths, but I believe that we must work to convert the provinces and make them see how useful the *despotisme lié* [limited despotism] would be to them.[77]

In other words, he intended to force them to be free, much as his ancestors had forced their subjects to be the true and loyal children of Holy Church.

Happiness, the blessing brought by the house of Habsburg, was a secular replacement for the old pietistic themes of the dynasty. The Habsburgs remained devoutly Catholic – Joseph himself said that he wanted to make all his people Catholic – but they now extended happiness to all their peoples, of whatever faith and beliefs. Maria Theresa prided herself on the traditional 'clemency' of the house of Habsburg, which she claimed had dealt less harshly with those who stood against it than other nations. Many Hungarians and Czechs, with memories of the gallows, burning flesh and the smell of blood, would have demurred. But this was the basis of the new theory of the dynasty, developed by Joseph and adhered to by all his successors. The Habsburgs were the first servants of all their nations, striving ceaselessly to create *Felix Austria*, the *happy state*.

7

The Last Cavalier

1790–1916

In the third act of Franz Grillparzer's epic drama, *Ein Bruderzwist in Habsburg* (Family Strife in Habsburg) the old Emperor Rudolf II, alone and afraid in Prague, tells Julius, Duke of Brunswick, that, despite all, he has confidence in the future.

> My house will last for ever, I am sure
> For it does not with human vain conceit
> Anticipate, encourage what is new.
> No, but because, joined with the universe
> Through moves unwise or wise, fast or delayed,
> It imitates eternal Nature's course
> And in the centre of its orbit, waits.[1]

However, Habsburgs were no longer content *to wait in their orbit*. A new spirit animated both Maria Theresa and her elder son Joseph. While her husband Francis Stephen lived, her passion for change was held in abeyance; after 1765 it had full reign. It is usually suggested that Maria Theresa applied the brake on Joseph's radicalism, but it is often hard to distinguish between the two in their zeal for change – 'a remarkable example of the imposition from above of a radical programme of change ... proud of the ruthlessness of [the] internal measures, despite the unpopularity they brought'[2]. Derek Beales was writing of Maria Theresa, but he could equally have been describing Joseph.[3] They disagreed about most matters, but they were in accord on the principle of alteration; as Khevenhüller morosely noted in the last chapter, the old order was dead.

As Maria Theresa's reign limped on (for old age slowed her down in the 1770s) many speculated what the Empire under the sole rule of Joseph II would be like. His oldest friend, the Prince de Ligne, had it most exactly: endless excitement, endless activity. However, he put it a little more pointedly. 'As a man he has the greatest merit and talent; as a prince he will have continual erections and never be satisfied. His reign will be a continual Priapism.'⁴ Joseph's restless and imperious energy made him a trial not merely to his mother but to all his family. His relationship with his brother Leopold was warm and close, but he never stopped behaving with the utmost boorishness and a callous disregard for the interests of his brother and his burgeoning family. Under normal circumstances this would not have mattered, but Joseph had no intention of marrying again, and thus one or other of Leopold's family would follow their uncle on the imperial throne.

The most likely candidate was the 'healthy, well formed young Archduke' whose birth on 12 February 1768 had so excited his grandmother that she had rushed into the court theatre and shouted, 'Der Leopold hat an Buam' (Our Leopold has a boy), to announce the new arrival to the world. One grandfather was the Lorrainer, the late Emperor Francis I, progenitor of the new house of Habsburg–Lorraine, the other a Bourbon, Charles III of Spain. He was christened Francis Charles Joseph; the Emperor Joseph, who was his uncle, installed him as a knight of the Golden Fleece before he was a month old. Francis was the first of a new generation of male Habsburgs, and part of his good fortune was to grow up in the relaxed splendour of Florence rather than constrained by the formality of the imperial capital. Maria Theresa had regarded all her children with almost obsessive affection, but it was in the next generation, and specifically in the family of her second son Leopold, that a new vision of children and childhood came to its full flowering. Leopold had been brought up in the heart of a large and affectionate domestic circle, where both his parents were intimately involved in all the details of their children's upbringing. For his own large (and ever-increasing) family, he devised an upbringing based on the spirit of freedom and self-expression.

The mid eighteenth century has been described as 'the golden age of childhood'. Children were a source of delight and wonder, especially in the house of Habsburg. Leopold commissioned the Bohemian artist Johann Zoffany to portray his family: in the painting he stands there a proud paterfamilias, bright-eyed and alert, while all the children, a little solemnly, follow his example. Only a family dog enthusiastically licking one of the younger children breaks the semi-solemnity. In the background a symbolic fountain splashes, an emblem of the cascade of new life that Leopold and María Luisa brought into the ancient lineage. Leopold was an apostle for a new approach to the young and immature. His preoccupation with the manner and objectives of child-rearing was obsessive. He instructed his younger sister, who had become Queen of Naples, on everything from the choice, care and management of wet nurses to what clothes children should wear. 'The boys, until they are nine, are dressed in sailor suit with large wide trousers, a small jacket at the neck and a round hat . . .' The girls wore simple dresses.

His children were all encouraged to express themselves, to run about freely and indulge in exuberant play, from the oldest to the youngest. When their aunt Archduchess Marie Christine came to Florence in 1776, she delighted in being 'rolled on the floor' with her nieces and nephews.[5] In 1774, he told the tutors of his younger children that: 'The princes must be very aware that they are human beings: that they hold their positions only through the sanction of other human beings; that for their part they must discharge all their duties and cares; and that other people must have the right to expect all the benefits that have been granted to them . . . True greatness is broad, gentle, familiar and popular; it loses nothing by being seen at close quarters.' Francis and his brothers were taught to respect all the virtues of the Enlightenment. Even the English Ambassador, Sir Horace Mann, was impressed.

The method of this young Prince's education ought to be followed, I mean, adopted, for all children of his and more inferior rank . . . He has been . . . attended by men of sense without the least tincture of pedantry.

His amusement even tends to his instruction. He played at Geography by the dissected maps that I was desired to get from England, and on all his walks and rides he is accompanied by people who amuse and instruct him. He has learnt the principal modern languages as the natives do, having attendants of the different nations who always speak their own language to him, by which means, they are familiar to him. By the whole plan of his education it is plain what progress a youth may make at the age of fifteen.[6]

Leopold applied to his own family the benign but autocratic paternalism that he operated in his toy-duchy of Tuscany. In the state, he was endlessly inquisitive and ever-active; Tuscany had the most effective secret police in Europe, a dubious benefit he extended to the Habsburg Empire when he succeeded his brother as Emperor in 1790. In respect of his family he required constant reports from the children's tutors and governesses. But with the call to duty went the need for happiness, and it was this quality that his brother in Vienna, his own life marred by sorrow, had all but forgotten. In 1784 Francis, whom his parents and tutors agreed was a difficult, sly child, was taken to the imperial court to be groomed as a future ruler. The benign indulgence of Florence was replaced by the spartan discipline of his surrogate father, the Emperor Joseph II.

Within weeks of his arrival Joseph, with customary brusqueness, handed him a long list of his flaws and weaknesses, written with a headmasterly severity.

When we consider that he is seventeen years of age, and compare him with others of the same age, we are at once struck with the conviction that his physical development has been completely neglected; that he is stunted in growth; that he is very backward in bodily dexterity and deportment; in short he is neither more nor less than a spoiled mother's child, who considers all that he does himself infinitely important and hazardous and never takes into account what he sees others doing or suffering for him. The manner in which he was treated for upwards of sixteen years could not have but confirmed him in the delusion that the preservation of his own person was the only thing of any importance.[7]

When he did not 'improve' sufficiently, his uncle told him that since he had failed to respond adequately to Joseph's good advice, other methods, of 'fear and unpleasantness' would be used.

Nothing would fully satisfy the imperial martinet. He would admit to Francis's tutor that he had made improvements, that he could sit a horse more easily, and would speak more freely. Yet, 'It still appears, from this journal [kept by Francis on his uncle's instructions, in which he noted every detail of his daily life] and from all my nephew's actions, that he fails to lead himself, to do his own thinking, and to demonstrate the possession of an independent, reflective mind.' He was writing of a gauche and lonely seventeen-year-old, and his sole remedy was isolation, a form of solitary confinement, to make the boy more self-sufficient. 'Left alone to himself, he will be forced to come to his own decisions.'[8]

There is an extraordinary contrast in tone and feeling between the letters which his father wrote to Francis and all the communications from his uncle. Thus, Leopold, in 1790: 'We are and should try to remain two friends who love each other cordially, and contribute together having the well being of the public and the state at heart. You will accomplish through your strength and youth those things which I can no longer do.' By contrast, Joseph in 1788 at his most relaxed and benign: 'I note with great satisfaction your desire to form yourself and grow more strong in the principles that have been dictated solely by my love for you. Join to this goodwill perseverance and efficiency in execution and you will eventually be delighted with the result, will indeed satisfy the world which has the right to expect and demand such an outcome from you.' To brother Leopold the Emperor voiced his true and naturally caustic feelings.

Permit me to speak with full frankness. The more I see at close hand of the training of [your] eldest children, the more convinced I am that pure as are your intentions and earnest as your endeavours for their good, just so defective is either the method or the group of individuals employed by you to educate them ... The oldest children have already taken their bent, but I beg you seriously to consider modifying the vicious training methods where the youngsters are concerned.

Leopold replied temperately that nearly all the tutors had been chosen by Joseph himself, and that he (Leopold) had 'spared neither care, nor assiduity, nor pains, for their education'.[9]

We can legitimately infer that Francis was subjected to a number of powerful and contrary influences, without invoking all the paraphernalia of psycho-history. At Vienna, he learned to control his feelings and the expression of his views, trimming them always to the insatiable and ever-changing demands of his uncle. Some parts of his life he found a relief from the endless inquisition of Joseph's court. He was sent to Hungary to join a regiment and he found the military life, with its set routines and clear requirements, was a society into which he could settle with ease. His naturally affectionate nature found an outlet in the marriage, long planned by Joseph for political reasons, with Elisabeth of Württemberg. But there too, the Emperor's yearning for discipline and subordination frustrated Francis's natural desires. He refused Elisabeth's repeated petitions for her young husband to be allowed leave in the last stages of her first pregnancy, and prolonged his service in the field. 'Yes, that's the way it is when one is the wife of a soldier' was his only response to her pleas. Nor was there time for them to enjoy the brief respites of a soldier's life. In the space of a few months, within a week of his twenty-second birthday, Francis was both a widower and the heir to the throne. Elisabeth died early on the morning of 19 February 1790, after she gave birth to a sickly daughter, while the Emperor, in conflict to the last, finally expired less than twenty-four hours later.

Francis was not at his uncle's deathbed, but on his birthday, 12 February, which was the day before his daughter was born, he had received a present of a diamond-studded dirk from Joseph with a note to say it was 'in memory of an uncle who will soon be no more'. Their relationship was complex: Francis both feared and inordinately admired a man whom he looked upon as a stern father.[10] On Joseph's part, his affection for his nephew was un-feigned, but he sincerely believed that he needed to steel him for the arduous role he was to fulfil. In his final days, he observed, 'I do not miss the throne; I feel at peace, but only a little hurt with so much painful effort to have made so few happy and so many ungrateful; but then, such is the fate of men on the throne.'[11] Constant pain dominated those dying months, with no relief. Nor could he look back to past success in his high-minded endeavours, since all his plans and schemes seemed doomed to failure. Those around him watched him weaken a little day by day, but Joseph refused to give in to the ravages of disease.

Every day he brought up ever larger amounts of blood from his ravaged lungs, often ounces at a time, but he worked on until the last moment. On the last full day of his life he signed eighty documents and then, late in the evening, tired of his dressing gown, he called on his servants to bring him his military uniform. At that late hour he dressed as a soldier once more, and then lay down on his day bed. At five the next morning he woke as normal, and remarked that the sun had not yet risen; he prepared to begin another agonizing day. He collected his papers and asked for a plate of soup for his breakfast, and then, with a sudden presentiment of death, he called for his confessor. But before he arrived, Joseph was racked by convulsions, and died in the space of four minutes, without the last rites of the Church.

His brother Leopold, a most unenthusiastic new Emperor, eventually left Florence for Vienna and was immediately confronted by problems on every side. He wrote to Marie Christine in June 1790,

The internal affairs here are the greatest confusion and there is a shortage of capable officials. It's enough to discourage anyone. The provinces are in ferment. Everyone – provinces, peasants, cities, the nobility, merchants, bishops, the clergy, monks – everyone is demanding rights and privileges and seeks to regain (without regard for justice or discretion) concessions dating as far back as Charlemagne; and they all want everything at once.[12]

He saw that the new priority was to end Joseph's failed political experiments, but above all to restore order and discipline. Consequently, his former tolerance for dissent diminished very rapidly. A political pamphlet criticizing his policy resulted in the following instruction to the governor of Lower Austria in September 1791.

I desire that you should do everything possible in close co-operation with the military and the police (if necessary by the promise of an attractive reward to informers) to discover and arrest one of those responsible for the dangerous and malicious leaflets which have been distributed in order to set a warning example through his appropriate punishment to others like him, and thus . . . to nip this mischief in the bud.[13]

Other problems seemed equally pressing, in the family domain: he needed to find a suitable second wife for Francis. He selected his sister's daughter Marie Theresa of Naples (the same sister he had advised about the care of infants). In this, as in matters of state, Leopold had a surer touch than Joseph, and the marriage was fulfilling to both parties, until she died sixteen years and twelve children later. When separated Marie Theresa sent letters to him daily, and her complaints were only that he did not respond quite as frequently. 'Dearest, best Francis,' she wrote on a sheet of writing paper which she had decorated with hearts, forget-me-nots and red flowers,

On some really pretty paper I am writing you a really thundering letter. I am angry at you, first because you sent me no news of yourself and I fear lest something has happened to you and second, because I am told that you will remain away longer than had been anticipated. But my entire anger will vanish immediately upon your casting your first glance upon me again. Please, dearest love, come back soon.[14]

Leopold hastened from place to place, winning back those alienated by his brother and seeking to confront the new perils of the Revolution in France. He left Francis as his deputy in the capital. Through the winter of 1791 he suffered various ailments, but, always fussily attentive to his health, his complaints were put down by his family and his doctors to his hypochondria. But in February 1792 it became clear that matters were serious, and the court bulletin of 1 March 1792 carried the following unexpected announcement:

His Majesty the Emperor was seized on 28 February with a rheumatic fever accompanied by pains in the chest; the ailment was at once fought with bloodletting and other necessary remedies. On 29 February, the fever increased but three bloodlettings seemed to bring some relief. The following night, however, proved very restless and greatly weakened his powers. On 1 March, the Emperor began to vomit, with horrible convulsions and was unable to retain anything of which he partook. At three thirty in the afternoon he expired, vomiting, in the presence of Her Majesty the Empress.

To his brother Charles the new Emperor Francis II wrote: 'The greatest misfortune which might befall our family now forces me to write to you. Our father died of a stroke at four o'clock today, without receiving the last sacrament, but in the arms of my mother. I am too frightened in my monstrous calamity to write any more.'[15] In the first year of his reign matters got much worse, to an extent he could scarcely have imagined. On 13 May, Marie Theresa suffered a miscarriage, and two days later his mother died, for him as much a shock and torment as the death of his father. Within twelve months the Jacobin leadership of the Revolution in France had cut off the head of its king, Louis XVI; in October 1793, Francis's own aunt, Marie Antoinette, would also meet her end under the democratizing blade of the guillotine.[16]

France was to rule Francis's life as much as the incandescent career of Louis XIV had mesmerized his predecessors. He saw the rise and fall of extremism, the reaction against the excesses of the Revolution, the emergence and triumph of Napoleon Bonaparte. He was instrumental in ending the first French Empire and restoring the old Bourbon line in 1814, only to see it expelled once again in 1830. Francis had become the epitome of reaction: he told the French minister Talleyrand that he had spent twenty years fighting the principles of revolution. But it was only after he had been on the throne for almost twenty years that he became rigid in his beliefs, certain that all change, of whatever sort, was in some way a victory for the forces of democracy and disorder.[17] He was undoubtedly suspicious of radical change from the time that he had first seen the dire effects of Josephinism when he took his father's place in the state council in 1791–2. But he also saw the weakness and incompetence that riddled the old order, and he struggled to make the system more efficient, a more potent instrument in the hands of the Emperor. Without the constant danger from France – which had first cost Austria her territories in the Netherlands and then threatened to dismember many of her other possessions – would Francis have followed the path of extreme conservatism? It was not his most natural course; an absolute monarch he would always have been, but perhaps a more 'enlightened' one.

Francis's invariable response to all issues, mindful of his uncle Joseph, was to work harder and with even greater zeal. In 1794, a conspiracy of 'Jacobins' was discovered in Austria and in Hungary, including both civilians and army officers. At the trial that followed one of the accused, Heinrich Jelline, publicly declared the source of his revolutionary corruption: 'The Enlightened reforms of the Emperor Joseph kindled a blazing fire within me; I devoured the Enlightened political literature with insatiable avidity and I became more and more republican.'[18] The trials revealed only the outer contours of the radical conspiracy. Francis's brother Leopold, who had been appointed the Palatine [Regent] in Hungary wrote to his brother in March 1795, 'Although we have caught a lot of the culprits, we have not really got to the bottom of this business yet.' And Count Pergen, the minister of police, told Count Collorado, Francis's trusted former tutor, 'neither unbelief . . . nor wild democratic aspirations have been destroyed at the source; the itch to criticise even the best actions of the monarch, and revolutionary leanings generally, have not been suppressed.' Radicalism was crushed ruthlessly, and with an eye to deterring others. Two army officers deep in the conspiracy were cruelly dealt with, under the full rigour of the penal code established by Maria Theresa. They were locked in the pillory for three days and nights and then, already battered and half-dead, were hanged in Vienna, and their bodies gibbeted. Other conspirators were sentenced to life imprisonment under the harshest conditions and many died in captivity. In Budapest seven died under the axe or on the gallows and a number were imprisoned. All tried and sentenced were found guilty of *lèse-majesté* and high treason, which carried the harshest penalties: unquestionably, after the executions of his aunt and uncle by marriage, Francis felt that he and his own family were in peril of their lives.

He took a personal and lively interest in the reports from the increasing number of police spies, and over time developed his own system of informers that bypassed the official structure. But for all the repression of the late 1790s and the ever growing network of spies and informers, this was not a 'police state' on the model of Tsarist Russia. C. A. Macartney had a better sense of the system, humanized by Austrian lack of enthusiasm and efficiency:

It was rare for persons to be arrested and kept in prison without trial on political grounds . . . Francis, like his father and uncle before him, used the police reports rather as a means of informing himself on current affairs, including public opinion, than for a more sinister purpose. Intercepted letters were never used against their authors or addressees. A man might have his doings and sayings reported for years and yet live quite unmolested. Francis's first Chief of police . . . although a thoroughgoing obscurantist, was no sadist, and . . . his deputy, was an exceptionally enlightened man.[19]

This all sounds suspiciously like the fabled 'Austrian clemency' of Maria Theresa's day, and if there were no torture chambers, the climate of fear and oppression became stultifying. The case of Franz Grillparzer is illuminating. He was unquestionably a Habsburg patriot, but at the same time also a man of principle. Trained as a lawyer, he hoped for a post in the civil service; his ultimate ambition was to take charge of the imperial library, one of the most desirable posts in the imperial service. However, despite exceptional qualifications, he was endlessly manoeuvred sideways, first into finance and finally into the archive departments. Time and again he was passed over by lesser men: his problem was a hint of political notoriety. What did they have against him? One of his poems roused official misgivings: might not his subject be 'subject to misinterpretation' by foreign governments? Then there was the matter of his first major play, *König Ottokars Glück und Ende*, which was submitted to the censor in November 1823. Two months later he received notification that it 'had not been approved for performance or publication'. No reason was given, and he told his friends, 'No one can understand why.' Fortunately, also in January 1824, the Empress received a copy of the manuscript and read it with pleasure; with her support the censorship was revoked and the play granted a licence. It was first performed to full houses in August 1824. Later Grillparzer met the censor responsible, a most amiable and intelligent person who greeted the author warmly. Informally, he assured the playwright that the ban was only a precautionary measure. When Grillparzer asked him in a most friendly fashion what he had found so disturbing in the play to warrant its suppression, the censor replied with some animation, 'Oh, nothing at all; but I thought to myself "One never can tell".'[20]

Nor did the author's travails end there. With a later play, the Emperor intimated that he wished to purchase the copyright, a

kindly way of ensuring that it never again saw the light of day.
Grillparzer was horrified and again the good offices of the Empress
Caroline Augusta were employed. She persuaded Francis to relent.
But Grillparzer thereafter failed to advance in the imperial service
as he had hoped, or at least within the areas that most interested
him. No doubt his dossier indicated that he was 'unsound'. Even
the slightest hint of any seditious tendency (and the poet-play-
wright's work constantly provided new fuel to the fertile and
inventive minds of the censorship office) was sufficient to keep him
away from the 'sensitive' area of the imperial library.

The Habsburg technique was not so much to punish its opponents
as to manipulate them. A real threat only existed for a few years in
the 1790s but a mortal fear of subversion, even in its mildest forms,
coloured the remaining thirty-two years of Francis's reign. He was
a 'reactionary' in the true and limited sense of the word: he
responded to the perils (real or imagined) of revolution. But he did
not hark back to some pre-Josephinian Golden Age, to a fossilized
autocracy on the traditional Habsburg model. He could see the
success of the new order, embodied in Napoleon's France. She
repeatedly defeated Austria, and all the powers of Europe on the
battlefield, and even, like the Minotaur of Greek legend, had
exacted a maiden tribute from Francis in the form of Napoleon's
marriage to his favourite daughter Marie Louise. As Leopold II had
looked with both suspicion and admiration at Louis XIV, so too
Francis was well aware of the success of the Napoleonic Grand
Style, especially as exemplified in the paintings of David, Gérard
and Gros. These works, both in their original form and in countless
engraved reproductions, carried the message of the French triumph
throughout the continent of Europe. Francis had the intuition and
the imagination to learn from his enemy.

∽   ∽   ∽

The Habsburgs had faced (and overcome) a crisis of legitimacy
when the old dynasty ended with Charles VI. At the death of
Leopold II the institution of monarchy itself had seemed under
threat, not only in the Habsburg lands but throughout Europe.
When the National Convention in Paris declared on 19 November
1792 that it would offer fraternal aid to 'any nation wishing to

recover its liberty' and in the following month ordered its commanders to 'revolutionize' the Austrian Netherlands, the danger was
both clear and immediate.[21] Facing this unparalleled threat was a
young man whom his own father (in his private moments) had
thought possessed of very mediocre talents. His younger brothers,
especially Charles and John, had shown infinitely greater capacities
even from their earliest years. The elements which made up what
the French call his *formation* (and for which there is no precise
equivalent in English)[22] are especially significant. It was the second
time in just over half a century that, at a moment of national crisis,
an inexperienced and callow heir had taken control of the Empire.
The outcome in each case had not been the catastrophe that so
many had confidently anticipated. Maria Theresa had triumphed,
to become the Mother of her country, while Francis, the 'good'
emperor, became the pattern for future rulers of the Habsburg
domains. When a crisis struck for the third time, in 1848, and the
eighteen-year-old Franz Joseph came to the throne, he looked to
memories of his grandfather for his inspiration.

Circumstances forced each of them – Maria Theresa, Francis I
and Franz Joseph – to push the monarchy into a new direction, not
merely because of their youth, but because they responded instinctively to the demands of the moment. In later years, each one of
them would become a totem to immobility, the living exemplar of
frozen convention. What later writers have remembered most powerfully is that final stage of absolute stasis, a memory which has
obscured their earlier and more vital moments. Most accounts start
from a false premise, that the Habsburg system was wholly retro-
grade, and entirely resistant to change. It indeed altered relatively
little over the centuries, but this was only because from the dynasty's
viewpoint its methods and practices continued to match the demands of the moment. However, like a lizard that has being lying
torpidly in the sun for hours on end, it could move with great speed
when threatened.

Biological or ecological hazard is a key stimulant in the process
of animal evolution. The process of genetic transformation does
not take place at an even or steady rate, but in rapid bursts of
activity followed by much longer periods of seeming inanition. In
the political or intellectual sphere, this is roughly the pattern

described by the historian of science, Thomas Kuhn, when he tried
to account for the erratic path of scientific advance. To use Kuhn's
terminology, the Habsburgs under Francis I experienced the effects
of a 'paradigm shift', a transformation in the political and intellectual framework of Europe. Less than two months after his accession
the revolutionary government in Paris had declared war on Austria,
and the prophecy of Prince Kaunitz, the doyen of the Empire's
government and now, in his old age, the protector of the Imperial
Academy of Arts, proved grimly apropos. The magistrates of Vienna
had wished to nominate an artist to provide a portrait of the new
ruler for their council chamber. The prince concurred, but suggested
that they should

have the new lord painted in marshal's uniform and armour; let there be a
reddish-blue sky and an army in the background ... Emperor Francis
will, against his wishes and judgement, become involved in wars ... His
heart will bleed for the suffering of his people but he will be forced to
wage wars. Happy he and the monarchy if his faithful people will not lose
their courage, but persevere steadfastly and bravely until the great fight
shall have been won. I myself will not live to see its conclusion.[23]

However much revisionist historians have managed to blur the
outworn categories such as 'The Age of Revolution' or 'The Industrial Revolution', something had changed. The situation faced by
the Habsburgs in the years of Francis's rule had no precedent or
parallel. His response to the task was neither thoughtless nor
unimaginative, as has been claimed; he did not have the benefit of
hindsight.

๛   ๛   ๛

Francis knew from both his father and his uncle of the power of
public opinion, of the 'will of the people' long before the French
bourgeois revolutionaries had expropriated the term. He had seen
as a child how Leopold had gained the affection of the Florentines
as much by the open manner of his rule as from its actual content.
'Pietro Leopoldo' is still remembered as a true son of Florence
and not some foreign interloper. He had also observed during
the Turkish campaign of 1788 how an ailing Joseph II was revered
by the common soldiers, who would kiss his hands and fall

on their knees before him, like some Alexander.[24] How consciously, then, did Francis decide to try a new tack, presenting himself first as *leader* and then as *father* of his peoples? We do not know directly but it is certain that he encouraged and funded a new 'Imperial cult' that from the first years of the nineteenth century stressed both these qualities.[25] Both leadership and fatherhood were expressed through openness and approachability. He was informal to a degree that even Maria Theresa, who thought of herself as always open to her people, would never have countenanced. The young monarch first presented himself to his peoples at a succession of coronation ceremonies – on 6 June 1792 in Hungary, as Holy Roman Emperor on 15 July and as King of Bohemia in Prague on 6 August 1792. Thereafter he did not retreat into the palace, but remained more accessible to his people, or at least to the Viennese, than any of his predecessors.

He spent two full mornings each week, from seven in the morning to one-thirty in the afternoon, receiving the public. In the open audience on a Friday, anyone could attend, simply notifying the court on the previous Monday so as to obtain a number for a place in the queue.[26] Usually two to three hundred people came on those days, sometimes many more. One disdainful official wrote that 'all the world and his wife, in rags and in riches, as the case happened to be, mingling with the refined odour of perfumed elegance were the ramlike stench of befurred shepherds and the peculiar poverty smell of the needy'.[27] The emperor would receive his people in groups of about thirty, and Francis would talk quietly, in his easy Viennese German, to each individual. He preferred to speak in German, but if his petitioner were Czech, Hungarian or Italian, he would use that language to put them at their ease. He was especially concerned with the pleas of women and children, as Johann Peter Krafft caught in a depiction of Francis in audience in his last years.[28] The Emperor's decision was recorded by his secretary and speedy action invariably followed. He often gave small (but welcome) gifts of money, but in most cases it was the imperial stick applied to the bureaucracy that was the desired and effective outcome.

At these audiences, Francis always wore a simple officer's uniform, without decoration or elaboration, in the manner popularized by

Joseph II. Much of the first twenty years of his reign was either occupied by war or preparation for it. War was unpopular, and Francis took pains to make it plain that he was a man of peace. However, he did see the advantage for Austria to be portrayed as the guardian of German liberties and the principal agent of the 'War of Liberation' from the French, and this image emerged as a constant theme in the new Habsburg iconography. The small image, *The Holy Alliance, 1815*, painted by Heinrich Olivier, who had come from Dessau to Vienna with his brother Friedrich in 1811, encapsulates this new idea of the Austrian emperor in the centre of the struggle against Napoleon. Olivier presents the three leaders of the liberation, the Tsar, and the King of Prussia, with Francis, in an idealized Gothic chapel. Francis stands radiantly in the centre, under a statue of St George, a potently Habsburg emblem. He wears the lambent golden armour of a medieval Habsburg ruler, an image out of the pages of Burgkmair, a gilded man like his ancestors, Maximilian, Rudolf I and Charles V. The other two monarchs stand respectfully to each side, set back a little to enhance Francis's divinely ordained primacy.[29]

Francis responded to the challenge of revolution at a number of different levels. On the first, he sought to make the administrative and governmental structure function more responsively. No Habsburg since Philip II generated so much paper, or harried his officials so consistently.[30] He was unsentimental about old structures that had outlived their usefulness. His decision in 1804 simply to declare that, by virtue of his authority as *Holy Roman Emperor*, he permitted himself to become *Emperor of Austria*, was a breathtaking piece of constitutional trickery, and many questioned its legality. The outrage at this personal aggrandizement became a roar of anger when he declared the old Empire at an end in November 1806, at a stroke sweeping away the traditions of centuries. There was no provision in law for the Empire to be wound up, like some bankrupt business.[31] Francis did so under the doctrine that his will was sovereign.

However, the old order cast away, nothing very much distinguished his new Empire of Austria (vintage 1804) from the despised new Empire of France (vintage 1804). Just as in the years before and after 1740, a new style of legitimization of the Habsburg

destiny was developed.[32] Metternich was well aware of the importance of legitimizing the state's authority in the eyes of the people.
He had learned as much from his time as Ambassador to Paris, as
he wrote, 'Public opinion is the most powerful of forces . . . which
like religion penetrates the most obscure recess, where administrative actions are ineffective; to misunderstand public opinion is as
dangerous as to misunderstand moral principles.'[33] The transmutation of *Holy Roman* Emperor into *Austrian* Emperor (and R. J. W.
Evans has pointed out how 'Austrian' carried virtually no resonance
or meaning in any part of the non-German-speaking provinces)
required a rewriting of the past, in both image and text.

By the last quarter of the eighteenth century, for the first time in
more than two centuries, the Habsburg dynasty had some meaning.
The profusion of the lineage, male and female, many grown to
maturity, was also endowed, for once, with a wealth of talents.
Maria Theresa's sons and daughters, and Leopold's extensive
brood, encompassed men and women of unexpected distinction. Of
Francis's brothers, both John and Charles, achieved real eminence,
the former as a scholar and connoisseur, and the latter as a commander, perhaps the only Habsburg who merits the description, 'a
really talented strategist and a serious student of the art of war'.[34]
John was also unusual in contracting a morganatic marriage – the
first since the sixteenth century – to Anne Plöchl, the daughter of a
postmaster who lived close to Graz in John's native Styria. Charles,
who was slightly built, sickly and suffering from epilepsy, was
'adopted' by his aunt Marie Christine and joined her and her
husband, the Duke of Saxe-Teschen, the joint regents of the Austrian Netherlands. There he received his baptism of fire against the
invading French armies. Like many good generals, he was no fire-
eater, and was strongly against recommencing the war with France.
It was written of him: 'The Archduke Charles is averse to the war
in a degree which no one would believe, if one had not had daily
proofs of it; he would have opposed war under any circumstances,
even if the French had taken Vienna and demanded the Tyrol for
themselves.'[35]
This image of family unity was not wholly matched by the

reality. Francis became increasingly suspicious of his two talented younger brothers, and frequently sought to undermine their position. He set spies on both Charles and John and all their meetings and activities were reported to him. But nevertheless, he gave his support to Archduke John's effort to fabricate an 'Austrian identity', beginning in the years just before the declaration of the *Empire of Austria*.[36] The development began more or less by chance. A noted Swiss historian Johannes von Müller, who served as John's tutor, was invited to become head of the imperial library. His *History of the Swiss Confederation*, published in 1780, had been a defining work of Swiss nationhood; and Archduke John developed the idea of an Austrian equivalent to von Müller, but based on the history of the house of Habsburg.

His protégé, the Innsbruck scholar Joseph Hormayr, was appointed court secretary in Vienna, and worked closely with Müller to manufacture this notion of a national identity from the ancient myths, from Rudolph and the Priest onwards. The result was a cascade of publications. The first was Hormayr's biography of Andreas Hofer, the Tyrolese hero of resistance to the French (1809); then came his *Handbook for a National History* (1810), quickly followed by the twenty massive volumes of his '*Austrian Plutarch*', published under the patronage and with the official financial support of Archduke John. These volumes provided the source material for a great number of writers and artists, as Claudio Magris has observed, 'an authentic patriotic almanac, embracing the totality of the happy Habsburg past, gathering together the greatest figures from the Austrian and Bohemian past in a kind of pantheon, as *a source of edification and emulation*, as the author declared in his introduction'.[37]

Hormayr was not the first of the 'patriotic' writers and others quickly followed in his path, but he was unquestionably the most potent, partly from his vast output and also by virtue of his exalted connections in the *Hofmafia*.[38] In 1816 he was appointed the official historiographer of the Empire, a position of unique power and command, but one which also increasingly brought him into conflict with the chancellor Metternich, and with Francis himself. They saw that the notion of national patriotism which had been so useful against Napoleon could prove a dangerous survival. Hormayr himself, who had assiduously fostered the Tyrolese national revolt against the French, became a suspect character. But in true Habsburg style, he was not disciplined or sanctioned. The authorities tried a more indirect approach, quietly sabotaging his scheme for a continuing archive for history, statistics, literature and art, while constantly praising his dedication and sense of patriotic duty. In 1825, he proposed that the state should fund 'great works of art', which he defined as possessing the appropriate *religious*, and *national*, elements and linked above all to the concepts of fatherland and dynasty. Again lavish praise, but very few commissions, and then inactivity. In 1828, Hormayr left Vienna to take service in Bavaria, and immediately turned his pen to bitter attacks on Francis I and his 'creature', Prince Metternich.

The Hormayr episode illustrates the labyrinthine strategy and practice of the Franciscan 'system' after the final defeat of Napoleon in 1815. It is more usual to call this structure the 'Metternich system' after Francis's chancellor, but this obscures the fact that it was the Emperor who provided its guiding ethos, while managing to remain publicly detached. Francis stood above the fumblings of the bureaucracy. Although the old Empire had ended, he was presented as the natural guide and guardian of Germany's future. Francis's return to the city of Vienna after the battle of Leipzig was made the excuse for a ceremonial entry through a forest of triumphal arches. At the Kärntnertor, he rode beneath a great Roman vault surmounted by his own image displayed as a triumphant Roman emperor, while in the sky (according to the engraving produced to commemorate the events) the Habsburg eagle hovered, with the palm of peace in its claw.[39] Francis's greatest moment of triumph was the Congress of Vienna of 1814–15, where as the Allied dignitaries debated the shape of Europe he played the part of a welcoming host, eager to secure the comfort of his guests.

The price of this gigantic masquerade was 50,000 florins per royal (or merely noble) guest for each day of the congress, an impossible sum for a nation nearly bankrupt from war. But while the congress was debating, Francis was secretly negotiating with the restored French king, busily undermining the position of his two allies, the Tsar Alexander I and Frederick William, the King of

Prussia, with whom he was so frequently portrayed on terms of stately amity.

When Napoleon returned triumphantly to Paris from Elba this secret treaty was discovered and soon found its way into the hands of the Tsar, who was still attending the congress in Vienna.

This treaty, which Francis had secretly concluded against Alexander and Frederick William – his allies and guests who were staying under his roof – had all the time remained a secret from the monarchs and their ministers. A scene now followed which is thus described by General Wolzagen in his memoirs: '. . . the Emperor Alexander sent at an early hour for Stein [the Prussian minister] and said, "I have requested Prince Metternich also to attend and I wish you to be present as a witness of this interview." When the prince entered the room, Alexander held out the paper to him and asked "Do you know this?" The prince tried to answer evasively, but the Emperor cut him short, saying to him, "Metternich, as long as we shall live, this subject shall never be mentioned between us again; now, however, we have something else to do – Napoleon is returned; our alliance must therefore be closer than ever." With these words, he flung the treaty into the grate by his side and dismissed both gentlemen. From that time Alexander who until then had always disliked Metternich and had even tried to remove him from about the Emperor Francis, kept good friends with him to the last day of his life.'[40]

The Tsar like many others, had been taken in by the light touch and superficial amiability of Austrian autocracy; the story of the treaty had revealed that there was steel beneath the furs, silks and velvets.

Francis succeeded in outwardly maintaining the air of the bemused functionary, doing his duty, not understanding the higher issues of policy, and contentedly tending his garden, until the end of his very last days: a sort of *Hofrat Biedermeier*. His spare stooping figure, with his high narrow forehead, sparse fair, ultimately, silver, hair, and stern blue eyes, was a familiar sight in the city of Vienna. To his people he united the majesty of the Habsburgs with the homeliness of the man in the street. He consciously preserved this unique combination, speaking in his lightly accented Viennese,[41] uttering the banal sentiments on the lips of every gentleman. Thus on matters of censorship, he once expressed his amazement that a poem had been banned, saying, 'Our censorship really is silly'; once a well-known actor noted in his diary, in 1832, that he had personally given Francis a play to read, with a view to ensuring its performance. But the Emperor had said to him 'I'll read it, but you'll see – I have no influence.'[42] Nothing could be further from the truth. The system was created to Francis's specification and monitored by his own spies and informers. He trusted no one, least of all his own family.

This unique structure was designed to blur the lines of initiative and responsibility for the execution of the autocracy. This makes it difficult to say that Francis was 'implicated' in the torrent of patriotic propaganda that was created during the last thirty years of his reign. But nothing could enter the public domain without his acquiescence. The censorship commission had oversight over all published works, whether image or text, oral (as in plays) or written. Even objects like sculpture, tableware and textiles could sometimes fall under the restrictions: Metternich defined the objectives of the censorship as 'to block the manifestation of ideas that confound the peace of the state, its interests, and its good order'. Virtually no possible source of contamination was ignored: the censors were as alert to the subversive effect of a saucily exposed breast[43] as to potentially dangerous political ideas. Books would often be licensed for sale only to those who carried a certificate guaranteeing their impermeability to new ideas, or at a price that would restrict sales to the rich.

The model of what was wholesome and acceptable was defined by patronage, with the imperial family playing a major role. Once again, Archduke John took the lead. He recognized that written history could only partially effect the patriotic end he had in mind. So he commissioned a young Viennese artist, Carl Russ, who had won second prize in the Imperial Academy exhibition of 1809 to produce a series of thirty-one paintings drawn from Austrian history, based on Hormayr. These paintings were so successful that he was rewarded by a lucrative official appointment as the curator of the magnificent collection of art in the Belvedere. All Russ's work was of an enthusiastically dynastic stance, showing the part played by the house of Austria in the nation's past, and set a standard for the content of 'dynastic art'.[44]

Russ with a number of other painters and engravers portrayed the *past* glories of the Habsburgs. Francis himself played an active part as a patron, in presenting the role of the Habsburgs in the nation's *present* and *future*. This task required an artist with the capacity to match the great French masters who had glorified Napoleon. Johann Peter Krafft was a pupil of David, although indubitably a lesser painter, but he was much more direct and didactic in his imagery. His assigned task was twofold. First, he was required to show the Habsburgs' association with victory on the field of battle, which produced a long succession of group and individual portraits. He painted the same subjects time and again: Francis in uniform, Archduke Carl victorious on the field of Aspern, Francis meeting his allies, the Tsar of Russia and the King of Prussia, Francis receiving news of victory on the battlefield at Leipzig, plus various other archdukes arrayed in their military splendour. These works established an iconography of military prowess. There were few battle scenes, because there had been only a single victory, at Aspern in 1809. In his images of the Archduke Charles, Krafft pointed to Habsburg courage and Habsburg authority triumphing over the havoc of battle.

Krafft's second task was almost the obverse of the first, to show Francis as a man of the people, beloved by them and also working in their service. The principal vehicle for this new image was a set of three paintings commissioned through his fourth wife, the Empress Caroline Augusta, and painted between 1828 and 1832. They were placed in the great Audience Chamber of the Hofburg. The first represents the return of Francis from the Diet held at Pressburg in 1809. Francis is barely visible in his coach, almost swamped by the cheering crowd, throwing their hats in the air. Men, women and children all vie to shout the loudest in his praise. In the second, Francis returning from the Paris Peace, is more along the lines of a Roman triumph, with the Emperor sitting erect upon his horse, a general leading his troops. The enthusiasm of the people, who throng the picture just as densely, is more respectful and muted: hats waved in loyal greeting but not spiralling up in enthusiastic abandon. The bystanders represent every class and group within the city, united in their gratitude.

For the third image Krafft had at first suggested a moment from the life of the Emperor Joseph II, but the Empress shrewdly proposed an episode in more recent history. Francis had been very ill in April 1826, and she asked the artist to present the first time that the Emperor was seen in public after his illness. Here the crowd are quieter, seemingly anxious and concerned. Francis is dressed in civilian clothes looking drawn and dignified. His devoted subjects crowd the roof of the newly built Burgtor[45] in the background of the painting, standing above a large inscription of the emperor's motto, *Justitia regnorum fundamentum* (Justice is the foundation of kingdoms). These are the only words visible; the painting is an eloquent statement of Francis's gifts to his grateful people. This was a contract: he gave them justice and good government, they gave him their loyalty and their love.

This theme, of the Emperor beloved by his people, became the motif of Krafft's later work. He shows him in an audience, his hand outstretched to a beseeching mother while he looks on with affection and concern at her child. In another, the Emperor is walking with only a single companion (he needs no guards because he is safe in the love of his people) but stands respectfully at the side of the road while a coffin passes by; it was draped in the Habsburg colours, so perhaps it signified one of his old soldiers. In a third, Francis, a humble water-boatman, paddles his visitors in a skiff across the lake at his little castle of Laxenburg. Many of these didactic images were made into engravings for popular consumption, and had a huge success. Few homes in the Empire were without some visual token of their loyalty and patriotism; prying eyes noticed those that did not display one of the approved icons.[46]

The other visual element, sedulously fostered, was the Emperor as a man who took delight in his family. The adulation of children and childhood had developed from the eighteenth-century enchantment with innocence into a topic that was 'safe' under the Franciscan censorship. Adult interests were stifled, so cosy images of childhood could be used to criticize an infantalized society.[47] But these were also popular themes for German Romantic painters such as Philipp Otto Runge, who did not labour under such constraints.[48] The most noted of the Austrian artists specializing in scenes of children was Peter Fendi (hotly pursued by Joseph Danhauser, one of Krafft's pupils) and his picture of the Emperor and Empress happily playing with their grandchildren[49] was the first of many such idealized scenes in which the Habsburgs were shown sharing the delights of family life.

One of the cardinal points that Francis made in his 'Political Testament' to his elder son Ferdinand was 'Preserve unity in the family and regard it as one of the highest goods',[50] and this harmony and unity was displayed many times in formal group portraits of the old Emperor and his family. Leopold Fertbauer painted them in 1826 in a garden setting, under a rustic shelter.[51] Three strapping youths – the two sons and the grandson of Francis, the Archdukes Ferdinand and Franz Karl, and the Duke of Reichstadt, the son of Napoleon and Marie Louise – stand proudly erect, while the women – the Empress, Marie Louise and the Empress's half-sister, Sophie – sit in relaxed ease. Francis stands with his hand affectionately on the chair of the Empress, proud of the green shoots of his progeny, echoing the burgeoning green leaves which threaten to overwhelm the painting on every side. Its counterpart, produced almost a decade later by Peter Fendi, was painted a few months before the Emperor's death. The Fertbauer portrait was on an intimate scale: Fendi, by contrast, produced a grand set-piece of the Habsburg lineage, a family reunion, which is its title.[52]

Here the emperor, 'the father of his people', is also father of his immediate family, which is plainly flourishing through the fourteen young children quietly at play or doted upon by their parents. Francis himself is almost submerged by his multitudinous descent, an echo of the portraits made by Meytens and Zoffany for Maria Theresa and Leopold II. And prominent at the back of the painting is a classical statue depicting an old hero[53] passing the banner of the future to a naked youth. Within months, this prophetic utterance became fact. On 2 March 1835, the day after the anniversary of his father's death, Francis died quietly of a sudden fever, surrounded by his family and with all the spiritual comforts of the Church. A popular lithograph by Wolf shows the dead Emperor on his deathbed, with ordinary Viennese citizens kneeling in sorrow before him, while he is guarded by his soldiers and officers.[54] The cult of the Good Emperor Francis began immediately after his death. Noble ladies in Vienna fought for one of the feathers taken from the three pillows on which he rested as he breathed his last. A vast profusion of engravings, booklets and trinkets commemorating his long reign began to appear. Within five days of his death a competition was launched for a great statue of Francis the Good in Vienna, and towns throughout the Empire vied to have a statue of the old Emperor before their rivals.

The funeral was celebrated in traditional style, but for the first time in St Stephen's cathedral, with a vast catafalque surmounted by a towering column topped by a double-headed eagle. For three days, the people of Vienna filed past to pay their last respects.[55] Then the customary procession assembled and wound its way to the Capuchin church, where the traditional last rites for an Emperor were performed. The best and most honest summary of Francis's career is that of C. A. Macartney.

He was neither a bad man nor a stupid one ... an affectionate husband and father ... he inspired in at least one of his four wives a really passionate and romantic devotion and other members of his family circle seem to have liked and respected him ... He was shrewd above the average, with a disconcerting gift of drawing from any situation the conclusions which were right for his own premises, and possessed, incidentally, of a sardonic sense of humour for which the shocked modern chroniclers of some of his apparently more outrageous sayings have made insufficient allowance.[56]

He goes on to say that Francis had 'no trace of Leopold's genuine constitutional beliefs' while adhering to Joseph's 'unqualified faith in the doctrine of complete monarchic absolutism – not merely, as Eisenmann writes,[57] as a means, but as an end.'

After a reign of forty-three years few could remember a time before Francis, and developing the cult to his memory became one of the principal tasks of his son and successor Ferdinand. He has always been depicted as some kind of amiable idiot, so stricken by epilepsy that he was incapable of exercising any kind of control at all.[58] Some portraits attempted to disguise his oversized head, sparse hair and bulging eyes, and a high colour that always made his cheeks seem as if on fire, in a permanent high blush. Most did not. Like his ancestor Carlos II of Spain he seemed unlikely to have any children, but unlike Carlos, he had a strong constitution; it was not until 1875 that he finally died in Prague, where he was much respected, as he had been when he resided in Vienna. But if he had no children, the succession was assured through his brother Franz Karl, who had married Sophie of Bavaria, the half-sister of the Empress Caroline Augusta. Their four sons, Franz Joseph (born 1830), Ferdinand Maximilian (born 1832), Karl Ludwig (born 1833) and Ludwig Victor (born 1842), were the promise of the future. A single daughter, Maria Anna Pia, was born in 1835, but died in her sixth year.

These were some of the children who delighted Francis I's last years, and who dart in and out of the sugary portraits of Peter Fendi; but his first grandson, born to Franz Karl and Sophie, was his favourite. He paid for the little Franz Joseph to be painted by Waldmüller at the age of three, almost vanishing under a grenadier's cap;[59] the young child was photographed endlessly from as early as 1835.[60] His first communion in 1842 was made into an engraving and widely sold: almost from his birth Franz Joseph was a familiar image to his future people. Hans Pauer has listed over 3,300 separate images made over a lifetime, but these are only those which have been found and are collected. Of necessity the total excludes innumerable popular images, postcards and the like which have been lost to view. In the age of the camera, the capacity to create and replicate an image makes it impossible to hazard an accurate guess at the true total.

So, beyond question, Franz Joseph was the most visible of all the rulers of the house of Habsburg. Yet, despite this profusion of images, the constant chronicling of his daily life, the speculation that accompanied the tragedies of his family in later years, the hundreds of studies, both academic and popular, of his personality and empire, he remains opaque, resistant to inspection or interrogation. Many have made the mistake of regarding him as dull or stupid, wooden in his behaviour and unfeeling in his human relationships.[61] They have been deceived. Franz Joseph guarded his privacy despite the perpetual gaze of the public. He was perhaps the most complex of the Habsburgs since Maximilian I, a man who was forced to come to terms with a world in which power was slipping from the fingers of those who had formerly ruled by right of birth. He did not fail, although many have questioned the nature and style of his success.

ᔆ   ᔆ   ᔆ

I was once wrapped smartly over the knuckles[62] by the late A. J. P. Taylor for talking carelessly about Franz Joseph as 'an autocrat'. He was right, because the Emperor never possessed such a plenitude of power.[63] The Rule of One had vanished in Western Europe. Yet if Franz Joseph was not an autocrat, in fact he yearned to be one, through instinct and training. It was hard to predict this outcome, although from infancy he was brought up with the expectation that he would rule the Empire. He enjoyed a loving and affectionate childhood, surrounded by adults who were entranced by his sheer vitality, glowing pink skin and shock of fine blond hair. His uncle, the Duc de Reichstadt, called him a strawberry ice-cream topped with whipped cream. His doting grandfather gave the little boy a carriage drawn by six horses, and everywhere the imperial guard gave him a royal salute. He took the little boy for walks in the palace grounds. Peter Fendi shows Francis holding him up to put a banknote in the ammunition pouch of a sentry; the Emperor had given him the tiny sabre he is wearing in the picture.[64] He sat him on his knee and taught him to say his first few words of Italian, perhaps remembering his own idyllic childhood in Florence. Toy soldiers were Franz Joseph's passion and he was given his first uniform as a little hussar for his fifth birthday.

Of all the influences in his life, after his mother, his grandfather was probably the most powerful, though he died in Franz Joseph's sixth year. One of the little boy's most vivid early memories had been of his grandfather lying dead and having to control his emotions when he wanted to burst into tears. Francis continued to dominate his grandson's life from beyond the grave. When the boy was older, the educational scheme devised for him by his mother (his father had virtually no influence, then or later) depended strongly on the instructions which Francis had given for the upbringing of his own children. These bear the mark of the terrible two years he had experienced at the court of Joseph II, especially when the Emperor virtually placed him in solitary confinement. In his instructions Francis was explicit: no young archduke was to be left alone, but was to be under supervision and guidance at all times. Tutors and teachers were to confer daily and the programme was designed to equip the young of the house of Habsburg with the required physical and professional skills.

Physical and professional rather than intellectual skills were Francis's prescription, revealing his deep and perpetual prejudice against the over-stimulated brain. Again the example of his uncle Joseph was evident, and he emphasized Joseph's capacity for hard work and his dedication to duty rather than his passion for reform and change. Later critics have commented adversely on the nature of the young archduke's education. Thus Alan Palmer in his study of Franz Joseph remarks,

As an educational programme the scheme had grave defects, even by the standards of the time: there was too much rote learning, too little emphasis on how to think, and – apart from his brothers – virtually no contact with other children in the classroom. Despite half a century of social upheaval there was little difference between what Franz Joseph was learning in the late 1830s and what his grandfather had been learning sixty years before, except for increased attention to the minor languages of the empire.[65]

In fact, there were many differences from the enlightened education that Francis had received under Leopold's programme and that prescribed for Franz Joseph; and it was precisely because of the half-century of social upheaval that it was so much more constrained and rigorous.

The educational scheme was designed to allow no time for idle thought, for straying from the defined path. Palmer goes on to compare the education received by Albert of Saxe-Coburg and the plan devised for the children of Albert and Queen Victoria. Precisely how successful that extraordinary system of indoctrination was for his eldest son, the Prince of Wales, is open to doubt. Franz Joseph's training, which is a better term, was over-elaborate, but it was related to the realities of life for a future ruler. It was more important that he should ride well than that he should enjoy the poems of Goethe, or even the history of Hormayr. In fact both featured, although Franz Joseph's favourite pastime was drawing and sketching, for which he displayed some talent. The influence of Francis was again apparent, first in the stress on military experience – his own days with the regiment had been his happiest time in Vienna – and then in the imperative need for linguistic mastery. That Francis had been able to talk in Hungarian to his Hungarian subjects had eased his path, and his grandson displayed the same aptitude.

I have taken some space to rebut the criticisms levelled at the training given to Franz Joseph, because for the most part they apply standards that are either anachronistic or irrelevant to the real needs of a future ruler of the Austrian empire. More malign were the moral principles drummed into all Sophie's elder children, although her youngest son, Ludwig Victor, had a much easier passage. His mother's favourite, he was rather the runt of the litter, and perhaps his future career would have been less chequered if he had also been instructed in the need for responsibility and a sense of duty. Franz Joseph was taught the simple creed of the Habsburgs. The family had been chosen by God to do his bidding, and they would live their lives in his service. They were called upon to rule according to the traditional precepts for the good of their people. They would sacrifice their lives and their comfort to bring their subjects' contentment and happiness. Unfortunately these principles, honourable as they were, allowed no free will to the people of the Empire, no right to decide for themselves where *their* happiness was to be found.

'Pietas Austriaca', which had languished under Joseph II, was reborn. The image of the three little children of Sophie, in a water-colour by Peter Fendi,[66] kneeling before an image of Christ and the Virgin Mary, watched over by the vigilant figure of their mother, is a silent emblem of the renewed importance of the traditional Habsburg values. Franz Joseph, in addition to receiving his political education each week from Prince Metternich, was also taught by Archbishop Rauscher of Vienna, an apostle of the revived force of Catholicism after the rationalist attacks of the eighteenth century. The words which were being poured into his ears from every side were Legitimacy, Duty, and the need for Faith. He dutifully absorbed them all.

It was, years later, rightly said that he had all the qualities of an ideal regimental officer, limited in his outlook, utterly loyal and, as it turned out, fearless. His education was designed to create a product; as Jean Bled has observed, 'However we judge Franz Joseph's education, it had the merit of coherence. Although it was broadly based, his tutor's concern was always to inculcate an aversion to liberalism in the prince and to prepare him for authoritarian methods of government. This aspect of his education left an indelible mark on him.'[67] The product was right for the times, since no one could imagine the end of established order. Some parts of the Habsburg lands were experiencing a surge of prosperity and industrial development. The contented fleshy burghers, male and female, who populated the paintings of the 'Biedermeier era', were taken from life. The upheaval of 1830 in France and Belgium had left the Austrian lands virtually untouched. There was no seething discontent, just a little political dyspepsia; Franz Joseph was educated and trained to rule, in the fullness of time, during a continuation of these Good Old Days.

When Revolution erupted in March 1848, few governments in Europe had any notion as to how to deal with it.[68] In Vienna, they havered between taking a firm line and making concessions. In the end it was ruthless suppression that worked, although not quite so bloody as the destruction of the Paris Commune of 1870. Ultimately, the real threat to the established order came from Hungary and not Vienna. Prince Metternich fled from the capital, some said disguised as a washerwoman, and any clear sense of direction vanished with him. In this vacuum, Archduchess Sophie's influence grew stronger within the family; she was at this time 'the only man in the House of Habsburg'. She had been convinced from the outset that the revolution would end in blood, either her family's, in a ghastly rerun of Marie Antoinette in 1793, or that of the 'unspeakable rebels'. She was prepared to go to any extremity to protect her children, and not for the first time the women of the House of Habsburg revealed greater talent and capacity for command than the men. She sent Franz Joseph south to the Tyrol and thence to the protection of the Austrian army in Italy commanded by Field Marshal Radetzky, a hero of the war against Napoleon. She wrote to Radetzky. 'I am about to place my most precious Heart's Blood in your hands! Lead my child along your path, for he will then progress fearlessly and with honour. Be a good father to him – for he is a good and honest boy and ever since his childhood he has loved a soldier's career.'[69] Radetzky, who faced the threat from the kingdom of Savoy with an inadequate army that only his energy and personality held together,[70] cannot have relished the additional nursemaid's burden. But he realized that the dynasty's future lay with the shy young man, not old enough to be a lieutenant but who already wore a colonel's uniform. Franz Joseph's presence in Radetzky's army gives an added meaning to Grillparzer's famous line in praise of 'the oldest soldier in the army': 'In your camp is Austria.'[71]

The journey to Italy in the spring of 1848 left an indelible impression on the young archduke. First, he saw the deep springs of loyalty and affection for the Habsburgs among the country people around Innsbruck, quite different from the surly truculence of the Viennese. Second, once with the army, he felt at home; like his grandfather he found an answer to all his doubts in the unquestioning certainties of military life. He took part in a battle, at Santa Lucia, on 6 May 1848, a small but significant victory for Austrian arms over the army of the king of Savoy. His elated note to his mother written at eight in the evening after the battle told how he faced the cannonballs for the first time and how lucky he had been to escape injury.[72] As their letters flowed back and forward, he told her how any sign of Habsburg firmness galvanized the army. Six hundred copies of the Emperor's manifesto, he noted, were printed in Italian and were loyally read by the troops.[73]

By the time he returned north to rejoin his family on 5 June 1848, Franz Joseph had undergone a rite of passage. He had stood shoulder to shoulder with his fellow soldiers through the repeated dangers of war. He saw the events of the capital in a new light, contrasting the disloyal Viennese civilians with those soldiers who like him had risked their lives in the service of their country. Undoubtedly he loved the colour and glory of battle (in so far as he had seen it – Radetzky had ensured that he was kept away from most perilous situations). But it was more that he felt that he had done his duty and achieved adult status. Before Santa Lucia, he wrote dutifully as a little boy to his mother, and afterwards, exultantly, with a man's confidence.[74] Previously he had worn the uniform because his rank and station entitled him to it; now he had earned it through his own achievement. To the very end of his life, his habitual dress when working quietly at his desk was a version of that simple uniform he had worn at Santa Lucia, more than sixty-five years before.

It is hard not to feel the appeal of the young Franz Joseph. He was affectionate and concerned about his brothers and their family life. His love for his mother was all-embracing; he was dutiful and respectful to his aunt the Empress. The Emperor Ferdinand remarked that he had 'a good heart'. Yet the surface appeal is deceptive. Franz Joseph possessed the Habsburg stubbornness and obstinacy to an almost pathological degree. His responses to any situation were not based on reason and inner debate, but on a visceral sense of certainty. And, like his ancestor, Ferdinand II,[75] he would simply accept the will of God, whether it were good or ill. Ferdinand's remark to his confessor in the Bohemian crisis of 1619 could just as easily have come from the lips of Franz Joseph: 'I have weighed the dangers that approach from all sides and since I know of no further human aid, I asked the Lord for his help. But if it should be the will of God that I go under in this struggle, so be it.'

In October 1848, the situation in Vienna took the violent turn that Sophie had long expected. A large contingent of hussars under Count Lobkowitz had been sent by the commander of the Northern army, Prince Windischgrätz, to protect the imperial family, gathered within the ancient fortress walls of the Hofburg. The hussars camped in the inner courtyard, and stood guard at all the doors and windows. The gates to the city were kept closed, but from within, they could hear tumult in the streets. Late in the afternoon of 6 October, almost within sight of the windows, the naked body of the minister of war, Count Latour, 'bestially mutilated' as the contemporary accounts discreetly put it, and still bleeding profusely from countless cuts and slashes all over his body, was hanged from a lamp standard.

Lobkowitz decided immediately that the imperial family would leave at dawn on the following day and seek the protection of Windischgrätz's large army. The night was spent in feverish packing and preparing the coaches for the long journey. Franz Joseph wished, as an officer, to ride with the escort, but he was told that it was too dangerous and he should travel in a closed coach. Shortly after first light on Saturday, 7 October, the outer gates of the Hofburg were opened and the first troop of hussars rode slowly out, their sabres drawn. They were followed by the first of the coaches, their blinds down, and surrounded on each side by lines of hussars with their carbines at the ready. A sharpshooter sat next to the driver, and others took the place of the postilions. The atmosphere was tense as the caravan of black coaches left as if heading for Schönbrunn. The escort was prepared for an attack, especially at the city gate, but nothing happened; there were even some cheers for the Emperor from the few Viennese around at that early hour who recognized the imperial crest.

Within the hour they were well beyond the city limits, and a sense of relief and anticlimax came over the whole party. The blinds of the coaches were raised, to allow the thin winter light to reach the occupants, and the hussars sheathed their sabres and carbines. It is unlikely that the family was ever in any danger, for the people's anger was directed solely at the ministers and army commanders. Wrongly, the Viennese assumed that the Emperor was unquestionably on the side of his people, evidence perhaps of the success of the imperial image fostered by Francis and inherited by Ferdinand. The procession of carriages travelled slowly, stopping about twenty miles from Vienna on the first night and, after crossing the Danube, headed for the town of Olmütz in Moravia, where the Bishop's palace had been prepared as their temporary residence. They arrived there on 14 October, just as the huge army led by Windischgrätz was moving south-east against the city they had recently abandoned. The two events were not coincidental.

As Windischgrätz's force manoeuvred and encircled the city, it was the first time that Vienna had been besieged since the Turks encamped around it in 1683. The municipal council, after a few days of skirmishing in the suburbs, agreed to open the gates of the city and surrender. But then, hearing that a relieving force of their Hungarian allies was at hand, the citizens' militia repudiated the agreement and prepared to fight on. Windischgrätz, who had ranged over 200 artillery pieces around the city, and was anxious to purge the city, relished the chance to take it by storm. The bombardment was concentrated and quite short, but it did enormous damage, and cowed those within the walls. Engravings made at the time by artists standing with the general on the Kahlenberg hill showed the whole city lit up by innumerable fires from the shelling. When the army stormed the city walls, there was little resistance but a few die-hards made a stand, and the imperial troops sometimes had to fight from street to street. Two thousand armed citizens and non-combatants were killed in the bombardment and the fighting and another 2,000 were arrested for sedition. But 'Austrian clemency' was the rule, and the victors abandoned the idea of a general purge. Only twenty-five of the leaders were shot, but a great many more citizen-soldiers were conscripted and sent under guard to join the army in Italy. Those responsible for the murder of Latour were tried and immediately hanged.

It was another month before the final scene was enacted. The senior Habsburgs, led by Archduke John, had already decided that while Ferdinand was an acceptable figurehead for peacetime, supported by a strong team of ministers and 'advisers', he could not be expected to rule in such troubled times. However, no Habsburg had ever abdicated, although Maria Theresa and Joseph II had ruled in tandem. There was no constitutional provision under the family statute of 1839[76] for an Emperor to abdicate, and the assumption was that primogeniture would always operate, as it had in Francis's last years when the question of his successor arose. He would not hear of the proper order, established by the Pragmatic Sanction, being disturbed. It was God's will that Ferdinand should succeed him, and echoing the words of the Austrian national anthem, God would protect both the Emperor and Austria, whatever the circumstances.[77] In the summer of 1848, the proposal was, as it had been in the seventeenth century when the succession to the Emperor Matthias was agreed, that the throne should be handed on to a new generation. Not only would Ferdinand abdicate, but he would be succeeded not by his brother, next in line, but his nephew who would only reach his eighteenth birthday in August 1848. Even then, he would not officially have come of age in a number of the Habsburg dominions.

The deed that was enacted in the early morning of 2 December 1848 was of questionable legality. In the seventeenth century, there had been only family custom; now there was a legal family agreement, signed and binding on all parties. None the less, setting all such doubts aside, orders had been issued by Ferdinand the previous evening for the family and the local notables to assemble in formal dress in the grand salon of the Bishop's palace at 8.00 a.m. Sophie wore a court dress of white moiré silk and a jewelled rose in her hair. Franz Joseph, Maximilian and Karl Ludwig wore uniform, and the six-year-old Ludwig Victor a new suit appropriate to his age. None of the boys except Franz Joseph had any idea why they had been summoned. The Emperor and Empress entered, amid complete silence and the former read a short speech from a piece of paper handed to him by Prince Schwarzenberg, the new prime minister since October. He spoke in a low voice and stumbled over the words.

It has been the motto of Our Government [he said] to be the protector of the law . . . it has been its aim to promote the welfare of its peoples. But the impact of events, the unmistakable and conclusive desire for a far-reaching and comprehensive modification of constitutional forms, which we have endeavoured to initiate in March of this year, have, however, convinced us that younger shoulders are needed to foster the lofty work and to bring it to a fruitful completion.[78]

Then Schwarzenberg read the decree of abdication, which included a statement that Franz Karl waived his own claims, repeating the Emperor's assertion that a younger person was needed. Then Franz Joseph came forward and knelt before his uncle, who placed his hand on his head and gave him his blessing saying, 'God bless you. Bear yourself bravely. God will protect you. I don't mind. It is done gladly.'[79]

But profound concerns remained. Just before the Emperor had entered the room where the ceremony was to take place he had had second thoughts; he had been in doubt all through the summer and only pressure from his wife and other members of his family, especially his uncle, had convinced him. Franz Karl too had been most reluctant to stand aside for his son, and had suffered sleepless nights until his father had appeared to him in a dream and had given his assent, by laying his hand on his grandson's head. The pressure for change had come from a small group – General

Windischgrätz, the Empress, Archduke John and latterly, the Archduchess Sophie – but it was a revolutionary act not at all in accord
with tradition.

After all the documents had been signed and the imperial seal
affixed, a peal of trumpets announced the transfer of power outside
the Bishop's palace, and the proclamation was read from the steps
of the cathedral. The former Emperor recorded the day's events in
his diary. 'The affair ended with the new Emperor kneeling before
his old Emperor and Lord, that is to say, me, and asking for a
blessing, which I gave him, laying both hands on his head and
making the sign of the Holy Cross ... then I embraced him and
kissed our new master, and then we went to our room. Afterward
I and my dear wife heard Holy Mass ... After that I and my dear
wife packed our bags.'[80] Early in the afternoon, they took their
carriage to the station, with the new Emperor riding beside the
carriage on his horse. At the station he bade them farewell, as
their train pulled out for Prague and their new home in the
Hradčany palace. Perhaps it was appropriate that Ferdinand took
up residence in the palace which had been the home of the unfortunate Rudolf II, the last emperor of the Habsburg line to be
similarly spurned.

An elaborate mythology was erected around the events of
2 December. It could not be called a coronation, so it was normally
described as an 'enthronement'. But there was no throne, nor any
of the traditional regalia, although many of the popular engravings
inserted crowns, orbs and the like to give the event some degree of
authenticity. It was, in truth, a *coup d'état* and the Hungarians in
particular were quick to recognize its illicit nature. For almost
twenty years, until Franz Joseph made his pact with Hungary in
1867 and was crowned in Budapest, dissident Hungarians continued
to recognize only their crowned king, Ferdinand, in his retirement
in Prague. In 1848, the family swept away the legal niceties to
achieve the result that they wanted. There were precedents in the
tribal customs of the family, for there was the long tradition of
'partible inheritance' that antedated the strict enforcement of primogeniture. What mattered in the end was not so much the letter of
the family law, but the collective sense of the Habsburg lineage. In
1848, as in previous situations,[81] the clan spoke through the senior

archdukes, who were consulted and gave their assent, just as they had done since the fifteenth century. A. J. P. Taylor once called the Habsburgs 'the toughest organization in the history of modern Europe'.[82] Tough, and resilient.

The first task that confronted the new Emperor was to bring the rebellion in Hungary to an end. The King of Hanover, who was kept well informed and had managed to keep the revolutionary contagion out of his little kingdom, received a personal communication from Franz Joseph outlining his plans. The king wrote: 'It seems to me that with such an immense force as is now employed, Hungary is completely surrounded and thus cannot hold out . . . I own that I was staggered when I was informed of the abdication of Ferdinand in favour of his nephew Francis, being doubtful if in the present state of Hungary this might not lead to a complete disavowal of the kingdom ever to return the sovereignty of Austria.'[83] The suppression was achieved with the utmost severity, but not without great difficulty, and the humiliating need to call for aid from the armies of Russia. The principle which the Austrian commander, General Haynau, then adopted was 'to hang all the chiefs, shoot the Austrian officers who have taken service with the enemy and have Hungarian officers who had formerly been civilians or NCOs in our army conscripted as private soldiers'.[84] On 6 October, thirteen generals were shot or hanged, and about 500 death sentences were passed, of which 114 were carried out, and nearly 2,000 people imprisoned for long periods. Seventy-five notables who had fled the country were hanged in effigy. To that must be added the night searches, rapes and thefts by imperial troops, especially the wild Balkan irregulars, that went on for months. Order and quiet were finally restored throughout the Habsburg lands, but the bitterness in Hungary destroyed all hope of a lasting settlement.

Franz (*Franzi* was what he was always called within the family) decided on that first day in Olmütz that his imperial title should be *Franz Joseph I*, resonant with memories of both his grandfather and his great uncle. From the beginning, a concerted effort was made to create a cult of this new monarchy. At first it emphasized youth and vigour; then after his marriage to Elisabeth of Bavaria, the young lover; and, soon, the affectionate father of a family. And, latterly, it was said that children in the Habsburg monarchy all knew what God looked like, for his benign bewhiskered features looked down on them in every schoolroom. In his novel *The Radetzky March*, Josef Roth described what all his contemporaries would instantly have recognized.

Carl Joseph stared at the Emperor's portrait hanging on the opposite wall. There, in the flower-white of a general's uniform stood Francis Joseph, with the wide, blood-red sash across his chest, and at his throat, the Order of the Golden Fleece ... Carl Joseph remembered how the sight of the portrait had, in the first weeks after he joined the regiment, afforded him a kind of proud consolation. Then it was, as if the Emperor might at any instant have stepped out of the narrow black frame and come down to him. But gradually the Supreme War Lord had taken on the indifferent, habitual aspect of his stamps and coins. His portrait in the officer's club hung like some esoteric sacrifice offered to himself by a god ... At home this very portrait hung on the District Commissioner's study [his father]. It hung in the great hall of the Cadet School. It hung in the colonel's office in the barracks. The Emperor Francis Joseph was scattered a hundred-fold, throughout the length and breadth of his Empire, omnipresent among all his people as God is omnipresent in the world.[85]

Franz Joseph built a unique image of the monarch, as the 'first servant' of his peoples, in the manner of Joseph II and Leopold II. He never hesitated to take direct and personal responsibility for all the many problems and failures of his rule, in war and peace. He has been the subject of many studies, yet he remains enigmatic. Most of the personal accounts were written when he was already an old man. Those reminiscences, often affectionate, still portray him as merely an accumulation of pedantries and mannerisms. At times, he is the Kindly Old Emperor, so simple in his own needs that he slept on a simple iron bedstead in a small room behind his office; or, at others, the Military Autocrat, furious that an officer did not have the regulation number of buttons on his sleeve. Once at dinner the Emperor kept staring at a young orderly officer at the far end of the table. After the meal was over, and the guests adjourned to the garden, Franz Joseph

went straight up to the lieutenant and thundered at him 'What do you mean by not being dressed according to regulations?' The officer turned deathly pale in his utter amazement; he was deprived of speech and simply stared at his sovereign. It was only too plain that he had not the remotest idea to what the Emperor's angry remark referred. The Emperor understood and continued even more angrily: 'You've no buttons on your sleeves. Didn't you know it?' The lieutenant glanced desperately at his sleeve on which there were no buttons and replied in a broken trembling voice: 'No, your Majesty, indeed I did not!' Quivering with rage, the Emperor exclaimed, 'Then you don't know the regulations. It's monstrous.'[86]

There was, however, an unrecorded sequel to the story. The Emperor continued to fulminate on the following day about declining standards, until he was told by his staff that the officer was not at fault. Whatever the regulations might say, most of the military tailors had simply ceased to make uniforms with the buttons, which had now become purely decorative. Franz Joseph listened quietly, and said 'It is quite wrong' and gave instructions that his own tailor was to make up a new set of uniforms for the young officer, complete with buttons, at his expense. He also made sure that on a subsequent occasion he singled out the orderly officer for a mark of special favour. Whether 'It is quite wrong' referred to his own uncharacteristically harsh behaviour, or to the turpitude of the military tailors, is not clear.[87]

It is impossible to penetrate the mind and character of an individual long dead. It was especially so with Franz Joseph. The journalist Henry Wickham Steed asked Count Khuen Héderváry, who had served the Emperor for thirty years, what he was like. The count thought and finally answered.

I do not know the Emperor, that is I have probably had more experience of him than any other minister in Austria or in Hungary, but I do not, and never shall feel that I know him. Often when he has been in a good humour because something had gone well and he has begun to laugh and chaff, I have thought, 'Now I am going to see the real man', but at that very moment, an invisible veil has fallen between him and me, insulating him, as it were, from any current of human sympathy. Behind the veil would be, not a man but a monarch, persuaded of his own Divine Right, and of his responsibility to none save the Deity. If you want to study the Emperor you must study Austro-Hungarian history for the last sixty years.[88]

Most of the accounts of Franz Joseph have followed this approach and tried to present him in terms of his surface and then assumed that, behind the veil, he was just the same. The surface, then, was the whole man.

Franz Joseph was indeed, as Margutti remarked, 'an apostle of method'. As an old man he liked an ordered life, free from disruption and disturbance. He had his own ways of doing things, and the authority to ensure that his whim was law. His wilfulness defined the conduct of government in the first years of his reign. His early biographer, Joseph Redlich, remarked:

It has been said of the Habsburgs that many of them had the traits of the genuine artist in their make up in so far as they had the powerful impulse to mould the inchoate in accordance with their will ... This mystic inheritance of his ancestral house does not fit readily with the dry matter-of-factness of Francis Joseph. And yet in the rigid calm, the almost somnambulistic appearance, with which the young man of twenty conceived the idea of a modern, technically efficient autocracy as the only possible reply of revolution in almost every part of his inherited realm, and carried it through, simply and solely by the force of his own resolution – in this there is something analogous to the relation of the artist to the material through which he seeks to convey his thoughts and visions to the outside world.[89]

But did he carry the habits of the office into other and more intimate areas of his life? Was he, perhaps, a stuffy, soulless, bureaucrat at home, and, most particularly, in the bedroom?

There is an alternative view. Far from being an empty husk of a man, a man, to adapt Robert Musil's phrase, 'without qualities',[90] void of emotions and strong feelings, and sustained only by the carapace of order, Franzi was a man driven by his will and his passions. These he set himself to curb and discipline. Order, pattern and system were a way of keeping that incipient chaos in check. But at times throughout his life, feelings ruled him. There are a number of occasions when the veil was lifted. First, and most significantly, there was the matter of his marriage. His father's marriage had been arranged, while Joseph II and Leopold II selected his grandfather's first two partners. The Archduchess Sophie looked upon him as a dutiful son, and expected him to follow her wishes (and family custom) in the matter. But he chose not the wife she had selected for him, but her younger sister. He first met his cousin Helene of Bavaria (his putative bride) and her sister Elisabeth in their holiday hotel at the little spa town of Bad Ischl, three days before his birthday in 1853. At their first meeting, although he paid dutiful attention to Helene, his attention constantly wandered to Elisabeth (Sisi) who had been paired off with his younger brother. Afterwards, Karl Ludwig told his mother, 'Mama, Franzi likes Sisi very much, better than Néné. You will see, he will choose her instead of the elder one. "What an idea" said the Archduchess, "That Romp (Fratz)!"'[91] But his brother was right and nothing would dissuade Franz Joseph. In the most whirlwind of romances, over the space of two days, he had pressured his mother to secure the consent of her sister, Elisabeth's mother, and by the end of the following day, 19 August, he and the sixteen-year-old Sisi were engaged. At mass on the next morning, at the end of the service, Franz Joseph led Elisabeth to the altar steps, and asked for the priest's blessing on him and his future wife.

He had fallen in love with her 'luxuriant and beautiful hair, in exquisite harmony with her eyes, as shy as those of a doe',[92] with a vision rather than the reality. The reality was a gauche and rather difficult girl, flattered yet terrified by his overwhelming passion. In his uniform, with his good looks, to say nothing of his exalted rank, he was indeed the fairy-tale prince. His passion, from those first moments, seems never to have wavered, hers seems never to have been truly roused. In the last days of their stay in Ischl, he took her on a long drive in the woods in an open carriage. As the sun set and evening chill descended, he wrapped his military cloak around her shoulders and whispered in her ear, 'You know, I can hardly say how happy I am.' That wrapping was an emblem of their future relationship. In time she came to resent his enveloping, stifling care, and could not understand his sense of rebuff when she refused his protective arm. His love overflows in his letters to her. Whenever they were parted he wrote with punctilious regularity, to his 'Dear Angel', or to his 'Dear, dear, only Angel'. From 1867, when she conceived her passion for Hungary and the Hungarians, he always began his letters with a Hungarian phrase, 'My sweet, dearest soul', or 'My Heart's Love'. Then he no longer signed himself 'Franz', but 'Your little Man', or 'Your little one'. His last letter, on 12 September 1898, concluded with, 'Farewell my most beautiful, best and sweetest Angel', which was prophetic, for she never received it. When it reached Geneva, she was lying dead, stabbed to death with a sharpened file by an Italian anarchist.

When the news was brought to Franz Joseph he snatched the telegram from the hands of the messenger, tearing it open in his anxiety. When he read 'Her Majesty the Empress has just passed away', he sat down at his writing desk and wept uncontrollably. He muttered, 'So I am to be spared nothing in this world ... Nobody knows the love we had for each other.' Then he contained himself, and said, 'First of all, the children must be informed.'[93] That conflict, between the demands of feeling and the call of duty, had been a source of contention between him and Elisabeth throughout their marriage. He tried to adapt to her needs, accepting her wish to live outside the constraints of the imperial role, to travel and establish her own life, whether in the Greek islands, hunting in the English shires, or roaming incognito through France and Germany. He tried every means to attract her home, most successfully by creating the home in Hungary that she had long desired, at Gödöllö.[94] He lavished money and presents upon her. But it was in vain. If not precisely 'the bureaucrat in the bedroom', he remained the Emperor, a role which had become second skin.

But to the world, their relationship seemed an idyll. Visually they were an ideal match, the slim young officer and the willowy bride with her cascade of dark-brown hair. One eyewitness was the Countess of Westmoreland, who saw Elisabeth arrive in Vienna.

They are the most charming couple and the best matched one can imagine. She is a thousand times better than her portraits; none of them give an idea of her freshness, her air of candour and gentleness and intelligence, and of the perfect grace of all her movements. If her features are not perfect, they are delicate; her complexion white and clear, her lips like coral, her brown eyes not large, rather deep set, but bright, pretty hair . . . Her figure is charming, medium size, slender and lissom, pretty shoulders and round arms, a most distinguished air and a young soft voice. I saw her arrive on the boat at Nussdorf . . . Hardly had the boat touched than the Emperor ran on to the bridge and embraced her openly. I can't tell you the effect of this simple natural act. Not only thousands of spectators on the banks burst into prolonged cheers, but many eyes besides mine were wet . . .[95]

The demand for memorabilia was insatiable. One popular souvenir at the time of their engagement was a portrait painted on porcelain. The artist did not quite know what the mysterious young bride actually looked like, so he has the colour of her hair entirely wrong. The Vienna porcelain works produced a set of three biscuit statuettes.[96] In the first, they are dressed as Tyrolese peasants, she sitting and looking up, as he stares down protectively; then, in the second, as the bridal pair, arm in arm exchanging loving glances; and, finally, as the proud young parents, she holding their first child, Sophie, born in April 1855, while he looks down in pride and wonder. The reality was different.

The struggle between two strong personalities, Elisabeth and her mother-in-law Archduchess Sophie, began shortly after the marriage, and was made more complex by their additional relationship as aunt and niece. Elisabeth's mother felt as much loyalty to her sister as to her daughter. Elisabeth bitterly resented her mother-in-law's interference with the upbringing of her first daughter, also called Sophie, and her second, Gisela (born in July 1856). Against her mother-in-law's advice, she took her elder daughter with her when she and Franz Joseph visited Venice in 1856, and both her children when they went to Budapest in the spring of 1857. Soon after their arrival on the second trip both children fell ill with a high fever and Elisabeth had wished to cancel an official visit to rural Hungary which was imminent. She and Franz Joseph were 'in the greatest distress', for as he wrote to his mother, 'The little thing cries and screams incessantly in the most heartrending way . . . what Sisi and I are suffering, you can imagine.'[97] But, in the end he had insisted that the duties of state meant that they had to fulfil their obligations, and she had had to leave Budapest without her elder daughter, who was vomiting blood and bile, but with the memory of those incessant cries. Their journey was almost completed when on 28 May they received news that Sophie had worsened, and when they returned to the Hungarian capital 'Baby' had only a few hours to live.

Elisabeth never fully recovered from the death of Sophie, a little after the child's second birthday. But a little over a year later, on 21 August 1858, she fulfilled her Habsburg destiny and gave birth to the son and heir for whom they had all longed. Tears ran down the face of Franzi when he saw his son, whom he described as 'not beautiful, but magnificently built and very strong'. He was named 'Rudolf Franz Carl Joseph', but the name Rudolf stressed the contact with the Habsburg past. A coloured engraving celebrated his birth, with the infant, the order of the Golden Fleece around his neck, in a cradle supported on what can only be described as a 'Plus Ultra' column, under a portrait of the first Rudolf, with an angel flying above his happy parents.[98] His special position was recognized in another manner. Franz Joseph granted him the title 'Crown Prince' to distinguish him from all the other archdukes, rather as the elder son of the Holy Roman Emperor might be King of the Romans. But by Rudolf's second birthday, the relationship between his parents was almost at the point of rupture. In November 1860, Elisabeth insisted on travelling to Madeira for an extended stay, for the sake of her health. Her doctor could find nothing wrong with her, but in public suggested some tubercular infection.[99] Queen Victoria placed a yacht at her disposal. She spent the winter in Madeira, returning to Vienna at the end of May 1861. A little over a month later Franz Joseph was saying goodbye to her again, as she set off for Corfu. In October Franz Joseph went to visit her in her Mediterranean retreat and agreed that she would return to him when her health was better. In August 1862, she suddenly arrived in Vienna four days before his birthday.

She continued to alight like a bird of passage, sometimes staying for months (or even years) at a time, and at others staying away for almost as long. A brief reconciliation in 1867 resulted in the birth of their last child, Marie Valerie, in April 1868. She grew even more beautiful as she became older. Baroness Bloomfield, the wife of the English Ambassador, saw her for the first time in 1860.

She was very beautiful, tall, and had the greatest profusion of rich brown hair, which hung in curls down her back. She wore a magenta-coloured satin train, and when the folding doors were thrown wide open, she appeared like a beautiful vision . . . Her eyes were very fine, her complexion brilliant, and altogether most striking. She spoke in English, which she informed me she had learned from her father's grooms! She was passionately fond of dogs and horses, rode splendidly, and sometimes drove four in hand.[100]

She became concerned that she would put on weight, and had a private gymnasium installed in the Hermesvilla, which he had built for her in Vienna. She rode to hounds in England and Ireland, with a fearless bravado, over the highest fences, which gained her the nickname 'The Queen of the Chase'. Her name was linked with an equally daring young Scot, called Bay Middleton. The only bonds that remained with the Habsburg Empire, and with Franz Joseph, were her children and her passion for Hungary. The old wound, from the brutal suppression of Budapest was finally healed with the political 'Compromise' (the Ausgleich) of 1867, which restored and extended Hungary's historic rights.[101] The outward sign of reconciliation was the coronation of Franz Joseph and Elisabeth in Budapest. She had discovered in the Hungarians the human and spiritual qualities she found lacking in Vienna; she learned Hungarian, acquired a Hungarian lady-in-waiting and other Hungarian servants, and made clear her passion for all things Magyar. This was a stroke of good fortune for Franz Joseph, for Elisabeth achieved enormous popularity in her own right in Hungary.

The coronation in Budapest began on 6 June 1867 when, in accordance with custom, she set to work with needle and thread repairing the ancient mantle of St Stephen, darning the slightly less ancient Coronation Stockings, and putting a lining into the Crown of St Stephen, which was much too large for Franz Joseph's narrow head. At seven in the morning of the following day,

a Coronation procession of unexampled brilliance moved off from the Royal Palace. The great ones of the land, in numbers never seen before, dressed in their picturesque magnates' costumes, and riding on noble horses with trappings gleaming with gold, assembled to do honour to the Kingdom, but at the same time to display their own pomp and power. The Emperor, wearing the uniform of a Hungarian Marshal, and riding on horseback, Elisabeth, looking bewitchingly lovely in [Hungarian] national costume with a diamond crown on her head and driving in a state coach drawn by eight horses, the Life Guards with Leopard skins floating from their shoulders and riding on their grey horses, made up a picture of bewildering brilliance, which recalled the proudest splendours of the Kingdom and the aristocracy in the palmiest days of the Middle Ages.[102]

'The plateau' of Franz Joseph's long reign began with the Compromise of 1867. He was in his thirty-eighth year, with a wife and three children whom he adored, as is evident from his many letters. His hair began to thin early on, making him look older than he was but he always retained a great deal of animal vigour. Films taken in his eighties show that he could still mount and ride a horse with ease. In his fifties he was still a young and highly energetic man. He suffered numerous shocks and reverses, but he had become largely impervious to them.[103] It was within days of his coronation in Budapest that he heard that his brother Maximilian, who had engaged in a French-backed venture to create a Mexican Empire, had been tried and shot by his subjects. It was all the more painful because the brothers had quarrelled over Maximilian's decision to accept the proffered 'throne'. With his brother dead, he did what he could. The Austrian navy was sent to bring back the body to Trieste where it was met by his younger brother, Karl Ludwig, and Ludwig Victor. In Vienna, he was given all the honours due to an archduke[104] and carried through the snow to the church of the Capuchins in January 1868.

More positively, perhaps, after almost twenty years of marriage, he reached an accommodation with Elisabeth, finding his physical comfort elsewhere. In 1875, he struck up a relationship with a young woman, Anna Nahowski, and developed a regular liaison; her diary records the regularity of the visits.[105] There may well have been other women who did not similarly document his attentions. There has always been speculation as to whether his relationship with the noted Burgtheater actress Katherina Schratt was merely the platonic connection that both parties claimed. His letters to her can bear both interpretations, but I believe, with her biographer Joan Haslip, that at least at one point she was his mistress in the full sense.

In a letter carefully omitted in the correspondence edited by Baron Bourgoing, we read: 'Yesterday it was exactly six weeks since I left you in your bed, hoping that in two days I should be sitting on it again, and look what has happened. But now at last the sad time is drawing to an end and we will have a wonderful reunion.' ... Evidently the actress did not always receive the Emperor coifed and corseted in the breakfast room at Hietzing. There were other, more intimate occasions, when the coffee and kipferls would be served on a table beside her bed, and Katherina, looking ravishing in a beribboned and ruffled negligée, would lie back among the lace pillows and satin quilts.[106]

Elisabeth approved of the connection, whatever its nature, and she engineered their first meeting; hitherto, Franz Joseph had simply admired 'Kathi' from the royal box at the Burgtheater. She had arranged for the painter Heinrich von Angeli to paint the actress's portrait as a present for her husband, and at the last of her sittings, she made sure that they met. Looking at the painting today, there is a striking similarity between Angeli's view of Katherina Schratt and Franz Joseph's favourite painting of his young wife, by Winterhalter, with her tresses falling to below her waist.

At the great Paris Exposition of 1900, the Austrian army won a major prize. But it was not for the best rifle or the most deadly field gun, but for the most elegant uniform. Louis Eisenmann, writing of the old army, remarked:

The army had only one vision of Austria, which was as a vast army. In the regiments, discipline, passive obedience, the commander's-word-as-law obliterated all diversity of origins and all nationalistic sentiments. Under the regimental banners all Austrians were only Austrians: the cult of the dynasty, of the emperor as the supreme commander, brought all together. By applying the same method to the population at large to give, would it not be possible to create the sense of a single Austria, just in the same way that a single army had been created?[107]

After 1867, the mechanism was more complex, with the *kaiserlich* (imperial) element of Austria and the *königlich* (royal) entity of Hungary. Written together as '*k.k.*', they provided the abbreviation for the full name of the new state, as USA stands for the United States of America. However, a subsequent imprint has been overlaid on this image of the Empire. In his novel *The Man Without Qualities*, Robert Musil defined it as '*Kakania*', another fanciful central European state, like Anthony Hope's *Ruritania*.[108]

Here one was in the centre of Europe, at a focal point of the world's old axes ... There was some display of luxury, but it was not, of course, as over-sophisticated as the French. One went in for sport, but not in madly Anglo-Saxon fashion. One spent tremendous sums on the army; but only just enough to ensure one of remaining the second weakest among the great powers.

The capital, too, was somewhat smaller than all the rest of the world's largest cities, but nevertheless quite considerably larger than a mere ordinary large city. And the administration of this country was carried out in an enlightened, hardly perceptible manner, with a cautious clipping of all sharp points, by the best bureaucracy in Europe, which could be accused of only one defect: it could not help regarding genius and enterprise ... unless privileged by high birth or State appointment as ostentation, indeed presumption.

But who would want unqualified people putting their oar in, anyway? And besides, in Kakania it was only that a genius was always regarded as a lout, but never, as sometimes happened elsewhere, that a mere lout was regarded as a genius.[109]

All of which was true; and the final joke was in the name of this 'state' itself, for as spoken it evoked the German nursery word '*caca*', meaning faeces. So *Kakania* might best be rendered in English as *Shiteria*.

This state over which Franz Joseph ruled, so much mocked and burlesqued, was indeed in constitutional terms like no other. But its ambience, as Musil suggests, was also unique. For the old Emperor this notion of a single multinational Empire, based on the same fundamental principles as informed the single army, was the truest expression of the Habsburg dynastic ideal. His only means of expressing it personally was through his scrupulous attention to duty, and by being Emperor to all his peoples. But when his son Crown Prince Rudolf suggested a means whereby the public could be persuaded of this ideal, he provided his full support, both of money and prestige.

Rudolf's idea was for a popular encyclopedia of the Austro-Hungarian monarchy, presented in words and in pictures, and sold to a wide public. As a project it had some precedents. The King of Bavaria had patronized a massive work on his nation, edited by W. H. Riehl, which was published between 1859 and 1867. But this was intended for an educated and wealthy market. Rudolf first presented his proposal early in 1884, and the initial report from the finance minister was damning. He had control of the imperial printing office, and in his view the project could not be published without a large loss, and at any event he stipulated that 'the cost must be kept down to the margin of absolute necessity'. This would mean a standard of production no better than that of official government literature, with few illustrations and a survey much shorter and less comprehensive than Rudolf had envisaged. The Crown Prince believed that he was seeking to sabotage the project, in the time-honoured fashion of the Habsburg official.

He appealed directly to the Emperor. At an audience in March 1884, he formally read an address: 'Your Majesty . . . The Austro-Hungarian Monarchy still lacks a great ethnographical work which, founded on the most advanced scientific research of the present day, and embellished by the highly perfected artistic means of reproduction, shall while stimulating and instructing, present a comprehensive picture of our Fatherland and its race of peoples.' The Emperor immediately grasped the motive and intention of the project, and told his son that he had his full support, then asked him to continue. Rudolf concluded by observing:

The literary and artistic circles among the peoples of this Empire would be united in a common undertaking; well-known names would shed lustre on the work, and opportunity would be provided for younger, aspiring intellects to make themselves known and use their gifts . . . This work will show at home and abroad what a rich treasure of intellectual power this Monarchy possesses in the peoples of all her countries, and how these co-operate in a splendid achievement, which is bound to serve to develop the consciousness and power of the common Fatherland.[110]

The study of the peoples living within the boundaries of this empire does not only present a highly important sphere of activity for scholars, but is also of practical use in the development of united patriotism.

By the growing recognition of the qualities and characteristics of the single ethnographical groups and of their mutual and material dependence, that feeling of solidarity which is to unite all the peoples of our Fatherland must be strengthened.

The Emperor provided immediate and direct support. The finance minister was told that this was a project sanctioned by personal command of Franz Joseph, and no constraints were to be placed upon it. He sent letters to all the imperial ministries and institutions of art and science instructing them to cooperate fully with the Crown Prince. He personally approved the establishment of the supervisory board proposed by Rudolf, and asked for regular reports on the progress of the great scheme. In its final form it was planned as twenty-four substantial volumes, but published in small sections each week in paper covers, so that they could be afforded by individuals. Each area of the empire would have one or more volumes covering every aspect of its society, history and topography, some with coloured illustrations. The whole text would be profusely illustrated and two special studios were set up, one in Vienna and one in Budapest, to cope with the more than 4,000 images that would be required. A Hungarian edition was published, simultan-eously, in Budapest as a manifestation of the collaboration embodied in the joint venture.

The first volume was presented to the public in 1886, but Rudolf had been able to give his father the first part of that volume on 1 December 1885.[111] From 1886 it continued with weekly publica-tion, until the final chapters on Croatia, Bosnia and Herzegovina ap-peared in 1902, sixteen years later.[112] Perhaps the closest comparison is with Herrgott's two great works in the eighteenth century, but the audience and focus have changed radically. Rudolf's aim was to create a sense of patriotic identity among individual citizens, not to produce volumes that would sit unread on shelves in libraries and law offices. The method of publication that he chose, in fascicles, or what we would now call a part-work format, was designed to disseminate the work as widely as possible. This was how novels and other popular works were still distributed by some publishers. The imperial printing press subsequently produced a number of other works, including studies of the imperial collections, and a multi-volume survey of the industrial development of Austria-Hungary, but none aimed at the same mass audience as Rudolf's work.

But publications could not reach into every corner of the monarchy, satisfying that elusive 'public opinion' which had so preoccupied Metternich. Not all citizens were literate, and with the ethnic and linguistic diversity of the Habsburg lands the written word was not an effective means of instilling a sense of popular patriotism. Yet the need to create loyalty to the dynasty was paramount, especially when other forces – nationalist and class-based – were pulling in the opposite direction. The resources that the Habsburgs could deploy were the personality of the Emperor and Empress, and the sense of a majestic past. The milestones of Franz Joseph's life were the natural focus for staged expressions of public loyalty, beginning with the imperial couple's silver wedding in April 1879, and the wedding of Rudolf and Stephanie of Belgium in 1881, then the celebration of 1,000 years of Hungarian monarchy in 1896, the 1898 silver jubilee of the Emperor's accession, and in 1908, a pageant honouring sixty glorious years.

The desire to promote both the past identity and future direction of the monarchy took a number of forms. The first, and most permanent, were buildings. The Votivkirche, erected to commemorate Franz Joseph's lucky escape from an assassin's knife in 1853, set the pattern, and in subsequent years the towns of the Empire showed their patriotism by taking collections and erecting buildings, from hospitals to schools and orphanages, generally named after the Emperor or Empress. In many cases either the Emperor himself or one of the imperial family would perform the opening ceremony. This, in its way, did do something to bring the monarchy closer to the people. The Emperor became not merely a portrait on the wall, but a living being, whom many had seen with their own eyes. The celebration of the silver wedding of Franz Joseph and Elisabeth in April 1879 was planned as a great festival of the Habsburg past. The public commemoration of the event in the capital was an enormous pageant designed by the artist Hans Makart, in which some 10,000 people took part, all dressed in the lavish costumes of Habsburg Flanders in the era of Charles V.

The attention to detail, the careful presentation of an appropriately enticing past – the theme was the overflowing bounty of the land and of art and industry under the benign rule of the Habsburgs – made the event hugely expensive. Makart was not used to working on a limited scale. He produced a vast array of drawings, sketches, and paintings, costume designs, and working plans for all the floats, and finally stage-managed the entire event.[113] On the great day the floats were prepared and dragged through the city streets to the cheers of the population. Then in a procession extending over many hours, they paraded before the Emperor and Empress, who sat in a box on the Ringstrasse, close to the Hofburg. Makart himself appeared as the master of ceremonies, riding a black horse and dressed, a little anachronistically, as Rubens. Franz Joseph described it as, 'A lasting family celebration for all the peoples of my empire.'[114]

Had Maximilian I's Triumphal Procession ever been staged, it would have had much the same effect. There was a sense of the overwhelming antiquity and energy of the Empire as each of the floats trundled by. The imperial family had prepared their own more private celebration. A few days before the great parade, Archduke Karl Ludwig gave a dinner after which members of the family staged tableaux from Habsburg history before Franz Joseph and Elisabeth; many of the costumes and jewels that the young archdukes and archduchesses wore were those which had originally belonged to the characters they represented. Attics and museums were scoured for appropriate costumes and Rudolf raided the imperial treasury for orbs and sceptres. He appeared first as his namesake, Rudolf I, then as Charles V, and then as Charles of Lorraine, who had defeated the Turks.[115] On the following day there was a solemn thanksgiving mass in the Votivkirche.

When the imperial couple went to Budapest to receive congratulations from the Hungarians, there was 'almost wild' enthusiasm.[116]

But this was nothing to the surge of excitement in 1896, when the Emperor, dressed in the uniform of a general of hussars, drove with Elisabeth in Maria Theresa's 'glass coach' to the new (and still unfinished) Parliament building above the Danube. There they received the holy crown of St Stephen, the emblem of Hungarian nationhood, and later in the evening, on a great open field to the west of Castle Hill, oxen were roasted and given to the people. All that night the city blazed with the newly installed *electrical illuminations*.[117]

When Franz Joseph's sixty glorious years as Emperor were celebrated in 1908, the scene was darker. Elisabeth had been dead for a decade,[118] and Rudolf for almost twenty years. The events at Mayerling, where he had shot himself and his mistress Marie Vetsera, remain one of the great 'unsolved mysteries', although the main outlines are now clear. But it is untrue that his relationship with his father had become so difficult that he preferred suicide to confronting Franz Joseph with some scandal – sexual or political. Those close to the Emperor were becoming thin on the ground. Seven years after Rudolf's suicide, Franz Joseph's brother Karl Ludwig died from drinking the holy – but contaminated – waters of the River Jordan while on a pilgrimage to the Holy Land, and only a year later, he suffered the devastating loss of Elisabeth. Only his youngest brother Ludwig Victor survived to see out his brother's golden jubilee, and he was something of an embarrassment. After creating innumerable scandals in low bars and houses of ill repute, he had been effectively banished to a castle near Salzburg.

The celebrations in 1908 lacked Makart's showman's touch.[119] But they were more truly national. Each of the provinces sent their contingent, the great events of Habsburg history were once again re-enacted on the streets of Vienna. The frontispiece of the programme showed the old Emperor greeting each of his ancestors, and looking very much as if he were about to join them himself. It was as if the Emperor, now almost eighty, had become a saintly icon, consigned to the Capuchin crypt before he was actually dead. Vienna and the Habsburg Empire, in the new century, were moving forward, and Franz Joseph had become fixed as the emblem of a distant and happy past. The correspondent of *The Times*, however, saw it all in a rosy light:

On June 12 there passed before the Emperor, in a procession which lasted more than three hours, 12,000 of his subjects, of all races and tongues, in costumes of historic periods, shouting their loyal greetings. Nobles and warriors have assembled before the monarch before but never before has there been so complete a muster of the peoples of the empire. The Austrians, who are a nation without knowing it, found themselves that morning, and the people of Vienna cheered each race and clan, in the consciousness that not only common loyalty to a common dynasty personified in a venerable Sovereign, but also a common history, common interest, common enemies and a common destiny, all unite them. Nor was an omen for the future wanting. Towards midday, with scarcely a cloud on the horizon, and none overhead, there appeared a rainbow, pale but distinct and lying, as it were, horizontally in the form of a crescent along the vault of the sky, the arch of the bow pointed southwards and the two extremities of the bow northwards. The rainbow, as the omen foreshadows, is pointed southwards.[120]

It turned out to be an omen of doom, pointing to 28 June 1914, to the encounter of an archduke and an assassin on the streets of Sarajevo.

∽   ∽   ∽

Although the line of succession was assured, first to his nephew Franz Ferdinand (although that was to be overturned by the archduke's murder in Sarajevo) and then to his great-nephew, Karl,[121] and eventually to Karl's son, Otto, Franz Joseph had come to see himself as standing at the end of the line. He met the American statesman Theodore Roosevelt in 1910 and remarked, only half-jokingly, that he was the last representative of the old system. He knew of the new currents in culture and in society. He did not like them, but he was unquestionably aware of their existence. How could he not be, when he had visited the Secession exhibition or, for the celebrations of 1908, had sat on a podium designed, jointly with Josef Urban, by the apostle of Austrian modernism, Otto Wagner? (That podium eschewed velvets and brocade for a huge imperial crown and a clump of gigantic columns used as flagpoles.)[122]

Franz Joseph stood above the interests and prejudices of his peoples. He abhorred the populist anti-Semitism of Karl Lueger, and he refused to confirm his election as mayor of Vienna on four separate occasions. Yet change, of itself, did not trouble him: it was Franz Joseph who sanctioned a 'leap in the dark' and extended the franchise. In some matters he was adamant, as when he felt that the unity of the army or the state were challenged; in others he amazed his ministers by his elasticity and political shrewdness. However, his values were those of an older society, increasingly under challenge. Many now called him the 'old gentleman in the Hofburg', others thinking of his courtly values, and perhaps the pageantry of 1908, called him 'the Last Knight'. Someone named him, most aptly of all, 'the Last Cavalier', and that, to an English ear, creates the most powerful resonance. For it embodies devotion to a lost cause and loyalty unto death.

8

Finis Austriae: The End?

1916–1995

At a little before dawn on the 19th of June 1867, Archduke
Ferdinand Maximilian, Emperor of Mexico, prepared to make a
good death. His attempt to create an empire for himself in Mexico
had failed: all that remained was to die like a true Habsburg. On
the execution ground he was to be shot with two of his officers.
One did not wish to stand on the left, because it reminded him of
the thieves who had died on either side of Christ – so Maximilian
exchanged places with him. They had no blindfolds and looked
directly at the squad of peasant conscripts who faced them with
their muskets at the ready.

Just before the officer gave the order to fire, Maximilian spoke
in a loud voice, in Spanish, that could be clearly heard by the 3,000
soldiers drawn up in an open square around the execution ground.
'Mexicans,' he shouted, 'Men of my class and race are created by
God to be the happiness of nations or their martyrs ... I forgive
everybody. I pray that everyone may also forgive me and I wish
that my blood which is now to be shed may be for the good of the
country. Long live Mexico, long live independence.' As the last
echo of 'Viva Méjico, viva la independencia' was still reverberating,
the soldiers fired and Maximilian dropped dead, with six bullets in
his body.[1]

The word he used – *raza* – race, is confusing because it has now
changed its normal meaning so profoundly. When Maximilian used

it, the word meant *pedigree* (as in a pedigree dog)[2] or *lineage*, not some claim for racial superiority over the inferior Mexicans. He had not taken up 'the white man's burden', in Kipling's phrase. Maximilian meant: I am a Habsburg, and we serve our peoples. Words spoken under such circumstances are not uttered carelessly, and Maximilian had his eye on posterity. But he spoke also to his brother and his family, thousands of miles away in Vienna. His last words said to them: 'I die in the faith, both of Holy Church and of our lineage.'

This book has ignored the normal landmarks of history. Sometimes, with some difficulty, and especially in the last chapter, I have turned away from the events that I have been trained to consider important, to those other issues that loomed as large in the minds of my subjects. Many of these concerns seem pointless to us today, as they did to many of their contemporaries. Many of the critics of Franz Joseph condemned – or marvelled at – his sense of detachment. Sometimes his control broke: the wife of his heir, Karl, remembered a meeting shortly after the first news of an Austrian victory arrived early in the First World War. As Zita congratulated the Emperor, 'He replied in a resigned tone of voice, "Yes it is a victory, but that is the way my wars always begin, only to end in defeat. And this time it will be even worse. They will say that I am old and cannot cope any more, and that after that revolutions will break out and then it will be the end."' She was shocked at his note of gloom and responded hotly: 'But that's surely not possible – the war we are fighting is a just one.' He smiled and tipped his head on one side as he looked straight at her, 'Yes, one can see that you are very young, that you still believe in the victory of the just.'[3] But as so often when he made that characteristic gesture with the head, he was speaking in riddles.

He did believe in the ultimate victory of the just, but not victory in the military or even the temporal sense. We have to accept, I think, that Habsburgs are indoctrinated with the sense and ethos of their past; I use the present tense quite deliberately. They are conditioned to see as important matters that to the non-Habsburg have no meaning or real significance. That does not mean to say that they are fixed with their eyes resolutely on the past, because part of their success over so many centuries has been a vision that embraces both the past and the present.

Allan Janik and Stephen Toulmin, in their superb book on Wittgenstein's Vienna, suggest that the Habsburgs attempted to 'abolish history'.[4] By that they mean a number of things, but principally, that the Habsburgs removed the distinction between 'then' and 'now', creating a boundless continuum.

In the communal situation as it actually existed, genuine moral principles and aesthetic values could be arrived at only by an idealized abstraction . . . There was a strict sense in which – failing any occasion for the corresponding language games – these abstract, idealized values were 'unsayable'. The accepted communal language games really gave the term 'good' no use more rigorous than its use in the phrase 'good taste', while for the strictly loyal Austrian, the question whether Francis Joseph's political decisions were correct or mistaken was meaningless. (What else did the divine right of the Habsburg *Hausmacht* imply?) So, a situation developed from which, as a by-product of conscious social policies, the normal language games of valuation had been eliminated.[5]

That is to say, the Habsburgs, over time, constructed an environment in which things meant what (as in Humpty-Dumpty's universe) you wanted them to mean.

On reading that passage in Janik and Toulmin's book, I remembered the story about Emperor Francis I, which John Osborne used as the title for his play about the Austrian spy, Colonel Redl. When Francis was told that the Tyrolese leader, Andreas Hofer, fighting bravely against the French, was a great patriot, he is supposed to have replied: 'Yes, that is all very well. But is he a patriot for me?' If not true, it ought to be, for the story is quintessentially Habsburg. It can be read in many ways and it takes the normal sense of the words, and twists them into a 'dynastic logic' almost as complex as the investigations that Wittgenstein was making.

Language games were, I suggest, at the essence of the Habsburg system, games that embraced both words and images, that manipulated the interplay of symbols and the concepts attached to them. The theme of this book has been of the Habsburg preoccupation with the image and not the fact.[6] Over the centuries, they became extraordinarily adept at playing the games for which they set the rules, and occasionally rewrote, as in the eighteenth century. Far from staring fixedly backwards, my sense is that the Habsburgs had a strong sense of the here-and-now. However, because their collective past was their greatest, and sometimes only, asset, the Habsburgs give the impression of perpetual retrospection. For them, as Franz Joseph implied in the passage quoted above, the present, and objective reality have a transitory quality. Musil, inevitably, has an observation on this matter. 'What a strange affair history was, come to think of it! ... This history of ours looks pretty unsafe and messy, when looked at from close at hand, something like a half-solidified swamp, and then in the end, strangely enough it turns out there is after all a track running across it, that very "road of history" of which nobody knows whence it came.' Sitting in his tramcar on the way home, Ulrich chewed over these thoughts and finally came to the conclusion: 'The law of world history, it now occurred to him, was nothing but the fundamental principle of government in old Kakania, namely that of "muddling through". Kakania was an immensely shrewd state.'[7]

Which drags us back again to that ferment, variously described as 'Vienna 1900', the 'Waltzing Volcano', or more prosaically, 'The Origins of Modernism'. Janik and Toulmin, and in a less sprightly fashion, William M. Johnston in his study *The Austrian Mind*, point to the astonishing array of talents in the Habsburg monarchy, and especially its capital, before the First World War. Musil remembered it.

People were standing up on all sides to fight against the old way of life ... Talents developed that had previously been choked or had taken no part at all in public life. They were as different from each other as anything well could be and the contradictions in their aims were unsurpassable ... one had faith and was sceptical, one was naturalistic and precious, robust and morbid; one dreamed of ancient castles and shady avenues, autumnal gardens, glassy ponds, jewels, hashish, disease and demonism, but also of prairies, vast horizons, forges and rolling mills, naked wrestlers, uprisings of the slaves of toil, men and women in the primeval Garden, and the destruction of society. Admittedly, these were contradictions and very different battle cries, but all breathed the same breath of life.[8]

Contradictions or not, there was a network, and one ostensibly in opposition to the established order.

In the Habsburg Empire, however, *opposition* was also embraced within the long arms of officialdom. Gustav Klimt, Otto Wagner and Sigmund Freud were on both the *inside* and the *outside*; Carl Schorske suggests that, indirectly, Freud got his chair at the University of Vienna because Klimt had failed to achieve his expected appointment to the Academy of Fine Arts.[9] The journal of the Secession, *Ver Sacrum*, both outraged the established bourgeois order,[10] and carried advertisements for all the leading stores in Vienna that served that market. Klimt, Wagner, Freud, as well as others much more radical, all benefited in one form or another, from the power of connection, the old Habsburg tradition of *Protektion*.[11] All of them, loyalist, dissident and disaffected alike, grew up in an education system suffused with Habsburg values, under the benign eye of the Emperor – in the schoolroom, at the place of work, and in the newspapers. It was possible to react against *Habsburgica*, but it also permeated the air that they breathed.[12]

So what does this mean? I am suggesting that the Habsburg ethos (in particular, the Habsburg preoccupation with image and affect), provided an ideal growth medium, the agar jelly, for the luxuriant hothouse outgrowths of *fin de siècle* Vienna. It was not intentional, just an accidental by-product, like penicillin.

ᕥ   ᕥ   ᕥ

Many studies of the Habsburgs draw a line underneath their long history and draw a balance in 1918: *Finis Austriae*. One or two record the pitiful exile of the last Emperor Karl, who probably merited the title *The Good* rather more than his ancestor Francis I. But this is not how the Habsburgs see it themselves. Karl, dispossessed and dying of pneumonia in exile in Madeira, told his wife: 'I must suffer like this so my peoples can come together again.'[13] He died, consciously or unconsciously echoing the last moments of Charles V and Philip II, holding a crucifix to his lips, and looking through an open door from his bedroom to mass being celebrated in the adjoining drawing-room. And like Charles he asked for the sacrament a second time before he died, and perhaps for the same reason. Little wonder, then, that a proposal for his beatification was set in motion in 1949, perhaps in the hope that there might at last be a true and undisputed Saint in the house of Habsburg.

But Karl was not the Last Habsburg, which is the title of Gordon Brook Shepherd's biography, any more than Franz Joseph, who saw himself as the end of the line. When Karl was on the point of withdrawing from the throne of Austria in 1918, his wife, the Empress Zita, bitterly rejected the notion of abdication. 'A sovereign can never abdicate. He can be deposed and his sovereign rights be declared forfeit. All right. That is force. But abdicate – never, never, never. I would rather fall here at your side. Then there would be Otto. And even if all of us here were killed, there would still be other Habsburgs.'[14] Maximilian's wife Charlotte had said much the same when her husband had contemplated abdication in Mexico in 1865. Karl's son, Otto, succeeded his father, so his supporters believed, as the rightful King of Hungary and the true Emperor of Austria. He has continued the Habsburg role but by new means.

One means was entirely traditional. The eldest child of a large family, he himself has seven children; and the total extent of the Habsburg lineage now scattered throughout the world numbers six or seven hundred. Of that family, both nuclear and extended, he remains the head. No archduke can marry outside the 'permitted degrees' without permission of the head of the House. In the 1980s Otto relaxed the rules, still based on the 1839 statute. He did so in the customary manner, consulting with the senior archdukes, and getting the agreement of the clan. Characteristically, he finally settled the matter indirectly, not by rewriting the family law but through blurring its most inflexible requirements.[15]

One unexpected consequence of that revision affected Otto directly. His elder son, Karl, was able to marry outside the narrow circle of royal princesses or ancient aristocracy, previously the only option for a Habsburg. In February 1993, the Archduke Karl married Francesca, daughter of Baron Heinrich von Thyssen-Bornemizza, in the basilica of the seven-hundred-year-old shrine of Mariazell.[16] Quite the most flamboyant figure at the wedding was not the bride, but the baron himself, as perhaps befits one of the richest men in the world. Clad in the scarlet, gold braid, fur, silks and egret plume of a Hungarian magnate, he added an operatic note (more Franz Lehár rather than Richard Strauss) to the event. The costume, he said, had belonged to his father.

By contrast, the Habsburg party appeared dowdy. The mother of the bridegroom dressed more in the restrained style of the English landed gentry than of European High Society. But in their button-holes the Habsburg men all wore the tiny emblem of the order of the Golden Fleece, a distinction which even the wealth of the Thyssens could not buy. It was a meeting of two distinct and divergent worlds. As the Archduke Karl made plain in a long interview after the wedding,[17] he and his family had little money, and they had to work for a living. That work, however, was the continuation of the Habsburg mission.

Almost from the first days after his father's death in 1922, at the age of twelve, Otto has borne the burden of Habsburg destiny. He managed to survive the Depression and the war, he avoided capture by the Nazis, and worked hard for the restoration of a free Austria. A generation of Austrians still looked to him as their leader. One such was Josef Roth, who in the 1930s was rapidly drinking himself to death. His friends had tried every means to cure him but without success. Then one had the idea of asking Otto to intervene, knowing Roth's infatuation with the Habsburgs. As Otto himself tells the story, he summoned Roth, who arrived a little tongue-tied, in the Exalted Presence. In his best Franz Joseph manner, Otto barked, 'Roth, I, as your Emperor, order you to cease drinking.' The author, standing at attention was shocked, but stammered his agreement and left the room. For a while the Imperial Will had the desired effect, although he eventually succumbed again to his compulsion.[18]

Otto's vision was broader than Austria, and in the decades after the Second World War he became a prime advocate of European union, east and west, partly through the European Economic Community, now the European Union, but more actively with the Pan-European Union which he now heads. He has written a sheaf of books and articles that have advanced the cause for more than forty years, and this is the work now jointly undertaken with his son. Otto relinquished his personal claim to the family's territories to Karl in 1961, and his elder son and heir is careful in his choice of words when asked if he still harboured hopes of a return to the monarchy. 'I am too much of a realist. But let me put it this way. It would be ridiculous to ask for a republic in the United Kingdom, just as it would be to ask for a monarchy in Switzerland. But in Austria – who knows? It's an open question.'

That comes to the heart of the Habsburg philosophy: it is an open question. If not now, later; what has been, may be again. History has been 'abolished',[19] in the sense that historians use the term to ghettoize the past. For the Habsburgs, there is only a continual present. The archdukes and archduchesses have no doubts: they embody the essence of empire. The members of the family will work, serve the ideal, lead sober, respectable, boring lives, from generation to generation, sure in the knowledge that destiny will turn again in their direction. The dynasty continues, like the perpetual flame on the grave of John Fitzgerald Kennedy, which is an emblem for future greatness rather than past glory.[20]

FAMILY TREES

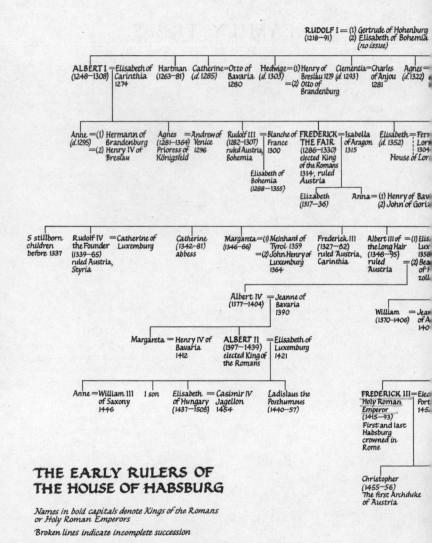

THE EARLY RULERS OF
THE HOUSE OF HABSBURG

*Names in bold capitals denote Kings of the Romans
or Holy Roman Emperors*

Broken lines indicate incomplete succession

RUDOLF I = (1) Gertrude of Hohenburg
(1218–91)   (2) Elisabeth of Bohemia
              (no issue)

ALBERT I = Elisabeth of   Hartman   Catherine = Otto of   Hedwige = (1) Henry of   Clementia = Charles   Agnes =
(1248–1308) Carinthia   (1263–81)   (d. 1285)   Bavaria   (d. 1303)   Breslau 1279 (d. 1293)   of Anjou   (d. 1322)
             1274   1280   = (2) Otto of   1281
                                                              Brandenburg

Anne = (1) Hermann of   Agnes = Andrew of   Rudolf III = Blanche of   FREDERICK = Isabella   Elisabeth = Fer
(d. 1295) Brandenburg   (1281–1364) Venice   (1282–1307)   France   THE FAIR   of Aragon   (d. 1352)   Lor
       = (2) Henry IV of Prioress of   1296   ruled Austria, 1300   (1286–1330) 1315   1304
            Breslau   Königsfeld   Bohemia   elected King   House of Lor
                                                                        of the Romans
                                      Elisabeth of   1314, ruled
                                      Bohemia   Austria
                                      (1288–1355)
                                                                        Elizabeth   Anna = (1) Henry of Bav
                                                                        (1317–36)   (2) John of Goriz

5 stillborn   Rudolf IV = Catherine of   Catherine   Margareta = (1) Meinhard of   Frederick III   Albert III of = (1) Elis
children   the Founder Luxemburg   (1342–81)   (1346–66)   Tyrol 1359   (1327–62)   the Long Hair   Lux
before 1337   (1339–65)   abbess   = (2) John Henry of   ruled Austria,   (1348–95)   1358
               ruled Austria,   Luxemburg   Carinthia   ruled   = (2) Bea
               Styria   1364   Austria   of I
                                                                                                                             zoll

                          Albert IV = Jeanne of
                          (1377–1404) Bavaria
                                       1390   William   = Jea
                                                                                     (1370–1406)   of A
              Margareta = Henry IV of   ALBERT II = Elisabeth of   140
                          Bavaria   (1397–1439) Luxemburg
                          1412   elected King of 1421
                                         the Romans

Anne = William III   1 son   Elisabeth = Casimir IV   Ladislaus the   FREDERICK III = Elec
       of Saxony   of Hungary   Jagellon   Posthumous   Holy Roman   Port
       1446   (1437–1505) 1454   (1440–57)   Emperor   145
                                                                                (1415–93)
                                                                                First and last
                                                                                Habsburg
                                                                                crowned in
                                                                                Rome

                                                                                Christopher
                                                                                (1455–56)
                                                                                The first Archduke
                                                                                of Austria

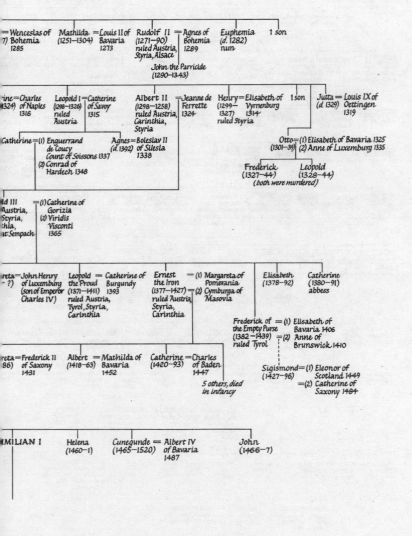

= Wenceslas of 7) Bohemia 1285 — Mathilda (1251–1304) = Louis II of Bavaria 1273 — Rudolf II (1271–90) ruled Austria, Styria, Alsace = Agnes of Bohemia 1289 — Euphemia (d. 1282) nun — 1 son

John the Parricide (1290–1343)

rine = Charles 1324) of Naples 1316 — Leopold I (1298–1326) ruled Austria = Catherine of Savoy 1315 — Albert II (1298–1258) ruled Austria, Carinthia, Styria = Jeanne de Ferrette 1324 — Henry (1299–1327) ruled Styria = Elisabeth of Vyrnenburg 1314 — 1 son — Jutta (d. 1329) = Louis IX of Oettingen 1319

Catherine = (1) Enguerrand de Coucy Count of Soissons 1337 (2) Conrad of Hardech 1348

Agnes = Boleslav II (d. 1392) of Silesia 1338

Otto = (1) Elisabeth of Bavaria 1325 (1301–39) (2) Anne of Luxemburg 1335

Frederick (1327–44) Leopold (1328–44) (both were murdered)

ld III Austria, Styria, hia, at Sempach = (1) Catherine of Gorizia (2) Viridis Visconti 1365

reta = John Henry – ?) (son of Emperor Charles IV) of Luxemburg — Leopold the Proud (1371–1411) ruled Austria, Tyrol, Styria, Carinthia = Catherine of Burgundy 1393 — Ernest the Iron (1377–1427) ruled Austria, Styria, Carinthia = (1) Margareta of Pomerania = (2) Cymburga of Masovia — Elisabeth (1378–92) — Catherine (1380–91) abbess

Frederick of the Empty Purse (1382–1439) ruled Tyrol = (1) Elisabeth of Bavaria 1406 = (2) Anne of Brunswick 1410

Sigismond (1427–96) = (1) Eleonor of Scotland 1449 = (2) Catherine of Saxony 1484

reta = Frederick II 86) of Saxony 1431 — Albert (1418–63) = Mathilda of Bavaria 1452 — Catherine (1420–93) = Charles of Baden 1447

5 others, died in infancy

MILIAN I — Helena (1460–1) — Cunegunde (1465–1520) = Albert IV of Bavaria 1487 — John (1466–7)

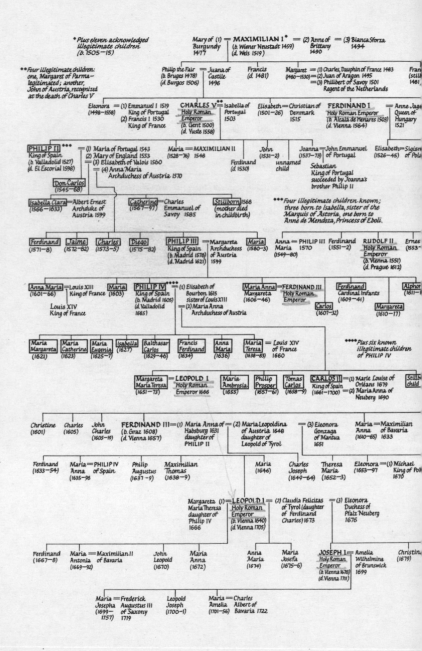

THE HABSBURGS AT THEIR ZENITH

Names in bold capitals denote Kings of the Romans, Holy Roman Emperors or Kings of Spain

Names enclosed within boxed outlines indicate the Spanish line

Broken lines indicate incomplete succession

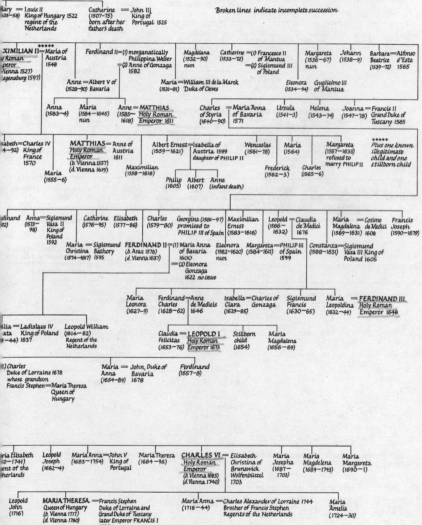

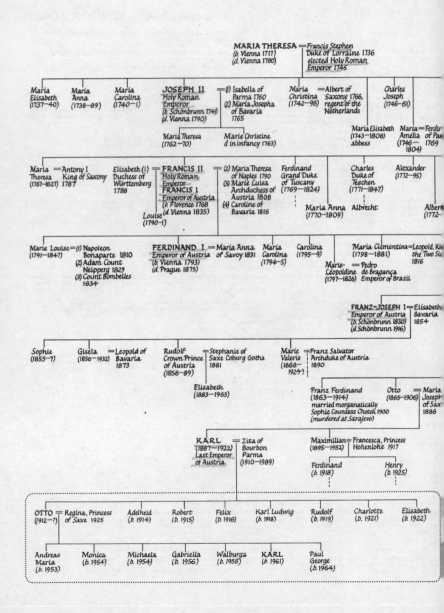

MARIA THERESA = Francis Stephen
(b. Vienna 1717) Duke of Lorraine 1736
(d. Vienna 1780) elected Holy Roman
Emperor 1745

Maria Elisabeth (1737–40) | Maria Anna (1738–89) | Maria Carolina (1740–1) | JOSEPH II Holy Roman Emperor (b. Schönbrunn 1741) (d. Vienna 1790) = (1) Isabella of Parma 1760 (2) Maria Josepha of Bavaria 1765 | Maria Christina (1742–98) = Albert of Saxony 1766, regent of the Netherlands | Charles Joseph (1745–61)

Maria Theresa (1762–70) | Marie Christine d. in infancy 1763

Maria Elisabeth (1743–1808) abbess | Maria = Ferdin Amelia of Pa (1746– 1769 1804)

Maria Theresa (1767–1827) = Antony I King of Saxony 1787 | Elisabeth (1) Duchess of Württemberg 1788 = FRANCIS II Holy Roman Emperor FRANCIS I Emperor of Austria (b. Florence 1768) (d. Vienna 1835) = (2) Maria Theresa of Naples 1790 (3) Marie Luisa Archduchess of Austria 1808 (4) Caroline of Bavaria 1816 | Ferdinand Grand Duke of Tuscany (1769–1824) | Charles Duke of Teschen (1771–1847) | Alexander (1772–95)

Louise (1790–1)

Maria Anna (1770–1809) | Albrecht | Albe (1772–

Marie Louise = (1) Napoleon Bonaparte 1810 (1791–1847) (2) Adam Count Neipperg 1829 (3) Count Bombelles 1834 | FERDINAND I = Maria Anna Emperor of Austria of Savoy 1831 (b. Vienna 1793) (d. Prague 1875) | Maria Carolina (1794–5) | Carolina (1795–9) | Maria Clementina = Leopold, Kin (1798–1881) the Two Sic 1816

Marie-Léopoldine = Pedro (1797–1826) de Bragança Emperor of Brazil

FRANZ-JOSEPH I = Elisabeth Emperor of Austria Bavaria (b. Schönbrunn 1830) 1854 (d. Schönbrunn 1916)

Sophie (1855–7) | Gisela (1856–1932) = Leopold of Bavaria 1873 | Rudolf Crown Prince of Austria (1858–89) = Stephanie of Saxe Coburg Gotha 1881 | Marie Valerie (1868– 1924) = Franz Salvator Archduke of Austria 1890

Elisabeth (1883–1963)

Franz Ferdinand (1863–1914) married morganatically Sophie Countess Chotek 1900 (murdered at Sarajevo) | Otto (1865–1906) = Maria Joseph of Sax 1886

KARL (1887–1922) Last Emperor of Austria = Zita of Bourbon Parma (1910–1989)

Maximilian = Francesca, Princess (1895–1952) Hohenlohe 1917

Ferdinand (b. 1918) | Henry (b. 1925)

OTTO (1912–?) = Regina, Princess of Saxe 1925 | Adelheid (b. 1914) | Robert (b. 1915) | Felix (b. 1916) | Karl Ludwig (b. 1918) | Rudolf (b. 1919) | Charlotte (b. 1921) | Elisabeth (b. 1922)

Andreas Maria (b. 1953) | Monica (b. 1954) | Michaela (b. 1954) | Gabriella (b. 1956) | Walburga (b. 1958) | KARL (b. 1961) | Paul George (b. 1964)

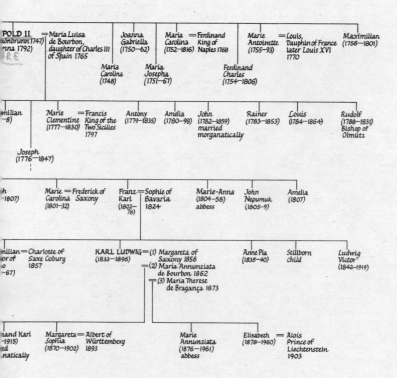

POLD II
(önbrunn 1747) = Maria Luisa
(nna 1792)   de Bourbon,
            daughter of Charles III
            of Spain 1765

Joanna   Maria   = Ferdinand   Marie   = Louis,   Maximilian
Gabriella   Carolina   King of   Antoinette   Dauphin of France (1756—1801)
(1750—62)   (1752—1816)   Naples 1768   (1755—93)   later Louis XVI
                                                              1770

        Maria   Maria   Ferdinand
        Carolina   Josepha   Charles
        (1748)   (1751—67)   (1754—1806)

milian   Marie   = Francis   Antony   Amelia   John   Rainer   Louis   Rudolf
-8)   Clementine   King of the (1779—1835) (1780—98)   (1782—1859)   (1783—1853) (1784—1864) (1788—1831)
            (1777—1830)   Two Sicilies   married   Bishop of
                           1797   morganatically   Olmütz

        Joseph
        (1776—1847)

h   Marie   = Frederick of   Franz = Sophie of   Marie-Anna   John   Amelia
-1807)   Carolina   Saxony   Karl   Bavaria   (1804—58)   Nepumuk   (1807)
            (1801—32)   (1802—   1824   abbess   (1805—9)
                                      78)

milian = Charlotte of   KARL LUDWIG = (1) Margareta of   Anne Pia   Stillborn   Ludwig
or of   Saxe Coburg   (1833—1896)   Saxony 1856   (1835—40)   child   Victor
o   1857   = (2) Maria Annunziata   (1842—1919)
-67)   de Bourbon 1862
                                           = (3) Maria Therese
                                                 de Bragança 1873

nand Karl   Margareta = Albert of   Marie   Elisabeth = Alois
-1915)   Sophia   Württemberg   Annunziata   (1878—1960) Prince of
ed   (1870—1902) 1893   (1876—1961)   Liechtenstein
naticaly   abbess   1903

THE LATER HABSBURGS

*Names in bold capitals denote Emperors of Austria
(Heads of the House of Habsburg)*

The section outlined indicates the post-Imperial Habsburgs

Broken lines indicate incomplete succession

Notes

Chapter 1: The Castle of the Hawk

1. Hungarian, Serb, Cuman and Bohemian mercenaries all fought in the armies of western Europe. Some clerical writers saw no difference between these easterners and the Turks and Tartars.
2. See Joseph Planta, *The History of the Helvetic Confederacy*, London, 1807, vol. 1, p. 436.
3. See L. Hug and R. Stead, *Switzerland*, London, 1890, pp. 168–9.
4. This was already in existence in 1064, according to the *Acta Murensia*: see Emil Mauerer, *Die Kunstdenkmäler des Kantons Aargau*, Basel, 1954, pp. 256ff.
5. These were still used in east and central Europe although they had become less common in the west.
6. It was Albert, grandfather of Leopold, son of the first Habsburg emperor, Rudolf I; the use of this knife at the battle of Göllheim enabled him to dispose of his rival for the imperial throne and become the second Habsburg emperor. Ironically, he was himself stabbed to death.
7. See Keith Thomas, *Man and the Natural World. Changing Attitudes in England, 1500–1800*, Harmondsworth, Middx, 1983, p. 64.
8. For a good description of the halberd (the *halmbarte*, an axe with a long handle), see Hans Delbruck, *History of the Art of War*, vol. 3, p. 6. The Scottish clansman's claymore, the Great Sword, two-handed, with a blade four to five feet in length, struck much the same kind of fear into English hearts.
9. They had chosen their battleground well. Behind them lay the forest, and they drew up their ranks in a square about thirty men deep and thirty men wide. When the battle began, and the larger army of Fribourg moved to the attack, the Bernese city-dwellers fled, leaving the mountain men to face the enemy alone. Soon they were surrounded on three sides by the Fribourgers, who had toiled up the hill under a barrage of stones and arrows. Towards evening the 1,000 Schwyzers charged down the hill, embedding themselves into the mass of the knights who jabbed at them with spears, and tried to hack down on them with swords and daggers. All were drawn into the mêlée, which rolled slowly backwards down the hill. The impetus lay with the attack, but it was gradually brought to a halt. The impasse was broken when the forces that had fled earlier in the day rallied, and returned to attack the

embattled Fribourg knights in the rear. Once the pressure was taken off the 1,000 spearmen and halberdiers, they began to lay about them, slaughtering the knights who were now trapped on two sides.

10. Led by Enguerrand de Coucy, Count of Soissons, half a Habsburg, the ostensible purpose was to claim Habsburg territory that, he asserted, was due to his mother from his cousin Leopold. In reality, the object was plunder.

11. The story concludes: 'He sprang forth from among his friends, rushed into the thickest of the enemy and sought his doom: he fell, and while weighed down in vain [attempting] to raise himself, he was approached by a common man from Schwitz who levelled a blow at him. Leopold called out: "I am the Duke of Austria", but the man either heard him not [or] believed him not, or thought that in the thick of battle the highest rank conferred no privilege; the duke received a mortal wound. Martin Mattered, the banneret of Freiburg-im-Breisgau, saw the disaster: he stood appalled: the banner dropped from his hand: he threw himself upon the corpse of his slaughteréd sovereign to preserve it from insult, and there met his own fate.'

12. C. W. O. Oman, *The Art of War in the Middle Ages*, AD 378–1515, rev. and ed. J. Cornell Beeler, New York, 1953, pp. 77–8.

13. The Habsburg knights were 'oppressed by their heavy armour, by heat, thirst and fatigue ... were impeded ... by their unskilfulness in the evolutions of well-trained infantry; and even their native prowess, [being more] adapted to deeds of knight errantry than to the tactics of a disciplined army, was moreover relaxed by the sovereign contempt they entertained for the Swiss peasantry'.

14. The point of the *Chanson*, of course, was that he would not, not even to save his own life.

15. Oman cited in R. E. and T. N. Dupuy, *The Encyclopedia of Military History from 3500 BC to the Present*, London, 1970, p. 205.

16. See E. Bonjour, H. S. Offler, and G. R. Potter, *A Short History of Switzerland*, Oxford, 1952, p. 49, where they point out that by the end of the eleventh century the Alemannian dukes had 'lost their hold south of the Rhine'. It was in this vacuum that the Habsburgs flourished.

17. Technically, Rudolf was only King of the Romans, but he was always counted in the imperial pedigree.

18. See Adam Wandruszka, *The House of Habsburg. Six Hundred Years of a European Dynasty*, tr. Cathleen and Hans Epstein, Garden City, NY, 1964, p. 28.

19. For example, William Coxe, *History of the House of Austria ...*, London, 1895, vol. I, p. 5. I have preferred Coxe's retelling of many of these traditional tales, because his language is sprightly, and expresses the energy of the original. And, as he explains, 'For the reign and character of Rhodolph have been consulted numerous annals, chronicles and histories, both of contemporary and subsequent authors; as well as the various dissertations on his reign and the diplomatic and genealogical labours of Herrgott and Gerbert.'

20. See Janet L. Nelson, 'The Lord's anointed and the people's choice: Carolingian royal ritual', in David Cannadine and Simon Price (eds.), *Rituals of Royalty:*

Power and Ceremonial in Traditional Societies, Cambridge and New York, 1987, p. 156.

21. He was, of course, not Holy Roman Emperor until crowned by the Pope in Rome, which he was never able to achieve. In practice this did not weaken his hold over the vassals of the Empire. Rudolf is always counted among the Holy Roman Emperors, and I have taken the liberty of calling him 'Emperor' knowing that this is technically incorrect.

22. Ottokar had acquired the duchy of Styria by election and secured his position by marriage to the widow of the last Babenberg duke, Frederick the Quarrelsome; he defeated the King of Hungary and forced him to cede his claim to Austria, and in 1269 he inherited the duchy of Carinthia from the last duke, who had been persuaded to make Ottokar his heir. Thus his territories stretched from the Sudeten mountains in the north to the shores of the Adriatic.

23. The account as given by Coxe, vol. 1, p. 25.

24. Ottakar's banner was the white lion of Bohemia, which allowed Grillparzer to create a scene in which Rudolf's accession was foreshadowed (the triumph of the red lion over the white lion).

25. *König Ottokars Glück und Ende* was published in 1825, and in it Rudolf became the embodiment of the subtle, intangible power of the Habsburgs, who by their dogged persistence had overcome the febrile power of an Ottokar – or a Napoleon Bonaparte. In Grillparzer's hands, the mythology of Rudolf became the justification for his descendant, Francis, last Habsburg Holy Roman Emperor, who had completed the cycle begun by Rudolf. And as Rudolf was transformed from man to Emperor, so too Francis became the incarnation of a newly minted Habsburg Empire. Incredibly, it at first fell foul of the Metternichean censorship, to Grillparzer's amazement. He confessed to Beethoven that he could not imagine any reason why so patriotic a piece should have attracted suspicion. Eventually it was performed and became a favourite both of the Emperor Francis I and the Viennese public. And it was not just for Grillparzer that Rudolf functioned as the inspiration of the dynasty, in time of trouble. In 1808 the poet Heinrich von Collin had summoned the spirit of Rudolf to the aid of Francis in his poem 'Österreich über alles': 'Ruft Rudolf von des Himmels Höhen/Zu Franz herab: Es wird bestehen,/Weil Österreich will,/Hoch Österreich' (Called Rudolf from the height of heaven/To Franz beneath: It will survive,/Because Austria wills it,/Hail Austria) (in *Deutsche Literatur, Politische Dichtung* II, p. 59).

26. 'The historian dissatisfied with the evidence of the practical record can turn to narrative sources. Though marred by errors, they contain a wealth of interpretation and comment invaluable for a retrospective sociology ... charters, narrative histories, epics and courtly romance all deserve our attention. Each is attuned to a different level of authenticity; each constructs its own fictions.' See Dominique Barthélemy, 'Civilising the fortress: eleventh to thirteenth century', in Philippe Aries and Georges Duby, *A History of Private Life II: Revelations of the Mediaeval World*, tr. Arthur Goldhammer, Cambridge, Mass., and London, 1988, p. 85.

27. The connection of the sun and empire has pre-Christian origins, but it was a claim strongly asserted by the Habsburgs, who followed on solid Carolingian precedents. For example, the verse epistle *Ermold the Black* cited by Nelson

(p. 67) echoes the same theme: 'As the sun illuminates the whole earth with its rays/And with his warmth puts all the clouds to flight/Signalling joy to trees, crops and sailors/Just so does the king in his coming bring joy to his people.'

28. Act III, scene 1.

29. See J. J. Fugger, *Spiegel der Ehren des hochtlöblichsten Kayser und Königlichen Erzhauses Österreich*, Nuremberg, 1682, p. 58, 'Rudolphus ehret das H. Sacrament', anno 1261.

30. It, of course, appears from the fourteenth to the seventeenth century, but it was also popular with German Romantic painters and poets. The paintings by Franz Pfarr and Friedrich Olivier were widely known.

31. Not, however, Joseph II, and even Maria Theresa, although personally devout, was not so attached to baroque flummery as her father, Charles VI. See D. Beales, *Joseph II*, vol. 1: *In the Shadow of Maria Theresa*, Cambridge and New York, 1987, pp. 441–55. He cites Kovacs's useful 1979 article in *Mitteilungen des Österreichischen Staatsarchivs*, to the effect that 'If one surveys the change in ceremonial observance of public worship in the period from 1765–6 to 1780–1, one sees the almost complete destruction of the Pietas Austriaca, of Habsburg piety, as it had developed since the beginning of the seventeenth century . . .' Perhaps 'suspension' rather than 'destruction' would be a better choice of words, for the 'apostolic' quality of Habsburg rule was emphasized once more in the nineteenth century. One of the most popular and characteristic images of the Emperor Franz Joseph, available on picture postcards and in prints for display on the walls of patriotic citizens, was of the Emperor at prayer.

32. See Baron von Margutti, *The Emperor Francis Joseph and His Times*, London, n.d., pp. 181–3.

33. See Fugger, ibid., 'K. Rudolph's Krönungs Handlung'.

34. See Coxe, p. 57, who quotes this 'just eulogy of a contemporary writer'.

35. It was Pope Boniface VIII who suggested that his external disfigurement suggested a spiritual distortion – had he not killed the elected Emperor with his own hand? The story that his appearance was due to being held up by his heels at birth by his doctors is apocryphal.

36. Philip resolved the problem by having Boniface kidnapped at the town of Anagni by a sworn enemy whose family he had traduced.

37. There is some dispute as to the precise location of these events. Many of the histories have Albert murdered either on the bank of the river in sight of his family, or on the site of the future abbey of Königsfelden. Both are problematical. Autopsy indicates that if the Emperor's party watched the murder from the far bank of the Reuss, as the story explicitly states, then it cannot have taken place at the point where the church was built. The landfall cannot have changed that much over the centuries. My suggestion is that the choice of the site for the church was based on motives other than topographical specificity.

38. There were subsequent Habsburg candidatures, but none were successful.

39. See Mauerer, Bd III, *Das Kloster Königsfelden*, Basel, 1954. Although other Habsburg monuments are well documented in terms of the history of the family, for example the tomb of Maximilian I in Innsbruck, Königsfelden features in none of the standard modern literature, and seems to have been

entirely forgotten outside Switzerland. I am grateful to Hippolyt and Brigitte Meles in drawing my attention to it, and informing me of its later history, including the translation of the Habsburg remains in the eighteenth century.

40. Not surprisingly, the issue of the power of symbols has loomed larger in anthropology than in history, with a few exceptions, notably Marc Bloch and the French tradition of the history of *mentalités*. Rodney Needham, in his useful short book on *Symbolic Classification*, observes: 'In human society many things are important, and we can expect that in any social aggregate these will be marked by symbols that focus attention on those things and perhaps also indicate the kind of importance these possess.' See Rodney Needham, *Symbolic Classification*, Santa Monica, Calif., 1979, p. 4. This also introduced me to two other books which have been very valuable: A. M. Hoccart, *Kings and Councillors: an Essay on the Comparative Anatomy of Human Society*, Chicago and London, 1970, and A. N. Whitehead, *Symbolism: Its Meaning and Effect*, Cambridge, 1927, reprinted 1958.

41. See *The Cambridge Mediaeval History*, vol. vii, Cambridge, 1932, p. 147. 'He accordingly caused to be forged five documents purporting to emanate from earlier emperors, one being ostensibly a confirmation by Henry IV of edicts issued ... by Julius Caesar and Nero ... The fraud was not badly executed, but Charles's suspicions were apparently aroused by Julius Caesar and Nero, and he referred the documents to his friend Petrarch, who decisively rejected them.'

42. There is no documentary evidence for the Roman claims of Rudolf. But it seems likely that these were based on some family tradition, a likelihood enhanced by the fact that these assertions were deemed to be so improbable to the sceptical eye that they damaged his legal case, and were used to expose the whole set of documents as forgeries. The *Privilegium maius* was overall an attempt to embody an oral tradition – like the ancient legend of the origin of the archducal title – within a written construct.

43. See Marcel Beck, Peter Felder, Emil Mauerer and Dietrich W. H. Schwarz (eds.), *Königsfelden: Geschichte, Bauten, Glasgemälde, Kunstschätze: Iconographie der Glasgemälde*, Olten und Freiburg im Breisgau, 1983, pp. 115–26.

44. See Whitehead, pp. 61–2: 'Symbolism is no mere idle fantasy or corrupt degeneration: it is inherent in the very texture of human life.'

45. Like St Denis for the House of Valois.

46. But the death of Albert and its aftermath revealed another trait seen less often, and even more rarely discussed: their ruthlessness. Even in 1308, their exercise of the 'Blutgericht' was seen as excessive. Vindictiveness clothed in the apparel of the law is a recurring theme down the centuries, justified by the need to protect the line of Habsburg. In the pursuit of that end, no measure was too extreme.

Chapter 2: Cosa Nostra (Our Cause)

1. See Barthélemy, in Aries and Duby, p. 397.
2. See Roberta Gilchrist, *Gender and Material Culture: The Archaeology of Religious Women*, London, 1994, p. 150.

3. Of course, in the renewal of war in both France and England in the fourteenth and fifteenth centuries, the possession of castles and fortified towns became a key issue, but even so, 'the soaring walls of castle and city were capable of keeping out any enemy who was not prepared to devote weeks, perhaps months, to the work of reducing them'. See Christopher Duffy, *Siege Warfare. The Fortress in the Early Modern World 1494–1660*, London, 1979, p. xiii.

4. The kings of France from Clovis onwards were anointed with oil from a sacred ampoule. The legend was that at the baptism of the heathen King Clovis, the vast crowd gathered to witness the deed prevented the priest carrying the oil for the King's anointing from reaching the Bishop, St Remi. The Bishop, seeing all his plans endangered, fell on his knees and prayed to God for help. A milk-white dove appeared from Heaven bearing a vial of the holy chrism with which Clovis was then anointed. When Charles the Bald was crowned at Rheims four hundred years later, the Bishop, Hincmar, told the congregation that 'Charles – of the race of Clovis who was baptised with heaven-sent Chrism, some of which we still possess – was anointed and consecrated king'. See F. Oppenheimer, *The Legend of the Sainte Ampoule*, London, 1953.

5. Rudolf's cult, like that of Leopold, was very localized. But, unlike Leopold, Rudolf was never recognized as a saint or even beatified. Leopold was sanctified in 1485, as Maximilian was beginning his programme of propaganda. Charlemagne was never a saint, but merely accorded the lesser rank of 'Blessed', although these categories were not precisely drawn until the seventeenth century. In Habsburg chronicles, and imagery, all three are presented with all the attributes of a saint. However dubious technically these claims may have been, the constant linking of these 'saintly' lives to the Habsburg line was thought to prove the special election of the House of Austria.

6. M. T. Clanchy, *From Memory to Written Record: England 1066–1307*, Oxford, 1993, pp. 148–9.

7. This crown was also used on coins and in images of Albert V before he became Emperor.

8. This was not merely a theoretical problem in the past. In 1400, Charles IV's successor, his elder son Wenceslaus, was deposed as Emperor and replaced by Rupert III, Count Palatine.

9. Article 4.

10. A bull (Latin *bulla*) takes its name from the seal with which a public document was authenticated. Without this seal the document had no validity. Most documents were given a lead seal but some documents of great public importance were sealed with a golden seal, hence the name, 'Golden Bull'.

11. It was at this point that the tradition of their Roman origin took concrete form.

12. Cited in Alphons Lhotsky, *Privilegium maius. Die Geschichte einer Urkunde*, Munich, 1957, pp. 81–90. They were purportedly from Emperor Henry IV in 1058 to Ernest of Babenberg, Margrave of Austria; from the Emperor Frederick I in 1156 to Duke Henry of Babenberg; from Emperor Henry VII in 1228 to Duke Leopold of Babenberg; from Emperor Frederick II in 1245 to

Frederick Duke of Austria and Styria; and a decree from Emperor Rudolf I to his two sons in 1283.

13. Except, of course, in the brief but convincing work by Alphons Lhotsky (see note 12).

14. See Coxe, p. 120.

15. See Clanchy for the situation in English jurisdictions; the issues relating to the validity of testimony were not very different.

16. See Jack Goody, *The Logic of Writing and the Organisation of Society*, Cambridge, 1986, p. 136.

17. Alphons Lhotsky suggests that his chancellor, Johann von Platzheim, was the alternative candidate. See *Privilegium*, p. 16.

18. These appear only in the 'privilege' of Henry IV in 1058 as grants conceded by the ancient pagan emperors. As the remainder of the document makes clear it is the Emperor in his plenary power who makes the grants, to which the Roman precedents form only an illustrative preamble. None of the other four documents even refer to the Roman origin.

19. See Marie Tanner, *The Last Descendant of Aeneas*, New Haven, Conn., 1993, p. 88ff. The particular linkage to the Habsburgs was presented by Anna Coreth in her study of *pietas austriaca*.

20. See M. Dugast-Rouillé, *Les Maisons Souveraines d'Autriche*, Paris, 1967, p. 81.

21. A godfather was not distinguished from a natural father in terms of affinity.

22. See Lhotsky, pp. 16–17. He himself speculates on the origin of the *Privilegium* and remarks that both his father and the widow of Albert I at Königsfelden had expressed similar attitudes to those which found their way into Rudolf's document.

23. See Barthélemy, in Aries and Duby, p. 90, who makes the point, too often forgotten, that kinship was as much a matter of the imagination as of 'reality' in the narrow (and limited) sense of the word.

24. See ibid., p. 97. 'In the early Middle Ages a man's first name was his real and basic identification. Family names were indicated by the repetition of the same names generation after generation. Names were transmitted as hereditary attributes from father to son and uncle to nephew . . . The *virtus* of the ancestors flowed in the blood of the homonymous descendants.'

25. In the Middle Ages many saints were not recognized by the hierarchy of the Church, but were created by the strength of the cults surrounding them. See Aviad M. Kleinberg, *Prophets in Their Own Country: Saints and the Making of Sainthood in the Late Middle Ages*, Chicago, Ill., and London, 1992.

26. See Michael Wilks, *The Problem of Sovereignty in the Later Middle Ages*, Cambridge, 1963.

27. Cited in Brian Tierney, *The Crisis of Church and State 1050–1300*, Englewood Cliffs, NJ, 1964, pp. 131–2. Innocent was emphatic that all temporal power derived from God through the agency of the Pope.

28. Unless of course he were a Habsburg; the Emperor Frederick III gave imperial sanction to the *Privilegium* in 1446.

29. See Barbara W. Tuchman, *A Distant Mirror. The Calamitous Fourteenth Century*, London, 1979, pp. 92–125.

30. Although Clement VI did so obliquely in his bull of September 1348, which talked of the pestilence with which God was afflicting the Christian people.

31. See Norman Cohn, *The Pursuit of the Millennium*, London, 1957, p. 67, citing Jean le Fevre, 'Les lamentations de Matheolus'.

32. Jean Gerson, *De auferibilitate sponsi ad Ecclesia*, p. 300, cited in Steven Ozment, *The Age of Reform, 1250–1550. An Intellectual and Religious History of Late Mediaeval and Reformation Europe*, New Haven, Conn., 1980, p. 163.

33. There had been a strong tendency towards anticlericalism (centred on the whole issue of ecclesiastical poverty) and to antipapalism from the late thirteenth century. But it grew inexorably in the fourteenth.

34. See Ozment, p. 164.

35. *Reformatio Sigismundi*, tr. and cited in Gerald Strauss, *Manifestations of Discontent in Germany on the Eve of the Reformation*, Bloomington, Ind., and London, 1971, pp. 4–8. Strauss observed that new and 'up to date' versions were regularly prepared in the years after its first appearance, and it was one of the most popular early printed tracts, with no less than eight printings between 1476 and 1522. As he noted: 'Everyone writing on the question of reform in the late fifteenth and early sixteenth century was familiar with it.'

36. Sigismund's uneasy relationship with his half-brother, Wenceslaus, who as Emperor would have been the logical sponsor of the crusade, was also a strong motive. He was keen to demonstrate that he and not Wenceslaus was the natural leader of Christendom. For the intention to go on to Jerusalem, see Froissart's Chronicle.

37. As at the battle of Sempach, there is great confusion among the chroniclers as to precisely what happened at each stage of the battle. I have tried to follow a course of probable action from the various accounts.

38. Edward Gibbon, *The History of the Decline and Fall of the Roman Empire*, J. B. Bury edn, London, 1909, vol. vii, p. 36.

39. Cited in Margaret Aston, *The Fifteenth Century: the Prospect of Europe*, London, 1968, p. 79.

40. Hus could have saved his life by yielding to oppression, but he chose death instead. The immolation of Hus was taken as embodying the spirit of the whole nation. In 1968, more than five centuries later, a Czech student, Jan Palach, sat in Wenceslaus Square in Prague, and burnt himself to death as a protest against the Russian invasion of his nation. His name is now bracketed with that of Hus, in Czech political mythology. It is perhaps a small irony that the man most instrumental in preparing the case against Hus was a former friend and colleague, Stefan Palech.

41. Perhaps the greatest achievement of Constance was the decree *Frequens*, requiring that the Pope summon general councils on a regular basis, something that would have radically altered the balance of power in the Church, to the permanent detriment of papal authority.

42. His principal objective was to retain a controlling voice in the determination of the candidacy for the papal throne, for which purpose the council was summoned to Constance. His remarks at the deposition of Frederick were

very pointedly aimed at the ecclesiastical delegates and those of the Italian cities.

43. This was the *reductio ad absurdum* of the Great Schism, which was resolved by the Council of Constance depriving all three claimants of their papal titles, and electing Martin V in their place.

44. His enmity for Sigismund was of long standing. He had supported the opposing candidates to the imperial throne, and he had hitherto refused, in the spirit of the *Privilegium maius*, to do homage for his imperial fiefs.

45. Yet it was not unknown elsewhere. In Scotland John Balliol had been ritually divested of his kingship on the orders of Edward I. I am grateful to Professor Anthony Goodman for this observation.

46. See Coxe, p. 198.

47. ibid., p, 160,

48. Cited in Paul Frischauer, *The Imperial Crown*, London, 1939, pp. 80–81.

Chapter 3: Universal Empire

1. Written anonymously in 1162 to celebrate his victory at Milan.

2. Cited in Cohn, pp. 110–11. According to Cohn this is attributed to Regebogen, as one of the *Meistersinger*, and is but one of many prophecies of the returned Frederick.

3. Some research suggests that this was not the case, but there is no conclusive answer.

4. This seems highly improbable, given his generally poor state of health. But it is a classic case of the medieval penchant for *post hoc, ergo propter hoc*, and for the moral lesson that a death from surfeit implied.

5. Friedrich Heer, *The Holy Roman Empire*, tr. Janet Sondheimer, London, 1968, p. 124.

6. Coxe, p. 214.

7. However, she found many problems with Frederick's lethargy, and the cold climate of Wiener Neustadt. See Bernd Rill, *Friedrich III, Habsburgs Europäischer Durchbruch*, Graz, 1987, pp. 110–26.

8. This little walled town on the route from Vienna to Graz was founded by the Babenbergs in 1192. Frederick built extensively here in the 1450s, enlarging the castle and decorating the chapel, which was dedicated to his favourite, Saint George. Inside, a set of superb stained-glass windows is echoed outside by a display on the main entrance to the courtyard where a statue of Frederick is surrounded by the coats of arms of all his territories and connections, real and imagined – eighty-nine in all. At the heart of the display is his cryptic motto AEIOU.

9. 'Wer spricht von Siegen? Übersteh'n ist alles.'

10. See Coxe, p. 216.

11. ibid., p. 212.

12. After his coronation as king of the Romans at Aachen a more general confirmation of the privileges of the house of Austria was issued; but the archducal title was only claimed after the imperial authorization of 1453. See Lhotsky, p. 33. Frederick went further than the letter of the *Privilegium*

demanded, reflecting perhaps the attempt to dispossess Duke Frederick of the Empty Purse in 1415. Henceforward, the Dukes of Austria became archdukes, and were considered to have been automatically invested in their domain if they did not receive confirmation after demanding it three times from the Emperor. They were to be invested within the boundaries of Austria, on horseback, wearing a royal mantle, and a ducal coronet surmounted with the imperial arch and cross and holding what was called 'the staff of command' – a form of sceptre. The archdukes were declared by birth to be privy councillors of the Emperor and their territories could not be put under imperial ban. Any attempt, by act or thought, against their persons was to be considered high treason, nor could they be challenged to single combat. They were to be free from the duty of attending the Diet, and exempt from all imperial taxes, except the duty to maintain twelve men-at-arms for one month against the Turks in Hungary. The liberties given to them were comprehensive. They could levy taxes and grant letters patent; they could create counts, barons and all inferior titles. If the male line of the family failed, then the female line were to enjoy the rights of succession, and in the failure of heirs the archdukes could dispose of their territories at will. Any lands of the Empire might be alienated in their favour, and their subjects could not be summoned out of their lands for a lawsuit, to give testimony, or to receive a fief.

13. See Lord Twining, *A History of the Crown Jewels of Europe*, London, 1960.

14. Honorius of Augsberg wrote in *Gemma Animae*: 'The crown of the emperor represents the circle of the whole world. The [Emperor] Augustus therefore bears it as evidence that he possesses the sovereignty of the world. An arch is bent over the diadem in order to represent the ocean by which the world is divided.' Cited in Twining, p. 49.

15. The only two occasions on which the Crown of Charlemagne was specifically recorded as having been used were for the coronations of the two Habsburgs, Rudolf I, and Frederick III in 1442. At the coronation of Rudolf it was noted that this was the first time that the crown had been used since Charlemagne, but this may have been an exaggeration. Again it was these two Habsburgs who were the only emperors to make much of the symbolism of the crown. Frederick struck a commemorative coin to celebrate the coronation at Aachen, and the crown was used on this as a symbol appropriate for a King of the Romans.

16. 'Rex et sacerdos.'

17. Twining, p. 43: 'A description of the coronation of the Emperor Sigismund by Eugenius IV in 1433 relates that the Pope first placed upon the Emperor's head a small red cap, then a mitre of white with horns worn at the side and over that, a crown. It will be apparent that the wearing of the mitre by these emperors who formally received it at Rome remained customary throughout the Middle Ages.'

18. ibid. 'In 1442 the Emperor Frederick III commissioned a new set of imperial regalia from a Nuremberg goldsmith. The crown included in this regalia incorporated an innovation for it was *fitted* with a mitre on the inside as an integral part of the ornament.'

19. See Helmuth and Stulhofer Grössing, 'Versuch einer Deutung der Rolle der Astrologie in den persönlichen und politischen Entscheidungen einiger

Habsburger des Spätmittelalters', in *Österreichische Akademie der Wissenschaften, Philosophisch-historische Klasse: Anzeiger*, 117 (1980), pp. 267–83.

20. As a loyal Siennese, he may have been a little prejudiced in favour of his native town.

21. Celebrated in a famous painting by Pinturicchio.

22. The oath declared: 'I Frederick, king of the Romans, promise and swear by the Father, Son and Holy Ghost, by the wood of the revivifying cross, and by these relics of saints [which he had brought with him] that if by permission of the Lord, I shall come to Rome, I will exalt the holy church and his holiness who presides over it, to the utmost of my power. Never shall he lose life, liberty or honour, by my counsel, consent, or exhortation. Nor will I, in the city of Rome, make any law or decree touching upon those things which belong to his holiness, or the Romans, without his consent. Whatever part of St Peter's patrimony shall fall into our hands, we will restore to his holiness; and he to whom we shall commit the administration of the kingdom of Italy, shall swear to assist his holiness in defending St Peter's patrimony to the utmost of his power. So help me God and his holy evangelists.' Fugger, *Spiegel der Ehren*, p. 575. Despite the subdued tone of this document, it is defiantly imperialist. All these concessions were allowed by grace from the Emperor to the Pope; the implication is that he could do otherwise.

23. Much of the ideology attributed to Maximilian more properly belongs to Frederick, which is why this chapter considers them as a unit.

24. His calculations went awry with Maximilian, who was born under the inauspicious sign of Saturn; all his life he believed that he had to fight against the qualities of a saturnine personality – moodiness and melancholia.

25. Although he was initially reluctant to accept it.

26. Adam Wandruszka writes (pp. 73–4): 'Frederick III is undoubtedly one of the most problematic and peculiar, and certainly not one of the most attractive, figures in Habsburg history. Hardly any other Habsburg has been so ill-treated.'

27. 'Erzschlafmütze.'

28. See H. Wiesflecker, *Kaiser Maximilian I: Das Reich, Österreich und Europa an der Wende zur Neuzeit*, Vienna, 1971–80, vol. 1, p. 352, cited in G. Benecke, *Maximilian I 1459–1519. An Analytical Biography*, London, 1982, p. 186.

29. The origin of the name 'Corvinus' is significant, for it shows that it was not only the Habsburgs who were obsessed with 'Romanity'. Like the Habsburgs Matthias was convinced he had a Roman descent. He traced his line back to a Roman consul, Marcus Valerius Corvinus, from whom he adopted the patronymic. From Marcus Valerius, he took the line of descent still further back to one of the sons of Zeus, a procedure very comparable to Habsburg claims of descent from Noah. Equally, Matthias claimed descent from Attila, a hero in Hungarian eyes. This line of argument was contained in Antonio Bonfini's *History of Hungary*, commissioned by Matthias.

30. The causes were complex. Matthias Corvinus had been elected King of Bohemia, but Frederick refused to crown him, on the grounds that another candidate had a good claim. In retaliation, Matthias occupied his lands in

Styria, Carinthia and a part of Lower Austria, and made Vienna his western capital until his death in 1490.

31. 'Rerum irrecuperabilis felix oblivio.'

32. 'Tene mensuram et respice finem.'

33. In Petrus Lambecius, *Diarium sacri itineris cellensis interrupti*.

34. 'Austria est imperare orbi universo.' In fact it can be found in a set of his notebook jottings dating from the time before he became Emperor, indicating that these ideas of the house of Habsburg as God's elect were in his mind long before he achieved the imperial purple.

35. 'Hic regit, illa, tuetur.'

36. See J. G. Fraser, *The Golden Bough*.

37. Literally, the bearer of Christ, from the legend of St Christopher; but it echoes the family legend of 'Saint' Rudolf and the Host, which tells the same story.

38. Quite against the family tradition; he died in his first year, ill-fated, some said, because he had been named after the parricide.

39. See the modern edition of Joseph Grünpeck, *Die Historia Fridericii et Maximiliani* (first published 1514), ed. O. Benesch and E. M. Auer, Berlin, 1957.

40. Later he was claimed as the reincarnation of the German Ur-hero, Arminius. See Simon Schama, *Landscape and Memory*, New York and London, 1995, pp. 100–110. Other chapters of this remarkable book relate directly to my theme, for example chapter 4, iv, 'The verdant cross', and chapter 5, 'Streams of consciousness', but the whole text demonstrates the full range and potential for this new style of history.

41. Leonora, on the other hand, came from a family of high spirit and adventure. But she died in his eighth year.

42. Of his granddaughters, Elisabeth married the King of Denmark in 1515, another, Mary, married Louis, King of Hungary and Bohemia in 1522, while a third, Catherine, became the wife of the King of Portugal.

43. From a letter to Prüschenk; see C. A. J. Armstrong, 'The Golden Age of Burgundy: Dukes That Outdid Kings' in A. G. Dickens (ed.), *The Courts of Europe, Politics, Patronage and Royalty 1400–1800*, London, 1977, p. 72.

44. In the Netherlands the States-General had claimed this right for themselves. He was even held prisoner in Bruges, while the people of Ghent talked of executing him. .

45. Wiesflecker's great biographical study embraces both points of view, but he sees, on the whole, Maximilian the planner rather than Maximilian the pragmatist. Perhaps his capacity to take the long view was most effective in his dynastic and 'propaganda' activities, rather than in his political and financial dealings.

46. 'Since Maximilian was hardly ever solvent for more than a few weeks or days he was always robbing Peter to pay Paul, which quickly resulted in bureaucratic muddle that only Maximilian in person could resolve. The more that happened, the more he set himself good resolutions and planned marvellously elaborate departments and institutions, only to see them break down as of necessity during the next cash or credit crisis.' See Benecke, pp. 125–6.

47. See ibid., pp. 123–5, and personal communication.

48. Her attraction was the large dowry offered with her.

49. Maximilian's brood of eleven bastards by a variety of mothers suggests that this was the case.

50. The death of Philip was a windfall for Ferdinand, because the young Duke of Burgundy had come to Spain to claim Juana's Castilian inheritance after the death of her mother Isabella in 1506. Ferdinand, relying on Isabella's will, claimed the regency for himself. Spanish society was polarized and it seemed likely that a civil war might break out. Philip's death and Juana's madness settled the matter in his favour.

51. Of course, the crowns of both nations were elective, even if a strong pressure towards a hereditary succession had been slowly growing.

52. Maximilian's own daughter, Margaret, had been formally promised to the Dauphin, and was sent at the age of three to be brought up at the French court. She spent eight years there before she was repudiated.

53. Indeed, he had, as the head of his own house, to assent to the Hungarian espousal of his sister.

54. Ferdinand of Aragón, who following the death of Philip the Fair was Ferdinand's guardian, planned to use his grandson's marriage to build closer ties to France; a Hungarian marriage was out of the question.

55. 'Felix Austria nube . . .'

56. It was painted in 1515 or 1516 and is now in the Kunsthistorisches Museum in Vienna. It is suggested (see Wolfgang Hilger, *Ikonographie Kaiser Ferdinands I (1503–1564)*, Vienna, 1969, p. 18) that this figure is in fact Joanna of Castile, or Bianca Sforza. However, the resemblance to other images of Joanna is not exact. His argument is that as wife and the mother of Charles and Ferdinand it is more logical to include her than Mary, dead since 1482, or Bianca. There are two other pieces of evidence that, however, might lead to Mary. First, Maximilian's passion for her and his sense that she was the co-progenitor of his line, and the point of contact to the Burgundian past. Second, her attitude – looking up to heaven – might indicate that this was now her abode, while Joanna was still very much alive in Tordesillas. The arguments against Bianca are probably conclusive.

57. The connection with Dürer's famous engraving of the Knight, Death and the Devil (1513) and Burgkmair's equestrian portraits is unclear. Erwin Panofsky says the Dürer is 'Generally reminiscent' of the Burgkmair, which he suggests was derived from an earlier Dürer. Later Burgkmair equestrian studies for the tomb of Maximilian echo the Dürer Knight.

58. The emphasis here is 'painted', and perhaps it would be fair to add, 'in his prime'. The Dürer engravings of Maximilian are eloquent and accomplished; by contrast, the painting of 1518 is lifeless, although from autopsy, he sat for Dürer 'high up in the palace in his little tiny cabinet'. But by 1518 he was ailing and in constant pain from his leg. Indeed, and for a long time, it was wrongly thought not to be by Dürer's hand. Certainly, it was much disliked by his daughter Margaret to whom the artist tried to present the portrait in 1521. No doubt she wanted to remember her father in a more heroic guise.

59. Maximilian had the unique experience of fighting twice at Guinegate, once in 1479 and again in 1513, and beating the French on both occasions.

60. On the development of printing see Elisabeth Eisenstein, *The Printing Revolution in Early Modern Europe*, Cambridge, 1983, and the first volume of her

larger work, *The Printing Press as an Agent of Change*, Cambridge, 1979. Also Lucien Febvre and Henri-Jean Martin, *The Coming of the Book: The Impact of Printing 1450–1800*, London, 1976. On the development of printing technology, the best short study is S. H. Steinberg, *Five Hundred Years of Printing*, Harmondsworth, Middx, 1955.

61. See K. Wehmer, *Mit Gemälde und Schrift. Kaiser Maximilian I und der Buchdruck*, Stuttgart, 1962.

62. The ten works that were actually published, produced in manuscript, or issued as uncompleted fragments were: 'The Triumphal Procession', 'The Triumphal Arch', *Theuerdank*, 'Tournaments and Masked Balls', 'The Holy Relatives of Emperor Maximilian', 'The Genealogy of the Emperor Maximilian', 'The Books of Artillery', 'The Book of Hunting', 'Weisskunig', 'Historia Frederici et Maximiliani', and the 'Tirolean Book of Hunting'. Another eighteen books were projected, but were not in progress at his death.

63. For Maximilian's literary work, see Gerhild Scholz-Williams, *The Literary World of Maximilian I: An Annotated Bibliography*, St Louis, Mo., 1982.

64. He began work on his *Autobiography* in Latin in the 1490s. In 1499 he showed the Nuremberg scholar Willibald Pirckheimer some parts in draft, and apologized for his rough 'soldier's Latin' ('Reiterlatein'). Pirckheimer retold the story to Melanchthon, who reproduced it in *Cronica Carionis aucta* (1563).

65. ibid., pp. 10–11.

66. See for example the engraving by Hans Springinklee, 'Maximilian I wird das Allmacht Gottes empfohlen', which is a form of 'apotheosis'. See Österreichische Nationalbibliotek, Vienna, *Biblos Schriften*, Bd 23. *Maximilian I, 1459–1519, Austellung*, Vienna, 1959, p. 134.

67. See Tanner, *The Last Descendant of Aeneas*, p. 103, Yale, New Haven and London, 1993.

68. Future Habsburgs were to follow this pattern pioneered by Maximilian: Rudolf in his court at Prague in the late sixteenth century, Leopold I amid his books and music in the late seventeenth, and even, a long step forward, the Crown Prince Rudolf in the late nineteenth, with his plan for a vast encyclopedia paying tribute to the wisdom and accomplishments of the Habsburgs.

69. His intervention was persistent: sometimes he would send an image back several times to be redrawn.

70. This puns on the two meanings of 'Weiss'.

71. See Scholz-Williams, p. 13: '*Weisskunig* changes the chaos of life into a well planned matrix of cosmic order and to a logical motivational matrix that controls all facets of Maximilian's turbulent life.'

72. Maximilian actually did much to standardize the German used in official documents throughout the Empire, and also, by commanding the cutting of the Fraktur type for the production of *Theuerdank*, left a lasting impact on German written culture until the 1940s.

73. When it was finally published by Joseph Kurzböcken in Vienna in 1775, it contained no less than 237 woodcuts.

74. This is largely because of the acute angle of observation. See Paul Veyne, 'Conduct without belief and works of art without viewers', *Diogenes*, vol. 143, 1988, pp. 2–4.

75. See Erwin Panofsky, *The Life and Art of Dürer*, Princeton, NJ, 1967, p. 179. My description of the Arch is adapted from his preceding pages 176-8.
76. See Marie Tanner, pp. 102-4. She observes: 'Maximilian burst the bounds of conventional ancestor stalking. In construing his mythical past, Maximilian concentrated on a single idea: the widening of the net of races that converged in his pedigree. Cultural borders offered no barrier to the medley of figures that were swept into the common genealogical root: the uninterrupted flow of the divine blood and not the rivalry of races impelled the vision here. The archaeological intensity with which he pursued this ancestral quest set Maximilian apart from his predecessors, as historians were sent throughout Europe to document his legendary past. The most renowned humanists of the Northern renaissance, including Johannes Aventinus, Heinrich Bebel, Conrad Celtis, Hieronymous Gebwiler, Wolfgang Lazius, Jacob Mennel, Johannes Naucler, Conrad Peutinger, Johann Stabius and Franciscus Irenicus give some indication of the prodigious talents devoted to these endeavours.'
77. *Heiligen aus der Sipp-, Mag-, und Swagerschaft.*
78. See *The Triumph of Maximilian I. 137 Woodcuts by Hans Burgkmair and Others* ... with a translation of descriptive text, introduction and notes by Stanley Applebaum, New York, 1964, p. 18.
79. 'Quod in celis sol hoc in terra Caesar.'
80. See Victor von Kraus, *Maximilians I Vertraulicher Briefwechsel mit Sigmund Prüschenk, Freiherrn zu Stettenberg*, Innsbruck, 1875, p. 48.
81. See G. E. Waas, *The Legendary Character of Kaiser Maximilian*, New York, 1941, p. 80.

Chapter 4: El Dorado (*The Golden One*)

1. Heer suggests the identification with Constantine, but Panofsky is dubious of the identification with the Holy Lance, on the grounds that 'this venerable but rather unwieldy object, with a nail from the Cross of Christ strapped to the blade, looks very different'. But he says that Titian portrayed Charles as the *miles christianus* as in Dürer's well-known engraving, but specifically also as a Roman emperor, who habitually carried a spear which was the embodiment of their supreme power. See E. Panofsky, *Problems in Titian, Mostly Iconographic*, London, 1969, pp. 84-6.
2. These are also the traditional colours of Burgundy.
3. See Frances Yates, *Astraea, the Imperial Theme in the Sixteenth Century*, London, 1975, pp. 1-28.
4. Gattinara writing to Charles on 12 July 1519, after the imperial election; see Karl Brandi, *The Emperor Charles V*, tr. C. V. Wedgwood, London, 1965, p. 112.
5. He spoke and wrote in Spanish to his immediate family, and in the first years in French to his brother and nephews; he had a natural ear for languages: speaking virtually no Spanish when he arrived in 1517, he quickly made it as good as a second mother tongue.
6. Philip, according to Panofsky, was habitually portrayed by Titian with the formal collar and, if seated, with a sceptre in his hand; Charles seemed much

more at ease with the more informal portrait. However, as Emperor, he could afford an ease of manner, while Philip was always conscious that he lacked the supreme accolade.

7. It was his original intention that his mausoleum, with thirty-four busts of his Roman 'antecedents', statues of the hundred saints which had been discovered as pertaining to the house of Habsburg, and the statues of his immediate forebears, should be built in the chapel of St George in Wiener Neustadt. This later developed into the less elaborate plan for Innsbruck, but it illustrates how highly Maximilian regarded the Order of St George, as epitomizing the virtues and essence of his lineage. He also planned a rotunda of twelve columns to be placed before the high altar at Speyer; each one topped by a statue of an emperor, all holding up a huge crown. See Heer, *The Holy Roman Empire*, p. 144.

8. Lost to France after Charles's death. Charles was determined to recover the full extent of his Burgundian inheritance, including Dijon.

9. Retranslated from the original cited in J. Huizinga, *The Waning of the Middle Ages*, tr. F. Hopman, London, 1924, reprinted Harmondsworth, Middx, 1972, p. 84.

10. It is not clear whether this was, like the pheasant, the real thing.

11. See Brandi, pp. 30–31.

12. The inspiration of the new order was Philippe de Mézières, tutor to the kings of France.

13. Huizinga, p. 195.

14. ibid., pp. 196–8.

15. This was the same period that produced Sir Thomas Malory's *Morte d'Arthur*. The stories of Arthur and the Grail legend were immensely popular throughout Europe. Arthur was one of the ancestors that Maximilian included among the bronze guardians of his tomb.

16. Vasari first used the word *rinascità*, in his *Lives of the Most Excellent Italian Architects, Painters and Sculptors* in 1550; Jules Michelet first used the word in the extended sense in 1855.

17. For example, the definition of the Renaissance as 'a distinct period in western history, a transition from a tradition-minded mediaeval world to a new change-orientated society of plural, moral and religious values'; see Ilan Rachum, *The Renaissance*, London, 1979, p. 458.

18. J. H. Plumb, in J. H. Plumb, *The Horizon Book of the Renaissance*, New York and London, 1961, p. 7.

19. This has been described by Mary Carruthers in a most important study as *a memorial culture*: 'It is my contention that mediaeval culture was fundamentally memorial, to the same profound degree that modern western culture is documentary. This distinction certainly involves technologies – mnemotechnique and printing – but it is not confined to them . . . Books . . . which were much more available in the late Middle Ages than ever before, did not profoundly disturb the essential value of memory training until many centuries had passed. Indeed, the very purpose of a book is differently understood in a memorial culture like that of the Middle Ages than it is today.

'A book [in this context, anything that is written or printed] is not necessarily the same as a text. *Texts* are the material out of which human beings make *literature*. For us texts come only in books and so the distinction between the two is blurred and even lost. But in a "memorial culture" a *book* is only one way among several to remember a "*text* to provision and cue one's memory".' See Mary J. Carruthers, *The Book of Memory. A Study of Memory in Medieval Culture*, Cambridge, 1990.

20. Elisabeth Eisenstein is careful to call it *an* agent of change, but its primacy is hard to deny, if only because it eventually undermined the centuries-old pattern of memorial culture. Eventually: but the habits of the old were a long time dying and for almost three centuries the new print culture was shot through with traces of the old. Nor was the birth without pain and difficulty, for the developing culture of the printed text had to accommodate the discordant forces of image and symbol within its structure. Again, the word *text* itself carries a set of twentieth-century assumptions.

The new techniques of printing followed the familiar form of the manuscript texts. The first typefaces in Germany mirrored the letter-shapes, punctuation and arrangement of handwriting. Moreover, the use of images in text followed, as far as possible, the conventions created for manuscript illustration, except that the technology did not allow images to be freely scattered in and around the text, and especially at its margins, but only as blocks dispersed within the body of the text. The function of these images was taken over from the manuscript. Often they were light relief from a 'heavy' text. But more often they were to 'cue the memory' or to act as chorus or commentator on the content in the written text. The importance of images in this process was fundamental. Mary Carruthers cites a late-fifteenth-century French MS on memory technique: 'One best learns for studying from illuminated books, for the different colours bestow remembrance of the different lines and consequently of that thing which one wants to get by heart' (p. 9). But because of the limitations to the new printed form, some of those functions began to drop away (colour included). Gradually the monochrome engraved or woodblock image assumed the role as the focal point of the text, usually compacting or concentrating the meaning contained in the ambient words. Symbolic images made that intensification all the more potent. This process of compaction blurred the medieval distinction between marginal and in-text images, or rather tried to express some of the same conventions in a different manner within the new format. Not all images were pictorial and early printers developed a whole range of 'devices', or ornaments, that could also be implanted within the body of the text. However, 'ornament' was not mere decoration, but, rather in the sense that 'the hand was the ornament of the body', an essential attribute of the text. For the development of punctuation, see M. B. Parkes, *Pause and Effect. An Introduction to the History of Punctuation in the West*, Aldershot, UK, 1992. On marginal images, see Michael Camille, *Images on the Edge: The Margins of Mediaeval Art*, London, 1992; and 'Seeing and reading: some visual implications of medieval literacy and illiteracy', *Art History*, VIII, 1985, pp. 26–49.

21. 'Maior erit Hercule.'

22. Fernando Checa Cremedes cites the little-known book of Alfonso Guerrero, *El Palacio de Fama* (The palace of fame), which suggests that Charles had not only broken the geographical boundaries, but also exceeded all heroes of the

past, had broken the bounds of time itself: 'plus ultra que Nestor, plus ultra en la Vida'; see Fernando Checa Cremedes, *Carlos V y la Imagen del Héroe en el Renascimiento*, Madrid, 1987, p. 199.

23. Notably, Edward Armstrong and, to a lesser degree, William Robertson.

24. See M. J. Rodríguez-Salgado, *The Changing Face of Empire: Charles V, Philip II and Habsburg Authority, 1551-1559*, Cambridge, 1988, p. 3.

25. 'The balance sheet which Charles might have drawn up on his death bed . . . must surely have been summed up in the words: *in vain.*' Karl Burckhardt, *Gedänken über Karl V*, cited in Otto von Habsburg, *Charles V*, tr. Michael Ross, London, 1970.

26. See Janet Cox-Rearick, *Dynasty and Destiny in Medici Art: Pontormo, Leo X, and the Two Cosimos*, Princeton, NJ, 1984, p. 214. Charles shared the sign of Capricorn with Cosimo di Medici, and used the Capricorn imagery assiduously propounded by the Medici, who welcomed the connection with imperial dignity. Charles used the Capricorn imagery when he made his grand entry into Milan in 1541.

27. See E. Vehse, *Memoirs of the Court and Aristocracy of Austria*, tr. Franz Demmler, 1896, vol. 1, p. 32.

28. See Royall Tyler, *The Emperor Charles the Fifth*, London, 1956, pp. 30-31. Tyler notes that de la Marche's *Le Chevalier Délibéré* ingeniously managed to present a case that Austria, the other element of his future inheritance, had once been a kingdom. De la Marche discovered 'in ancient chronicles' that Austria had been founded by a Trojan prince, Priam; at the same time another Trojan prince called Paris founded the city of the same name in France. His son Francio gave the name to 'France'. But after his death, the men of Paris chose Marcomire of Austria, son of Priam to be their new king. In turn his son, Pharamond founded the French monarchy. Moreover, the first arms of Austria were five golden larks, apparently 'the same as those of Troy'.

29. He had had a Spanish tutor, Luis de Vaca, since the age of eight but plainly had not made much progress.

30. See Brandi, p. 88.

31. See F. Braudel, *The Mediterranean and the Mediterranean World in the Age of Philip II*, tr. Sian Reynolds, London, 1973, vol. 1, pp. 361-4.

32. Transatlantic communication increased until 1550, when there were 133 ships westbound and 82 eastbound; then there was a sudden decline until it stabilized at about 60-65 westbound and rather fewer eastbound. But the ships grew larger and could carry more. See J. H. Parry, *The Spanish Seaborne Empire*, London, 1966, pp. 121-3.

33. Luther's basic attack was on the wholesale vending of indulgences, which for the first time promised remission of sin without any need for repentance on the part of the purchaser. He was not alone in his disgust for this blatant attempt to raise money by the exploitation of papal privilege. The indulgence campaign was stopped, but not before Luther had broadened his attack to wider issues of privilege and abuse. It is possible to argue that Luther's novelty was not doctrinal, but in the use of the printing-press and pamphlets (*Flugschriften*) to push the issue outside the traditional academic and ecclesiastical circles. In the first years of Luther's campaign, thousands of pamphlets flooded Germany, raising the debate over doctrine and authority. Little

wonder that Luther described printing as 'God's highest and extremest act of grace, whereby the business of the Gospel is driven forward'. See Eisenstein, pp. 148–55.

34. Cited in Brandi, pp. 131–2.

35. Many would argue for the opposite case and there are many contemporary tales of Charles being offered a compromise by the Lutheran princes and refusing. He wrote to Philip on 10 August 1546: 'You know already from my previous letters the main reasons for declaring war on the Protestants and how it could not be avoided, so I do not need to return to that theme. All I would like to say at this stage is that though my goal and intention has been, as you know, to make war for the sake of religion, it is considered politic to allege that the war is for the purpose of punishing rebellious subjects ...' Cited in F. Manuel Fernández Álvarez, *Charles V: Elected Emperor and Hereditary Ruler*, tr. J. A. Lalaguna, London, 1975, p. 131. But had the promised general council of the Church accommodated to the Lutheran position, the logic of Charles's position was that he would not set himself up as the arbiter of doctrine.

36. The physician, geographer and astronomer Petrus Apianus sought to present the forces underlying the natural order. In his new cosmography, *Astronicum Caesareum*, the twin figures of Jove and Charles were depicted, Charles governing the world and his alternate aspect, Jove, controlling the cosmic forces. This was one of the few books Charles took with him into his final retreat at Yuste. See Marie Tanner, 'Titian: the Poesie for Philip II', unpublished PhD thesis, New York University, 1976, p. 6.

37. He issued detailed instructions on which titles were to be used in every context, and on how the heraldic presence of the Emperor should be denoted. Each coat of arms was differently presented to take account of the varying relationships Charles enjoyed with his territories. For example, the arms of Castile and Aragón are *conjoined* with the personal coat of arms of the Emperor rather than appearing underneath it. In Burgundy, by contrast, the arms of the duchy are *incorporated* within the larger crest of the imperial crown. These were not petty matters, because these crests appeared on the seals that gave the force of law to documents and decrees.

38. It was in fact steel, but elaborately gilded and silvered. Much the same was thought of his father when he made his 'entry' in 1506.

39. See J. H. Elliot, *Imperial Spain, 1469–1716*, London, 1963, pp. 141–5.

40. The tradition of the *domus Austriae* – of partible inheritance constrained by a unitary head of the family – had been developing since Rudolf IV.

41. The *Lex Salica* was the ancient Frankish law, revised and codified by Charlemagne. It did not, as is often thought, prohibit *rule* by females; but it did in the section concerning descent of land '*de alode*' prohibit female inheritance of land, which was used to create the prohibition.

42. Juana inherited the crown of Castile from her mother, but Isabella herself took the crown from another female claimant, Juana 'la Beltraneja', who was kept imprisoned by Charles until her death in 1530. But 'la Beltraneja' always signed her letters and documents 'I, the Queen' in the traditional fashion.

43. *Orlando Furioso*, canto XV, 18, tr. Sir John Harington, 1634 edn. Cited in Yates, *Astraea . . .*, p. 53.

44. He abandoned a pre-contract to marry Princess Mary of England, whom his son Philip later married in 1554.
45. But see Rodríguez-Salgado, pp. 20–24.
46. ibid.
47. *London Gazette*, 1690, 2553/1; ibid., 1705, 4161/2.
48. See Paula Sutter Fichtner, *Protestantism and Primogeniture in Early Modern Germany*, New Haven, Conn., and London, 1989.
49. He had only taken minor orders and so found it easy, with a papal dispensation, to 'change tracks'.
50. See Rodríguez-Salgado, p. 128.
51. See ibid., pp. 86–7, citing F. Fernández Álvarez, *Corpus Documental de Carlos V*, Salamanca, 5 vols., 1971–81, vol. 2, p. 12. Charles to Philip, 9 April 1548. This was also the Ottoman practice, where age mattered as much as gender. A post-menopausal woman could exercise power more freely than any man.
52. See Andrew Hess, *The Forgotten Frontier. A History of the Sixteenth Century Ibero-African Frontier*, Chicago, Ill., and London, 1978.
53. Until 1529, the Spanish had held the fortress, the Peñón, which they had taken in 1510, and its loss opened Algiers as a base for Barbarossa's corsairs.
54. Tunis was recently captured by the Ottomans from a weak Muslim ruler, Muley Hacen in 1534.
55. Published in F. Walser, *Berichte und Studien zur Geschichte Karl's V*, pp. 167–72, cited in Fernández Álvarez, *Charles V*, p. 102. It was also a factor that Charles intended to attack Tunis, which would benefit the Italian ports but not the Spanish traders who suffered principally from the Algerine corsairs.
56. His objective was ostensibly to restore the deposed Muslim sovereign of Tunis, Muley Hacen. In creating any polarity of opposition between Islam and Christianity, we should bear in mind Braudel's wise observation: 'Between two enemy religions it would be unwise to imagine a watertight barrier. Men passed to and fro, indifferent to frontiers, states and creeds. They were more aware of the necessities of shipping and trade, the hazards of war and piracy, the opportunities for complicity or betrayal provided by circumstances' (Braudel, *The Mediterranean*, vol. 2, p. 759).
57. See W. Prescott, *History of the Reign of Charles V*, George Routledge edn, n.d., pp. 262–3, where he cites the contemporary sources.
58. See Braudel, p. 818.
59. ibid., p. 270.
60. Cited in Tanner, *The Last Descendant . . .*, p. 113.
61. Prescott, p. 264.
62. See ibid. and Fernández Álvarez, *Charles V*, p. 106.
63. See Joanneath Spicer, 'The renaissance elbow', in Jan Bremmer and Herman Roodenburg (eds.), *A Cultural History of Gesture*, Ithaca, NY, and London, 1991, p. 85.
64. See Hugh Trevor Roper, *Princes and Artists, Patronage and Ideology at Four Habsburg Courts, 1517–1633*, London, 1976, p. 28.
65. See Terzi (Franciscus Tertii), *Pictoris aulici austriacae gentis imaginum*, pt 1, 1569. The mural crown also signifies, according to Ripa, dominion over the inhabited parts of the earth.

66. See Jonathan Brown and J. H. Elliott, *A Palace for a King. The Buen Retiro and the Court of Philip IV*, New Haven, Conn., and London, 1980, pp. 147–56.
67. See Tanner, *Titian . . .*, pp. 159–60.
68. Cardinal Santa Cruz, cited in Rodríguez-Salgado, p. 30.
69. See Prescott, *History of the Reign of Charles V*, pp. 470–71. On the transfer of power and the issues involved, see Rodríguez-Salgado, pp. 126–35.
70. Rodríguez Salgado, p. 126.
71. See Geoffrey Parker, *Philip II*, Boston, Mass., 1978, p. 160.
72. Historical parallels are dangerous, but this so closely echoes the response of the Emperor Franz Joseph to the death of his wife Elisabeth; we know that Franz Joseph admired his great predecessor.
73. See William Stirling, *The Cloister Life of the Emperor Charles the Fifth*, London, 2nd edn, 1853, pp. 129, 142.
74. ibid., p. 217.
75. ibid., chap. IX.
76. Patrimonio Real, legajo 29, fol. 12. 'Ordena y manda que su cuerpo esté y se deposita en este dicho monasterio hasta quel Rey nuestro Señor su hijo ordena donde a de ser su enteramiento.'

Chapter 5: A War to the Last Extremity

1. These could still be seen until recently, in my personal experience, in some of the more traditional and 'folkloric' Spanish customs, especially in the processions surrounding Holy Week, and in the local festivities of *Cristianos y Moros*.
2. Only once, when the Archduke Matthias, the younger son of Maximilian II, allowed himself to be entrapped by the Protestant dissidents in the Netherlands into declaring against his Spanish cousins, was this common front broken. In 1576, Don John of Austria (the illegitimate son of Charles V), the victor at Lepanto over the Turks, had been appointed governor of the Netherlands in an attempt to stem the Dutch revolt. The States-General of the Netherlands had invited Matthias, a true Habsburg and a descendant of Charles the Bold, to become their governor. He accepted in 1577 and remained their nominee until 1581. An anonymous broadsheet widely circulated in the Netherlands has Don John and his predecessor Requesens in their coffins (each has the Golden Fleece around his neck) but to the right and left of the image, mounted and in armour, are two figures: on the left Matthias, and on the right William of Orange, both depicted as heroes of the Dutch resistance to the tyranny of Spain. The figure labelled Worthiness is handing Matthias a crown. A figure of a jester carries a stick which is topped by a tiny figure of Philip II, to which he points in a parody of the famous statue by Leone of Charles V overcoming Heresy. There are two issues of interest in this image. The first is the sense that the Dutch were not attacking the Habsburgs, but only their servants: almost all the images relate to the atrocities of Alva, who is also the central figure of this image, mocked by Time and the jester. It is rare that Philip himself is lampooned directly.

Secondly, there is the sense that the Austrian Habsburgs were the potential allies of the rebellious Dutch, with an equal claim to government. See James Tanis and Daniel Horst, *Images of Discord. A Graphic Interpretation of the Opening Decades of the Eighty Years War*, Bryn Mawr, Pa, 1993, pp. 108–9.

3. See Earl Rosenthal, *The Palace of Charles V in Granada*, Princeton, NJ, 1985, p. 252. 'The metaphysical and allegorical implications of the circle and the square would inevitably have been invoked by the more philosophically minded of the courtiers. Of course, the meanings associated with the square and the cube have less range than those attributed to the circle. Fundamental to the idea of the square or cube is the idea of stability, of constancy, of *virtù*, but there is also a secondary association with the earth and the terrestrial. The symbolism of the circle includes eternity, endless continuity, autonomy and perfection, but it is likely that most entrants to the round courtyard would have recalled the associations of the circle with the globe of the earth over which the emperor had been given dominion ... In Charles's case, the fiction of universal rule became more plausible as his Spanish subjects advanced in the New World. If the round courtyard was to have been a peristyle garden and its plants imported from all over his two empires, the pertinence of the circular form of the courtyard to his claim to global rule would have been very clear. If that was the case the shape of the garden into which he retreated would have symbolized the burden from which he withdrew for relaxation and renewal. One other symbolism of the circle could hardly be avoided and that is Charles V as the unique and immobile centre of a circle to which the whole refers.' Rosenthal cites Cesare Ripa on the meaning of the circle and the square. He writes principally as an architect, but despite the high quality of his study, the importance of the palace in Granada remains understated. The vision of the world as an enclosed garden (*hortus clausus*) applies equally to the courtyard garden of the Generalife, only a few hundred yards from the Arab and Christian palaces on the Alhambra hill. Here, the outer world is seen at a distance, with the hills and the Vega of Granada perceived through the apertures in the walls, but viewed over the ordered planting on either side of the fountains and moving streams of water that run the length of the building. The calm of the garden is dominated by the sound of water, and that same sense (and the smell of water) pervades the palace of Charles V; indeed the whole of the Alhambra site, a verdant island in an arid landscape, is built around a complex set of sensations, of light and shade, of aural, visual and olfactory sensations. These same influences would have been in play in the new garden to be built in the palace. On a personal note, based on many months working in the palace and in the Alhambra complex, the symbolic functioning of the palace quickly impresses itself upon those who work within its boundaries. For this reason, and by reason of its location, embedded in the heart of a Muslim environment, it possesses a set of intricate symbolic meanings which have yet fully to be unravelled.

4. There were other reasons why Madrid was an unusual choice. To the Burgundian nobleman Johannes Wyts, 'What you have in Madrid is by far the filthiest and most disgusting of all the cities of Spain, from the point of view that the streets are nothing more than great open sewers (as they are

called), cascades of shit and piss, emptied into the streets, which engenders an indescribable foetidity.' He no doubt visited the city in the summer. Cited in A. Alvar Ezquerra, *Felipe II, la Corte y Madrid en 1561*, Madrid, 1985, pp. 62–3.

5. Cited in Brown and Elliot, p. 2; Luis Cabrera de Córdoba, *Filipe Secundo, Rey de España*, I, Madrid, 1876, p. 298. See also Alvar Ezquerra for an anonymous poem of the 1580s, freely translated: 'In the city of Madrid/Royal seat of our great King Philip/he has placed the court of the Kingdoms of Castile, Aragón and Portugal/It is the centre of Spain/under a crystal sky . . . There he makes laws and rules the wide world . . .' (p. 69).

6. That is in the Christian world. The great monuments of the Ottomans and the Mughals are undoubtedly its equal.

7. See also Peter Pierson, *Philip II*, London, 1976.

8. It was to the Christian comfort of San Jerónimo that Isabella withdrew from the alien atmosphere of the Nasrid palace of the Alhambra during her honeymoon, and within whose walls Philip may well have been conceived.

9. See Parker, *Philip II*, pp. 171–2. Precisely why he did not bring the bones of Ferdinand and Isabella is not clear. Many thousands of bones and skeletons of assorted saints found their way to El Escorial. It is possible he had regard to Isabella's express instructions that she and Ferdinand should lie in Granada, the jewel of their joint crowns and symbol of the triumph of Christianity. Philip was always dutiful in such matters and not a little superstitious. To have moved Los Reyes Católicos might have been a symbol of abandoning Granada. Their shrine gave a purchase on a land still alien, and whose Morisco inhabitants broke into open revolt in 1568.

10. The 'Austrian Escorial' – the Emperor Charles VI's reconstruction of the abbey of Klosterneuburg outside Vienna – was never completed, and remained largely an architect's ideal.

11. He was not actually present on the battlefield, but commanded from a position some twenty-five miles away.

12. See Anton Capital, 'Planimetría y tradición. El Escorial como sistema de claustros', in *IV Centenario del Monasterio de El Escorial: Ideas y Diseño (La Arquitectura)*, Madrid, 1986, pp. 73–86.

13. There are many explanations for the origins and purpose of these life-size bronze figures. Similar figures are to be found in the chapel of the kings of France at St Denis, but they are not located close to the altar in an attitude of prayer. They are, first, a particularly Spanish phenomenon, with other examples in the family of Ferdinand and Isabella in the Capilla Real in Granada, but also in the abbey of Miraflores where the parents of Isabella are to be found in a similar attitude, and dating from the late fifteenth century. But, second, it became a Habsburg tradition, as in the statue of an archduke in the cathedral at Innsbruck, where his figure is pinned to a wall some distance from the altar, regarding the Crucifixion for all eternity. See B. von Barghahn, *Age of Gold, Age of Iron: Renaissance Spain and Symbols of Monarchy*, New York and London, 1985, pp. 55–8, and Adolf Reinle, *Das Stellvertreterbildnis*, Zürich, 1984.

14. The High Baroque pantheon that we see today was built by Philip III, and

Philip IV who 'paved, encrusted and embellished' it with 'the most exquisite work in marble, jasper and gilt bronze'.

15. Cited in Tanner, *The Last Descendant . . .*, p. 167.
16. ibid., p. 223.
17. What happened to the larger objects I have not been able to establish.
18. The literature on the Escorial is enormous, both in terms of its architecture and also as to the themes and ideas which underpinned the building. Its models were Roman, and it has been suggested that its architects would have been familiar with Diocletian's villa at Split, which was also a royal residence, a temple, and a mausoleum, and although the Escorial was not a military site, its tall towers at each corner gave it the image of a fortress. See von Barghahn, pp. 50–54.
19. See Capital, pp. 73–86.
20. Cited in James C. Davis (ed.), *Pursuit of Power: Venetian Ambassadors' Reports on Turkey, France and Spain in the Age of Philip II 1560–1600*, New York and London, 1970, pp. 83–4.
21. Sadly not the paragon whom Charles V had hoped for in his speech in Brussels when he had resigned his kingdoms to Philip II.
22. Cited in Parker, *Philip II*, p. 35.
23. The new building of the Real Chancillería in Granada dates from Philip's reign.
24. See Parker, *Philip II*, pp. 200–205.
25. Philip was devastated, too, by the death of his second wife, Elisabeth of Valois. see Parker, *Philip II*, pp. 84–6.
26. See Parker, *Philip II*, p. 30.
27. But not continuously. For example, the death of Suleiman the Lawgiver in 1566 provided a slight respite from the Turkish onslaught. Equally, the triumph of his half-brother Don John of Austria at Lepanto on 7 October 1571, which destroyed the Ottoman naval power. Yet three years later, in 1574, the Ottomans returned with a new fleet and recaptured Tunis, the prize taken by Charles V. In 1578, although Philip was not directly involved, the death of the Portuguese King Sebastian in battle in Morocco at Al Kasr al Kabir led to the incorporation of Portugal within the Spanish empire.
28. The key work on the Moriscos is Julio Caro Baroja, *Los Moriscos del Reinado de Granada. Ensayo de Historia Social*, Madrid, 1957. His description of the life of the Alpujarras destroyed after the revolt is a classic of historiography. He also points conclusively to the survival of Moriscos in Granada, especially in the famous Inquisition trials of 1724–8 that ferreted out no less than 300 families in the city of Granada still practising their faith. See pp. 258–63.
29. See for example Archivo del Alhambra, A. 60 Pieza. 9. 1566. For other references, see Sources and Bibliography. The unpublished PhD thesis of Kenneth Garrad, 'The Causes of the Second Rebellion of the Alpujarras', is the key source and has, inexplicably, never appeared in book form.
30. See William Stirling Maxwell, *Don John of Austria*, vol. 1, London, 1883, pp. 123–30. The traditional Protestant picture of the processes of the Inquisition largely misses the target. The mechanism of both accusation and trial was controlled by complex regulations designed to ensure consistency and

avoid personal bias. By the revision of the regulations published in 1561, the Holy Office moved through eight stages: denunciation, decision by the judges to pursue the case, gathering and evaluation of the evidence, decision of the judges to continue, hearings with the accused, defence by the accused, decision by the judges, sentence. Torture was used probably more sparingly than by many secular courts. However, once the judges had decided to pursue the case, the presumption was that the accused was guilty, and the whole process was simply designed to ensure a confirming confession. For an account of the Inquisition in practice, see R. Kagan, *Lucrecia's Dreams. Politics and Prophecy in Sixteenth Century Spain*, Berkeley, Calif., and London, 1990, pp. 136–8.

31. See Andrew Hess, 'The Moriscos: an Ottoman fifth column in sixteenth century Spain', *American Historical Review*, LXXIV, October 1968, pp. 1–25.

32. In fact many Moriscos remained or infiltrated back to their old homes. See Anwar O. Chejne, *Islam and the West: The Moriscos – a Cultural and Social History*, Albany, NY, 1983.

33. He failed. Caro Baroja calculated that many thousands of Moriscos remained, often protected by their Christian landlords.

34. See Parker, *Philip II*, p. 109.

35. My translation from the Spanish in the *Papiers d'État de Granvelle*, t. VI, p. 421, cited in W. H. Prescott, *Philip II*, London, n.d., p. 211.

36. This iconoclastic rage eventually spread over almost the whole of the Netherlands.

37. ibid., p. 275.

38. ibid., p. 282.

39. ibid., p. 279, citing *Correspondance de Philippe II*, vol. 1, p. 455.

40. Cited in Geoffrey Parker, *The Army of Flanders and the Spanish Road 1567–1659*, Cambridge, 1972, p. 132.

41. Cipher to Philip II, 13 April 1568, 'Se prendieron cerca de quinientos . . . He mandado justiciar todos', *CODOIN*, vol. 4, p. 488.

42. Prescott, *Philip II*, p. 343.

43. ibid., pp. 347–87, citing *Correspondance de Philippe II*, vol. 2, p. 27.

44. 750,000 ducats in 1566–7, 4.4 million in 1570–71. See Parker, *Philip II*, p. 97.

45. See David Kunzle, *The Early Comic Strip. Narrative Strips and Picture Stories in the European Broadsheet from c. 1450 to 1825*, Berkeley, Calif., and London, 1973, pp. 60–64, 438. Kunzle notes that 'the catalogue of horrors depicted in this beautifully engraved broadsheet is actually a selection in miniature from the illustrations to two historical works published as companions at this time: the *Spanish Tyranny in the Netherlands* and the *Spanish Tyranny in the West Indies*'. The text of the West Indies volume was based on the account of Bartolomé de Las Casas, which circulated widely among the enemies of Spain, with constant reprints in French and Dutch. The *Spanish Tyranny in the Netherlands* was published, with twenty large illustrations, after the truce between Spain and the United Provinces came to an end. The strip was entitled 'Verklaringe van dit Visoen ofte ghesichte /over den eyndelicken odegangh ende val van Castilien'. Numbered in the 1609 listing in the Van Stolk collection in Rotterdam, the example there has no text other

than the biblical phrase, meaning, 'Thou art weighed in the balances and found wanting.' The text and the explanation were published by Frederick Muller, *De Nederlandische Geschiednis in Platen. Beredeneerde Beschrijving van Nederlandsche Historieplaten, Zinneprenten en historische Kaarten*, Amsterdam, 1863–82.

46. Reported in Martin Hume, *The Court of Philip IV. Spain in Decadence*, New York, n.d., pp. 23–4.

47. On these issues, see Rodrigo de Zayas, *Les Morisques et le Racisme d'État*, Paris 1992, and Louis Cardaillac, *Morisques et Chrétiens: un Affrontement Polémique*, Paris, 1977.

48. Cited in Parker, *Philip II*, p. 193.

49. The attitudes of the Habsburgs were on the whole more positive. They tended to defend the Jews, for the financial benefits that their presence could bring. Frederick III was accused of being their protector, and both Maximilian I and Charles issued orders preventing their harassment. Rudolf II, following his father's benign policies, was tolerant, to the extent that while he banned all non-Catholic worship, he excluded the Jewish faith from the prohibition. Later generations were less benign, on the Spanish model. Leopold I expelled the Jews from all his lands in 1669–70, and only admitted them again under strict conditions – a yellow badge, ghettoization, and increased taxes. Both Charles VI and Maria Theresa followed the same line, and it was only under Joseph II that the restrictions were lifted.

50. See R. Po-Chia Hsia, *The Myth of Ritual Murder. Jews and Magic in Reformation Germany*, New Haven, Conn., and London, 1988, pp. 127–8.

51. See Bernard Seeman, *The River of Life. The Story of Man's Blood from Magic to Science*, New York, 1961, p. 36.

52. See Hsia, p. 145.

53. See Mary Elizabeth Perry, *Gender and Disorder in Early Modern Seville*, Princeton, NJ, 1990, p. 28.

54. Juan Martínez de Silica, Archbishop of Toledo and Philip's tutor, wrote the first comprehensive statute in 1548, which said that only those who could prove that they had no Jewish blood in their veins could hold office in the Church in Castile. Confirmed by Philip in 1556, that is, after he became king; Charles had not agreed to it.

55. See Parker, p. 101.

56. Albert Sicroff, writing in the *Encyclopaedia Judaica*, vol. 11, p. 255.

57. Henry Kamen interestingly suggests that *limpieza de sangre* – purity of blood – evolved into *limpieza de oficios* – purity from manual labour – which removed some of the problematical 'democratic' aspect of the older designation. See Henry Kamen, *Spain in the Later Seventeenth Century, 1665–1700*, London, 1980, p. 262.

58. See also Americo Castro, *Cervantes y los Casticismos Españoles*, 1974 (rev. edn), pp. 34–8.

59. See Manuel Alvar, *Léxico del Mestizaje en Hispanoamérica*, Madrid, 1987, and Jack D. Forbes, *Africans and Native Americans. The Language of Race and the Evolution of Red–Black Peoples*, 2nd edn, Urbana, Ill., 1993.

60. In his *History of Melanesian Society* (1914).

61. A contemporary example of the persistence of such patterns can be found among Ashkenazi Jewish families in the Diaspora. To marry 'out' breaks the chain of lineage and although it is devastating if the maternal line of connection is broken, either gender marrying out is considered socially harmful. However, the close kin connections which the Habsburgs accepted are frowned upon or completely prohibited.

62. The prohibition of Leviticus, chap. 18, depends on the definition of 'own flesh of his flesh', which varied from society to society.

63. See Jack Goody, *The Development of the Family and Marriage in Europe*, Cambridge, 1983, p. 176.

64. Cited in J.-L Flandrin, *Families in Former Times*, Cambridge, 1979, p. 164; see also, J.-L. Flandrin, *Un Temps pour Embrasser: Aux Origines de la Morale Sexuelle: VIe–XIe Siècle*, Paris, 1983.

65. Jack Goody (see above) provides an excellent general introduction, but does not comment on the Habsburg particularities. But in Françoise Héretier-Auge and Elisabeth Copet-Rougier, *Les Complexités de l'Alliance*, vol. 2: *Les Systèmes Complexes d'Alliance Matrimoniale*, Montreux, 1991, the chapter by Gérard Lenclud, 'Marriage, transmission des biens et réproduction sociale dans la Corse traditionelle', pp. 147–76, especially pages 150–52, on 'Famille, parenté, consanguinité', reflects many of the attitudes also common among the Habsburgs.

66. Many societies were preoccupied with the problems posed by these patterns of marriage. See Lévi-Strauss, where he observes: 'We have encountered a single logical conception of the opposition with the mother's brother's daughter and the marriage with the father's sister's daughter throughout the whole area of generalized exchange, extending from Assam to Indonesia and from Burma to eastern Siberia. The Batak of Sumatra forbid marriage with the father's sister's daughter, saying "How is it possible that water can flow up to its source?" On the other hand the Lubu of the western part of Sumatra justify marriage with the mother's brother's daughter by invoking the proverb "the leech rolls towards the open wound". It will be recalled that Tibet and China condemn marriage with the patrilineal cross-cousin as being a "return of bone and flesh" which runs the risk of "piercing the bone"' p. 449. Cross-cousin marriage was more widely practised and there were traditional structures that antedated the ecclesiastical prohibitions. 'There is no need for us to reconstruct some archaic state in which Indo-European society practised cross-cousin marriage . . . We need only note that Europe in its present state, or its still recent past, provides or provided a body of structural features all relating to what we call generalized exchange, the functional relationships of which are still observable in the study of simple forms of this type of exchange. What are these features? First and foremost is the Germanic classification of kinsmen and affines in "speermungen" and "schweitmagen" on the one hand, and "spillmagen" and "kunkelmagen" on the other: paternal relatives and maternal relatives, "relatives by the spear and the sword" and "relatives by the distaff and the spindle". With this we again encounter the Indo-Oriental distinction between "relatives of the bone" and "relatives of the flesh", between "wife givers" and "wife takers"'; see also chap. 28, 'The transition to complex structures' and chap. 29, 'The principles

of kinship'; see Claude Lévi-Strauss, *The Elementary Structures of Kinship*, London, 1969.

67. That is an endogamous rather than an exogamous presumption. Of course, there were pressures: possibly, a lack of suitable marriage partners outside the clan. But the Austrian branch found many acceptable marriages.

68. The relative infertility of the Spanish line may have been a contributory factor; this would not have prevented them marrying their Austrian cousins.

69. See Jean-Paul Roux, *Le Sang – Mythes, Symboles, et Réalités*, Paris, 1988, p. 152.

70. One or two of those marrying the Austrians converted from Protestantism.

71. A number were second or even third marriages. The mortality rate among young women of childbearing age was frighteningly high. No Habsburg male ever died on the battlefield after the fourteenth century; the number of Habsburg wives who died giving birth or subsequently of associated diseases is well in excess of 70 per cent.

72. *De iustitia et iure* (2,122, no. 4), cited in J. Höffner, *La Ética Colonial Española del Siglo de Oro: Cristianismo y Dignidad Humana*, Madrid, 1957, p. 455. The issues and problems posed by the American empire provided a field for experiment, both theoretical and practical. The theory, at least, quickly filtered back into the European context.

73. However, in the Dutch engravings of the Eighty Years War it seems comparatively rare that Philip is attacked in person. Alva was a frequent target even years after he had left the Netherlands. In literature, there was no such restraint, from William of Orange's *Apologia* of 1581 onwards. For a brief survey see Parker, *Philip II*, pp. 201–7.

74. For example, J. Bérenger, *A History of the Habsburg Empire 1273–1700*, tr. C. A. Simpson, London, 1994, p. 214. 'Philip II was afflicted with the Habsburgs' lack of resolution that had so hindered Charles V and was also evident in the Viennese branch of the family.' This conclusion is compromised by the immediately following sentence that continues, 'Moreover, Philip stuck firmly to his resolutions from the moment that he settled on a line of policy. Lacking confidence in his own ability to make decisions, he was too proud and too imbued with a sense of personal mission to consult advisers other than when he consulted clerics, who would see the problem from a moral or theological standpoint.'

75. See R. J. W. Evans, 'The imperial court at the time of Archimboldo', in *The Arcimboldo Effect*, London, 1987, p. 40.

76. This was the famous *Bruderzwist* that gave Grillparzer his greatest subject. In 1606 Matthias convoked a meeting of all the archdukes, and they collectively declared that Rudolf was incapable of rule, a clear indication of the collective sense of the family that ran beneath any tendency to a solitary imperialism.

77. Notably the excellent biographical study by Paula Sutter Fichtner, *Ferdinand I of Austria. The Politics of Dynasticism in the Age of the Reformation*, New York, 1982.

78. See W. H. Prescott, *History of the Reign of Ferdinand and Isabella*, London, 1886, p. 701.

79. That is, until the publication of R. J. W. Evans, *Rudolf II and His World*, Oxford, 1973, and many subsequent studies by the same author, which have forced a re-evaluation of the Court of Prague.

80. Rudolf ennobled him as a Count Palatine.

81. This feeling extended across the whole field of nature, into the design of gardens in particular. In the great gardens of Italy, natural objects were often given anthropomorphic form, most dramatically perhaps in the 'rocky giant', *Il Appennino*, in the Medicis' garden at Pratelino, near Florence. I am indebted to Dr Sheena Goulty for this observation.

82. See ibid., p. 167.

83. For example, *Mars and Venus*, 1588, and the highly suggestive *Hercules and Omphale*, c. 1600.

84. By contrast Ferdinand II and Ferdinand III were both dutiful and thorough in their administration.

85. John H. Elliott, 'Philip IV of Spain, prisoner of ceremony', in A. G. Dickens (ed.), *The Courts of Europe: Politics, Patronage and Royalty 1400–1800*, London, 1977, p. 182.

86. ibid.

87. See Brown and Elliott, pp. 114–15.

88. ibid., p. 114, citing Jean Muret, in García Mercadel, *Viajes de Extranjeros por España y Portugal*, 2 vols., Madrid, 1952.

89. Martin Hume, *The Court of Philip IV: Spain in Decadence*, New York, n.d., pp. 378–9.

90. There were, of course, already Spanish troops in the Netherlands when he arrived.

91. See Wandruszka, p. 11.

92. Most were provided with a good living, either in the Church or with an estate.

93. Three entered the Church but seem to have found no problem in resigning their orders to marry.

94. Many of the same motives brought the young Franz Joseph to the throne in 1848, illicitly, as his critics argued.

95. C. V. Wedgwood suggested that his confessor, the Jesuit from the Netherlands, Martin Becan, advised him to 'dissimulate' but she also remarked that he knew that Protestant extremism would allow him to rescind the concessions. See p. 76. On this topic generally, see Perez Zagorin, *Ways of Lying. Dissimulation, Persecution and Conformity in Early Modern Europe*, Cambridge, Mass., and London, 1990.

96. C. V. Wedgwood, *The Thirty Years War*, London, 1938, p. 12.

97. This was not the first or the last time that the Czechs hurled their rulers out of windows. When the last foreign minister of a free Czechoslovakia, Jan Masaryk, 'fell' from a window in 1948, the Czech memory was immediately of the Catholic ministers of Ferdinand, Martinits and Slavata, who had been pushed out from an upper floor of the Hradčany, while their assailants hammered at their fingers and knuckles until they let go of the sill. Masaryk may not have been thrown from the window, but instead may have committed a *Symbolic Suicide*, another Czech tradition.

98. Cited in Robert Bireley, *Religion and Politics in the Age of the Counter-*

reformation. *Emperor Ferdinand, William Lamormaini S.J. and the Formation of Imperial Policy*, Chapel Hill, NC, 1981, pp. 14–15.

99. See Therese Schüssel, *Kultur des Barock in Österreich*, Graz, 1960, p. 24.

100. *Ferdinandi II Romanorum Imperatoris Virtutes*, Vienna, 1638.

101. Rather like the Arlington National Cemetery in Washington DC, where former soldiers and state servants have a right to be buried, all Habsburgs could claim their place in the Kapuzinergruft.

102. See Stephen Orso, *Art and Death at the Spanish Habsburg Court. The Royal Exequies for Philip IV*, Columbia, Mo., 1989.

103. The account is given in Vehse, vol. 2, pp. 76–7, which I have translated from the French. The account is of the death of Leopold II, and some of the ceremonial may have been more elaborate than for earlier rulers. But in its essence the ceremonial remained the same from the time of Ferdinand III.

104. Cited in R. Kann, *A Study in Austrian Intellectual History from Late Baroque to Romanticism*, New York, 1973, pp. 74–5.

Chapter 6: Felix Austria – the Happy State

1. A Spaniard resident in England reported, 'in pompous ceremonies a secret of government doth much consist', cited in Dickens, p. 165. Under Charles I, the wealth and power of England was deployed in an even more potent ceremonial fashion. See Hart Vaughan, *Art and Magic at the Stuart Court*, London, 1994.

2. From an MS by a contemporary courtier, Soto y Aguilar, cited in Hume, pp. 63–4.

3. See Peter Burke, *The Fabrication of Louis XIV*, New Haven and London, 1992, p. 66.

4. These were all portrayed in engravings by François Chauveau, in the volume, with a text by Charles Perrault, *Festiva ad annulumque Decursio*, 1670.

5. 'le premier divertissement de quelque éclat'; see Burke, ibid.

6. Simon Schama points out that in 'the Netherlands the joyeuse entrée had been turned on its head. The Netherlandish version of the royal progress went back to the Burgundian Middle Ages and was periodically revived to greet visiting royalty, and on occasion, to acclaim a triumphant stadholderian retinue. It was, however, no slavish prostration before a crypto-monarchical conqueror. Built into its ceremonies was a formalised recognition by the visiting magnate of the rights and privileges embodied in the town charters and customary law. The symbolic connotations of the triumphal arch, then, had been cunningly reversed . . . instead of an acceptance of Caesarism, it signified the barrier through which military power passed in order to regain access to literally "civilised" society. In doing so, the victor who once paraded his spoils now accepted the conditions imposed upon his sovereignty. This ritual was respected by royal dignitaries, even in the captive south, where successive Habsburg viceroys in the seventeenth and eighteenth centuries appreciated the need to make tactful concessions to civic *amour propre* in Brussels, Ghent and Antwerp. The Emperor Joseph II who treated such antics with contempt, as an obscure relic of a dysfunctional past, brought down a violent revolt on himself when he attempted their suppression.' See Simon

Schama, *The Embarrassment of Riches. An Interpretation of Dutch Culture in the Golden Age*, London and New York, 1987, p. 66.

7. Coxe, vol. 3, pp. 515–16.

8. The whole issue of the expulsion of the Jews has been recently covered by John P. Spielman, *The City and the Crown. Vienna and the Imperial Court, 1600–1740*, West Lafayette, Ind., 1993, pp. 123–35. Spielman points out that Leopold's council strongly advised him against the expulsion, first on grounds that he would appear as someone whose word could not be trusted, and second, on financial grounds. The reasons for his actions are still unclear. Although his court preacher, Abraham a Sancta Clara, was a comprehensive anti-Semite, hating both Jews and Muslims, Leopold himself registered no particular prejudice and his individual relationship with his 'Court Jew', Samuel Oppenheimer, was warm and friendly.

9. See Vehse, vol. 2, pp. 440–48.

10. See Clifford Geertz: *Negara: the Theatre State of Nineteenth Century Bali*, Princeton, NJ, 1980; *The Interpretation of Cultures*, London, 1993.

11. See F. Hadamowsky, *Barocktheater am Wiener Kaiserhof, 1625–1740*, Vienna, 1955, pp. 48–71, for a full list of these performances.

12. Now in the collection at Schloss Ambras.

13. This emblem was used by a number of saints.

14. See Burke, pp. 95–6.

15. ibid., pp. 192–3.

16. The huge, over-life-size picture (over six feet high) of the Emperor Napoleon in his coronation robes, by François-Pascal-Simon Gérard, is in the state collection in Dresden, number 2518.

17. See John Stoye, *The Siege of Vienna*, London, 1964, p. 65.

18. See R. J. W. Evans, *The Making of the Habsburg Monarchy 1550–1700*, Oxford, 1979, p. 314. 'There is excellent information for the reign of Leopold about how its resources were actually used. Lambeck's *Commentarii* [was] a vast project, supervised by the emperor, to advertise its treasures to the scholarly world. Only a fraction could be published (twenty-five volumes were planned), but this suffices to show the emperor's close concern for the legacy of Greek theological, legal, medical, philosophical and historical manuscripts.' To that tally, I would add, 'genealogical', since this was a particular preoccupation of Leopold's, and forms a prominent feature of the first volume of the *Commentarii* and may be read in tandem with J. J. Fugger's *Spiegel der Ehren . . .*, published in 1682.

19. My own research in the political use of graphic images and printed text by the Habsburgs is still in progress, but preliminary results were presented to the SHARP meeting in Washington DC, July 1994, and to the meeting of the Graphic Cultures of Europe Group, at the European University Institute, in October 1994. My initial conclusion, that the Habsburg practice was singular, and also remarkably consistent in its objectives, seems to have been confirmed by discussing parallel activities with other scholars at those meetings.

20. See *Dissertio de Sacro-Sancti Romana Caesareo-Graeco Franco Germanici Augustissima Habsburgica Austriaco Germanica Dono iusque Regnis ducatibus praerogativis* of Don Joannes Felipe de Inazaghi, Baron de Kymburg,

Freiburg im Breisgau, 1671. I used the copy in the Zentralbibliotek, Luzern, but I have subsequently found copies in a number of libraries in the United Kingdom and the United States, suggesting that it had quite a wide circulation, although only presented as the defence of a thesis. He merits a two-line mention in Anna Coreth, *Österreichische Geschictschreibung in der Barockzeit (1620–1740)*, Vienna, 1950, pp. 67–8.

21. The Latin texts used as captions are equally to the point. I have concentrated here on the symbolic force of the images alone, which were even accessible to those who could not read. In the case of this text, intended for an educated audience, comprehension of it could be assumed. The use of the image is to focus attention on the underlying and implicit meanings of the text, 'subtexts' that are nowhere stated in written form. Thus the image becomes the key to the true intention ('the illuminating force') of the text.

22. Hellmuth Lorenz has pointed out that a 1696 engraving of the Plague Column, erected by Leopold on the Graben in Vienna to commemorate the ending of the Plague, also showed him as the mediator between heaven and earth, and the means of distributing divine favour. See Hellmuth Lorenz, 'The imperial Hofburg. Theory and practice of architectural representation in baroque Vienna', in C. Ingrao (ed.), *State and Society in Early Modern Austria*, West Lafayette, Ind., 1994, pp. 93–109.

23. 'réunions.'

24. There is, for example, no parallel to Simon Schama's *The Embarrassment of Riches*, which analyses Dutch society through its artistic production.

25. See Ernst Wangermann, *The Austrian Achievement, 1700–1800*, London, 1973, pp. 29–30.

26. See E. Crankshaw, *Maria Theresa*, London, 1969, p. 136. See also Hans Sedlmeyr, 'Die politische Bedeutung des deutschen Barock', *Epochen und Werke*, II, Vienna, 1980. 'Architecture which so completely dominates its terrain had probably not been seen in Europe since Palestrina built the Temple of Fortune in Rome, whose very ruins were Bramante's inspiration for the courts of the Vatican; not even the terraces of St Germain, the "hanging gardens" so much admired by Wren, can compare with this.'

27. See *Fontes Rerum Austriacum*, LVII, (2) *Privatbriefe der Kaiser Leopold I und der Grafen F. E. Pötting 1662–1673*, ed. A. F. Pribram and M. Landwehr von Pragenau, Vienna, 1904, no. 336, 14 March 1673, written at Schönbrunn. Leopold's curious private language to Pötting has led some to conclude that he was a poor linguist: quite the reverse, he was fluent in German, French, Spanish and Italian.

28. Cited in J. H. Elliott, *Spain and Its World 1500–1700*, New Haven, Conn., and London, pp. 254–5.

29. See John Nada, *Carlos the Bewitched*, London, 1962, p. 125, citing A. Legrelle, *La Mission de M. de Rébenac à Madrid et la Mort de Maria Luisa: Reine d'Espagne 1688–9.*

30. ibid., p. 140.

31. ibid., pp. 237–8.

32. Cited in Heer, *The Holy Roman Empire*, p. 226.

33. The pamphlet was a homily on the text *Aquila insidet corporibus*.

34. See Vehse, vol. 2, p. 85.
35. See Charles Ingrao, *In Quest and Crisis: Emperor Joseph I and the Habsburg Monarchy*, West Lafayette, Ind., 1979.
36. Charles VI for a long time effectively refused to regard Maria Theresa as his heir.
37. ibid., p. 90.
38. For example, Crankshaw, p. 149.
39. Maria Theresa did not actually learn to ride until the early 1740s.
40. See Vehse, vol. 2, pp. 123–4.
41. The Karlskirche, the new Hofbibliotek, where Leopold's wooden theatre had once stood, and the Winter Riding School, better known colloquially as the 'Spanish' Riding School, were only the most notable.
42. See Heer, *The Holy Roman Empire*, p. 236.
43. A Pragmatic Sanction, like a *bulla*, was simply a category of public document. There were many pragmatic sanctions, which were merely public decrees of the Emperor that had not been sanctioned by the Diet; but only Charles's decree has the singularity of capitalization.
44. There were very few challenges to either the content or the method of Herrgott's work. A short pamphlet was published in Venice under the name of the French Benedictine scholar Augustin Calmet, and the abbey of Muri, piqued at his cavalier treatment of their records, produced a claim restating their pre-eminence. But, otherwise, the assertions of the *Genealogia* went by default. See A. Calmet, *Illustrissimi et reverendissimi domini, Domini Augustini Calmetii . . . Refutatio systematis genealogici a R. P. Marquardo Herrgott . . . compositi e gallico in latinum sermonem*, Venice, 1748; and Fridolin Kopp, *Vindiciae Actorum Murensium pro & contra R. D. P. Marquardum Herrgott Genealogiae Diplomaticae Augustae Gentis Habsburgicae*, n.p., 1750.

  Herrgott's treatise book is technically in two volumes, but the second is divided into two equal parts, so there are three massive tomes on the shelf. The full title is: *Genealogia Diplomatica Augustae Gentis Habsburgicae* (rubricated) *qua continentur vera Gentis huius exordia, antiquitates, possessiones, praerogativae, chartis ac diplomatibus no. CMLIV, maxima parte hactantus ineditis asserta: adiectis sigillis, aliisque monumentis aere incisis, mappa item geographica et indicibus locupletissimis. Haec vero res non modo Habsburgicas universe corroborant, sed aliis etiam pluribus Illustrissimis Germaniae Nostrae Familiis* (rubricated like the title) *Germaniae nostrae familiis, et patriae medii aevi historiae lucem foenerantur.* Tomus I–Tomi II: Pars I: *Codicem probationum exhibens, quo continentur diplomata, chartae aliaque antiquitatis monumenta ab anno Christi DCCXLIV ad annum usque MCCLXIX numero D.* Pars II: *Complectitur codices probationum, diplomata, chartas et reliqua monumenta ab anno Christi MCCLXIX ad annum MCCCCLXXXI a numero DI usque CMLIV.*

45. See pages 196–7.
46. He had pointed out, although *in extremis*, that his chamberlains had not put out the number that befitted his status.
47. See the examples in Robert Pick, *Empress Maria Theresa*, 1966, facing p. 53,

and the example presented in Gerda and Gottfried Mraz, *Maria Theresa. Ihr Leben und ihre Zeit in Bilden und Dokumenten*, Munich, 1979, p. 58.

48. Medal commemorating the birth of Maria Theresa, on 13 April 1717, from an engraving by Carl Schütz, in *Schau- und Denkmünzen welche unter den glorwürdigen Regierung der Kaiserin Königin Maria Theresia geprägt worden sind*, Vienna, 1782.

49. A free translation of 'Renascens spes orbis'.

50. Jean Laurent Krafft, *Histoire Générale de l'Auguste Maison d'Autriche*, Brussels, 1744.

51. The image of childhood was transformed during the eighteenth century, but I do not believe it necessarily follows that parents had less concern for their children in earlier epochs, even if the manner of relating to them is less to our current taste. The *romantic* image of the child remains visually dominant in modern society.

52. Martin van Meytens, *The Seven Children of Maria Theresa*, 1749, now in the Historisches Museum der Stadt Wien, Index number 61011.

53. See an example Index number 78991, in the Historisches Museum der Stadt Wien.

54. The Lorraine family was much more fecund, and there is an example of a 'family circle' portrait of the Duke of Lorraine with the parents and eight siblings, some of them predeceased, of Francis Stephen. This painting by J. Renauld is now in the Kunsthistorisches Museum in Vienna. It was sent as a gift to Charles VI by Duke Leopold of Lorraine before his two sons Francis Stephen and Charles were dispatched to Vienna. The original prospect for Maria Theresa, his eldest son Clemens, died prematurely, and Francis Stephen took up the role. Whether Maria Theresa would have accepted the older brother is open to doubt. She was besotted with Francis Stephen. Nine years older than her, she had eyes for no one else. Shown a portrait miniature at Christmas 1730, her ayah (governess) Mme Fuchs, noted that 'she contemplated the painting for a long time, her face changing colours'. Her descendant Franz Joseph I behaved in much the same fashion: he refused the proffered older sister and declined to marry any except the younger, Elisabeth of Bavaria . . . For her reactions to Francis Stephen, see Pick, pp. 25–6.

55. Writing in September 1768. See Beales, p. 177.

56. See Carol Blum, 'Of women and the land', in John Brewer and Susan Staves (eds.), *Early Modern Conceptions of Property*, London and New York, 1995, p. 163. Harriet Ritvo writing later in the same volume of animal husbandry uses the phrase 'genetic capital' and this could well be applied to the sense of value attributed to the ramifying Habsburg lineage.

57. Cited in Heer, *The Holy Roman Empire*, p. 247.

58. Speech to the troops at Tilbury, 1588.

59. See his perceptive and informative brief essay, 'Schönbrunn, the palace which symbolises the peak of Viennese maturity', in *Great Palaces*, London, 1964, pp. 212–22.

60. 'The most human of the Habsburgs', according to G. P. Gooch.

61. J. C. Goethe cited in Beales.

62. See Beales, p. 194.

63. He printed Kollar's *Analecta* and the new edition of the *Commentarii*.

64. ibid., p. 195.
65. The *Monumenta Augustae Domus Austriacae*, in eight huge volumes, monumental in every sense, were published over a twenty-two-year period between 1750 and 1772. Vol. 1, Parts 1 and 2, Vienna, 1750. Vol. 2, Freiburg im Breisgan, 1752–3. Vol. 3, Freiburg im Breisgan, 1760– , 2nd printing, St Blasien, 1773. Vol. 4, St Blasien, 1772. The frontispiece shows Maria Theresa in the imperial library receiving the first of the volumes.
66. 'One of the great monuments of contemporary bibliography' was how R. J. W. Evans described the work (see R. J. W. Evans, *The Making of the Habsburg Monarchy*, p. 296). His reference is to the second edition, published between 1766 and 1782; the first was smaller in format and without the illustrative elaboration, in terms of head and tailpieces, of the second edition. But all the images used in the original volumes have been redrawn. I have used the sets of both editions in the University Library Cambridge for purposes of comparison, but it may be that other printings have variant forms. What is interesting, perhaps, is not so much the bibliographical detail, but why this vast enterprise was set in train at all in the 1760s.
67. Adam Francis Kollar, *Analecta Monumentorum omnis aevi Vindobonensia*, Vienna, 1761–2, 2 vols.
68. It was paid for by Joseph Kurzböcken, the Imperial Oriental Printer and bookseller.
69. See E. Mauerer, *Die Kunstdenkmäler des Kantons Aargau*, Bd III, *Das Kloster Königsfelden*, Basel, 1954. For the reburial in St Blasien, see *Kunstdenkmäler des Grossherzogtums Baden*, Bd III, p. 65.
70. Cited in Beales, p. 154.
71. ibid., p. 159.
72. ibid., p. 159.
73. ibid., p. 135.
74. See Vehse, vol. 2, pp. 291–2.
75. See D. Beales, 'Was Joseph II an enlightened despot?' in Ritchie Robertson and Edward Timms, *The Austrian Enlightenment and Its Aftermath*, Edinburgh, 1991, p. 1.
76. Cited in E. Wangermann, *From Joseph II to the Jacobin Trials. Government Policy and Public Opinion in the Habsburg Domains in the Period of the French Revolution*, Oxford, 1959, p. 20.
77. Cited in Beales, 'Was Joseph II an enlightened despot?', pp. 8–9.

Chapter 7: The Last Cavalier

1. See Franz Grillparzer, *Family Strife in Hapsburg, Tragedy in Five Acts*, tr. Arthur Burkhard, Yarmouth Bay, Mass., 1940. Act III, Rudolf II to Julius, Duke of Brunswick.
2. Beales, *Joseph II*, p. 54. He continued: 'The emperor and empress took apparently irreconcilable positions on the unification of the Monarchy's administration, on the balance between civil and military, on territorial aggrandisement, on the place of Catholicism in the state and on the role of the monarch. She found his attitudes both subversive and wounding, and

often talked of abdication ... Each accused the other of inconsistency and vacillation. Each claimed to be prevented by the other from achieving anything worthwhile.'

3. ibid., pp. 488–9.

4. Ligne, *Fragments*, vol. 1, p. 183. A rather more proper version incorrectly has Ligne (somewhat meaninglessly) saying that Joseph would always be sneezing. Cited in Beales, *Joseph II*, p. 491.

5. See Walter Consuelo Langsam, *Francis the Good, the Education of an Emperor 1768–1792*, New York, 1949, pp. 17ff.

6. ibid., p. 17.

7. Quoted in Vehse, vol. 2, pp. 326–7.

8. ibid., pp. 63–4.

9. ibid., pp. 72–3.

10. In February 1793, he ordered that a requiem should be said on the anniversary of Joseph's death as well as that of the late Emperor, as was the custom. Francis wrote in explanation: 'Although it has not been customary to observe the anniversary of the demise of any but the latest ancestor, I intend to deviate from this custom inasmuch as my uncle, the blessed Joseph II, was like unto a father to me.' Handwritten note to Prince Adam von Starhemberg, cited in Langsam. It was at his suggestion that his first grandson was christened Franz *Joseph*.

11. See Saul K. Padover, *The Revolutionary Emperor: Joseph II of Austria*, New York, 1967, p. 289.

12. Cited in Langsam, p. 88, from Wolf, *Leopold und Marie Christine*, pp. 69–70.

13. See E. Wangermann, *From Joseph II to the Jacobin Trials*, p. 89.

14. Ibid., p. 101, citing Wolfsgrüber, *Franz I*, vol. 2, pp. 201–7.

15. Ibid., pp. 106–7.

16. The guillotine for the first time provided an equal means of capital punishment for all classes and both genders, which its advocates were keen to press as a social advance. See Camille Naish, *Death Comes to the Maiden*, London, 1991.

17. Dr Jonathan Steinberg first applied these words to the German Junkers in his book, *Yesterday's Deterrent*. But they apply with equal – perhaps even greater – force to Francis.

18. See Wangermann, *From Joseph II to the Jacobin Trials*, p. 169.

19. Macartney, *The Habsburg Empire*, p. 164.

20. See Douglas Yates, *Grillparzer: a Critical Introduction*, Cambridge, 1972, pp. 11–12.

21. See Simon Schama, *Patriots and Liberators. Revolution in the Netherlands, 1780–1813*, London, 1977, p. 8.

22. In German, *Bildung* hits the same note.

23. See Langsam, p. 107, citing A. J. Gross-Hoffinger, *Leben, Wirken und Tod des Kaisers. Ein Charakter und Zeitgemälde ... entworfen bei Gelegenheit des Todes Franz I am 1 März 1835*, Stuttgart, 1835, pp. 15–16.

24. However, he himself told petitioners who knelt before him: 'Get up. Get up. Kneel before God; I am only a man.'

25. It is possible that Francis was more comfortable with 'art' than with 'words'. He wanted to ban all newspapers except the official news-sheet, while it was

Metternich who promoted Friedrich Schlegel's journalistic activity in the Habsburg cause, and supported a set of public lectures in 1810, 'Towards an Up-to-date History' (Über die neuere Geschichte), in which with the help of Josef Hormayr he created an image of the true, Habsburg, empire as opposed to the illicit French simulacrum. See Edward Timms, 'National memory and the "Austrian Idea" from Metternich to Waldheim', *Modern Language Review*, 86, 1991, pp. 898–1910.

26. This mechanism continues to exist in the Majlis system, which still persists in a number of traditional Arab governments. The parallels are instructive: see J. C. Matejka, 'Political Participation in the Arab World: the Majlis Mechanism (Middle East, North Africa)', Unpublished PhD, University of Texas at Austin, 1983.

27. See F. A. von Schönholz, *Traditionen zur Characteristik Österreichs, seines Staats- und Volkslebens unter Franz I*, ed. G. Gugitz, Munich, 1914, vol. 1, p. 320.

28. For the Krafft image, 'Kaiser Franz I erteilt eine allgemeine Audienz', 1836, see Marianne Frodl-Schneemann, *Johann Peter Krafft, 1780–1856, Monographie und Verzeichnis der Gemälde*, Vienna, 1984, p. 161.

29. Brigitte Buberl has recently (1994) written of this image: 'Heinrich Olivier celebrates the peace, Napoleon's defeat and the Congress of Vienna, by showing the victorious allied monarchs – as knights in shining armour in a lofty Gothic chapel. Like St George (whose figure stands in a niche behind them) they are Christian warriors with a mission from above. The Prussian King's gesture [an outstretched arm] makes the scene into a loyalty oath, invoking God as witness to the fraternal bond. The Nazarene's utopian mediaevalism and the dream of universal Christian monarchy find their apotheosis in the glittering, golden figure of Emperor Francis.' See Keith Hartley (ed.), *The Romantic Spirit in German Art 1790–1990*, Edinburgh and London, 1994, p. 473. The picture is in the Anhaltische Gemäldegalerie, Dessau.

30. Joseph II certainly tormented his officials with his ceaseless demands, but in the manner of a whirlwind. Once he had passed, matters settled down again. Francis, more naturally bureaucratic and methodical, purposed his ends inexorably.

31. On the consequences, see Joachim Whaley, 'Austria, "Germany", and the dissolution of the Holy Roman Empire' in Ritchie Robertson and Edward Timms (eds.), *The Habsburg Legacy, National Identity in Historical Perspective*, Edinburgh, 1994, pp. 3–12.

32. See Timms, 'National memory and the "Austrian idea".'

33. Cited in Timms, ibid., p. 901.

34. John Keegan, in J. Keegan and A. Wheatcroft, *Who's Who in Military History*, London, 1987, p. 65.

35. Letter from Metternich's 'publicist', Friedrich von Gentz, to Johannes Müller, 6 July 1805, cited in Vehse, vol. 2, p. 357.

36. His third wife Ludovica, who died in 1816, actively patronized both writers and painters, while his fourth wife, Caroline Augusta of Bavaria, whom he married late in 1816, increasingly commissioned on Francis's behalf as he became older and frailer.

37. See Claudio Magris, *Le Mythe et l'Empire dans la Littérature Autrichienne Moderne*, tr. Jean and Marie-Noëlle Pastereau, Paris, 1991, pp. 68–9.

38. See André Robert, *L'idée autrichienne et les guerres de Napoléon: l'apostolat du Baron Hormayr et le Salon de Caroline Pichter*, Paris, 1933.

39. See Hans Tietze (ed.), *Das Vormärzliche Wien in Wort und Bild*, Vienna, 1925, p. 17.

40. Quoted in Vehse, *Court*, vol. 2, pp. 405–6.

41. This too became an imperial pattern for the future, the *Schönbrunndeutsch*, very characteristic of Franz Joseph, who spoke with 'a light Viennese accent' (personal information).

42. Cited by Günther Duriegl, 'From revolution to revolution', in R. Waissenberger (ed.), *Vienna in the Biedermeier Era, 1815–48*, London, 1986, p. 38.

43. Carl Schuster's *Oriental Slave Market*, 1839, and Carl Leybold's *The Importunate Flea*, 1846, were both banned for this reason. Conversely, salacious images were used in the revolution of 1848 to demonstrate opposition to the hated *ancien régime*, as in prints produced by Johann Christian Schoeller.

44. Russ later turned to other themes. Much of the 'dynastic art' appeared on the walls of Archduke John's 'farmhouse' at the Franzenhof in Styria, at Laxenburg, or in his brother Charles's neo-classical country palace at Weilberg, at Baden not far from Vienna, or in his town house, the Albertina. See Roberts, pp. 409–11.

45. This was designed and built by Peter von Nobile between 1815 and 1824, having taken over from a Milanese architect who would not follow the Emperor's instructions in respect of its design. Francis exercised a close supervision over his commissions.

46. For example, in 1831 Alexander Clarot produced a series of sepia prints, one illustrating the audience, like Krafft, and another in which the Emperor and Empress informally visit the workers building a canal designed to prevent the city suffering a recurrence of cholera. For these images see *Bürgersinn und Aufbegehren. Biedermeier und Vormärz in Wien 1815–48*, Vienna, 1988, pp. 70–71.

47. Fendi and others matched the rosy-cheeked children of the aristocracy with rosy-cheeked children of the poor, dressed in near rags: social criticism achieved by subterfuge, and under the watchful eye of the censors. Some censors were shrewder than others and could see the underlying text. But the artists could argue that they simply portrayed the winsome and the picturesque. There are many examples, but I have in mind *The Little Violin-Player* (1833) or the *Boy Selling Pretzels on the Dominikanerbastei*, 1828. For these images, see Gerbert Frodl and Klaus Albrecht Schröder (eds.), *Wiener Biedermeier: Malerei zwischen Wiener Kongress und Revolution*, Munich, 1992.

48. For a good brief survey of these issues, see Hans Bizanz, 'Authentic Biedermeier painting and graphic art', in Waissenberger, pp. 161–89.

49. For this image see Tietze, p. 40.

50. Cited in Peter Paranzan, 'The development of taste in home decoration', in Waissenberger, p. 109.

51. In the Historisches Museum der Stadt Wien.

52. Listed in Pauer, p. 113, item 113. In the Historisches Museum der Stadt Wien.

53. Actually, a centaur.

54. See Tietze, p. 69.
55. ibid., p. 57.
56. See *The Habsburg Empire, 1790–1918*, 1969, pp. 147–8. This volume which Norman Stone, in the disguise of 'Severin Kameneff' ('Norman Stone' in Russian), dismissed as a 'nine hundred page entry in the Encyclopaedia Britannica', to the considerable ire of its author, contains many brilliant and incisive judgements, plus (it must be admitted) vast *longueurs*.
57. Louis Eisenmann, *Le Compromis Austro-Hongrois de 1867*, Paris, 1968(1904), p. 54.
58. In fact, he kept a perfectly coherent, if tedious, daily journal, and had a sharp wit. His seizures could affect his short-term memory, and certainly proved very disconcerting for those around him. It was said that he could have as many as twenty seizures a day, but these must have been, for the most part, of an experiential rather than a physically traumatic form.
59. See Hans Pauer, *Kaiser Franz Joseph I. Beiträge zu Bild-Dokumentation Seines Leben*, Vienna, 1966, p. 43, item 2.
60. See the comprehensive listing in Pauer, ibid., pp. 43ff, 112–14.
61. The new study by Alan Palmer (see note 65 below) goes a long way to correcting this misapprehension.
62. In a review of *The Habsburg Empire: The World of the Austro-Hungarian Empire in Original Photographs*, and subsequently in person.
63. Joseph Redlich entitled chapter 7 of his biography 'The autocrat', but as he makes clear, it was an autocracy of laws and system not monarchic whim.
64. 'The Emperor Francis and the Sentry at Laxenburg', 1836. See Frodl and Schröder, listed in Pauer, p. 112.
65. See Alan Palmer, *The Twilight of the Habsburgs. The Life and Times of the Emperor Francis Joseph*, London and New York, 1994, p. 16.
66. *Evening Prayers*, painted 1839, now in the Albertina.
67. See Jean Paul Bled, *Franz Joseph*, tr. Theresa Bridgeman, Oxford, 1992, p. 7.
68. There had been disturbances in Galicia in 1846.
69. See Otto Ernst (ed.), *Franz Joseph as Revealed by His Letters*, tr. Agnes Blake, London, 1927, p. 130.
70. General Radetzky succeeded in transforming a heterogeneous army into a military force that was at the least capable of winning battles. For Radetzky's clear-sighted view of the situation, military and social, in 1848, see Alan Sked, *The Survival of the Habsburg Empire. Radetzky, the Imperial Army and the Class War, 1848*, London, 1979.
71. 'In deinem Lager ist Österreich.'
72. See Franz Schnürer, *Briefe Kaiser Franz Josephs an seine Mutter, 1838–1872*, Munich, 1930, pp. 93–8.
73. ibid., p. 107, 26 May 1848.
74. ibid., p. 68ff.
75. Also selected, of course, out of the direct line of succession, and viewed by the Habsburgs as their saviour in their hour of danger.
76. Microfilm copy in the Library of Congress, Lloyd Mitis Collection.
77. 'Gott erhalte, Gott beschütze/Unser Kaiser, unser Land/Mächtig durch den Glaubens Stütze/Führt er uns mit weisser Hand.'
78. Cited in Adolph Schwarzenberg, *Prince Felix zu Schwarzenberg, Prime*

Minister of Austria, 1848–1853, New York, 1946, pp. 34–5, quoting Helfert, *Geschichte Österreichs vom Ausgang des Wiener October-Aufstandes, 1848,* vol. 3, p. 333.

79. Schwarzenberg, p. 35.
80. Egon Caesar Conte Corti and Hans Sokol, *Vom Kind zum Kaiser. Kindheit und erste Jugend Kaiser Franz Josephs I und seiner Geschwister,* Graz, 1951, p. 332.
81. And also with subsequent problems, up to the present day.
82. See *The Habsburg Monarchy,* p. 127.
83. *Letters of the King of Hanover to Viscount Strangford,* London, 1925, pp. 169–71.
84. Quoted in Macartney, *The Habsburg Empire,* London, 1971 p. 431.
85. See Josef Roth, *The Radetzky March,* tr. Eva Tucker, London, 1974, pp. 66–7.
86. Lt-Gen. Baron von Margutti, *The Emperor Francis Joseph and His Times,* London, n.d., p. 38.
87. This coda is jotted down in the papers of Arthur von Bolfras in the Kriegsarchiv, Vienna. It is not clear whether he or Margutti told the Emperor about the tailors. See Bolfras, *Nachlasse,* Kriegsarchiv, Vienna.
88. Henry Wickham Steed, *Through Thirty Years. 1892–1922. A Personal Narrative,* London, 1924, vol. 1, p. 239.
89. See Joseph Redlich, *The Emperor Francis Joseph of Austria. A Biography,* London, 1929, pp. 222–3.
90. Robert Musil's uncompleted novel sequence, *Der Mann ohne Eigenschaften* (tr. E. Wilkins and E. Kaiser, *The Man Without Qualities,* 3 vols., London, 1953–60), 1930–43, rev. edn 1952, remains one of the key points of reference for the Empire of Franz Joseph. Musil, born at Klagenfurt in 1880, produced a text that is, of course, fictional; but it is also a refined commentary on the nature of the Empire, and more acute in its judgements than many works of a more factual nature. Ulrich, his hero, is *without qualities* because he is a blend of so many of them, a human consequence of the homogenizing and synthesizing intentions of the Empire.
91. See Count Corti, *Elizabeth, Empress of Austria,* tr. Catherine Alison, New York, 1946, pp. 33–4.
92. ibid., p. 29–30.
93. ibid., p. 384–5.
94. Later, he had the Hermesvilla in the Lainzertiergarten built for her as well.
95. Lady Westmoreland to Comtesse Pauline Neale, 26 April 1854, in Lady Rose Weigall (ed.), *The Correspondence of Priscilla, Countess of Westmoreland,* London, 1909, p. 202.
96. These are depicted in Ernst Trost, *Franz Joseph I,* Vienna, 1980, p. 80, and in more detail in Rupert Feuchtmueller and Wilhelm Mrazak, *Biedermeier in Österreich,* 1963, plate 90. The statues are in the Österreichisches Museum für angewandte Kunst.
97. See Schnürer, p. 266. Letter written from Ofen (on their journey) on 19 May 1857.
98. See *Rudolf, ein Leben im Schatten von Mayerling,* 1990, p. 157. The engraving was later reproduced in 1859 and a copy is in the Hermesvilla, Vienna.
99. In fact it may well have been some venereal infection, caught from Franz

Joseph. That, coupled with her desire not to have endless children in the Habsburg fashion, may have cooled their relationship.

100. Baroness Georgiana Bloomfield, *Reminiscences of Court and Diplomatic Life*, London, 1883, p. 270.

101. The pros and cons of the Ausgleich have been debated since the moment it was signed. The only worthwhile book remains Louis Eisenmann's brilliant study of 1904, *Le Compromis Austro-Hongrois*.

102. Corti, *Elizabeth of Austria*, p. 141.

103. The shock of Elisabeth's murder made the idea of a true jubilee celebration in 1898 impossible.

104. I have not been able to establish whether he was given the honours of 'Emperor of Mexico'.

105. See F. Saathen (ed.), *Anna Nahowski und Kaiser Franz Joseph: Aufzeichnungen*, Vienna, 1986.

106. Joan Haslip, *The Emperor and the Actress*, London, 1982.

107. Eisenmann, p. 155.

108. As in *The Prisoner of Zenda*, 1894, and *Rupert of Hentzau*, 1898.

109. Musil, vol. 1, pp. 66–7. The whole of chapter 8, 'Kakania', pp. 64–9, is relevant.

110. This appeared as the introduction to volume 2, and in a modified holograph form in volume 6, which noted the Crown Prince's death, of *Die österreichisch-ungarische Monarchie in Wort und Bild; Auf Anregung und unter Mitwirkung Kronprinzen Erzherzhog Rudolf*, Druck und Verlag der kaiserlich-königlichen Hof- und Staatsdruckerei, 24 vols., 1887–1902.

111. An engraving was made of the occasion, and there is a copy in the Österreichisches Bildarchiv.

112. At the outset, its obvious political intentions caused it to be boycotted by many Slavs and, particularly, the Young Czechs. Rudolf regarded the opposition as a sign of the work's success in a dynastic sense.

113. See Gerbert Frodl, *Hans Makart, Monographie und Werkverzeichnis*, Salzburg, 1974.

114. Cited in Palmer, *Twilight*, p. 217.

115. See Mara Reissberger, 'Lebende Bilder zu einem historischen Familienfest – Kronprinz Rudolf als Erbe und Ahn', in *Rudolf, ein Leben im Schatten von Mayerling*, pp. 129–39.

116. See Corti, *Elizabeth*, p. 238.

117. See J. Luckacs, *Budapest, 1900*, London 1988, p. 72.

118. Her death was commemorated annually, both publicly and in private, by Franz Joseph.

119. The political motivation was more closely thought out than in 1879. See Elisabeth Grossegger, *Der Kaiser-Hüldigung-Festzug Wien 1908*, Vienna, 1992.

120. *The Times*, 13 June 1908, cited in Geoffrey Drage, *Austria Hungary*, 1909, p. 53.

121. Franz Ferdinand's children could not inherit because his marriage fell outside the restrictions of the family statute of 1839. But Wickham Steed rightly points out that the matter was not so clear-cut. His wife, Sophie Chotek, came from the old Czech nobility, which had not recognized the

German view of 'equal birth'. However, the family law of 1839 is precise on the topic. See the microfilm of the 1839 family statute in the Lloyd Mitis collection, Library of Congress, and also Steed, *The Hapsburg Monarchy*, pp. 42–9.

122. Compare this with the decorations that Wagner prepared for the wedding of Rudolf in 1881, all swags, corinthian columns, eagles and gilt. The drawings are in the Historisches Museum der Stadt Wien, no. 96.014. There is a parallel with Klimt's commission for the ceilings of the university, where the authorities expected that they were going to get another version of his ceilings for the Burgtheater. The shock when they received the 'obscene nakedness' that he had painted is easy to understand. But respectable and conventional court artists had become the leaders of the 'rebellion' against convention. On this topic, see *Kaiser Franz Joseph von Österreich oder der Zerfall eines Prinzips*, Vienna, 1981, and Carl E. Schorske, *Fin de Siècle Vienna: Politics and Culture*, New York, 1981, esp. chaps. 2 and 5.

Chapter 8: Finis Austriae: The End?

1. The event is described in Jasper Ridley, *Maximilian and Juarez*, New York and London, 1992, pp. 276ff.
2. French dog-breeders will still talk of a 'chien de race'.
3. Zita's meeting is described in G. Brook Shepherd, *The Last Habsburg*, New York, 1968, p. 29.
4. See Allan Janik and Stephen Toulmin, *Wittgenstein's Vienna*, New York, 1973, p. 267.
5. ibid., p. 266.
6. This might be considered by some to be a thoroughly post-modern activity.
7. Musil, vol. 2, p. 73.
8. Musil, vol. 1, p. 92.
9. See Schorske, p. 245.
10. See Peter Vergo, *Art in Vienna, 1898–1918*, London, 1975.
11. This means much more than its literal translation into English, because it is rooted in a different social system. To the Spanish it is an *enchufe*, being plugged in; to the French, a *piston* is the force that carries you forward in business or profession. Ulrich, in *The Man Without Qualities*, is a prime beneficiary, as he is co-opted on to the collateral committee, planning yet another celebration, this time of the Emperor's seventieth Jubilee.
12. See Stefan Zweig, *The World of Yesterday. An Autobiography*, London, 1943, pp. 13–103.
13. Brook Shepherd, *The Last Habsburg*, p. 328.
14. ibid., p. 213, citing Karl Werkmann, *Deutschland als Verbündete*, Berlin, 1931. He was the Emperor's press secretary and was present at the events of November 1918.
15. The old Habsburg tradition of '*fortwursteln*', muddling through.
16. This shrine was a source of special reverence to the Habsburgs, for whom

it had been the spiritual heart of the empire ever since Ferdinand II made the Virgin of Mariazell his generalissimo. According to the interview in *Hello* magazine, it had a deep significance for the bride's family as well.

17. *Hello*, 13 February 1993, pp. 4–18.

18. I owe this story to Dr Gary Schwartz, who saw the interview on Netherlands TV.

19. Hannah Hickman, in her study of Musil, suggests a better translation for the (probably untranslatable) 'Seinesgleichen geschieht' is 'History repeats itself', or 'There is nothing new under the sun'. In the title to chapter 83, Musil also adds the phrase, 'Or, why does one not invent history?' See Hannah Hickman, *Robert Musil and the Culture of Vienna*, London, 1984, pp. 144–5. A new and far superior translation of *The Man Without Qualities* was published in 1995, too late to allow its use for this work.

20. For example, the press conference given by Jacqueline Kennedy some time after her husband's burial. She declared: 'I don't think we should forget President Kennedy . . . is [his presidency] just going to be forgotten or is some way going to be found to make it keep going? [Perhaps some seed had been planted in the mind of some other young people, like Kennedy, full of ideals at university.] Then someone else like President Kennedy will come along. And these are the kind of men who are going to save the world.' From the text of a press conference included in *Jackie – Secret Lives*, broadcast 16 March 1995 on Channel 4 (UK). I am very grateful to Anneyce Wheatcroft for recalling and tracking down this information.

Sources and Bibliography

A bibliography always poses a problem. Inevitably, it involves some process of weeding or selection. What I have tried to offer here are the books that I have found stimulating, some positively and others not because of intrinsic merit, but because they have prompted me to think things out differently, for myself. If there is an English version of a book I have used it in preference to the original in another language. Sometimes, as with Corti's biography of Elisabeth, the original has some valuable additional material not found in the translation.

Bürgersinn und Aufbegehren. Biedermeier und Vormärz in Wien 1815–1848, Vienna, 1988

Franz Joseph I in 100 Bildern, Vienna, 1935

Hispania Austria: arte intorno al 1492. I re cattolici, Massimiliano I e gli inizi della casa d'Austria in Spagna, Milan, 1992

Hundert Berge in hundert Sinnbilden des allerhöchsten und durchlauchtigsten Erzhauses Österreich mit 20 Sprachen ausgezieret, mit gehöriger Genehmhaltung, Freiburg im Breisgau, 1765

Kaiser Franz Joseph von Österreich oder der Zerfall eines Prinzips, Vienna, 1981

Maximilian I, 1459–1519, Biblos Schriften-Band 23, Vienna, 1959

Die österreichisch-ungarische Monarchie in Wort und Bild. Auf Anregung und unter Mitwirkung Seiner kaiserlichen und königlichen Hoheit des durchlauchtigsten Kronprinzen Erzherzhog Rudolf

Rudolf, ein Leben im Schatten von Mayerling, Vienna, 1990

The Triumph of Maximilian I, 137 woodcuts by Hans Burgkmair and others . . . with a translation of descriptive text, introduction and notes by Stanley Applebaum, New York, 1964

Adams, Alison, and Harper, Anthony J. (eds.), *The Emblem in Renaissance and Baroque Europe: Tradition and Variety. Selected Papers of the Glasgow International Emblem Conference, 13–17 August 1990*, Leiden and New York, 1992

Albrecht, Erherzog, *Gedanken über den Militärischen Geist*, Vienna, 1869

Alhambra, Archivo del, *Acusación contra Isabel Cajinar y Consortes. Vecinos de Nijar, sobre Trato con los Turcos*, Legajo A-35, Pieza 9, 1564

——, *Aviso, sin Principio, sobre Averigüacion de Haberse Pasado a Berberia Lope Caluca y Consortes*, Legajo A-51, Pieza 2, 1563

——, *Justificación que Hicieron los Vecinos del Lugar de Turre de no Quere Pasarse a Berberia, por ser Buenos Cristianos y Leales al Rey*, Legaojo A-51, Pieza 51, 1563

——, *Autos de Justificación de Haberse Pasado a Berberia, Lorenzo el Guari y Consortes*, Legajo A-54, Pieza 4, 1564

——, *Justificación contra Cristianos Nuevos, Vecinos de Guesija y Haberse Querido Pasar a Berberia*, Legajo A-57, Pieza 6, 1565

——, *Justificación contra Majamud, que antes se Llamaba Juan Griego, por ser Cristiano Nuevo de Nacion, Vecino de Almeria, sobre Delito de Transfugaba a Berberia*, Legajo A-57, Pieza 8, 1565

——, *Autos de Justificación sobre Moriscos que se Pasaron a Berberia de la Ciudad de Almeria*, Legajo A-60, Pieza 9, 1566

——, *Causa contra Diego Hernández sobre Transfugia en Berberia*, Legajo A-63, Pieza 6, 1569

——, *Causa contra Miguel Zoli y Consortes, Vecinos de Nortaez que los Fueron Condenados a Muerte y Ejecutados en Justicia en la Puerta de Elvira, sobre Paso a Berberia*, Legajo A-64, Pieza 44, 1562

——, *Carta sobre . . . Socorro de Sus Costas contra Cualquiera Armada del Turco*, Legajo 1930, 1543

——, *Carta sobre . . . la Gente y las Armas para el Socorro contra el Turco*, Legajo 1930, 1558

Altenberg, Hermann, *Um Recht und Umrecht im Hause Habsburg*, Vienna, 1966

Alvar, Manuel, *Léxico del Mestizaje en Hispanoamérica*, Madrid, 1987

Alvar Ezquerra, A., *Felipe II, la Corte y Madrid en 1561*, Madrid 1985

Americo Castro, *Cervantes y los Casticismos Españoles*, rev. edn, Madrid, 1974

Amman, ektor, 'Die Habsburger und die Schweiz', *Argovia, Jahreschrift der Historischen Gesellschaft des Kantons Aargau*, vol. 43, 1931, pp. 125–53

——, *Das Kloster Königsfelden*, Aargau, 1933

Andics, Hellmut, *Die Frauen der Habsburger*, Vienna, 1969

Andrews, Marian, *Maximilian the Dreamer. Holy Roman Emperor*, London, 1913

Anon, *Epitaphia ac series Annorum natalis et obitus corporum Agg. Regg et sereniss. Personarum e domo Austriaca in Mausoleo Caesareo subtus ecclesiam PP. Capucinorum Vienna in Neo Foro Erecto in Christo Quiescentum. Anno MDCCLXIII. De verbo ad verbum fidelitur ex originalibus desumpta, et concinnata ad codici baptismali aulico circa tempuds natale peritus conformata*, Vienna [1763]

——, *Genealogia: origines Murensis Monasterii*, 1627

——, *Germania Triumphans sub Aquilae Austriae*, 1745

——, *Der Herzlich Triumf un(d) Eintritt . . . in die Statte Rhom*, 15 April MDXXXVI.

——, *The History of the Imperial and Royal Houses of Austria and Bourbon, Traced from Their Original to Their Present Time by an Impartial Hand*, London, 1708

——, *Memoria gloriosa regiae stirpis Hapsburgicae; oder Ruhm-Angedecken des Erz-Hausen Oesterreich, in dessen vortrefflichsten Regenten, absersonderlich in dem Leben Leopoldi Magni gezeiget; vorbei zugleich ... Joseph I. Hohe Geburt, Krönung ... und Grossthaten hervorab was sich ... bis 1709 ... zugetragen, vorgestellt wird*, Francfort und Leipzig, 1709

——, *Origine e succesione delle Casa d'Austria e di Lorene*, 1793

Archi, Antonio, *Gli ultimi Asburgo e gli ultimi Borbone in Italia, 1814–1861*, Bologna, 1965

Arenal, Mercedes García (ed.), *Los Moriscos*, Madrid, 1975

Argan, Giulio Carlo, *The Empire of the Capitals, 1600–1700*, Geneva

Aries, Philippe, *Centuries of Childhood*, New York and London, 1962

Aries, Philippe, and Duby, Georges, *A History of Private Life*, II: *Revelations of the Medieval World*, tr. Arthur Goldhammer, Cambridge, Mass., and London, 1988

Asch, Ronald, and Brike, Adolf M. (eds.), *Princes, Patronage and the Nobility at the Beginning of the Modern Age, c. 1450–1650*, Oxford, 1991

Aston, Margaret, *The Fifteenth Century: the Prospect of Europe*, London, 1968

Auclères, Dominique, *Soleil d'Exil: le Bannissement des Habsbourg: Récit Historique*, Paris, 1974.

Auersperg, Anton Alexander, Graf von (ed.), *The Last Knight, A Romance-Garland*, tr. John O. Sargent, New York, 1871

Barghahn, Barbara von, *Age of Gold, Age of Iron. Renaissance Spain and Symbols of Modernity*, Lanham, NY, and London, 1985

Bath, Michael, *Speaking Pictures: English Emblem Books and Renaissance Culture*, London and New York, 1993

Bäuml, F. H., 'Varieties and consequences of medieval literacy and illiteracy', *Speculum*, LV, 1980, pp. 237–65

Bazin, Germain, *The Baroque: Principles, Styles, Modes*, New York, 1968.

Beales, D., *Joseph II*, vol. 1: *In the Shadow of Maria Theresa*, Cambridge and New York, 1987

——, 'Was Joseph II an enlightened despot?', in Ritchie Robertson and Edward Timms, *The Austrian Enlightenment and Its Aftermath*, Edinburgh, 1991

Beck, Marcel; Felder, Peter; Mauerer, Emil; and Schwarz, Dietrich W. H. (eds.), *Königsfelden. Geschichte, Bauten, Glasgemälde, Kunstschätze: Iconographie der Glasgemälde*, Freiburg im Breisgau, 1983

Bellucci, Paolo, *I Lorena in Toscana*, Florence, 1984

Benecke, Gerhard, *Maximilian I 1459–1519. An Analytical Biography*, London, 1982

Benedikt, Heinrich, *Die wirtschaftliche Entwicklung in der Francisko Josefinischen Zeit*, Vienna, 1957

——, *Die Monarchie des Hauses Österreich. Ein historisches Essay*, Vienna, 1968

——, *Kaiseradler über dem Apennin, Die Österreicher in Italien 1700–1866*, Vienna, 1984

Benesch, Otto, *The Art of the Renaissance in Northern Europe. Its Relation to the Contemporary Spiritual and Intellectual Developments*, 2nd edn, London, 1965

——, *German Painting, from Dürer to Holbein*, tr. H. S. B. Harrison, Geneva, 1966

——, *German and Austrian Art of the Fifteenth and Sixteenth Centuries*, ed. Eva Benesch, London, 1972

Benesch, Otto, and Auer, Erwin M. (eds.), *Die Historia Fridericii et Maximiliani ... von Joseph Grünpeck*, Berlin, 1957

Bérenger, Jean, *Histoire de l'Empire des Habsbourg, 1273–1918*, Paris, 1990

——, *A History of the Habsburg Empire 1273–1700*, tr. C. A. Simpson, London, 1994

Berthold, H., *Geschichte der Wiener Schriftgiessereien seit Einführung der Buchdruckerkunst im Jahre 1482 bis zur Gegenwart*, 1924

Bireley, Robert, *Religion and Politics in the Age of the Counterreformation. Emperor Ferdinand, William Lamormaini S.J. and the Formation of Imperial Policy*, Chapel Hill, NC, 1981

Bled, Jean Paul, *Franz Joseph*, tr. Theresa Bridgeman, Oxford, 1992

Bloomfield, Georgiana, Baroness, *Reminiscences of Court and Diplomatic Life*, London, 1883

Boazu Álvarez (ed.), Francisco J. *Cartas de Felipe II a sus Hijas*, Madrid, 1988

Bodmer, Beatriz Pastor, *The Armature of Conquest. Spanish Accounts of the Discovery of America*, Stanford, Calif.

Bonjour, E., Offler, H. S. and Potter, G. R., *A Short History of Switzerland*, Oxford, 1952

Bossi, Gieronimo. *La Genealogia della Gloriossima Casa d'Austria*. Per Gieronimo Bossi, gentilluomo Milanese al Seranissimo et Invitissimo Re Catolice, Filippo d'Austria, sue signore, sum privilegio, in Venetia, Venice, 1560

Bourgouing (ed.), Jean de, *The Incredible Friendship*, tr. Evabeth Miller Kienast and Robert Rie, New York, 1966

Bradford, Martha, *More Letters from Martha Wilmot: Impressions of Vienna, 1819–1829*, London, 1935

Brandi, Karl, *The Emperor Charles V. The Growth and Destiny of a Man and a World Empire*, tr. C. V. Wedgwood, London, 1965

Braudel, Fernand, *The Mediterranean and the Mediterranean World in the Age of Philip II*, 2 vols. (tr.), London, 1973

——, *Civilization and Capitalism, 15th–18th Century*, 3 vols. (tr.), London, 1985

Bregoli-Russo, Mauda, *L'Impresa come Ritnatto del Rinascimento*, Naples, 1990

Bremmer, Jan, and Roodenburg, Hermann, *A Cultural History of Gesture*, Ithaca, NY, and London, 1991

Brewer, John, and Staves, Susan (eds.), *Early Modern Conceptions of Property*, London and New York, 1995

Bridge, F. R., *The Habsburg Monarchy among the Great Powers, 1815–1918*, New York, Oxford, Munich, 1990

Brook Shepherd, Gordon, *The Last Habsburg*, London, 1968

——, *Victims at Sarajevo: The Romance and Tragedy of Franz Ferdinand and Sophie*, London, 1984

Brown, Jonathan, and Elliott, J. H., *A Palace Fit for a King: The Buen Retiro and the Court of Philip IV*, New Haven, Conn., and London, 1980

Bryce, James, *The Holy Roman Empire*, New York (reprinted edn), 1978

Bryson, Norman, *Word and Image. French Painting of the Ancien Regime*, Cambridge, New York, Melbourne, 1981

Burke, Peter, *The Fabrication of Louis XIV*, New Haven, Conn., and London, 1992

———, *The Art of Conversation*, Ithaca, NY, 1993

Busch, Harald, and Lohse, Bernd (eds.), *Baroque Sculpture*, New York, 1965

Cabanes, Agustín, *El Mal Hereditario*, Madrid, 1927

Cadden, Joan, *Meanings of Sex Differences in the Middle Ages. Medicine: Science: Culture*, Cambridge, 1992

Cadenas y Vicent, Vicente de, *Entrevistas con el Emperador Carlos V*, Madrid, 1983

———, *La Doble Coronación de Carlos V en Bolonia. 22–24/II/1530*, Madrid, 1985

Calmet, Augustín, *Illustrissimi et reverendissimi domini, Domini Augustini Calmetii ... Refutatio systematis genealogici a R.P. Marquardo Herrgott ... compositi e gallico in latinum sermonem*, Venice, 1748

Camille, Michael, 'The Book of Signs: writing and visual difference in Gothic manuscript illumination', *Word and Image*, I, 1985, pp. 133–48

———, 'Seeing and reading: some visual implications of mediaeval literacy and illiteracy', *Art History*, VIII, 1985, pp. 26–49

———, *Images on the Edge: The Margins of Mediaeval Art*, London, 1992

Cannadine, David, and Price, Simon (eds.), *Rituals of Royalty: Power and Ceremonial in Traditional Societies*, Cambridge and New York, 1987

Capital, Anton, 'Planimetría y tradición. El Escorial como sistema de claustros', *IV Centenario del Monasterio de El Escorial: Ideas y Diseño (La Arquitectura)*, Madrid, 1986

Cardaillac, Louis, *Morisques et Chrétiens: Un Affrontement Polémique*, Paris, 1977

Caro Baroja, Julio, *Los Moriscos del Reinado de Granada: Ensayo de Historia Social*, Madrid, 1957

Carruthers, Mary J., *The Book of Memory: A Study of Memory in Medieval Culture*, Cambridge, 1990

Cassels, Lavender, *Clash of Generations. A Habsburg Family Drama in the Nineteenth Century*, London, 1973

———, *The Struggle for the Ottoman Empire*, London, n.d.

———, *The Archduke and the Assassin: Sarajevo, June 28 1914*, London, 1984

Célerier, Max, *Regards sur la Symbolique de la Toison d'Or*, with preface by Otto de Habsbourg, Dijon, 1990

Chartier (ed.), Roger, *The Culture of Print*, tr. Lydia G. Cochrane, Oxford, 1994

Chastel, André, *Mythe et Crise de la Renaissance*, Geneva, 1989

Chaunu, P., *L'Espagne de Charles V*, Paris, 1973

Checa Cremedes, Fernando, *Felipe II: Mecenas de los artes*, Madrid, [1992]

———, *Carlos V y la Imagen del Heróe en el Renacimiento*, Madrid, 1987

Chejne, Anwar G., *Islam and the West. The Moriscos – a Cultural and Social History*, Albany, NY, 1983

Chudoba, Bohdan, *Spain and the Empire*

Ciavarelli, Maria Elisa, *El Tema de la Fuerza de la Sangre. Antecedentes Europeos. Siglo de Oro Español*, Madrid, 1980

Clanchy, M. T., *From Memory to Written Record. England 1066–1307*, Oxford, 1993

Cohn, Norman, *The Pursuit of the Millennium. Revolutionary Messianism in Mediaeval and Reformation Europe and Its Bearing on Modern Totalitarian Movements*, London, 1957

Cone, Polly (ed.), *The Imperial Style: Fashion of the Hapsburg Era*, New York, 1980

Contamine, Pierre, *War in the Middle Ages*, Oxford, 1984

Coreth, Anna, *Österreichische Geschichtschreibung in der Barockzeit (1620–1740)*, Vienna, 1950

——, *Pietas Austriaca, Ursprung und Entwicklung Barocker Frömmigkeit in Österreich*, Vienna, 1959

Corti, Egon Caesar Conte, *Elisabeth 'Die Seltsame Frau'. Nach dem Schriftlichen Nachlass der Kaiserin, den Tagebüchern ihrer Tochter und sonstigen unveröffentlichten Tagebüchern und Dokumenten*, Salzburg, 1934

——, *Elizabeth, Empress of Austria*, tr. Catherine Alison, New York, 1946

Corti, Egon Caesar Conte, and Sokol, Hans, *Vom Kind zum Kaiser. Kindheit und erste Jugend Kaiser Franz Josephs I und Seiner Geschwister*, Graz, 1951

——, *Mensch und Herrscher. Wege und Schicksale Kaiser Franz Josephs I zwischen Thronbestegung und Berliner Congress*, Graz, 1952

——, *Der Alte Kaiser. Vom Berliner Kongress bis zu Seinem Tode*, Vienna, 1955

Cox-Rearick, Janet, *Dynasty and Destiny in Medici Art. Pontormo, Leo X, and the two Cosimos*, Princeton, NJ, 1984

Coxe, William, *History of the House of Austria from the Foundation of the Monarchy by Rhodolph of Hapsburgh to the Death of Leopold II, 1218 to 1872*, 4 vols., London, 1895

Craig, Gordon A., *The Battle of Königgrätz*, London, 1964

——, *War, Politics and Diplomacy. Selected Essays*, New York and London, 1966

Crankshaw, Edward, *The Fall of the House of Habsburg*, London, 1963

——, *Maria Theresa*, London, 1969

——, *The Habsburgs*, London, 1971

Cruz, Anne J., and Perry, Mary Elizabeth (eds.), *Culture and Control in Counter-Reformation Spain*, Minneapolis, Minn., and Oxford, 1992

Cutler, Allan Harris, and Cutler, Helen Elmquist, *The Jew as the Ally of the Muslim. Mediaeval Roots of Anti-Semitism*, Notre Dame, Ind., 1986

Daly, Peter M., *Emblem theory: recent German contributions to the characterization of the emblem genre*. Nendeln/Liechtenstein, 1979

Darnton, Robert, and Roche, Daniel (eds.), *Revolution in Print. The Press in France 1775–1800*, Berkeley, Calif., and London, 1989

Davis, James C., *Pursuit of Power. Venetian Ambassadors' Reports on Turkey, France and Spain in the Age of Philip II 1560–1600*, New York and London, 1970

Deanesly, Margaret, *A History of the Medieval Church: 590–1500*, London and New York, 1972

Dedijer, Vladimir, *The Road to Sarajevo*, London, 1967

Delbruck, Hans, *History of the Art of War*, vol. 3: *Mediaeval warfare*; vol. 4: *Modern warfare*, Lincoln, Nebraska and London, 1982

Denham, James, *The Cradle of the Hapsburgs*, London, 1907

Díaz-Plaza, Fernando, *Vida Íntima de los Austriacos*, Madrid, 1991

Dickens, A. G. (ed.), *The Courts of Europe: Politics, Patronage and Royalty 1400–1800*, London, 1977

Drage, Geoffrey, *Austria Hungary*, London, 1909

Duffy, Christopher, *The Army of Maria Theresa*, Newton Abbot, 1977

——, *Siege Warfare. The Fortress in the Early Modern World 1494–1660*, London, 1979

——, *The Fortress in the Age of Vauban and Frederick the Great, 1660–1789*, London, 1985

——, *The Military Experience in the Age of Reason*, London, 1987

Dugast-Rouillé, M., *Les Grand Mariages des Habsbourg*, Paris, 1955

——, *Les Maisons Souveraines d'Autriche*, Paris, 1967

——, *Descendance, Ascendance de Charles et Zita de Habsbourg, Empereur et Imperatrice d'Autriche*, Saint-Herblain, France, 1985

Dupuy, R. E., and Dupuy, T. N., *The Encyclopedia of Military History from 3500 BC to the Present*, London, 1970

Durstmüller, Anton, *500 Jahre Druck in Österreich: die Entwicklungsgeschichte der graphischen Gewerbe von den Anfangen bis zur Gegenwart*, Vienna, 1985–8

Eckhart (1674–1730), Johann Georg, *Origines Serenissimae ac Potentissimae Familiae Habsburgoaustriacae ex Monumentis Veteribus, Scriptoribus Coataneis, Diplomatibus, Chartisque*, Lipsiae, 1721

Edelmayer, Friedrich, and Kohler, Alfred, *Maximilian II. Kultur und Politik in 16 Jahrhundert*, Vienna, 1992

Egg, Erich, *Die Hofkirche in Innsbrück. Das Grabdenkmal Kaiser Maximilians I und die Silberne Kapelle*, Innsbruck, 1974

Eisenmann, Louis, *Le Compromis Austro-Hongrois de 1867. Étude sur la Dualisme*, Paris, 1968 (1904)

Eisenstein, Elisabeth, *The Printing Revolution in Early Modern Europe*, Cambridge, 1983

——, *The Printing Press as an Agent of Change*, Cambridge, 1979

Elliott, J H, *Imperial Spain 1469–1716*, London, 1963

——, *The Old World and the New: 1492–1650*, Cambridge, 1970

——, *Spain and Its World: 1500–1700*, New Haven, Conn., and London, 1989

——, *The Hispanic World. Civilization and Empire, Europe and the Americas, Past and Present*, London, 1991

Erdmann, Knut (ed.), *Mobilmachung: die Habsburger Front in Auftrage des JEF-Bundesrortstandes*, Bonn, 1979

Ernst, Otto (ed.), *Franz Joseph as Revealed by His Letters*, tr. Agnes Blake, London, 1927

Evans, R. J. W., *Rudolf II and His World: A Study in Intellectual History 1576–1612*, Oxford, 1973

——, *The Making of the Habsburg Monarchy, 1550–1700*, Oxford, 1979

——, 'The imperial court at the time of Archimboldo', in *The Arcimboldo Effect*, London, 1987

Febvre, Lucien, and Martin, Henri-Jean, *The Coming of the Book. The Impact of Printing 1450–1800*, London, 1976

Ferdinand I, Emperor of Austria, Family Law of the House of Habsburg ('Unpublished documents drawn by Prince Metternich, Chancellor of the Austrian Empire ... to serve as a code of conduct enforceable ... by the emperor on members of the Imperial House of Austria'), Vienna, 1839

The state of the Imperial-Court of the Emperour Ferdinand the Second, tr. R. W., London, 1637

Fernanández Alvarez, Manuel, *Corpus documental de Carlo V*, 5 vols., Salamanca, 1971-81

——, *Charles V: Elected Emperor and Hereditary Ruler*, tr. J. A. Lalaguna, London, 1975

Fernández-Santamaria, J. A., *The State, War and Peace. Spanish Thought in the Renaissance 1516–1559*, Cambridge and New York, 1977

Feuchtmueller, Rupert, and Mrazak, Wilhelm, *Biedermeier Österreich*, Vienna, 1963

Feuchtmüller, Rupert, and Kovacs, Elisabeth (eds.), *Welt des Barock*, Vienna, 1986

Fichtenau, Heinrich, *Der junge Maximilian*, Vienna, 1959

Fichtner, Paula Sutter, *Ferdinand I of Austria. The Politics of Dynasticism in the Age of the Reformation*, New York, 1982

——, *Protestantism and Primogeniture in Early Modern Germany*, New Haven, Conn., and London, 1989

Fischer-Galati, Stephen, *Ottoman Imperialism and German Protestantism, 1521–1555*, Cambridge, Mass., 1959

Flandrin, J.[-L.], *Families in Former Times*, Cambridge, 1979

——, *Un Temps pour Embrasser. Aux Origines de la Morale Sexuelle: VIe–XIe Siècle*, Paris, 1983

Flesch-Brunnigingen, Hans, *Die letzten Habsburger in Augenzeugenberichten*, Düsseldorf, 1967

Forbes, Jack D., *Africans and Native Americans. The Language of Race and the Evolution of Red–Black Peoples*, 2nd edn, Urbana, Ill., 1993

Foucault, Michel, *The Order of Things. An Archaeology of the Human Sciences*, New York, 1970

Francis, Mark (ed.), *The Viennese Enlightenment*, New York, 1985

Freschot, Casimir, *Mémoires de la Cour de Vienne*, Cologne, 1705

Frey, Linda, *A Question of Empire. Leopold I and the War of the Spanish Succession 1701–05*, New York, 1983

Frischauer, Paul, *The Imperial Crown. The Story of the Rise and Fall of the Holy Roman and the Austrian Empires*, London, 1939

Frodl, Gerbert, *Hans Makart, Monographie und Werkverzeichnis*, Salzburg, 1974

Frodl, Gerbert, and Schröder, Klaus Albrecht (eds.), *Wiener Biedermeier: Malerei zwischen Wiener Kongress und Revolution*, Munich, 1992

Frodl-Schneemann, Marianne, *Johann Peter Krafft, 1780–1856. Monographie und Verzeichnis der Gemälde*, Vienna, 1984

Fugger, J. J., *Spiegel der Ehren des hochtlöblichsten Kayser und Königlichen Erzhauses Osterreich . . .*, Nuremberg, 1682

Fugger, Nora, *The Glory of the Habsburgs*, New York, 1932

Fussel, Stephan, *Riccardus Bartholinus Perusinus: humanistische Panegyrik am Hofe Kaiser Maximilians I*, Baden-Baden, 1987

Gagliardo, John G., *Reich and Nation: The Holy Roman Empire as Idea and Reality 1763–1806*, Bloomington, Ind., 1980

García Mercadel, *Viajes de Extranjeros por España y Portugal*, 2 vols., Madrid, 1952

Geertz, Clifford, *Negara: the Theatre State of Nineteenth Century Bali*, Princeton, NJ, 1980

——, *The Interpretation of Cultures*, London, 1993

Geramb, Ferdinand von, *Habsburg – ein Gedicht seiner k.k. Majestät Franz II [of Germany] bei Annahmeder Österreichischen erblichen Kaiserwürde zugeeignet*, Vienna, 1805

Gibbon, Edward, *The History of the Decline and Fall of the Roman Empire*, 7 vols. ed. J. B. Bury, London, 1909

Gilchrist, Roberta, *Gender and Material Culture. The Archaeology of Religious Women*, London, 1994

Girecour, Comte de, *Essai sur l'Histoire de la Maison d'Autriche*, 6 vols., Paris, 1778

Girtanner, Christoph, *Charakteristik der Kaisers Rudolph von Habsburg*, Leipzig, 1817

Glaise Horstenau, Edmund von, *Franz Josefs Weggefährte. Das Leben des Generalstabschefs Grafen Beck*, Vienna, 1930

Gollner, Carl, *Turcica: Die Europäischen Turkendrucke des XVI Jahrhunderts*, 2 vols., Bucharest and Baden-Baden, 1968

Gooch, G. P., *Maria Theresa and Other Studies*, Hamden, Conn., 1965 (reprint)

Goody, Jack, *The Development of the Family and Marriage in Europe*, Cambridge, 1983

——, *The Logic of Writing and the Organisation of Society*, Cambridge, 1986

Gottlieb, Theodor, *Büchersammlung Kaiser Maximilian I. mit einer Einleitung über alteren Büchbesitz in Hause Habsburg*, 1900

Grafton, Anthony, *New Worlds, Ancient Texts. The Power of Tradition and the Shock of Discovery*, Cambridge, Mass., 1992

Graphaeus, Cornelius, *Le Triumphe d'Anvers. La Tresadmirable, tresmagnifique, et Triumphante Entreé, du treshault et trespuissant Prince Philipes, Prince d'Espaignes, filz de Lempereur Charles Ve, ensemble la vraye description des Spectacles, theatres, archz trumphaulx. etc. lesquelz ont esté faictz et bastis a la tresdesireé reception en la tresrenommee florissante ville d'Anvers*. Anvers, 1550

Greenblatt, Stephen (ed.), *New World Encounters*, 1993

Greyerz, Kaspar von, *Religion and Society in Early Modern Europe, 1500–1800*, London, 1984

Gribble, Francis Henry, *The Life of the Emperor Francis Joseph*, London, 1914

Grierson, Edward, *The Fatal Inheritance: Philip II and the Spanish Netherlands*, London, 1969

Griffith, Antony, and Carey, Frances, *German Printmaking in the Age of Goethe*, London, 1994

Grillparzer, Franz, *Family Strife in Hapsburg. Tragedy in Five Acts*, tr. Arthur Burkhard, Yarmouth Bay, Mass., 1940

——, *King Ottocar, His Rise and Fall*, Yarmouth Port, Mass., 1825 [1962]

Grimschitz, Bruno, *Die Altwiener Maler*, Vienna, 1961

Gritzner, Erich, *Symbole und Wappen des alten deutschen Reiches*, Leipzig, 1902

Grossegger, Elisabeth, *Der Kaiser-Huldigung-Festzug Wien 1908*, Vienna, 1992

Grössing, Helmuth, and Grössing, Stulhofer, 'Versuch einer Deutung der Rolle der Astrologie in den persönlichen und politischen Entscheidungen einiger Habsburger des Spätmittelalters', in: *Österreichische Akademie der Wissenschaften, Philosophisch-historische Klasse: Anzeiger*, 117, 1980

Gurevich, Aron, *Mediaeval Popular Culture, Problems of Belief*, Cambridge, 1988

Habsbourg, Otto de, *Mémoires d'Europe: Entretiens avec Jean-Paul Picaper*, Paris, 1994

Habsburg, Otto von, *Charles V*, tr. Michael Ross, London, 1970

Habsburg, Walburga von, and Posselt, Bernd, *Einigen – nicht Trennen. Festschrift für Otto von Habsburg zum 75. Geburtstag am 20 November 1987*, Moers, Germany, 1987

Hadamowsky, F., *Barocktheater am Wiener Kaiserhof, 1625–1740*, Vienna, 1955

Hale, J. R., *Renaissance Europe: 1480–1520*, London, 1971

——, *The Civilisation of Europe in the Renaissance*, London, 1993

Hamann, Brigitte, *Die Habsburger. Ein biographisches Lexicon*, Munich, 1588

Hanover, King of, *Letters of the King of Hanover to Viscount Strangford, GCB. Now in the possession of his granddaughter Mrs Frank Russell*, London 1925

Hantsch, Hugo, *Die Geschichte Österreichs*, Graz, 1953

Harding, Bertita, *Golden Fleece. The Story of Franz Joseph and Elisabeth of Austria*, London, 1937

Hart, Vaughan, *Art and Magic at the Stuart Court*, London, 1994

Hartley, Keith (ed. in chief), *The Romantic Spirit in German Art 1790–1990*, Edinburgh and London, 1994

Haslip, Joan, *Imperial Adventurer. Emperor Maximilian of Mexico*, London, 1971

——, *The Emperor and the Actress. The Love Story of Emperor Franz Joseph and Katharina Schratt*, London, 1982

Hauser, Henri, *La Naissance de Protestantisme*, Paris, 1940

Hawlik van de Water, Magdalena, *Der schöne Tod: Zeremonialstrukturen des Wiener Hofes bei Tod und Begrabnis zwischen 1640 und 1740*, Vienna, 1989

——, *Die Kapuzinergruft. Begrabnisstatte der Habsburger in Wien*, Vienna, 1993, 2nd edn

Headley, John M., *The Emperor and His Chancellor. A Study of the Imperial Chancellery under Gattinara*, Cambridge, 1983

Heer, Friedrich, *The Holy Roman Empire*, tr. Janet Sondheimer, London, 1967

——, *Der Kampf um die österreichische Identität*, Vienna, 1981

Heller, Eduard, *Kaiser Franz Joseph I. Ein Charakterbild*, Vienna, 1934

Hellwich, C. de (ed.), *Origo et Genealogia gloriosissimorum comitum de Habsburg . . . ex antiquos et authenticis . . . monumentis . . . succinte quiden sed clare demonstrate [by] Dominicus, Abbot of Muris*, Wrctislavie, 1715; 1718

Henderson, Nicolas, *Prince Eugen of Savoy. A Biography*, London, 1964

Héretier-Auge, Françoise, and Copet-Rougier, Elisabeth, *Les Complexités de l'Alliance*. Vol. 2: *Les Systèmes Complexes d'Alliance Matrimoniale*, Montreux, 1991

Herrgott, Marquard, *Genealogia Diplomatica Augustae Gentis Habsburgicae . . .*, Vienna, 1737

——, *Monumenta Augustae Domus Austriacae*, 4 vols., Vienna, Freiburg im Breisgau, St Blasien, 1750–73

Herzig, Max (ed.), *Viribus Unitis. Das Buch vom Kaiser*, mit einer Einleitung von Josef Freiherr von Helfert, Vienna, 1898

Hess, Andrew, 'The Moriscos: an Ottoman fifth column in sixteenth century Spain', *American Historical Review*, vol. LXXIV, October 1968

——, 'The evolution of the Ottoman seaborne empire in the light of oceanic discoveries, 1453–1525', *American Historical Review*, vol. LXXV, December 1970, pp. 1889–1919

——, 'The battle of Lepanto and its place in Mediterranean history', *Past and Present*, no. 57, November 1972, pp. 53–73

——, *The Forgotten Frontier. A History of the Sixteenth-century Ibero-African Frontier*, Chicago, Ill., and London, 1978

Heuter, Pontus, *Opera historica omnia; Burgundica, Austriaca, Belgica . . . insertus est eiusdem de vetustate et nobilitate familiae Habsburgicae et Austriacae liber singularis*, Louvain, 1649

Heydte, Friedrich August von der, *Die Monarchie, eine europäische Idee: Österreich vom Wiener Kongress bis St Germain*, Vienna, 1933

Hickman, Hannah, *Robert Musil and the Culture of Vienna*, London, 1984

Hilger, Wolfgang, *Ikonographie Kaiser Ferdinands I (1503–1564)*, Vienna, 1969

Hindman, Sandra L., *Printing the Written Word. The Social History of Books circa 1450–1520*, Ithaca, NY, 1991

Hocart, A. M., *Kings and Councillors. An Essay in Comparative Anatomy of Human Society*, Chicago, Ill., 1970 (new edn)

Hodge, Robert, and Kress, Gunther, *Language as Ideology*, 2nd edn, London and New York, 1993

Hodl, Günther, *Habsburg und Österreich 1273–1493: Gestalten und Gestalt des österreichischen Spätmittelalters*, Vienna, 1988

Höffner, J., *La Ética Colonial Española del Siglo de Oro: Cristianismo y Dignidad Humana*, Madrid, 1957

Hopel, Ingrid, *Emblem und Sinnbild: vom Kunstbuch zum Erbauungsbuch*, Frankfurt am Main, [1987]

Hsia, R. Po-Chia, *The Myth of Ritual Murder. Jews and Magic in Reformation Germany*, New Haven, Conn., and London, 1988

Hug, L., and Stead, R., *Switzerland*, London, 1890

Huizinga, J., *The Waning of the Middle Ages*, tr. F. Hopman, Harmondsworth, Middx, 1972

Hume, Martin, *The Court of Philip IV. Spain in Decadence*, New York, n.d.

Hyatt Major, A., *People and Prints. A Social History of Printed Pictures*, Princeton, NJ, 1971

Inazaghi, Baron de Kymburg, Joannes Philippus D. ab, *Dissertio de Sacro-Sancti Romana Caesareo-Graeco Franco Germanici Augustissima Habsburgica Austriaco Germanica Dono iusque Regnis ducatibus praerogativis*, Freiburg in Breisgau, 1671 (?)

Ingrao, Charles, *In Quest and Crisis. Emperor Joseph I and the Habsburg Monarchy*, West Lafayette, Ind., 1979

Ingrao, Charles (ed.), *State and Society in Early Modern Austria*, West Lafayette, Ind., 1994

J. C. B. (Johann Christian Beer), *Der durchleuchtigsten Erz-Herzogen zu Österreich Leben, Regierung und Gross-Thaten: non dem allerpreiswürdigsten Urheber dieses Hauses Rudolpho an, bis in die höchst glückseelige regierung der Römanischen Kayserlichen Majestät Leopold I, unter Römanischen Koniglichen Majestät Joseph I*, Nuremberg, 1695, 1713

Janik, Allan and Toulmin, Stephen, *Wittgenstein's Vienna*, New York, 1973

Jászi, Oscar, *The Dissolution of the Habsburg Monarchy*, Chicago, Ill., 1929

Johnston, William M., *The Austrian Mind. An Intellectual and Social History 1848–1938*, Berkeley, Calif., and London, 1972

Judtmann, Fritz, *Mayerling. The Facts behind the Legend*, tr. Ewald Osers, London, 1971

Kagan, Richard L., *Lucrecia's Dreams. Politics and Prophecy in Sixteenth Century Spain*, Berkeley, Calif., and London, 1990

Kamen, Henry, *Spain in the Later Seventeenth Century, 1665–1700*, London, 1980

Kann, Robert A., *A Study of Austrian Intellectual History. From the Late Baroque to Romanticism*, London, 1960

——, *A History of the Habsburg Empire, 1526–1918*, Berkeley, California, and London, 1974

Kann, Robert A., and David, Zdenek V., *The Peoples of the Eastern Habsburg Lands, 1526–1918*, Seattle, Wash., and London, 1984

Kaufmann, Thomas DaCosta, *Variations on the Imperial Theme in the Age of Maximilian II and Rudolf II*, New York, 1978

——, *Drawings from the Holy Roman Empire*, Princeton, NJ, 1983

Keegan, John, and Wheatcroft, Andrew, *Who's Who in Military History*, London, 1987

Keen, Maurice, *Chivalry*, New Haven, Conn., and London, 1984

Kertesz, Johann, *Bibliographie der Habsburg Literatur, 1218–1934*, Budapest, 1934

Ketterl, Eugene, *The Emperor Franz Joseph I. An Intimate Study*, London

Kleinberg, Aviad M., *Prophets in Their Own Country: Saints and the Making of Sainthood in the Late Middle Ages*, Chicago, Ill., and London, 1992

Knappich, Wilhelm, *Die Habsburger Chronik. Lebensbilder, Charaktere und Geschichte der Habsburger*, Salzburg and Stuttgart, 1959

Koenigsberger, H. G., *The Habsburgs and Europe, 1516–1660*, Ithaca, NY, and London, 1971

Kolb, Karl, *Vom heiligen Blut: eine Bilddokumentation der Wallfahrt und Verehrung*, Würzburg, 1980

Kollar, Adam Francis, *Analecta Monumentorum omnis aevi Vindobonensia*, Vienna, 1761–2

Kopp, Fridolin, *Vindiciae Actorum Murensium pro & contra R.D.P Marquardum Herrgott Genealogiae Diplomaticae Augustae Gentis Habsburgicae*, n.p., 1750

Koschatzky, Walter, *Die Dürerzeichnungen der Albertina*, Salzburg, 1971

Koschatzky, Walter (ed.), *Maria Theresa und ihre Zeit: zur 200. Wiedenkehn des Todestages*, Salzburg, 1980

Krafft, Jean Laurent, *Histoire Générale de l'Auguste Maison d'Autriche*, Brussels, 1744

Kraus, Victor von, *Maximilians I Vertraulicher Briefwechsel mit Sigmund Prüschenk, Freiherrn zu Stetternberg*, I, Innsbruck, 1875

Kray, Stefan Baron, *Im Dienste der Kabinettskanzlei während des Weltkrieges. Episoden und Charakterbilder aus dem Leben der Kaiser Franz Josef und Karl*, Budapest, 1937

Kreutal, Richard E. (ed.), *Kara Mustafa vor Wien. Das Turkische Tagebüch der Belägerung Wiens 1683, verfasst von Zeremonienmeister des Hohen Pforte*, Graz, 1960

Krieg von Hochdfelden, Georg Heinrich, *Denkmäler der Hauses Habsburg in der Schweiz*, 1841

Kugler, Georg, and Hauptl, Herbert (eds.), *Des Kaisers Rock: Uniform und Mode am österreichischen Kaiserhof. 1800 bis 1918*, Eisenstadt, 1989

Kunzle, David, *The Early Comic Strip. Narrative Strips and Picture Stories in the European Broadsheet from c. 1450 to 1825*, Berkeley, Calif., and London, 1973

Kusin, Eberhard, *Die Kaisergruft bei den PP Kapuzinern in Wien*, Vienna, 1949

Lacarta, Manuel, *Felipe II: la Idea de Europa*, Madrid, 1986

La Feuille, Daniel de, *Symbola et Emblemata jussu atque Auspiciis Sacerrimae Suae Majestatis . . .*, Amstelaedami, 1705

Lambecius, Petrus, *Comentarii de augustissima Bibliotheca Caesarea Vindobonensi*, 1665–74; and 1766–82

——, *Diarium sacri itineris cellensis interrupti*, Vienna, 1665

Lambert, Malcolm, *Mediaeval Heresey. Popular Movements from the Gregorian Reform to the Reformation*, Oxford, 1992

Lanckoronska, Maria, *Die christlich-humanistiche Symbolsprache und deren Bedeutung in zwei Gebetbücher des frühen 16 Jahrhunderts*, Baden-Baden, 1958

Langer, Eduard, *Bibliographie der österreichischen Drucke der XV und XVI Jahrhunderte*, Vienna, 1913

Langer, William L., *European Alliances and Entanglements*, New York, NY, 1931

Langhans, Jacob, *Von Auff- und Abgang der Hertzogen zu Zahringen. Auch von auff- und abgang der uralten Hertzogen zu Oesterreich. Und von dem elten Edlen Stammen der Graffen von Habsburg. Und von der Stiftung dess Furstlichen Closters Königsfelden*, Bern, 1642

Langsam, Walter Consuelo, *Francis the Good. The Education of an Emperor 1768–1792*, New York, 1949

Lanier, Henry, *He Did Not Die at Mayerling: The Autobiography of Rudolf*, London, 1937

Lanz, Johann, *Kinder und Ahnen des letzten österreichischen Kaiserpaares*, Vienna, 1970

Lavandier, Jean Pierre, *Le Livre au Temps de Marie Thérèse. Code des Lois de Censure du Livre pour les pays Austro-Bohemiens. 1740–1780*, Bern, 1993

Lazius, Wolfgang, *Commentarium in Genealogiam Austriacam*, liber II, Basel, 1564

Leeper, A. W. A., *A History of Medieval Austria*, London, 1941

Levetus, A. S., *Imperial Vienna. An Account of Its History, Traditions and Arts*, London and New York, 1905

Lévi-Strauss, Claude, *The Elementary Structures of Kinship*, London, 1969

Lhotsky, Alphons, *Apis Colonna. Fabeln und Theorien über die Ankunft der Habsburger. Ein Exkurs zur Cronica Austria des Thomas Ebendorfer*, 1944

——, *Privilegium Maius. Die Geschichte einer Urkunde*, Munich, 1957

——, *Thomas Eberndorfer, ein österreichischer Geschictschreiber*, Stuttgart, 1957

——, *Europäisches Mittelalter das Land Österreich*, Munich, 1970

——, *Das Zeitalter des Hauses Österreich. Die ersten Jahre der Regierung Ferdinand I in Österreich, 1520–27*, Vienna, 1971

Liebenau, Theodor von, *Geschichte des Klosters Königsfelden*, 1867

Lindberg, David C. (ed.), *Reappraisals of the Scientific Revolution*, Cambridge, 1990

Lovett, A. W., *Early Habsburg Spain, 1517–98*, Oxford, 1986

Lübke, Wilhelm, *Die Glasgemälde im Chor den Kirche zu Königsfelden*, 1867

Luckacs, John, *Budapest 1900. A Historical Portrait of a City and Its Culture*, London, 1988

Macartney, C. A., *The Habsburg Empire*, London, 1971

——, *The Habsburg and Hohenzollern Dynasties in the Seventeenth and Eighteenth Centuries*, New York and London, 1970

McGuigan, Dorothy Gies, *The Habsburgs*, London, 1966

McKay, Derek, *Prince Eugene of Savoy*, London, 1944

Mackenzie, D. F., *Bibliography and the Sociology of Texts. The Panizzi Lectures 1985*, London, 1986

Maclean, Ian, *The Renaissance Notion of Women. A Study in the Fortunes of Scholasticism and Medical Science in European Intellectual Life*, Cambridge, 1980

McNeill, William, *Europe's Steppe Frontier 1500–1800*, Chicago, 1964

Magris, Claudio, *Le Mythe et l'Empire, dans la Littérature Autrichienne Moderne*, tr. Jean and Marie-Noëlle Pastereau, Paris, 1988

Mansel, Philip, 'Monarchy, uniform and the rise of the "Frac" 1760–1830', *Past and Present*, no. 96, August 1992, pp. 103–32

Margutti, Baron von, *The Emperor Francis Joseph and His Times*, London, n.d.

Martin, H. J., and Febvre, L., *L'Apparition du Livre*, Paris, 1971

Marx, Robert F., *The Battle of Lepanto*, 1571, Cleveland and New York, 1966

Mas, Albert, *Les Turcs dans la Littérature Espagnole du Siècle d'Or*, 2 vols., Paris, 1967

Matejka, J. C., 'Political Participation in the Arab World: the Majlis Mechanism (Middle East, North Africa), unpublished PhD, University of Texas at Austin, 1983

Mauerer, Emil, *Die Kunstdenkmäler des Kantons Aargau*, vol. 2: *Die Bezirke Lenzburg und Brugg*; vol. 3: *Das Kloster Königsfelden*, Basel, 1954

Megisser, Hieronymous, *Diarium Austriacum*, Augsburg, 1614

Mexia, Pero [Pedro], *The Imperial Historie or Lives of the Emperors from Julius Caesar, the First Founder of the Roman Monarchy to This Present Year*, London, 1623

——, *Le Vite de tutti gli imperadori romani da Giulio Cesare, fin a Massimiliano . . .*, Venice, 1625

Mikoletzky, Hans Leo, *Österreich. Das Grosses 18. Jahrhundert von Leopold I bis Leopold II*, Vienna, 1967

Mitchell, W. J. T., *Iconology. Image, Text, Ideology*, Chicago, Ill., and London, 1986

Mitchell, W. J. T. (ed.), *The Language of Images*, Chicago, Ill., and London, 1980

Mitis, Baron von, *The Life of the Crown Prince Rudolph of Habsburg with Letters and Documents Found among His Effects*, tr. M. H. Jerome, London, n.d.

Mollo, John, *Military Fashion. A Comparative History of the Uniforms of the Great Armies from the 17th Century to the First World War*, London, 1972

Mraz, Gerda and Gottfried, *Maria Theresa. Ihr Leben und ihre Zeit in Bilden und Dokumenten*, Munich, 1979

Mulcahy, Rosemarie, *The Decoration of the Royal Basilica of El Escorial*, Cambridge, 1994

Murad, A., *Franz Joseph and His Empire*, New York, 1968

Musil, Robert, *The Man Without Qualities*, tr. E. Wilkins and E. Kaiser, 3 vols., London, 1953–60

N. A., *La Sontuosa Intrata di Carlo V. sempre Augusto in la Gran Citta di Parigi con li Apparati, Triumphi, Feste, Archi Triomphali, etc.* (in Italian)

Nada, John, *Carlos the Bewitched. The Last Spanish Habsburg, 1661–1700*, London, 1962

Naish, Camille, *Death Comes to the Maiden: Sex and Execution 1431–1933*, London, 1991

Nash, Jane C., *Veiled Images: Titian's Mythological Paintings for Philip II*, Philadelphia, Pa, and London, 1985

Needham, Rodney, *Symbolic Classification*, Santa Monica, Calif., 1979

Newman, Francis William, *The Crimes of the House of Habsburg against Its Own Liege Subjects*, London, 1853

Nicholas, David, *The Evolution of the Mediaeval World*, Harlow, 1992

——, *Mediaeval Flanders*, London, 1992

Nicolson, Harold, *The Congress of Vienna. A Study in Allied Unity 1812–15*, London, 1946

Noel, Jean-François, *Le Saint-Empire*, Paris, 1976

Nostitz-Rieneck, Georg, *Briefe Kaiser Franz Josephs an Kaiserin Elisabeth 1859–1898*, Vienna, 1966

Novotny, Alexander, *Franz Joseph I. An der Wende vom Alten zum Neuen Europa*, Göttingen, 1968

Oberhammer, Vinzenz, *Die Bronzestatuen am Grabmal Maximilians I*, Innsbruck, 1955

Oettinger, Karl, *Die Bildhauer Maximilians am Innsbrucker Kaisergrabmal*, Nuremberg, 1966

Oman, C. W. O. (Sir Charles), *The Art of War in the Middle Ages, AD 378–1515*, rev. and ed. J. Cornell Beeler, New York, 1953; 1st edn, London, 1924

——, *The Art of War in the Sixteenth Century*, London, 1937

Oppenheimer, F., *The Legend of the Sainte Ampoule*, London, 1953

Orso, Stephen N., *Art and Death at the Spanish Habsburg Court. The Royal Exequies for Philip IV*, Columbia, Mo, 1989

Ortiz, Antonio Domínguez, *El Antiguo Régimen: Los Reyes Católicos y los Austriacos*, Madrid, 1973

Ortner, Josef Peter, *Marquard Herrgott (1694–1762). Sein Leben und Wirken als Historiker und Diplomat*, Vienna, 1972

Ozment, Steven, *The Age of Reform, 1250–1550. An Intellectual and Religious History of Late Mediaeval and Reformation Europe*, New Haven, Conn., 1980

Padover, Saul K., *The Revolutionary Emperor: Joseph II of Austria*, New York, 1967

Palacio Atard, Vicente, *Derrota, Agotimiento, Decadencia, en la España del Siglo XVII*, Madrid, 1956

Palmer, Alan, *The Twilight of the Habsburgs. The Life and Times of the Emperor Francis Joseph*, London and New York, 1994

Pangels, Charlotte, *Die Kinder Maria Theresias. Leben und Schicksal in kaiserlich Glanz*, Munich, 1980

Panofsky, Erwin, *The Life and Art of Albrecht Dürer*, Princeton, NJ, 1955

——, *Studies in Iconology. Humanistic Themes in the Art of the Renaissance*, New York, 1967

——, *Problems in Titian, Mostly Iconographic*, London, 1969

Parisot, Jacques, *La Descendance de François Joseph I, Empereur d'Autriche*, Paris, 1984

Parker, Geoffrey, *The Army of Flanders and the Spanish Road 1567–1659*, Cambridge, 1972

——, *Philip II*, Boston, Mass., 1978

Parkes, M. B., *Pause and Effect. An Introduction to the History of Punctuation in the West*, Aldershot, UK, 1992

Parry, J. H., *The Spanish Seaborne Empire*, London, 1966

Pauer, Hans, *Kaiser Franz Joseph I. Beiträge zur Bild-Dokumentation Seines Lebens*, Vienna, 1966

Paultre, Roger, *Les Images du Livre: emblemes et devises*, Paris, 1991

Peabody, Elizabeth Palmer, *Crimes of the House of Austria against Mankind*, n.p., 1852, 2nd edn

Perry, Mary Elizabeth, *Gender and Disorder in Early Modern Seville*, Princeton, NJ, 1990

Peter, Lazlo, and Pynsent, Robert B. (eds.), *Intellectuals and the Future in the Habsburg Monarchy 1890–1914*, Basingstoke, 1988

Pick, Robert, *Empress Maria Theresa. The Earlier Years 1717–1757*, London, 1966

Pierson, Peter, *Philip II*, London, 1976

Pirtzl, Leopold, *Stammbaum der Regenten Österreichs von Leopold I dem erlauchlen . . . aus Hause Babenberg vom Jahre 984 bis Ferdinand I aus den Haus Habsburg Lothringen*, Vienna, 1842

Pitt, J. N. U., *Curiosities of Heredity*, London, 1931

Planta, Joseph, *The History of the Helvetic Confederacy*, London, 1807

Plumb, J. H., *The Horizon Book of the Renaissance*, New York and London, 1961

Polzer-Hoditz, Arthur, *The Emperor Karl*, tr. D. F. Tait and F. S. Flint, London and New York, 1930

Pope-Hennessy, John, *The Portrait in the Renaissance*, London, 1966

Porta, W. de, *Die Devisen und Motto der Habsburger*, Vienna, 1887

Poull, Georges, *La Maison Ducale de Lorraine Devenue la Maison Impériale et Royale d'Autriche, de Hongrie et de Bohème*, Nancy, 1991

Praz, Mario, *Conversation Pieces. A Survey of the Informal Group Portrait in Europe and America*, University Park, Pa, and London, 1971

Prescott, W. H., *Philip II*, London, n.d.

——, *History of the Reign of Ferdinand and Isabella the Catholic*, London, 1886

——, *History of the Reign of Charles V*, George Routledge edn, n.d.

Pribram, A. F., and Pragenau, M. L. von (eds.), *Privatbriefe Kaiser Leopold I und der Grafen F. E. Pötting 1662–73*, Vienna, 1904

Primisser, Aloys, *Der Stammbaum . . . des Hauses Habsburg Österreich, in einer Reihe von Bildnissen Habsburgischen Fürsten und Fürstinnenen. Von Rudolf I bis Phillip den Schönen, nach den in k.k. Ambraserr Sammlung befindlichen . . . originalgemälde*, Vienna, 1820

Rachum, Ilan, *The Renaissance*, London, 1979

Radziwill, Princess Catherine, *Secrets of Dethroned Royalty*, New York, 1920

Rath, J. R., *The Viennese Revolution of 1848*, Austin, Tex., 1957

Redlich, Oswald, *Das Werden einer Grossmacht. Österreich in 1700– bis 1740*, Baden bei Wien, 1938

Reifenscheid, Richard, *Die Habsburger in Lebensbildern von Rudolf I bis Karl I*, Graz, 1982

Reinle, Adolf, *Das Stellvertreterbildnis*, Zürich, 1984

Remak, Joachim, *Sarajevo. The Story of a Political Murder*, London, 1959

Ridley Jasper, *Maximilian and Juarez*, New York and London, 1992

Rill, Bernd, *Friedrich III, Habsburgs Europäischer Durchbruch*, Graz, 1987

——, *Habsburg als Barocke Grossmacht*, Graz, 1992

Ripa, Cesare, *Baroque and Rococo Imagery*. The 1758–60 Hertel edition of Ripa's Iconologia with 200 engraved illustrations, ed. Edward. A. Maser, New York, 1971

Rivera, Luis N., *A Violent Evangelism. The Political and Religious Conquest of America*. Louisville, Ky, 1992

Robert, André, *L'idée autrichienne et les guerres de Napoléon: l'apostolat du Baron Hormayr et le salon de Caroline Pichter*, Paris, 1933

Robertson, Ritchie, and Timms, Edward (eds.), *The Habsburg Legacy. National Identity in Historical Perspective*, Edinburgh, 1994

Robertson, William, *History of the Reign of Charles the Fifth*, with an account of the Emperor's life after his abdication by William H. Prescott, London, n.d.

Rodríguez, O.F.M., Darío Cabenalas, *El Morisco Granadino. Alonso del Castillo*, Granada, 1965

Rodríguez Salgado, M. J., *The Changing Face of Empire. Charles V, Philip II and Habsburg Authority, 1551–1559*, Cambridge, 1988

Roo, Gerardus de, *Annales oder Historische Chronik*, Augsburg, 1621

Rosenthal, Earl E., *The Cathedral of Granada*, Princeton, NJ, 1967

——, *The Palace of Charles V in Granada*, Princeton, NJ, 1985

Roth, Norman, *Conversos, Inquisition and the Expulsion of the Jews from Spain*, New York, 1992

Rothenburg, Gunther E., *The Army of Francis Joseph*, West Lafayette, Ind., 1976

Roux, Jean-Paul, *Le Sang – Mythes, Symboles, et Réalités*, Paris, 1988

Rubbrecht, Oswald, *L'Origine du Type Familiale de la Maison de Habsbourg*, Brussels, 1910

Rudolf, Crown Prince, *Travels in the East: Including a Visit to Egypt and the Holy Land*, London, 1884

——, *Notes on Sport and Ornithology*, tr. with the author's permission by. C. G. Danford, London, 1889

Rumbold, Horace, *The Austrian Court in the Nineteenth Century*, London, 1909

Sánchez-Camargo, M., *La Muerte y la Pintura Española*, Madrid, 1954

Schaeffer, Emil, *Habsburger schreiben Briefe Privatbriefe aus fünf Jahrhunderten*, Vienna, 1935

Schama, Simon, *Patriots and Liberators. Revolution in the Netherlands, 1780– 1813*, London, 1977

——, *The Embarrassment of Riches. An Interpretation of Dutch Culture in the Golden Age*, New York and London, 1987

Scheicher, Elisabeth, *Die Kunst und Wunderkammern der Habsburger*, Vienna, 1979

Schiel, Irmgard, *Stephanie. Kronprinzezzin im Schatten von Mayerling*, Stuttgart, 1978

Schindel, J. C., *Das Habsburg–Österreichische Stamm Paar. Adelreich und . . .*

Schmid, Franz, *Genealogische Stammtafel des Allerhöchsten Kaiserhauses Habsburg-Lothringen von 1708 bis 1893 und graphische darstellung der sucession im Hause Habsburg von 1273 bis 1780*, Vienna, 1893

Schneider, Josef (ed.), *Kaiser Franz Joseph I und Seine Hof. Erinnerungen und Schilderungen aus den Nachgelassenen Papieren Eines Personlichen Ratgebers*, Vienna, 1919

Schnürer, Franz, *Briefe. Kaiser Franz Joseph an seine Mütter. 1838–1872*, Munich, 1930

Scholz-Williams, Gerhild, *The Literary World of Maximilian I: an Annotated Bibliography*, St Louis, Mo., 1982

Schönholz, F. A. von, *Traditionen zur Characteristik Österreichs, Seines Staats- und Volkslebens unter Franz I*, ed. G. Gugitz, Munich, 1914

Schorske, Carl E., *Fin de Siècle Vienna. Politics and Culture*, New York, 1981

Schramm, Percy Ernst, and Mutherich, Florentine, *Denkmäler der deutsche Könige und Kaiser*, Munich 1962

Schulte, Aloys, *Kaiser Maximilan I als Kandidat für den Papstlichen Stuhl, 1511*, Leipzig, 1906

Schüssel, Therese, *Kultur des Barock in Österreich*, Graz, 1960

Schütz, Carl, *Schau- und Denkmünzen welche unter den glorwürdigen Regierung der Kaiserinn Königin Maria Theresa geprägt worden sind*, Vienna, 1782

Schwarzenberg, Adolph, *Prince Felix zu Schwarzenberg, Prime Minister of Austria, 1848–1853*, New York, 1946

Sealsfield, Charles, *L'Autriche tell qu'elle est*, Paris, 1828

Sedlmeyr, Hans, 'Die Politische Bedeutung des Deutschen Barock', *Epochen und Werke*, II, Vienna, 1980

Seeman, Bernard, *The River of Life. The Story of Man's Blood from Magic to Science*, New York, 1961

Setton, Kenneth M., *Venice, Austria and the Turks in the Seventeenth Century*, Philadelphia, Pa, 1991

Simkowsky, Hans, *Es war Einmal Kaiser Franz Joseph I*, Vienna, 1959

Sked, Alan, *The Survival of the Habsburg Empire. Radetsky, the Imperial Army and the Class War, 1848*, London, 1979

Smets, M., *Wien in und aus der Türken Bedrängnis, 1529–1683*, Vienna, 1893

Spannager, G. P. von, *Bipertita commentario in tabulam hiero-glyphicam et geneographicam Domus Austriae et Lotharingicae aere incisam*, Vienna, 1744

Spielman, John P., *Leopold I of Austria*, London and New Brunswick, NJ, 1977

——, *The City and the Crown. Vienna and the Imperial Court, 1600–1740*, West Lafayette, Ind., 1993

Srbik, Heinrich Ritter von, *Aus Österreichs Vergangenheit. Von Prinz Eugen zur Franz Joseph*, Salzburg, 1949

Staatliche Museen zu Berlin, *Kunst der Reformationzeit*, Berlin, 1983

Steed, Henry Wickham, *The Hapsburg Monarchy*, London, 1913

——, *Through Thirty Years. 1892-1922. A Personal Narrative*, London, 1924

Steinberg, S. H., *Five Hundred Years of Printing*, Harmondsworth, Middx, 1974

Steinitz, Eduard von, *Erinnerungen an Kaiser Franz Joseph I. Kaiser von Öster-reich, Apostolischer König von Ungarn*, Berlin, 1931

Stettler, Michael, *Swiss Stained Glass of the Fourteenth Century*, London, 1949

Steurs, John de, *Aperçu Historique sur la Dynastie des Habsbourg (de Rodolphe I à Charles Quint) et le Déclin de la Branche Espagnole par Suite des Mariages Consanguins*, Geneva, 1942

Stirling, William, *The Cloister Life of the Emperor Charles the Fifth*, 2nd edn, London, 1853

Stirling-Maxwell, William, *Don John of Austria or Passages from the History of the Sixteenth Century 1547–1578*, London, 1883

——, *The Chief Victories of the Emperor Charles the Fifth, Designed by Martin Heemskerck in MDLV*, 1870

——, *The Procession of Pope Clement VII and the Emperor Charles V after the Coronation at Bologna, on the 24th February MDXXX*. Designed and engraved by Nicholas Hogenberg. Edinburgh, 1875

——, *Antwerp Delivered in MDXXVII*. A passage from the history of the troubles in the Netherlands . . . illustrated with facsimiles of designs by Martin de Vos, Franz Hogenburg and others, Edinburgh, 1878

Stone, Norman, 'Army and society in the Habsburg monarchy. 1900–1914', *Past and Present*, no. 33, April 1966, pp. 95–111

——, 'Constitutional crises in Hungary', *The Slavonic and East European Review*, vol. XLV, no. 104, January 1967

Stoye, John, *The Siege of Vienna*, London, 1964

Strauss, Gerald, *Manifestations of Discontent in Germany on the Eve of the Reformation*, Bloomington, Ind., and London, 1971

Strauss, Walter L., *Albrecht Durer* (woodcuts and woodblocks)

Strauss, Walter L., and Alexander, Dorothy, *The German Single Leaf Woodcut. 1550–1600. A Pictorial Catalogue*, New York, 1977

Strohl, Hugo Gerard, *Österreichische-ungarische Wappenrolle*, Vienna, 1900

Stubbs, William, *Germany in the Later Middle Ages, 1200–1500*, New York, 1969 (new edn)

Stumberger, Hans, *Kaiser Ferdinand II und das Problem des Absolutismus*, Munich, 1957

Sturminger, Walter, *Bibliographie und Ikonographie der Turkenbelägerungen Wiens 1529 und 1683*, Vienna, 1955

Sunthaim, Ladislaus, *Der Löblichen Fürsten in des Lands Österreich . . .*, 1491

Tanis, James, and Horst, Daniel, *Images of Discord. A Graphic Interpretation of the Opening Decades of the Eighty Years War*, Bryn Mawr, Pa, 1993

Tanner (ed.), J. R., *The Cambridge Medieval History*. Vol. vii: *Decline of Empire and Papacy*, Cambridge, 1932

Tanner, Marie, *The Last Descendant of Aeneas. The Hapsburgs and the Mythic Image of the Emperor*, New Haven, Conn., and London, 1993

——, Titian: the 'Poesie' for Phillip II, unpublished PhD thesis, New York University, 1976

Tanner, Paul, *Graphik des Manierismus. Raffaelisch-Michelangelesk im Kupfer-stichkabinett Basel*, Basel, 1989

Tapie, Victor-L., *The Rise and Fall of the Habsburg Monarchy*, tr. Stephen Hardman, London, 1971

——, L'Europe de Marie-Thérèse. Du Baroque aux Lumières, Paris, 1973

Taylor, A. J. P., Europe, Grandeur and Decline, London, 1967

——, The Habsburg Monarchy. A Survey of the Austrian Empire and Austria Hungary, Harmondsworth, Middx, 1970

Temimi, Abdejelil (ed.), Las Practicas Musulmanes de los Moriscos Andaluces 1492–1609, Zaghouan, 1989

Terzi, Francisco [Franciscus Tertii] (c.1523–91), Pictoris Aulici Austriacae Gentis Imaginum, pt 1, 1569

Thelen, Theodor, Der Publizistische Kampf um die Pragmatische Sanktion und Erbnachfolge Maria Theresias 1731 bis 1748, Mainz, 1955

Thomas, Julian, Time, Culture and Identity: An Interpretive Archaeology, New York and London, 1996 (forthcoming)

Thomas, Keith, Man and the Natural World. Changing Attitudes in England, 1500–1800, Harmondsworth, Middx, 1983

Thompson, I. A. A., War and Government in Habsburg Spain 1560–1620, London, 1976

Thorne, B., and Henley, N. (eds.), Language and Sex: Difference and Dominance, Rowley, Mass., 1975

Tierney, Brian, The Crisis of Church and State 1050–1300, Englewood Cliffs, NJ, 1964

Tietze Hans (ed.), Das Vormärzliche Wien in Wort und Bild, Vienna, 1925

Timms, Edward, Karl Krauss. Apocalyptic Satirist. Culture and Catastrophe in Habsburg Vienna, New Haven, Conn., and London, 1986

——, 'National Memory and the "Austrian Idea" from Metternich to Waldheim', Modern Language Review, 86, 1991, pp. 898–910

Tracy, James D., Holland under Habsburg Rule 1506–66, 1990

Trevor Roper, Hugh, Princes and Artists. Patronage and Ideology at Four Habsburg Courts 1517–1633, London, 1976

Trost, Ernst, Franz Joseph I, Vienna, 1980

Tuchman, Barbara W., A Distant Mirror. The Calamitous Fourteenth Century, London, 1979

Turba, Gustav, Geschichte des Thronfolgerechtes in allen habsburgische Ländern bis zur Pragmatischen Sanktion Kaiser Karls VI. 1156 bis 1732, Vienna, 1903

Turnbull, Peter Evan, Austria, London, 1840

Twining, Lord, A History of the Crown Jewels of Europe, London, 1960

Tyler, Royall, The Emperor Charles the Fifth, London, 1956

Typotii, Jacobi, Symbola Divina & Humana. Pontificum Imperatorem regem. Ex Musaeo Octavii de Strada, Civis Romani Accessit brevis & facilis Isagoge, Arnhem, 1673

Vacha, Brigitte, Die Habsburger. Eine Europäische Familiengeschichte, Graz, 1993

Varnodoe, Kirk, Vienna 1900. Art, Architecture, and Design, 1986

Vehse, E., Memoirs of the Court and Aristocracy of Austria, tr. Franz Demmler, 2 vols., London, 1896

Vergo, Peter, Art in Vienna 1898–1918. Klimt, Kokoschka, Schiele, and Their Contemporaries, London, 1975

——, Vienna 1900. Vienna, Scotland and the European Avant-garde, Edinburgh, 1983

Verheiden, Willem, *An Oration or Speech appropriated unto the most mighty and illustrious Princes of Christendom wherein The Right and Lawfullnesse of the Netherlandish Warre against Philip King of Spain is approved and demonstrated*, London, 1624

Veyne, Paul, 'Conduct without belief and works of art without viewers', *Diogenes*, 1988, vol. 143

Viuksic, V., *Cavalry: The History of a Fighting Elite. 650 BC–AD 1914*, London, 1993

Vocelka, Karl, *Rudolf II und Seine Zeit*, Vienna, 1985

Waas, Glenn Elwood, *The Legendary Character of Kaiser Maximilian*, New York, 1941

Waissenberger, Robert, *Vienna in the Biedermeier Era, 1815–48*, London, 1986

Wandruszka, Adam, *Leopold II. Erzherzog von Österreich, Grossherzog von Toskana, König von Ungarn und Böhmen*, Vienna, 1963–5

——, *The House of Habsburg. Six Hundred Years of a European Dynasty*, tr. Cathleen and Hans Epstein, Garden City, NY, 1964

Wangermann, Ernst, *From Joseph II to the Jacobin Trials. Government Policy and Public Opinion in the Habsburg Dominions in the Period of the French Revolution*, Oxford, 1959

——, *The Austrian Achievement, 1700–1800*, London, 1973

Wedgwood, C. V., *The Thirty Years War*, London, 1938

Wehmer, K., *Mit Gemälde und Schrift. Kaiser Maximilian I und der Buchdruck*, Stuttgart, 1962

Weigall, Lady Rose, *The Correspondence of Priscilla, Countess of Westmoreland*, London, 1909

Weissensteiner, Friedrich (ed.), *Lieber Rudolf. Briefe von Kaiser Franz Joseph und Elisabeth an ihren Sohn*, Vienna, 1991

Whitehead, Alfred North, *Symbolism. Its Meaning and Effect*, Cambridge, 1927

Wiesflecker, Hermann, *Kaiser Maximilian I: Das Reich, Österreich und Europa an der Wende zur Neuzeit*, vol. v: *Der Kaiser und Seine Unwelt Hof, Staat, Wirtschaft, Gesellschaft und Kultur*, Vienna, 1971–80, 1986

Wilks, Michael, *The Problem of Sovereignty in the Later Middle Ages*, Cambridge, 1963

Wistrich, Robert S., *The Jews of Vienna in the Age of Franz Joseph*, Oxford, 1989

Wittkower, Rudolf, *Allegory and the Migration of Symbols*, London, 1977

Wolf, Julius, *Blut und Rasse des Hauses Habsburg-Lothringen. Problem der Physiognomiengeschichte und Verbungslehre*, Zürich, Leipzig, Wien, 1938

Wurfbain, Leonhard, *Absonderlichen relatio historica Habspurgico Austriaca durch was mittel das Haus der Ertz Hertzogen zu Österreich in Europa, Africa, Asia und Amerika zu den Herrschaften kommen*, Nuremberg, 1636

Yates, Douglas, *Grillparzer: a Critical Introduction*, Cambridge, 1972

Yates, Frances, *The Rosicrucian Enlightenment*, London, 1972

——, *Astraea, the Imperial Theme in the Sixteenth Century*, London, 1975

——, *Ideas and Ideals in the Northern European Renaissance. Collected Essays*, vol. 3, London and Boston, Mass., 1984

Yerushalmi, Yosef Hayim, *Assimilation and Racial Anti-Semitism. The Iberian and German Models*, New York, 1982

Yonge, Charlotte M., *The Dove in the Eagle's Nest*, New York, 1913

Zagorin, Perez, *Ways of Lying. Dissimulation, Persecution and Conformity in Early Modern Europe*, Cambridge, Mass., and London, 1990

Zayas, Rodrigo de, *Les Morisques et le Racisme d'État*, Paris, 1992

Zelfel, Hans Peter, *Ableben und Begräbnis Friedrichs III*, Vienna, 1974

Zohn, Harry, *Karl Kraus*, New York, 1971

Zollner, Erich, *Geschichte Österreichs von den Anfangen bis zu Gegenwart*, Munich, 1961

Zweig, Stefan, *The World of Yesterday. An Autobiography*, London, 1943

Index